THE ANCIENT PAST OF MEXICO

by

ALMA M. REED

Foreword by

Dr. Eusebio Dávalos Hurtado

CROWN PUBLISHERS, INC.
NEW YORK

A.

GULF OF MEXICO

GUATEMALA

PIEDRAS PINTAS
BURRITA
REY
CRUILLAS
EL NOVILLO
C. VICTORIA
STAMANTE
STA. ISABEL
LA PIEDAD
S. TAMAULIPAS
XICOTENCATL
OCAMPO
FEWKE
LA CEIBA
TANINUL
LA PALMA
MAIZ
MIRADORES
ENCARNACION
SALADO
TAMPICO
MICOS
TAMUIN
TAMBOLON
TANCANHUITZ
NEBLINAS
TAMAZUNCHALE
HUEJUTLA
TELOMAL
TUXPAN
PETLALTOLUCA
BARRA DE CAZONES
C. DE TEAYO
MEZTITLAN
TAJIN
TECOLUTLA
ATOTONILCO
ZOZOCALCO
ACTOPAN
NAUTLA
PACHUCA
TULA
ZACATLAN
HUEHUETOCA
STA. CRUZ
CONTLA
CAMARONES
JALAPA
CEMPOALA
TEXCOCO
TLAXCALA
TEMEXTEPEC
VERACRUZ
TOLUCA
TIZATLAN
LA PALMILLA
SACRIFICIOS
TENANGO
CHOLULA
COSCOMATEPEC
ERNAVACA
PUEBLA
ATOYAC
NOGALES
XOCHICALCO
MALINALCO
TEPEXI
EL COCUITE
ALMOLONGA
HUEYAPAN
BUENAVISTA
ATENCINGO
TEHUACAN
PILCAYA
ACATEPEC
ZOQUITLAN
S. MARTIN
TUXTLA
HUITZUCO
ACATLAN
TEOTITLAN
ZOYULTEPEC
QUIOTEPEC
MEZCALA
SUCHIXTEPEC
S. CRISTOBAL
VALLE NACIONAL
S. CRISTOBAL
CUICATLAN
HUAJUAPAM
YUCUÑIDAHUI
OCOTEPEC
TLAPA
PUEBLO VIEJO
ANCINGO
TEXMILINCAN
YUCUNDO
IXTLAN
PANTLA
OZTOCINGO
JUXTLAHUACA
OAXACA
GUICHICOVI
TALCOAPA
MONTE ALBAN
MITLA
ACATEPEC
TLACOTEPEC
LLANO GRANDE
EJUTLA
ZOQUITLAN
OMETEPEC
SOLA DE VEGA
JUCHITAN
MIAHUATLAN
TEHUANTEPEC
JUQUILA
PAXTLAN
SALINA CRUZ
TUTUTEPEC
ASTATA
HUAMELULA
CICATELA
HUATULCO
POCHITLA
LA VENTA
COMALCALCO
CHILTEPEC
BALSILLO
VILLAHERMOSA
TORTUGUERO
ATASTA
LOS IDOLOS
PASO REAL
PALENQUE
CHANKALA
PLAYA LARGA
TEOPATAN
EL TORO
BOLOLCHON
C. VENADO
OCULUM
TUXTLA G.
CINTALAPA
ZANATEPEC
CHABIN
OSTUTA
DELICIAS
TONALA
CUSTEDEQUES
CHIMALAPA
MOTOZINTLA
PANAMA
HUIXTLA
HUEHUETAN
TAPACHULA
LIBERTAD
TECOLPAN
CHAKABA
PETENCHE
SULUSUM
TENOSIQUE
CALLEJONES
YOXIHA
LA MAR
TONINA
BUSILDNA
OCOCINGO
EL CAYO
AÑAITE
YAXCHILAN
STA. ELENA
JOTANA
S. LORENZO
INDEPENDENCIA
HUN CHABIN
COMITAN
TZENDALES
TENAM
CABO CATOCHE
I. MUJERES
EL MECO
PROGRESO
DZILAM
KATUNILKIN
AKE
TZEBTUN
MERIDA
IZAMAL
YAXCHEXLABPAK
ACANCEH
CHICHEN-ITZA
PALMUL
MAXCANU
MAYAPAN
COZUMEL
MUNA
OXKINTOK
COBA
CEDRAL
BECAL
ZAYI
TANCAM
TULUM
TANKUCHE
UXMAL
OXKUTZCAB
MUKIL
I. JAINA
LABNA
ICHMUL
BACABCHEN
TABI
CHACMULTUM
TAMPA
KALUM
CHACBOLAY
PUNTA SOL MAN
TAMPAK
KICHMU
CHICHAN-KANA
XLABPAK
MACOBA
ELEMAX
CAMPECHE
ETZNA
TIXMUCUY
PUNTA PAJAROS
DZIBALCHEN
PARAISO
YACALCHUK
CANCHE BALAM
KANKABCHEN
CHAMPOTON
NOHCHEN
SACBECAN
JERUSALEM
BACALAR
MOCU
IXPUHIL
HIGUERAS
NOH-ICHMUL
SILBITUK
MARIO ANCONA
CHETUMAL
KOHTUM
CHOMIL
TRES MARIAS
LA MUÑECA
RIO BEC
BUENTIL
OXDEMUL
XKULUB
KALAKMUL
VILLA HERMOSA
ALTA MIRA
NOHOCHNA

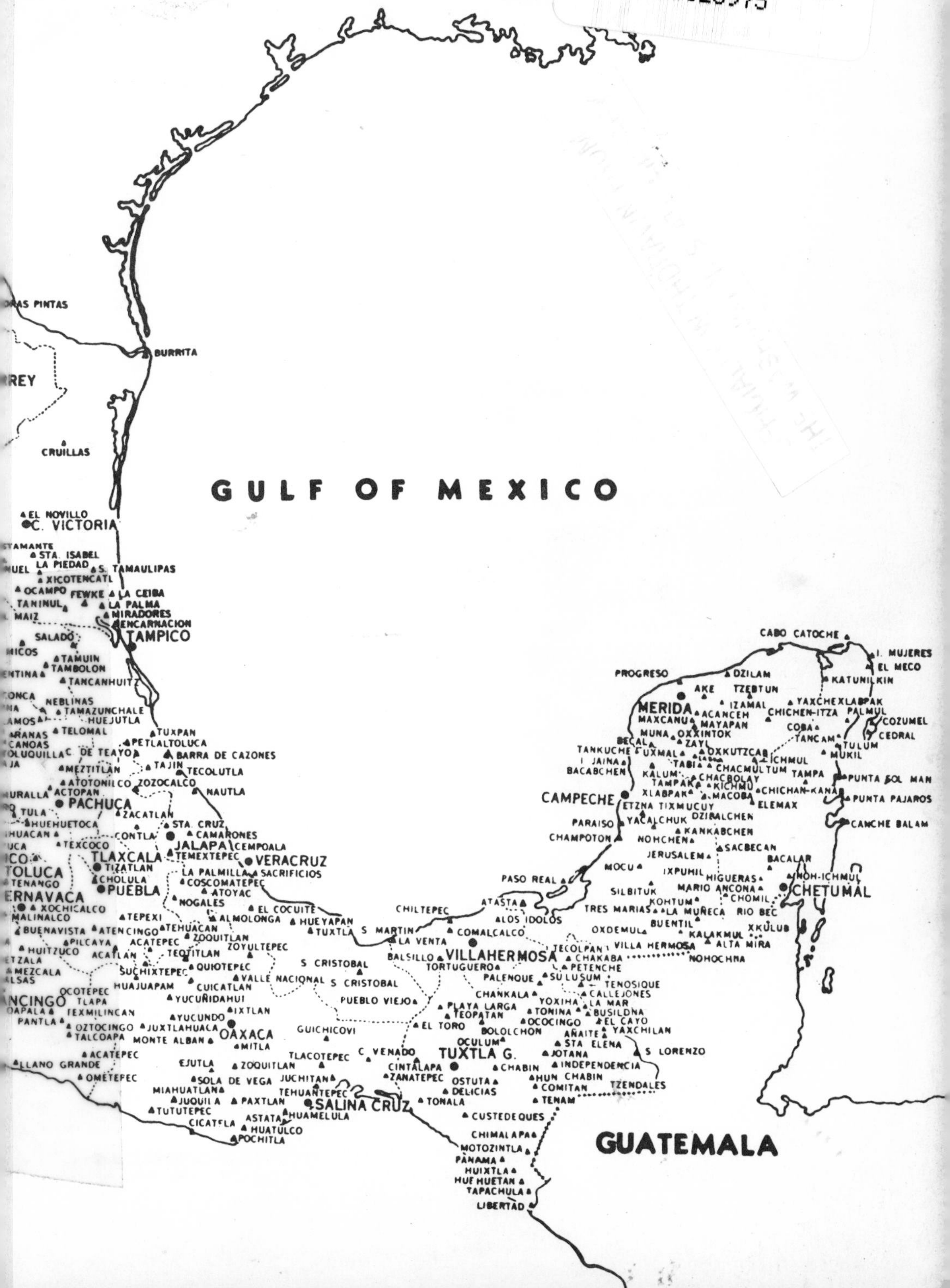

THE ANCIENT PAST OF MEXICO

Books by Alma M. Reed

THE ANCIENT PAST OF MEXICO
THE MEXICAN MURALISTS
OROZCO
JOSÉ CLEMENTE OROZCO
THE NATIONAL UNIVERSITY OF MEXICO
UXMAL AND THE LOW HILL CITIES OF YUCATÁN

Translations

DEDICATION BY ANGELO SIKELIANOS (from the Greek)
CUMAE BY CONSOLI (from the Italian)

To the memory of
Felipe Carrillo Puerto of Yucatán,
martyr to man's undying quest for freedom,
who, faithful to ancient Maya heritage
and to his personal vision of social justice,
linked the culture of the great American race
with the civilization of some distant liberated tomorrow

Library of Congress Catalog Card Number: 64–17847
Printed in the U.S.A.

Contents

Acknowledgments

INDIVIDUAL ACKNOWLEDGMENT of the many persons who, over the years, have contributed to the making of *The Ancient Past of Mexico* imposes upon me too complex a task. Certain names, however, constitute an inextricable part of a cumulative roster that began in the mid-twenties when, as a young American journalist, I was fortunate enough to encounter, on my first visit to Mexico, several leading scholars and scientists who gave me initial encouragement and guidance.

The eminent group included Dr. Manuel F. Gamio, then the director of the Mexican Government Department of Anthropology; Dr. Marshall H. Saville of the Museum of the American Indian, Heye Foundation; Dr. Charles Merriam and Dr. Sylvanus G. Morley of the Carnegie Institution; Dr. Aleš Hrdlička of the Smithsonian Institution; Dr. Thomas A. Joyce of the British Museum and Dr. Herbert J. Spinden of the Peabody Museum. It is to these dedicated men that I owe the sparking of my own interest in Mexico's past, which has developed into a major enthusiasm and never-ending quest. After a period of study of ancient art and religion in southern Italy and Greece, during which this interest was further stimulated by cultural, aesthetic and cosmogonic analogies I perceived in the early civilizations of the Mediterranean, I returned to Mexico to pursue independent investigations as a journalist. Here again I was aided by scholarly men and women, in whose diverse efforts to excavate and restore the lost cities of Middle America and to explore the values of ancient cultures I was frequently permitted to share.

To Dr. Eusebio Dávalos Hurtado, director of the National Institute of Anthropology and History, I am profoundly grateful for the many courtesies extended to me on my visits to various archaeological sites, often in the company of Dr. Eulalia Guzmán, that valorous defender of the autochthonous races of Mexico, to whom I owe a clearer understanding of the way in which Spanish chroniclers of the Conquest, through ignorance or fanatical intolerance, often left distorted evaluations of native cultures. My awareness of the perception and profundity of the aesthetic and cosmological concepts held by various peoples of ancient America has been broadened by Dr. Miguel León-Portilla's revelations of the beauty of Nahuatl poetry and the universality of Nahuatl philosophy. I am also indebted to Dr. Rául Noriega, mathematician and astronomer, for widening my appreciation of indigenous intellectual attainments. An increased admiration for the high technological standards of the artisans of ancient America, apparent in the quality of designs of objects in everyday use, has been stirred by the painter-scholar Dr. Jorge Enciso, subdirector of the National Institute of Anthropology and History. Discussions with Dr. Gordon F. Ekholm of the American Museum of Natural History regarding his study of Asian-American parallels have resulted in an enlarged vista of possible New World origins and cultural relationships. Many obscure issues and controversial texts have been clarified for me by Dr. Jésus Amaya Topete, author of several works on pre-Conquest and modern Mexican history. Professor José Farías Galindo has provided valuable assistance in translating ancient Nahuatl place-names. Inestimable help in efforts to trace the beginnings of the Maya story in Caribbean waters has been provided by the subaqueous research undertaken by C.E.D.A.M. (Club de Exploraciones y Deportes Acuaticos de México), sponsored by Pablo Bush Romero, in whose expeditions I have participated as official historian.

In the preparation of this book I am indebted to Helen E. Sterling for her invaluable services as editor and coordinator, and to Dorothy Cinquemani, lecturer on Middle America on the staff of the American Museum of Natural History, for technical consultation.

The illustrations have been derived from various sources. Most of the photographs of archaeological sites and objects displayed in Federal museums have been supplied from the archives of the National Institute of Anthropology and History. The State Museums of Puebla, Colima, Yucatán, Michoacán and Veracruz, the Mexican National Tourist Council, the Mexican Government Tourist Bureau and the Ministry of the Treasury have all contributed photographs, as have such agencies as Club de Viajes Pemex and C.E.D.A.M. Dr. Kurt Stavenhagen's famous collection of pre-Columbian art, many examples of which are reproduced in this book, has often been loaned to official Mexican exhibitions. Professional photographers whose pictures enrich this book include Mary Saint Albans and Manuel Alvarez Bravo of Mexico City, Edward Weston, James Webster and Ralph Payne of the United States, and Ferdinand Anton of Munich, Germany. Valuable records of ancient sites have also come from the ranks of amateur photographers, among them C. W. Ennis, Jr., and Dr. Richard Posner.

GRATEFUL ACKNOWLEDGMENT is also made to those authors and publishers listed below for their permission to include copyrighted excerpts. These and other sources are listed in detail on page 363.

Calder, Ritchie, *The World Man Created,* Simon and Schuster, Inc., New York.

Ceram, C. W., *Gods, Graves and Scholars,* Alfred A. Knopf, Inc., New York.

Codice Badiano, Seguro Social, Mexico City.

Colum, Padraic, *Orpheus: Myths of the World,* The Macmillan Company, New York.

de Camp, L. Sprague and Catherine C., *Ancient Ruins and Archaeology,* Doubleday & Company, Inc., New York.

Ferguson, Thomas S., *One Fold, One Shepherd,* Books of California, San Francisco, California.

Gardiner, C. Harvey, *Naval Power in the Conquest of Mexico,* University of Texas Press, Austin, Texas.

Guzmán, Dr. Eulalia, *Clarifications and Rectifications of the Invasion of Anáhuac,* Libros Anáhuac, Mexico City.

Heyden, Doris and Horcasitas, Fernando, editors, *The Aztecs,* The Orion Press, Inc., New York.

León-Portilla, Miguel, *La Filosofía Nahuatl,* Instituto Indigenista Interamericano, Mexico City; *Los Mexicanos Antiguos a Traves de Sus Crónicas y Cantares,* Fondo de Cultura Económica, Mexico City.

Lipps, Teodoro, *Fundamentals of Aesthetics,* Daniel Jorro, Madrid.
Mann, Thomas, *Joseph and His Brothers* (preface), Alfred A. Knopf, Inc., New York.
Marett, Sir R. H. K., K.C.M.G., O.B.E., *Archaeological Tours from Mexico City,* Ediciones Tolteca, S. A., Mexico City.
Morley, Sylvanus G. and Brainerd, George W., *The Ancient Maya,* third edition, Stanford University Press, Palo Alto, California.
Noriega, Rául, co-editor, *Esplendor de México Antiguo,* Centro de Investigaciones Antropológicas de Mexico, Mexico City; *La Piedra del Sol y 16 Monumentos Astronómicos del México Antiguo con Símbolos y Claves,* Editorial Superacion, Mexico City.
Richard, Paul, *Dawn Over Asia,* Ganesh & Co., Madras, India.
Saville, Marshall H., *Cruciform Structures Near Mitla,* American Museum of Natural History, New York.
Séjourné, Laurette, *Burning Water,* Fondo de Cultura Económica, Mexico City; *Un Palacio en la Ciudad de los Dioses,* National Institute of Anthropology and History, Mexico City.
Smith, Joseph Lindon, *Tombs, Temples and Ancient Art,* University of Oklahoma Press, Norman, Oklahoma.
Spengler, Oswald, *The Decline of the West,* Vol. II, Alfred A. Knopf, Inc., New York.
Vaillant, George, *The Aztecs of Mexico; Origin, Rise and Fall of the Aztec Nation,* Doubleday & Company, Inc., Garden City, New York.
Westheim, Paul, *The Sculpture of Ancient Mexico,* Doubleday & Company, Inc., Garden City, New York.

List of Illustrations

FOREWORD

ALMA M. REED, the American writer who for many years has been deeply involved with the past and present of her adopted country, Mexico, knows well not only the panorama of modern Mexican life but more particularly its ancient roots. Long associated with the scientists and scholars who have sought to trace its history, she continues to be a constant visitor to the increasing number of archaeological zones, finding out at first hand what has been determined by excavations at each site, in order to keep herself fully up to date on the latest discoveries. Her indefatigable research makes her conversant with the many recent advances in the various fields of investigation into Mexico's ancient past. This fresh knowledge imparts to her articles and books a vibrancy heightened by the ardor with which she describes its vanished splendors. Her personal reports on Mexican archaeology have won for her not only a wealth of Mexican readers but others elsewhere who are interested in the ancestral cultures of Mexico.

We salute Alma M. Reed—conscientious and stimulating author, dynamic journalist and charming *Peregrina*—for keeping so radiantly alive an interest in Mexico's past and for presenting its image to the world.

DR. EUSEBIO DÁVALOS HURTADO, *Director,*
National Institute of Anthropology and History

INTRODUCTION

IN WRITING *The Ancient Past of Mexico* my chief aim has been to link descriptions of recent archaeological discoveries with historical data in order to give a broad survey of what is now known of pre-Conquest Middle America.

While complete objectivity on a subject that has resulted in so many and such bitter controversies is difficult to achieve, I have attempted, at least, to present a summary of the various theories regarding the origins and development of autochthonous cultures. Some investigators have taken positive stands. Others are disinclined to draw final conclusions, aware that, with the next turn of the excavator's spade, some formidable new challenge to their cherished concepts may emerge. Wherever possible I have presented, in their own words, the opinions of Mexican and foreign archaeologists and anthropologists with whom I have been privileged to work as a journalist and often as a student-participant in the process of exploration of many of Mexico's ruined cities.

It is precisely because the revelations which still lie ahead may endow with dramatic possibilities efforts to penetrate Mexico's remote and enigmatic yesterday that today's "on-the-ground" observations may hold timely interest and make some contribution to the historic record.

ALMA M. REED

CHAPTER I

The Presence of Man in Middle America: Some Theories

THE RECORD OF THE ROCKS we have slowly amassed from careful study of prehistoric eras has yielded, to date, no conclusive evidence of the presence of man in Middle America before the end of the Pleistocene Era, now believed to have lasted more than a million and a half years, during which four great ice ages were interspersed with temperate periods. Leading anthropologists do not believe any preceding races of sub-men existed in the New World. No ancient remains of great apes or the advanced types of Old World monkeys have been found in the Western Hemisphere, nor are such species present here today. Of course the quest for fossils that might relate man to other species is comparatively recent. There has hardly been time, since Charles Darwin launched his theory of organic evolution, to locate even an infinitesimal part of the remains from former geological epochs. Yet the question recurs as to how long man, as Homo sapiens, has existed in the New World and from whence he came. Recent discoveries have upset some of the long-held theories of origin, and the probable date of the earliest occupation by man of the American continent is constantly being placed in an ever-more-remote past.

Many of the nineteenth-century speculations are regarded as nothing less than bizarre fantasies, while many of the early serious scholars of prehistory leaped too soon to conclusions after desultory explorations and unsystematic excavations of the lost cities of Mexico and Guatemala. In 1865 Abbé Brasseur de Bourbourg revived, with New World connotations, Plato's "Lost Atlantis" story, as related in 355 B.C. in his dialogues *Timaeus* and *Critias,* based on an account given by the Egyptian priests of Saïs to the Greek statesman Solon. After discovering what he believed to be "the Maya alphabet" in an account of Yucatán (*Relación de las Cosas de Yucatán*) by Bishop Diego de Landa, de Bourbourg obtained, through his "translation" of a section of an ancient Maya book, the *Codex Tro-Cortesianus,* what he accepted as an account of a frightful convulsion that destroyed the continent of Mu. Ignatius Donnelly expanded the theories of the French savant to embrace the similarities he believed existed between Mayan and Egyptian hieroglyphs. His *Atlantis: The Antediluvian World* has often been reprinted since its publication in 1882. Augustus Le Plongeon amplified the concept of a New World-Atlantis by his interpretations of murals found in the Akab-Dzib, or "The House of the Obscure Writing" in Chichén Itzá in Yucatán, where he and his wife labored for many years. Teobert Maler sought the lost Atlantis at Uxmal. In 1912 Dr. Paul Schliemann, the grandson of the discoverer of ancient Troy, published in the New York *American* an article entitled "How I Discovered Atlantis, The Source of All Civilization." He claimed that a 4,000-year-old Chaldean manuscript revealed the destruction of Mu, "Land of the Seven Cities," by an earthquake and an explosion caused by a falling star. Schliemann's claims evidently influenced James Churchward who, in his series of popular titles about submerged continents, placed Atlantis at the bottom of the Atlantic and Lemuria, or Mu, on the floor of the Pacific. The German writer Karl George Zchaetzch held that the Atlanteans were the original Aryans. He believed that the partial disintegration and fall of the former planet, Luna, the Moon, caused the sinking of Atlantis and Lemuria, a variation of concepts presented by Immanuel Velikovsky in his *Worlds in Collision.*

Apart from this body of Atlantis lore, the earlier serious scholars held, for the most part, that the Western Hemisphere had been populated by tribes who crossed the Bering Strait from Siberia between 2,000 and 4,000 years ago in a series of migratory waves. It was believed that they must have used the Aleutian Islands as steppingstones or walked across what may once have been, at the narrowest point between the North American and Asiatic continents, a land bridge known as Beringia. While an Asiatic migration has been supported by scientific evidence, the dates first set forth as the era of migration have long since been abandoned.

A few anthropologists, among them Dr. M. R. Harrington, contend that some migrations to the American continent may have taken place over the ice or over a now-submerged land bridge that once connected Greenland and Europe, a route supposedly used by great prehistoric mammals whose fossilized remains have been discovered in the Arctic wastes and in other parts of North America. It is his opinion that men of the Magdalenian period may have settled in the Arctic region.

The first real reversal among experts as to the degree of antiquity of American cultures came with the development in the late 1940's, by Dr. Willard F. Libby, of the Carbon-14 method, a technique that could be used to measure the age of ancient remains by testing them for radioactive carbon. Application of this method to pre-Columbian material was announced in 1950. The use of the Carbon-14 process resulted in revolutionary discoveries when charred animal bones, often found with the early flint weapons known as Folsom points, were tested. The conclusions pushed the presence of man in the New World back to at least 10,000, possibly even 15,000 years ago.

At Tule Springs, northwest of Las Vegas, Nevada, archaeologists found bones of primitive mammoths, bison and horses, two implements made from what are believed to be camel bones, stone scrapers and stone flakes, or chips, used by ancient man in the shaping of implements. These tiny stone tools may, according to some scholars, push back by many millennia the known date of the appearance of Homo sapiens in what is now the western United States. At this same site, as Dr. Ruth D. Simpson of the Southwest Museum of Los Angeles reported, "We have obtained a date of 28,000 years plus for carbon directly associated with a stone scraper. Tools there were very rare; one stone scraper and four or five bone tools from the earliest horizon. There is also an occupation level at 13,000 years." During her extensive work in the Mojave Desert, especially in the Manix Lake basin east of Barstow, California, Dr. Simpson found tufa on rocks marking a high shoreline of the lake. The date of occupation of this hand-axe site—where

Signs of early habitation in western North America have been found at several sites, including Santa Rosa Island, Manix Lake and Sandia Cave. In some cases, implements have been found alongside bones or the remains of campfires.

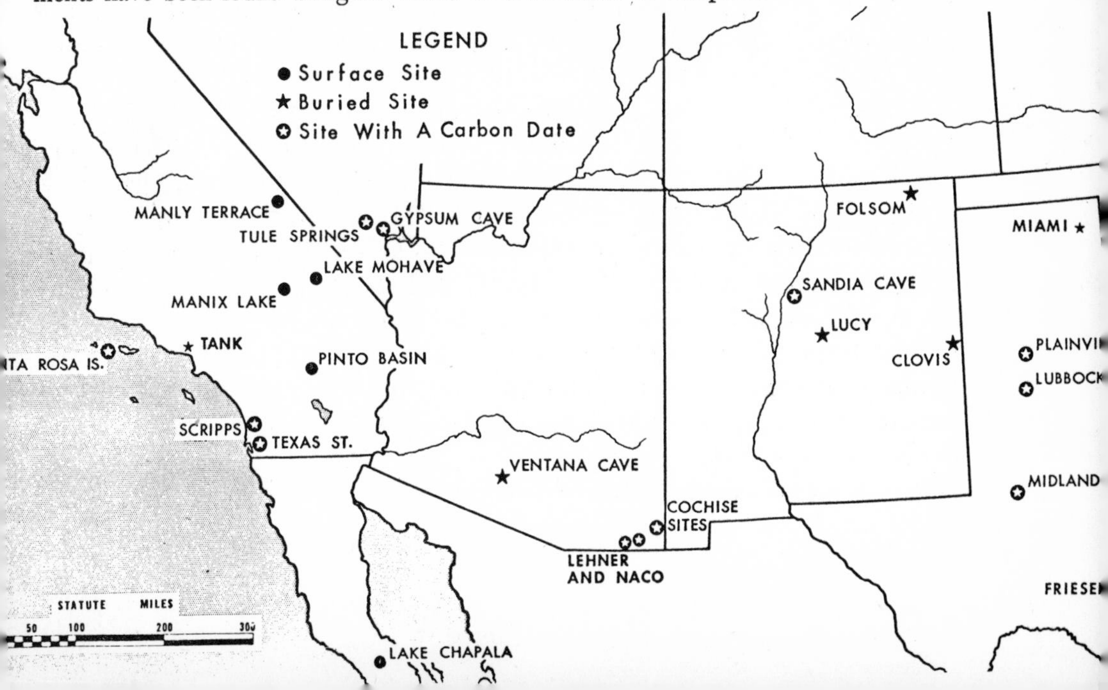

The carvings on the pelvis of a mastodon found near Tetela in the Valsequillo area by Dr. Juan Armenta Camacho may portray game being hunted by primitive man.

no weapon points but an abundance of artifacts were found—is believed to be about 19,700 years ago. The artifacts of Sandia Cave, New Mexico, found in a sealed layer below some Folsom points, which have been assigned an antiquity of between 9,000 and 11,000 years, are possibly 20,000 to 30,000 or more years old.

From datings made by Dr. Wallace Broecker of Columbia University, Dr. George E. Carter of Johns Hopkins University and Dr. Philip Orr of the Santa Barbara Natural History Museum, tools found alongside burned dwarf mammoth bones (a circumstance suggesting that the animal may have been hunted and killed by man) at Santa Rosa Island off the coast of southern California, have been placed at about 29,000 B.C. Dr. Carter found near San Diego what he believes to be primitive implements used at campfire sites. Although some archaeologists do not accept them as man-made, Dr. Carter attributes their use to men living some 40,000 years before our era.

A claim for man's great antiquity in Middle America was made in May of 1959 by Dr. Juan Armenta Camacho, of the Department of Anthropology of the University of Puebla, who offered evidence to support his theory of human habitation in Mexico for 30,000 years. Excavating along the banks of the Atoyac River about ten miles southeast of Puebla near Tetela in the area of Valsequillo, Dr. Armenta Camacho discovered in a stratum of earth of the Pleistocene era the pelvis bone of a mastodon showing carved figures that may represent animals being hunted with primitive lances. A few weeks later, near Apetizingo, three other fragments of cranial bones of animals were found with implements of bone and flint at the same cultural stratum.

In 1963 Dr. Armenta Camacho's excavations under the sponsorship of the National Science Foundation and the American Philosophical Society brought forth evidence that man hunted camels and mastodons with stone implements. Flint points were found still imbedded in mastodon bones. From the deepest Pleistocene layer were recovered bones of camels and horses. If the latter had survived in Middle America up to the period of the Conquest the history of the New World might have been far different. To the terrified native warrior the horses of the Spaniards were not only strange but supernatural, a significant factor in the success of the European invaders. Over a four-year period Dr. Armenta Camacho found in the Tetela region several hundred fragments of bones in the shape of knives or similar pointed weapons as well as bones of an order of mammals including elephants and other related extinct species which show faint traces of man-made drawings.

The discovery of bones of an ancient mastodon which had two long straight tusks, small ears and a thick hairy hide was reported in 1965 by José Oscos Colín, an amateur-paleontologist-anthropologist, at Ixtapan de la Sal. Similar remains have been found in Tequixquiác and Santa Catarina, Jalisco, near the Río Arrecifes in Argentina and in Tarija, Bolivia. His discovery included a rock bearing the impression of a handprint, a human femur from an eight-foot skeleton and the skull of a saber-toothed tiger.

In 1870 the ancient representation of the head of a coyote, wolf or peccary on a fragment of vertebra from an extinct species of llama was found at a depth of 40 feet by workmen digging a drainage ditch at Tequixquiác in the Valley of Mexico. In 1947 came the discovery of the

Remains of ancient animals, including a mastodon with two tusks, were found at Ixtapan de la Sal by José Oscos Colin, shown with some of the relics.

Tepexpán man (or woman) on the dried lake bed of Lake Texcoco. Although Dr. Helmut de Terra, one of the discoverers of the ancient remains, determined from his analysis that the skeleton was that of a man about sixty years old and 5½ feet tall, Dr. Santiago Genoves came to a different conclusion. "I have analyzed the problem of age by direct examination," he declared, "and indirectly by relating the Tepexpán Man with others living under equally difficult conditions, exposed to constant danger in a struggle with huge wild animals. I find no valid argument for assigning to this discovery a greater age than thirty years. And, basing my opinion on new calculations of the length of the femur, the height could not have been more than 5 feet, 2 inches." He further declared that a reexamination of the skull and other parts of the skeletal structure, particularly characteristic large bones, proved that the fossilized remains were those of a woman rather than those of a man. He believes that the thighbone offers the best guide for ascertaining the height of Middle-American skeletons, since Mexicans generally have short legs and long arms, and if height were judged by arm length the Mexican would be considered taller than he actually was. The opinion that the ossified remains were those of a woman was supported by the orthopedist Dr. Guillermo Velasco Polo at the National Congress on Orthopedics and Traumology held in Mexico City in May 1964.

On the question as to how the Tepexpán man and others "exposed to constant danger in a struggle with huge wild animals" and the generations who succeeded them in the New World developed their cultures, several

The remains of the Tepexpán man, found by Dr. Helmut de Terra on the dried lakebed of Lake Texcoco, may be those of a woman. The skull of the skeleton (*left*) served as the basis for the reconstruction (*right*).

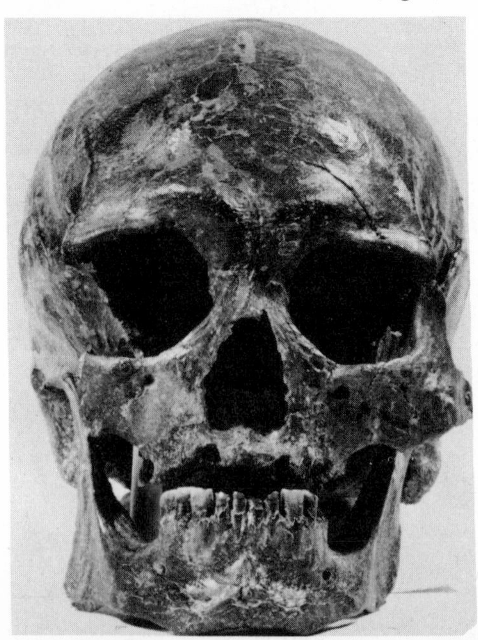

schools of thought on origins have evolved. There can, of course, be no clear, incontrovertible answer to the questions which have been raised until a preponderance of the evidence is at hand. Perhaps one or more of the now apparently conflicting views may, at some future date, be validated.

The proponents of one group argue that the indigenous peoples of America probably came "empty-handed" from Siberia, developing their arts and material cultures in this hemisphere. Such scholars as Professor Gutierre Tibón have contended that Asiatic peoples, with little more than the basket and the dog, migrated from Siberia, developing skills after their arrival on the American mainland. He has maintained that the culture of the Maya is an entirely independent and unique phenomenon. The late Dr. Aleš Hrdlička believed that the highly evolved culture of the Maya was brought from Siberia to Alaska. He has stated that the "ancient peoples of America brought it all with them from Asia when they crossed the Bering Sea. There is plenty of proof of this in the skulls I have dug up on the Alaskan coasts at points where, on a clear day, one can see Siberia. I have scores of these skulls with the same type of dental incrustation of semi-precious stones that one finds in examples in the National Museum of Mexico." He attributed the marked divergence in cultural development among indigenous American peoples to different environments and consequent conditions of life. Climate and the adaptability of the soil to agriculture, in his opinion, chiefly determined the way of life and the development of cultural patterns. He pointed out that the mode of living of primitive peoples on parched and barren islands resembles that of the ancient peoples of the Siberian tundras. Taking a unique position, the botanist José Ramírez Mateos has championed the idea that, since there are many species of flora and fauna exclusively indigenous to the New World and unknown in other parts of the earth, the human species might also have been indigenous.

According to the "Independent Inventionists," culture is imposed by natural conditions which drive man to the attainment of progress with inexorable determinism. Other theorists claim that simple diffusion never takes place but that there is always a readaptation, a truly creative process in which external influence is remolded by inventive genius. The "Diffusionist" school is concerned with significant resemblances between Old and New World objects, beliefs and cultural patterns and submits evidence purporting to show that there are American cultural traits which exhibit a remarkable similarity—difficult to dismiss as mere coincidence—to cultural traits of the ancient civilizations of Egypt, Greece, India, Sumeria, Ceylon and Cambodia. A chief spokesman, the anatomist Sir Grafton Elliot Smith, according to *Ancient Ruins and Archaeology* by L. Sprague and Catherine C. de Camp, "traced all civilization back to Egypt, whence it was carried all over the world by sun-worshipping, gold-seeking Egyptians . . . spreading out from Egypt, they came first to Mesopotamia, where they built or taught the natives to build ziggurats in imitation of their own pyramids, later repeating the performance in Cambodia and finally in Central America." Sources of culture favored by other Diffusionists include Brazil, the Ohio Valley, the Arctic and "Atlantis."

Some Diffusionists, among them W. J. Berry, have pointed out provocative resemblances between the vast mausolea built to guard the mummies of Egyptian pharaohs and the pyramid-temples of ancient Mexico. A tomb beneath the pyramid of the Temple of the Inscriptions in Palenque was found to contain the jewel-adorned remains of an exalted personage placed there some 1,300 years ago, demonstrating that in some cases the pyramid-temples of Middle America did serve as tombs. Another princely interment was found beneath a pyramid at Tikal in Guatemala which sustains the Temple of the Red Stele, thus establishing the custom of pyramid burial in the lowland Maya area. Samples of bacteria entombed here for more than a thousand years are being studied by microbiologists and may provide a clue to the mysterious decline of the Maya culture.

Middle American contact with Asia is a theory which has been argued by such scholars as Dr. Gordon F. Ekholm and Dr. Robert von Heine-Geldern. The late artist-archaeologist Miguel Covarrubias, commenting upon the design of Maya objects of polished jade recovered from the depths of the "Well of Sacrifice" at Chichén Itzá, has said, "It would be hard not to share the belief in stronger and more direct ties with the East." Dr. Antonio Pompa y Pompa believes that Mexico shares with Easter Island "cultural expressions of a common mythico-religious concept originating in some remote protohistorical epoch," that an ancient common culture encircled the littoral of the South Pacific. Recalling the opinion of Alfred Metraux, an authority on the culture of Easter Island, Dr. Pompa y Pompa has pointed out that the Islanders attribute their megalithic monuments to a race of giants who disappeared with the sinking of a great continent extending between America and Asia. It was Metraux's contention that Easter Island was the sole vestige of an advanced civilization whose ruins were destroyed in some mighty cataclysm and that the Maya and Inca cultures were merely offshoots of this vanished empire. Citing various monumental structures carved from rock in Mexico, Dr. Pompa y Pompa has also linked, through an analogous zoomorphic tradition, the gigantic stone frogs of Guanajuato with enormous sculptured forms in Peru representing the condor, the turtle, the monkey and other animals that were not found in America at the time of the Conquest.

Among the roster of candidates advanced as contenders for the title of "New World culture-bearers" are "Israelite," Celtic, Phoenician, Norse, Chinese and Polynesian voyagers. Of course new excavations and underwater explorations in Mexico's coastal waters may add new names to the lengthening list.

Thomas Stuart Ferguson, a lawyer of Orinda, California who is associated with the New World Archaeological Foundation, is of the opinion that Mexico's early high civilization was received from Mesopotamia in the third millennium B.C. and that about 600 B.C. two small groups of "Israelites" crossed the Atlantic to make new contributions to the existing Middle-American culture and to influence religious beliefs. He cited records of extensive early voyages from Crete to Britain and one from Ezion-geber to Ophir to bring gold to King Solomon. In his book, *One Fold, One Shepherd,* he has stated, "I suggest that transoceanic voyagers 'discovered' the New World hundreds of years before Columbus," offering as evidence the record of a voyage reportedly made to America in 587 B.C., as described in the earliest known Guatemalan manuscript. This chronicle was published in 1885 by the Société de Philologie of Paris in its official bulletin and by the University of Oklahoma Press as *The Annals of the Cakchiquels.* The document, compiled by the nobles of Totonicapán in 1554, relates the history of their ancestors and tells of their ocean journey, undertaken at the instigation of the "Great God," who wished it to be done "because they were the sons of Abraham and Jacob" and accordingly provided them with a sacred director, the *Giron Gagal.* The nobles believed that their ancestors were aware of the scriptural accounts of Adam and Eve, the Creation and the Deluge. Mr. Ferguson has conceded that the nobles of Totonicapán could have learned of the patriarchs from Spanish priests and "conspired to gain favor by adopting themselves into the House of Israel." Since the Jews had been expelled from Spain in the preceding century, for the nobles to say they were Jews, he believes, would, however, have been to make a statement not in their own interest. Mr. Ferguson has also cited the *Popul Vuh,* the sacred book of the Quiché Maya, written about 1550, with a reference to the Old World as a point of departure and of coming from "the other side of the sea."

Chroniclers and native historians have also speculated on the ancestral heritage of the people of Mexico. The Texcocan *mestizo* Fernando de Alva Ixtlilxóchitl, a sixteenth-century historian, spoke of a council meeting held at Huehuetulapalan in 132 B.C. and of early kings who were "high of stature, white and bearded like Spaniards." He stated that white and blond children were born to descendants of the early Toltecs of central Mexico as late as the tenth century. Fray Bernardino de Sahagún, who lived in Mexico from 1529 to 1590, spoke of a transoceanic voyage of the early settlers of Middle America, who "never ceased to have their prophets."

Juan de Torquemada, another early chronicler, described them as "a very wise people, skilled in shipbuilding and in working gold and silver," their garb resembling that of Turkey.

Because of his special interest in Semitic and Near Eastern origins Mr. Ferguson initiated in 1964 a linguistic project with the support of David Jordan Rust of San Leandro, California, and under the supervision of Professor Morris Swadesh of the National University of Mexico. Professor Swadesh and his assistants have compared a few hundred words of indigenous languages of Mexico with Hebrew to determine to what extent, if any, Hebraic influences may have survived in the tongues spoken today. "I was surprised," he commented, "at the number and closeness of the parallels between the Savi-Zaa (which includes the Zapotec and Mixtec) and the Semitic languages." A thousand basic words are to be compared in the linguistic research program. Mr. Ferguson has reported that, in the course of a pilot study in Oaxaca, the Zapotec vocabulary sampled contained from 18 to 20 percent recognizable (but corrupted by time) Hebrew words. Such a percentage, he maintains, is too high to be the result of chance parallels.

Mr. Ferguson has also compiled a list of 311 cultural elements common in ancient times to both Near Eastern and Middle American cultures. These include such objects as adobe bricks, blast furnaces, crested war helmets, nose rings, truncated pyramids, sundials, stucco masks on walls, thrones, wheeled toys made of pottery, hieroglyphics, genealogical records, fertility figurines, unleavened bread, tripod vessels and cylinder seals incised with identical designs. Also compared by him were such practices and concepts as the payment of a dowry by the bridegroom, New Year renewal ceremonies, Venus cycles, a zodiacal sequence, the idea of a scapegoat, the decoration of pottery surfaces with human features, the rite of human sacrifice, skull deformation and the principle of the corbelled arch.

In his detailed study of cylinder seals and their diverse designs Henri Frankfort of the Oriental Institute of the University of Chicago stated that "one must reckon to a greater extent than most of us were hitherto prepared to admit with the possibility of diffusion from the Middle East." The "amazingly abstract" quality of the designs used on ancient seals and spindle whorls place them, according to Dr. Jorge Enciso, "among the examples of outstanding art of all ages." Used from remote times in Mexico for personal adornment and ceramic decoration, some seals resemble rolling pins, while flat ones are equipped with handles. Many were fashioned from clay, although bone, stone and copper were also used. Designs of feet, hands and geometric forms, later of flowers, birds, animals and human figures, were made into molds which were inked with vegetable or mineral

Cylinder seals, the designs inked with vegetable or mineral dyes, were used from remote times. Some scholars have recently compared similar dyestuffs employed by pre-Columbian peoples of Middle America and the ancient Hebrews.

dyes and pressed against the skin, cloth, pottery or paper. Smoke and charcoal were used for dyes, as were chalk, gypsum and cochineal. *Escuahuitl,* the blood tree, provided a red coloring and *zacatlascal,* a tropical parasite, a yellow dye. Indigo was combined with alum and white chalk to obtain a turquoise shade.

Symbols of ancient art were of special interest to the artist and Egyptologist Joseph Lindon Smith, who observed in *Tombs, Temples and Ancient Art,* that he had found "striking features in common between the cultures of the Egyptians and of the Maya," among them the "flowing vase," symbolizing one of the earliest astral myths. With its undulating streams, flowing in opposite directions, it is a symbol of the "Milky Way," regarded by ancient peoples as the seed, or life-power, of deity, and known as early as 2400 B.C. to Mesopotamia and to the astronomers of pre-Columbian Mexico. Another shared symbol was the serpent, hailed as the river of the sky and the source of rain, as well as a symbol of life, rebirth and resurrection. The "Tree of Life" design, a motif found in ancient Sumerian, Egyptian, Assyrian, Hittite and Hebraic cultures and mentioned in the Books of Genesis and Revelations, may also be seen in the Maya area. Dr. Matthew W. Stirling has dated its appearance on a stele at Izapa in Chiapas at about the beginning of the Christian Era. A "Tree of Life" design appears in bas-relief on the lid of a sarcophagus in a chamber deep within the heart of the pyramid of the Temple of the Inscriptions at Palenque.

Altars and incense-burners horned at four corners, described in the Old Testament, are symbols common to the ancient Middle East and to ancient Middle America, as is the so-called "holy bucket," often pictured in the hands of religious personages. The six-pointed star, or shield, of David, formed by two equilateral triangles, found as early as the seventh century B.C. on a Hebrew tombstone at Sidon, appears, with the triangles similarly interlaced, on the wall of a Maya ruin in Uxmal. Count Goblet D'Alviella of Belgium in his *The Migration of Symbols,* published in London in 1894, called attention to the fact that the feathered "tail," or lower appendage, of the star found at Uxmal is like pennated tails attached to symbols from ancient Bible lands. It suggested, he remarked, "in a striking manner, the pennated tail of certain Assyrian, Phoenician and Persian globes." Lord Kingsborough, who compiled nine volumes of Aztec and Maya codices (*Antiquities of Mexico,* 1831–1848) subscribed totally to the notion of the colonization of Mexico by "The Lost Tribes of Israel." William H. Prescott commented wryly that to this theory "the whole battery of Lord Kingsborough's logic and learning was directed; for this hieroglyphics were unriddled, manuscripts compared, monuments delineated."

Other theorists have favored wandering Irish monks over migrants from the Middle East as "New World culture-bearers." Bolstering the case for an early Celtic diffusion, Hans Leip declared in *River in the Sea: Story of the Gulf Stream,* "The Irish legend of Saint Brendan seems to me to harmonize better with the Mexican-Toltec traditions and with those of Yucatán and Guatemala." In the Irish chronicles known as the *Imranas,* compiled up to A.D. 700, there are references to the evangelizing expeditions of Saint Brendan, who presumably left Galway A.D. 577, accompanied by seventeen monks, to sail toward the "Promised Land" on the other side of the ocean. These, according to some theorists, were the original "fair gods" of Middle American legends. In *They All Discovered America,* Charles Michael Boland placed the date of departure of the canonized Celtic navigator on one of his several voyages a few decades earlier than the

The Star or Shield of David, the Hebrew symbol, has been compared to a star with a "feathered tail" found at Uxmal, a Maya city of Yucatán.

Imranas date. He states that Saint Brendan "put out from Aran Mor on March 22nd in the year 551."

Hans Leip has suggested a link between the city of Tula and the legendary Norse isle of Thule. The Greek navigator Phileas of Marseilles was reputed to have visited Great Britain and Thule, or Tule, in 325 B.C., but scholars have argued whether Thule might be the Shetland Islands or Iceland. The Irish monk Discuile maintained that it could only have been Iceland. Mention is made in ancient Icelandic chronicles of expeditions to a "land of white men." Alexander von Humboldt inferred that this might have been to what is now Florida.

The late Professor Augustín Aragon Leiva of Mexico City has called attention to present-day Tula, not far from Tampico, where, some believe, Saint Brendan may have disembarked. Dr. Eulalia Guzmán has suggested that Tula of Tamaulipas might be traced to the custom observed by migratory Nahua tribes of naming new places in memory of their original cities. In the Nahuatl language "Tula," or "Tollan," signifies "Where Bulrushes Grow." Hans Leip is of the opinion that the name of the Maya deity Kukulcán, a designation of the Nahuas' "fair god," Quetzalcóatl, was that of a priest or ruler of Tula. This theory has been endorsed by Dr. Jorge Acosta. According to some interpreters the word "Kukulcán" has a strange etymology. The term "cucullated," applied by English botanists to hooded flowers, is derived from the Latin root *cucullus,* meaning "monastic habit." "Can," an ancient English vocable, signifies "to cover." It is claimed by some scholars that "Kukulcán" refers to a cowled monk. Mrs. Ethel D. Turner has pointed out that Cu Chulainn was the greatest of Gaelic heroes. Most Maya scholars trace the construction of the word to *cuc,* a Maya word for quetzal bird, and *can,* Maya for serpent.

Whether the legendary footprints of Saint Brendan's monks, who might have converted pagan natives without violence and taught them various arts and crafts, thus giving rise to the Quetzalcóatl myth, or whether, as argued by Constance Irwin in *Fair Gods and Stone Faces,* the footprints were those of Phoenicians bringing a legend of a fair-skinned god, it is clear that attempts to explain the dim cultural beginnings of the Middle American peoples have indeed proliferated. According to Charles Michael Boland, a Chinese monk, Hoei-Shin, left the Celestial Empire and encountered a king named Ichi in Mexico in A.D. 499. An overland journey was reportedly made by a Buddhist monk, Hsuan Tsang, across central Asia and India, as well as a voyage to Java six centuries before Marco Polo. An opinion advanced by a member of China's National Assembly holds that a Chinese monk, Fa Hsien, landed in Mexico in A.D. 412 and that it was he who became the Toltec culture-hero symbolized by the "plumed serpent" whose influence was so significant in the development of Middle

America. Fa Hsien and his companions, according to this theory, had apparently started for India but had become lost on an unknown coast, leaving it on April 16, A.D. 413 and making their way back at last to China.

Such a theory has been challenged by still other theorists who maintained that the mysterious voyager was none other than the Norse adventurer Leif Ericson, who is believed by many scholars to have reached Pánuco on the Gulf of Mexico at the end of the tenth century. The extensive voyages of the Vikings' "dragon ships" were cited in support of this claim. A theory of American cultural origins in Polynesia was advanced by Thor Heyerdahl, leader of the Kon-Tiki expedition, in his *American Indians in the Pacific*. George E. Carter speculated on unknown voyagers in an article in the *Pacific Review* in February 1957: "Botanists have discovered that an Asiatic cotton and a Peruvian wild cotton combined to produce a duplicate of the American domesticated cotton. Now, cotton seeds are not particularly tough. Plant men do not believe that they can float around the ocean and remain alive. To have got to America they must have been carried there by someone."

The quest for knowledge concerning the dawn of civilization in the New World will doubtless bring forth many more such speculations. Yet who can determine which is the true beginning? As Thomas Mann observed in his preface to *Joseph and His Brothers:* "For the unresearchable plays a kind of mocking game with our researching ardours; it offers apparent holds and goals, behind which, when we have gained them, new reaches of the past still open out—as happens to the coastwise voyager, who finds no end to his journey, for behind each headland of clayey dunes he conquers, fresh headlands and new distances lure him on."

Part One

CENTRAL MEXICO

CHAPTER II

The Settlement of the Valley of Mexico

THERE CAN BE, obviously, no simple, clear-cut answer to the question of when and how man arrived and developed his early culture in the Americas. With every advance in scientific methods for rediscovering and reconstructing lost civilizations, the potential field of research broadens. Yet whatever theory of provenance may be assigned to the earliest men in Middle America, anthropologists generally agree that the continent of North America has been inhabited for at least 20,000 years, with the time span steadily lengthening, and that the most likely route of exodus was from the Siberian coast to the mainland, to the Valley of Mexico and beyond. Once arrived in the Americas the early peoples were confronted by situations which will forever elude precise analysis. They slowly evolved a way of life until, in the Olmec, Teotihuacán, Toltec, Zapotec, Mixtec, Aztec, Tarascan, Maya and other ancient cultures of Middle America, they achieved advanced and unique forms of civilization.

For many millennia before the full flowering of the creative faculties that resulted in their highly original contributions to art, science and religious ritual, the earliest inhabitants of the Valley of Mexico, whether indigenous or migrant peoples, probably owed their survival, as Dr. Román Piña Chan has suggested, to native herbivorous animals. Mammoths, camels, horses and antelopes, existing under climatic conditions more humid than those of the present day, grazed on the abundant grasses and supplied the early hunters with meat, fats and skins for clothing as well as horn, bone and ligaments for a variety of useful tools, weapons and other artifacts.

These early peoples also gathered herbs, seeds, roots and various forest products. To protect themselves from cold they fashioned rude cloaks and sought the shelter of caves. Details of their primitive way of life emerged in the late 1940's when Dr. Helmut de Terra found two ancient sites in the Valley of Mexico known to scholars as the stone industries of San Juan and Chalco. These yielded scrapers, flakers, gravers, stone knives, hammers, slicers, projectile points and chipped pebbles of quartz, chalcedony and obsidian. Archaeologists believe the objects may have been fashioned and used by relatives of the ancient Tepexpán man (woman). At Santa Isabel Iztapan were found two points, one imbedded in the remains of a mammoth, three scrapers and an obsidian blade. A discovery in San Vicente Chicoloapan showed that seeds and grains were ground. Among a hundred tools, mainly of basalt, found alongside a skeleton believed to be between 6,000 and 7,000 years old were some crude millstones.

In any discussion of remote cultural origins in this territory, the date put forth by Dr. Herbert J. Spinden as marking the beginning of agriculture in the New World—c. 4000 B.C.—is significant. "It may be earlier," he has said, "but it can hardly be much later." It is his contention that besides developing agriculture, the making of pottery, weaving and other characteristic arts of sedentary peoples, the Maya of Middle America, at least, began at an early period to form the "elaborate social and religious structures that result from a sure supply of food and a reasonable amount of leisure." His estimate was verified by the work of scientists engaged in the botanical and archaeological project sponsored in the Tehuacán caves by the Robert S. Peabody Foundation under the direction of Dr. Richard S. MacNeish, in cooperation with the National Institute of Anthropology and History. It has been established by this study that the ancient inhabitants of the area grew calabaza, or squash, before 6000 B.C. and that *maíz*, or Indian corn, the "staff of life" of the New World, was apparently domesticated between 5000 and 4000 B.C. During a long period before the development of ceramics various cultivated plants, including beans, pumpkins, chile and amaranth, were added to the diet of aboriginal man in the Americas. Pottery appeared about 2000 B.C. in a very crude form, marking the end of the prehistoric period.

The earliest known settlement in Central Mexico dating from what has been called the Pre-Classic, or Formative, period, formerly known as the Archaic period, about 1350 B.C., is located near El Arbolillo in the Guadalupe Range foothills. Here ancient refuse heaps were excavated and studied in 1930–1931 by the late Dr. George C. Vaillant. Two years earlier, at nearby Zacatenco, he had excavated a settlement which was believed to have flourished about 1100 B.C. Both sites are located on the slopes of enormous hills overlooking old lake beds. At Zacatenco bodies sprinkled with red cinnabar were found together with funerary jade carvings, an ancient burial custom also followed in China.

Excavations at a large cemetery, **Tlatilco,** west of Mexico City, including the discovery of many full-figured female figurines, are believed to show the existence of a settlement illustrating the intermediate phase of the Pre-Classic culture. West of Tlatilco is the site known as Cerro del Tepalcate, which was occupied in the Late Pre-Classic period. This hillside settlement, overlooking the entire Valley of Mexico, appears to have been founded after the abandonment of Tlatilco, which flourished possibly as early as 2000 B.C. and could have ended by 150 B.C. Excavations have yielded quantities of pottery, imported from Chupícuaro in Guanajuato, in a style believed to have originated in western Mexico. Here, too, have been found clay masks and seals, terra-cotta figurines representing warriors, medicine men, acrobats and dancers and a variety of jade and pyrite objects. The remains of terraces indicate that a small temple with red-painted walls, built of irregularly cut, unworked slabs and tree trunks, and with a straw roof sharply elevated at each end, once rose upon a platform with a polished floor. One of the platforms covered graves of people with mutilated teeth and deformed skulls. Dr. Román Piña Chan has stated that in his opinion this construction is the most ancient temple in the Central Plateau region. He has cited its similarity to small models of pre-Hispanic structures originating in western Mexico.

Various full-hipped female figurines, along with pottery vessels, have been found at Tlatilco burial sites.

The Tlatilco figurines include many known as the "Pretty Lady" type (*left*) and other vessels (*right*). According to some scholars these were fashioned from clay by Pre-Classic peoples to invoke the help of magic forces to obtain abundant harvests.

In 1917 **Copilco** near San Angel in the Villa Obregón district was excavated under the direction of the late Dr. Manuel F. Gamio, revealing a variety of pottery and stone objects, together with several skeletons buried in cylindrical graves and in earthen jars. These have been dated by most authorities from the remote period between 1100 and 600 B.C. Beneath the igneous rock of El Pedregal were found stone pavements, small figurines and bone artifacts. The dwellings, sometimes floored with evenly cut blocks of *tezontle,* a local stone, were made of straw, tree trunks and clay. The dead were buried in an extended position with offerings that were believed to be of use to them in an afterlife. The quantities of vessels found, both for domestic use and of a funerary character, indicate that the practice of the ceramic arts was one of Copilco's main occupations.

Among the objects found at Copilco were ceramic vessels and primitive stone *metates* and *manos,* used to grind *maíz,* a staple food of Middle America.

The ceramic and lapidary arts reached an even higher development at **Cuicuilco** ("The Place of Song and Dance"), first explored in 1922, as demonstrated by figurines of clay, well-designed ear ornaments, whistles, flutes, ocarinas and a wealth of other decorative and useful objects. The theory that Cuicuilco may have been a large civil and ritual center organized by a priesthood for the worship of specific deities is borne out by a profusion of images of *el dios viejo,* "the old god," who is generally represented as an aged hunchback carrying a brazier on his back.

Cuicuilco, regarded as belonging to the latest of the three major phases in the development of the Pre-Classic culture, is a vestige of the era that marked the beginning of monumental religious architecture. One of the oldest edifices on the American continent, it rises from an expanse of petrified lava at Tlalpam in the suburbs of the Mexican capital. Here lived early peoples whose existence has been reconstructed from shreds of archaeological evidence hidden for centuries beneath the lava flow.

The precise source of the fiery torrents that successively engulfed the land and its culture, imbedding the base of the flat-topped mound, is still a matter of controversy. Some scientists claim that a series of mighty volcanic eruptions, occurring between 4,000 and 12,000 years ago, emanated from the giant Ajusco, the highest peak of the Cordilleras (13,000 feet above sea level), the mountain range dividing Morelos and the Central Plateau. Others maintain that El Pedregal was formed later by Xitli—the Nahuatl word for "navel"—a mouth of the extinguished Ajusco. This smaller volcano, southwest of Tlalpam, reaches a height of more than 9,000 feet and gives the appearance, at times, of having been thrust forward by the parent Ajusco to embark upon a destructive career of its own.

Cuicuilco is really a series of superimposed, truncated mounds and may have been modeled after the contours of surrounding volcanoes, of which there are about 1,500 in Mexico. R. H. K. Marett observed in his *Archaeological Tours from Mexico City* that "Cuicuilco is neither very beautiful nor very impressive in its ruined condition, but it makes up for these deficiencies by the interest it inspires." That interest centers on the fact that the mound, however crude, is the archetype of all the magnificent temple-pyramids that glorified the indigenous cultures of later epochs. Grim, fortress-like and primitive it may be in comparison with the brilliantly columned and carved structures of Teotihuacán, Tula or vanished Tenochtitlán.* Yet it stands as monumental evidence, in its orientation to the four points of the compass, that even in remote millennia men were observing the movements of celestial bodies, using the knowledge thus gained to plant crops in season. It shows also, in the various examples of early decorative art which have survived, that men felt a need for beauty and adornment. One of Mexico's earliest paintings, a representation of a large red serpent, was found in a megalithic-type crypt at Cuicuilco.

As with other regions of Middle America where a Pre-Classic cultural horizon existed between 3000 and 1500 B.C., the original provenance of the peoples responsible for the development of the community can only be surmised. The inhabitants of both Copilco and Cuicuilco were essentially agriculturists, raising *maíz,* which they ground on large basalt *metates,* or curved millstones, equipped with *manos,* cylindrical hand stones. However, they practiced a mixed economy, relying for much of their food supply on hunting, fishing and the gathering of grasses and herbs. *Metates,* identical in form with those used to grind corn and chile peppers in many Mexican villages today, were found beneath the lava. Fossilized *maíz* cobs were imbedded in the Pre-Classic stratum.

The skeletal remains indicate that these people were no different from contemporary inhabitants of the region, who still depend largely upon agriculture, fishing, hunting and the gathering of roots and wild grasses. The differences between the way of life of the earliest known occupants of the Valley of Mexico, as exemplified by the Tepexpán man (woman), and the subsequent inhabitants of El Pedregal stemmed mainly from the initiation of agriculture. By increasing the quantity and stability of the food supply, more leisure was available for other activities. With an increased population came a broader specialization, as evidenced by the elaborate burials and religious structures.

* Some Nahuatl scholars favor Tenochtítlan.

A reconstruction of flat-topped Cuicuilco, one of the oldest edifices on the American continent. *Drawing by Gregorio Gutierrez Balderas.*

The sides of Cuicuilco, a vast bulk about 60 feet high and 370 feet in diameter, were strengthened by its builders with river boulders. Proof of the sturdiness of its construction may be noted in the fact that it withstood the onrush of lava that buried Copilco. Its inhabitants may have gone to Tlapacoya, a smaller site only recently excavated. Eduardo Noguera and Byron C. Cummings made an opening at the base of Cuicuilco. The trench, almost exactly oriented toward the east, freed the circular platform from the stratum of lava on which the four superimposed tiers rested. Ignacio Marquina has noted the possibility that the original monument was a single circular structure of smaller dimensions than the present one, which was progressively enlarged at the base and heightened.

Between 1955 and 1957 Robert F. Heizer and J. A. Bennyhoff of the University of Southern California found at Cuicuilco four other early pyramids, among them one of a circular shape, with a sun-dried adobe surface and seven large stairlike levels. The remains of an ancient circular

structure may be seen at Chupícuaro in the southeast corner of Guanajuato. This mound, its convex surface faced with river boulders, is one of the few cylindrical-conical monuments similar to Cuicuilco.

Today gardens and tree-lined walks create a pleasant approach to ancient Cuicuilco, which rises just beyond the campus of the National University south of Mexico City. Here the flowering scarlet *colorín,* the sparkling white stone bordering the paths and a glass-walled museum provide a striking contrast to the black sea of volcanic rock that swirls around its base on three sides and extends on the north to the far horizon. Cuicuilco effectively points up the campaign to make Mexico's ancient sites centers of aesthetic as well as of scholarly interest. Here, in dramatic juxtaposition, are the opposite ends of the vast time trajectory linking cave and cyclotron, for, also rising out of the lava is the House of Higher Learning, with its towering, rectangular forms and its bizarre, horseshoe-shaped units containing reactors and other nuclear-fission devices.

Cuicuilco, its masssive bulk faced with river boulders, withstood the flow of lava from a nearby volcano that imbedded its base.

In Mexico City's Chapultepec Park now stands the new ultramodern, 65-acre National Museum of Anthropology, where vast collections of original items as well as reconstructions and reproductions of important discoveries of Mexico's ancient past are strikingly displayed in a complex of galleries. At its opening on September 17, 1964, Dr. Jaime Torres Bodet paid homage to Cuauhtémoc, the last leader of the Aztecs, and to the proud culture of his ancestors and all the cultures covered, "with firm and powerful wings, by the eagle of his lineage."

At San Pedro Tepetlapa, in the region once engulfed by Ajusco's streams of lava, towers the Anáhuacalli, its name, which means "Near the Water," recalling the vanished Nahuas of the Valley of Anáhuac. This museum was willed to the people of Mexico by the late Diego Rivera, who provided for its maintenance and presented to it his own extensive collection of ancient art. At the time of his death he had accumulated 59,400 pieces of pre-Hispanic sculpture. Rising from the lava and built of the porous, black stone, it is reminiscent of ancient temples. The people who once lived and worshipped in this Valley of Mexico left a powerful aesthetic impression not only upon the land but upon the stone and clay with which they worked.

The galleries of the new National Museum of Anthropology in Chapultepec Park (*top*) surround a central patio. Its collection of more than 100,000 relics and replicas presents an unrivaled panorama of pre-Hispanic cultures. The Anáhuacalli (*bottom*) was built by Diego Rivera, who bequeathed it and his own extensive collection of ancient Mexican art to the people of Mexico.

CHAPTER III

The Builders of Teotihuacán, Tula, Xochicalco and Tenayuca: Precursors of Tenochtitlán

ARCHAEOLOGISTS who are restoring many of the buried cities of ancient America have long sought to identify the people of the Valley of Mexico who built monumental structures and ornamented their pottery and tools, which they traded far and wide, centuries before the Aztecs' capital, Tenochtitlán, rose on the site of what is today Mexico City. After full-scale excavations, two early sites, Teotihuacán and Tula, have emerged from millennial obscurity. Xochicalco and Tenayuca, protected since the turn of the century by being designated as official archaeological zones, have long fascinated scholars as symbols of early cultures. The jewel of Anáhuac—dazzling Tenochtitlán on its many causeways—was razed by the Spaniards, surviving only in a few descriptions by those chroniclers who beheld its splendor before its fall in 1521.

Certain areas of Mexico have provided archaeologists with clues by which to document chronologies of various cultural zones. Date-bearing inscriptions on upright stelae, or stone slabs, have enabled scholars to trace with precision events occurring in some Maya areas as far back as 300 B.C.; by means of Mixtec codices, the broad outlines of the history of the Oaxaca region to A.D. 692 can be reconstructed; but the chronology of the Central Plateau before the end of the ninth century cannot, at present, be documented.

The year A.D. 900 is usually chosen to denote the end of the Classic period and the beginning not only of coherent record but of the dawn of the use of metal, ushered in with the arrival of the Toltecs in the Valley of Mexico. The Teotihuacanos had apparently preceded them, yet for all practical purposes the New World cultures were still in the Stone Age, as metal was used in Teotihuacán primarily for ornaments and rarely for tools.

The Toltecs, according to Dr. Wigberto Jiménez Moreno and other authorities, came from the northwest, traversing, in their advance, the plains of Ixtlahuaca north of Toluca. This presumed route coincides with the theory—supported by the presence of Toltec influence in the regions of Nayarit and Michoacán—that their cultures developed still farther north, probably in what are now northern Jalisco and southern Zacatecas, with the earliest phases originating in an unknown location. Some investigators place this cultural fount in the area of North America occupied by the states of New Mexico, Arizona, Colorado and California.

The identity of the Toltecs, however, poses one of the most confusing problems in the legendary and documented history of Mexico. Even the name has aroused controversy. According to Professor Ramón Mena, the word does not, as was generally believed, signify "artist," "artisan," "architect," or "inhabitant of Tollan," but rather "people who stuffed," from the Nahuatl word *tecatl,* or "people," and the verb *toloa,* "to stuff, or to feed gluttonously." He suggested that since there are no such terms as "Toltec" or "Aztec" in the Nahuatl language, even though both are in common use, a more correct practice would be to call the earlier (Toltec) group the "ancient Nahuas" and the much later (Aztec) tribe "the recent Nahuas."

Before the results of the excavations undertaken by Dr. Jorge R. Acosta at Tula and the research of Dr. Jiménez Moreno were coordinated, the Toltecs were generally credited with the building of **Teotihuacán,** recently excavated and restored in what has been called "probably the most ambitious archaeological exploration in this hemisphere." Evidence produced within the last decade has, however, shown that the earlier Teotihuacán epoch came to a close by or before the era of the Toltecs. As late as 1941, when Dr. George C. Vaillant published his *Aztecs of Mexico,* the story of the Teotihuacanos as related by the native historian Fernando de Alva Ixtlilxóchitl was believed to have applied to the Toltecs. But in the view of recent investigators the end of the Teotihuacanos as a political power came with the arrival in the Valley of Mexico of the Toltec-Chichimec and Otomi peoples, although the cultural influence of Teotihuacán was still felt over a wide area.

Led by the fierce warrior Mixcóatl, who has been called the "New World Genghis Khan" and who was deified by his own people, the Toltec hordes appeared with the suddenness of a cyclone, which the word "Mixcóatl" signifies. After burning and sacking Teotihuacán the energetic chieftain moved on, seeking a favorable site, finally settling on the southern shore of Lake Texcoco at Culhuacán ("The Place of the Turning" or "The

Place of the Bent Ancient Ones"). According to the *Anales de Cuauhtitlán,* he later moved the seat of the Toltec empire to Tula. The Culhuacán site, however, offered strategic advantages because of its peninsular location, numerous caves and proximity to the Cerro de la Estrella ("Hill of the Star"), where the annual "New Fire" ceremony was performed.

Five tombs have been discovered in Culhuacán (district of Ixtapalapa, near the old Dominican Convent of San Matias) with Teotihuacán-style ceramics. The artifacts were placed with the bones, which were interred in a fetal position, one above the other.

There is evidence that what has been called the Pre-Classic ceramic period began in the Valley of Mexico about 1500 B.C. and terminated possibly two centuries before the beginning of the Christian era. The Teotihuacán culture, as deduced from recent excavations at Teotihuacán, is believed to have coexisted with the latter Pre-Classic culture and to have ended by A.D. 900 or earlier, a date which, tradition holds, marks the foundation of Tula, thus spanning a time cycle of more than a millennium. The Teotihuacanos may have governed an area larger than that over which the Aztecs held sway in their prime. The latter did not arrive in the Valley of Mexico until 500 years after the Teotihuacanos as a great force had disappeared.

To date no one may say with certainty from whence came the Teotihuacanos or what language they spoke. Yet considerably more is known today of the builders of the extraordinary structures of Teotihuacán, about 33 miles north of Mexico City, than was known by the Aztecs. The "City of the Gods" actually presented more of an enigma to the Aztec emperors than it does to modern archaeologists, who have been able to extract some idea of its past grandeur.

This fabulous city, described by Mme Laurette Séjourné as a "vast poem, every detail an integral part of a highly inspired whole," seems to have emerged suddenly in all its full creative vigor. Although Teotihuacán's roots were deep in the Pre-Classic world, as a study of the ruins of Cuicuilco has indicated, the "City of the Gods" was clearly planned from the start, even to such features as the orientation and decoration of the buildings. Architects have pointed out that remarkable advantage was taken, not only of the terrain—a gentle, sloping valley, traversed from east to west by a small river, the San Juan—but especially of the hills encircling it, dominated by the extinct volcano Cerro Gordo. The architect or architects responsible for the complex and its harmonious relation to the environment must have stood on some distant mountaintop, calculating from afar the spatial requirements with much the same precision employed by a modern city planner.

The vast Teotihuacán achievement appears all the more remarkable

Abandoned for centuries, the city of Teotihuacán was the first real urban site in central Mexico. Built in rings, its core was bisected by a wide avenue. In the center were pyramids, temples, markets and plazas, with palaces and smaller dwellings on the outskirts.

when one considers that artistic perception and engineering technique had to be subordinated to the dictates of a cosmic ceremonial design. As R. H. K. Marett commented, "That astronomical genius should be revealed by architecture may seem strange until it is realized that the principal buildings of the city are quite possibly arranged according to a highly complicated astronomical scheme." Each temple was so placed that the sun's rays would strike a portion of it on a given day and at a given season, such an arrangement being a part of the calendrical system that played so dominant a role in ancient Mexican life. Central Teotihuacán was a religious focus rather than a city in the modern sense, and its layout conformed to the highly symbolic outlook of the priesthood. Teotihuacán was, in fact, the first real urban site in central Mexico, the most important and by far the largest.

A clue to the beginnings of Teotihuacán and its creative builders may be concealed in an ancient epic of four suns, or eras, during which life on earth evolved. The first era, *El Sol del Agua* (The Sun of the Water) existed, according to the historian de Alva Ixtlilxóchitl, at the creation of the world by the Nahuas' supreme deity. Tloque-Nahuaque. After 1,716 years, floods and catastrophic bolts of lightning apparently destroyed it. During the second era, *El Sol de la Tierra* (The Sun of the Earth), the world was believed to have been inhabited by a race of giants, the Quinametzin, who, before being vanquished by the Olmecs and the Xicalanca, were presumed to have built the pyramids of Teotihuacán. The new conquerors inherited the city's grandeur and opened up the great cultural epochs through the efforts of an inspired leader, teacher and spiritual guide, known as Huemac, or "Big Hand," and called, by some, Quetzalcóatl. The other two legendary eras were known as *El Sol del Viente* (The Sun of the Wind) and *El Sol del Fuego* (The Sun of the Fire).

While legend and history remain fused in any real attempt to explain the origin and development of Teotihuacán, the four legendary epochs may have some historic relevance. The first era, which was said to have come to an end in vast inundations, is analogous to the diluvial epics of other ancient civilizations. The giants were believed to have all but disappeared in the toll of violent earthquakes, and bones of huge prehistoric animals have been discovered in the Central Valley area. During the third period Quetzalcóatl, the god of the wind, is said to have prophesied that the fourth "sun" would end in a general conflagration. One of the most important deities of Teotihuacán was the "Old God," or the "Lord of Fire."

One of the deities honored at Teotihuacán was the god of fire. This representation in volcanic stone was made in the form of an old man bearing on his shoulders an incense burner.

Among the objects excavated at the site of the "Quetzal-Butterfly Palace" was a huge stone serpent head. Teotihuacán has been called "the place where the serpent learned to fly."

Associated with the night hours, the beneficient deity was portrayed in stone and clay, as at Cuicuilco, as an old man bearing on his shoulders a receptacle for burning incense. The worship of this god, continuous from the Upper Pre-Classic period through the Aztec supremacy, during which he was known as Huehuetéotl, represents the oldest known ritual honoring any Middle American deity.

The suffix *téotl,* found in Huehuetéotl, figures in the poetic version cited by Fray Bernardino de Sahagún for the naming of Teotihuacán, which in Nahuatl signifies "The City of the Gods," or "The Place Where Men Became Gods," also interpreted as "The Place Where Men Became Lords."

"The lords therein buried," Sahagún wrote, "after their death were canonized as gods, and it was said that they did not die, but wakened out of a dream and that they turned into spirits or gods . . . and so they said to the dead 'Lord, or Lady, wake, for it begins to dawn; now comes the daylight, for the yellow-feathered birds begin to sing, and the many-colored butterflies go flying.' And when anyone died, they used to say of him that he was now *téotl,* meaning to say he died in order to become spirit of god." In *Burning Water* Mme Séjourné observed that, "Far from implying any gross, polytheistic belief, the term 'Teotihuacán' evokes the idea of human divinity and shows that the 'City of the Gods' was the very place where the serpent learned miraculously to fly; that is, where the individual, through inner growth, attained the category of a celestial being."

Reconstruction of Teotihuacán, "The City of the Gods." *Drawing by Gregorio Gutierrez Balderas.*

Perhaps the enigma as to the rare degree of artistic development attained at Teotihuacán may find no other explanation than the elusive one offered Fray Sahagún. The Indians told him, he said, that when in response to a summons from their god the ancient wise men who had journeyed from their far-off land returned to the East, only four of the venerable members of the group remained. It was they who had the huge task of restoring the narrative of the destinies, the annals, the computations of the years and the "Book of Dreams" because the others had taken along with them the "red and black inks and the codices." That irretrievable "Book of Dreams" may contain the only reliable clues.

Archaeologists of the National Institute of Anthropology and History have endeavored to restore Teotihuacán "as a city that was lived in." Present-day visitors may gain some idea of the temples, the vast marketplaces, the quarters of the military and the palaces of the priests and nobles. The archaeological zone is about four miles long and two miles wide, but the ancient city extended far beyond the ceremonial center, embracing an area that, even by modern standards, would be regarded as immense.

As Dr. Frederick A. Peterson pointed out, "Many buildings are invisible to the casual viewer because they lie beneath cornfields or are buried under the rubble, dust and vegetation of centuries." From 1961 to 1963 a small army of workers under the supervision of Dr. Jorge Acosta cleared away debris and prepared the terrain. With his transference to the Department of Pre-Hispanic Monuments as director, the archaeologist Ponciano Salazar Ortegón assumed charge at Teotihuacán, with Dr. Acosta remaining as a consultant.

The main axis of the city is a broad highway designed to connect its two principal groups of buildings, located about a mile and a half apart. At the north is a structure which, with its annexes, is known as the Pyramid of the Moon; at the south is the Temple of Quetzalcóatl (or Tláloc) and the vast courtyard known as La Ciudadela; on the east is the majestic Pyramid of the Sun.

The quadrangular courtyard, occupying 38 acres enclosed by high stone walls, formed one of Teotihuacán's greatest ceremonial plazas. Although the temple is adorned with relief carvings of a plumed serpent, the rain god is also prominently represented by sculptured heads on the

The once splendid metropolis may have been devastated by fire, according to one theory for its abandonment. Char marks have been found on the 12-pillared "Quetzal-Butterfly Palace."

Masks of the rain god and plumed serpent heads adorn the façade of the Temple of Quetzalcóatl (or Tláloc).

plane surfaces of the sloping walls. According to Dr. Eulalia Guzmán, all of the representations are of Tláloc in symbols that might easily be confused with those of Quetzalcóatl, since both deities are identified with water. In the opinion of Mme Séjourné, the two heads are symbolic expressions of the basic Nahua concept, "the vital impulse arising from the unification of opposing elements." According to this interpretation Tláloc, like Quetzalcóatl, is "the bearer of luminous seed which converts matter—in this case the earth—into creative energy."

The highway, or Miccaotli, for a time mistakenly called "The Road of the Dead" because it was believed that the mounds flanking it contained tombs, is an artery built, according to estimates, between 200 B.C. and A.D. 250. Its 130-foot width is defined on both sides with platforms and groups of low buildings, a number of them containing connecting chambers arranged around sunken courtyards. The shrub-covered mounds which have been excavated reveal structures adorned with bas-relief carvings and masterly frescoes, none of which, in fact, served as tombs.

All small pyramids have been excavated and reconstructed in the plaza of the Pyramid of the Moon. Among the ruins unearthed at the rear of this complex was a vaulted passage. The upper stones of its arch were integrated with other stones and its curvature was covered with a clay facing. There are indications that it was devastated by fire. Dr. Acosta has pointed out that during the eighth century the temples and the houses of the priests were evidently sacked. The palace may well have been the scene of a revolt in which the violent passions of the populace were unleashed against the rulers and priests after centuries of blind obedience. Because some of the fragments of the bas-reliefs of the portico seemed to

Recent excavations at Teotihuacán have uncovered various platforms and dwellings in the plaza of the Pyramid of the Moon.

resemble a butterfly, this building received the name of Palacio del Quetzalpapalotl, or "Quetzal-Butterfly Palace." When the entire design was reassembled, the figures, encrusted with obsidian and glistening mica, emerged as quetzal birds in a striking decorative effect. It is thought that this palace may have been the residence of the high priest. Near it are structures which were probably occupied by lesser dignitaries.

On the east side of the Miccaotli is the great Pyramid of the Sun, which appears to have been built in the Late Formative period. Measuring about 720 by 760 feet at its base, it contains approximately a million cubic yards of material and is undoubtedly the most impressive structure at Teotihuacán. At present it rises, in five great elevations, to a height of about 216 feet. At the turn of the century Leopoldo Batres peeled more than 20 feet off the pyramid's southeastern side. In an attempt to reach a possible substructure, thousands of tons of cut *tezontle,* the coarse, reddish volcanic rock so plentiful in the region, were removed. The adobe masses within began to disintegrate with repeated exposure to heavy rains. The pyramid's fourth body was hastily covered with rough rock, resulting in a serious marring of the original symmetry. Projecting slabs, which enclosed sunken panels, had originally anchored the facing of the inclined surfaces. With the removal of the facing, the slabs still projected from the central mass but without an architectural or decorative function. Recent tunneling has, in fact, revealed the existence of older interior structures.

The innumerable archaeological discoveries made at Teotihuacán, including recent excavations in the Zacuala area southwest of the Pyramid of the Sun, described by Mme Séjourné in *Un Palacio en la Ciudad de los Dioses* (*A Palace in the City of the Gods*), testify to the development here of the roots and basic cultural molds that were to be diffused throughout the entire central zone. In nearby Tetitla are painted *tableros* framed by serpents with streams of water flowing from outstretched hands and a procession of jaguars and coyotes. Here, too, is the lavishly decorated triple-unit dwelling group of Atetelco. At Tepantitla, east of the ritual center, the paradise of Tláloc, Tlalocan, is portrayed in an animated fresco as a place of aquatic revels.

As Dr. Miguel León-Portilla has pointed out in his *Los Mexicanos Antiguos a Través de Sus Crónicas y Cantares* (*The Ancient Mexicans as Seen Through Their Chronicles and Songs*), Teotihuacán's "architecture and pyramids, plazas and palaces are like an implicit pattern for future creation." The same may be said, he declares, for its "mural painting, sculpture, marvelous ceramics and works of obsidian." According to the Nahuatl scholar, the paintings of Teotihuacán suggest "ancient codices incorporated in the walls," a description which is particularly apt in the case of the luminous deep red murals which adorn a succession of chambers in the Palace of Zacuala. "Apart from what Teotihuacán was in its era," Dr. León-Portilla has observed, "it has left on thousands of little clay figurines the profound expression on the faces of its savants, priests and ordinary people . . . Teotihuacán was, for the Nahuas of later times, the most ancient root of their religious beliefs and arts—in a word, of the principal institutions of the subsequent culture of Anáhuac."

The original symmetry of the Pyramid of the Sun was marred by the removal of a part of the facing at the turn of the century. Ceramic fragments discovered in recent tunneling indicate no important occupation of the site following the Early Classic period. The pyramid is believed to have been begun in the epoch known as "Teotihuacán I" and completed in "Teotihuacán III."

Murals have been found on plaster-coated walls of buildings which were presumably occupied by officials or priests, notably at the Palace of Zacuala (*top*). A single-dimensional mural depicting the presentation of offerings was found in the structure known as the Temple of Agriculture (*bottom*). A copy was made of it at once, as the colors of ancient frescoes fade when exposed to the elements.

This frieze of jaguars and coyotes was found at Atetelco (*top*). A jaguar provides the motif for the wall painting (*bottom*). The frescoes of Teotihuacán, executed in pigments including black, dark red, yellow, blue and green, have been likened to ancient codices.

Among the artifacts discovered at Teotihuacán are elaborate funerary vases of distinctive design.

The precise dating of the mighty monuments of Teotihuacán is still largely enveloped in mystery. Investigators are often entire millennia apart in estimates of the time of the construction of the city. Through a scholarly coordination of sources known up to 1940 Dr. Vaillant developed a sequence of five cultural phases, from the fourth century to the first quarter of the twelfth century. He dated "Teotihuacán I"—the era in which the sun-dried brick used in the interior of the Pyramids of the Sun and the Moon was made—between A.D. 510 and 666. To the era of the building of the first major structures, culminating with the Temple of Quetzalcóatl (or Tláloc) he assigned the designation "Teotihuacán II." During this period, which began in A.D. 66 and ended in A.D. 829, there was a wide diffusion of Teotihuacán culture in Cholula and Morelos. The era known as "Teotihuacán III–IV" (A.D. 829 to A.D. 959) witnessed commerce with the Maya, new religious manifestations, the construction of temples of the second period, such as the one superimposed on the Temple of Quetzalcóatl (or Tláloc), the use of molds for figurines, incursions by the Chichimecs and the abandonment of the city. During the era designated as "Teotihuacán V," which terminated in A.D. 1122, there was a marked development in religious ritual, a strong Oaxaca influence and the destruction of the city by the Culhua.

However, discoveries made subsequent to Dr. Vaillant's research would seem to place Teotihuacán's first two cultural phases in a far more remote period. Some archaeologists hold that the city was flourishing in 600 B.C.; others, as early as 1500 B.C. A third small group maintains that the construction of Teotihuacán goes back to an era before the eruption of the volcano Xitli, perhaps some 6,000 years ago. The supporters of this theory point out that the adobe of the Pyramid of the Sun contains ceramic pieces, bits of pottery and small clay heads that can be attributed to the Pre-Classic period.

The prevalence of shells from East-Coast species of molluscs in the sculptural ornamentation of the Temple of Quetzalcóatl (or Tláloc) have been cited to suggest that its builders hailed from the Gulf Coast and were probably Olmecs. One hypothesis is that the encounter of the Pre-Classic civilization with the Olmec culture produced the hieratic epoch in which the high priests combined religious and kingly functions. An indication that the Teotihuacanos may have been Nahuatl-speaking—and hence members of the great Nahua family—may lie in their use of a common calendrical system, a view sustained by Dr. Alfonso Caso. While the system itself, founded upon astronomical observation, was the same among the Nahuas, the Olmecs and the Maya, the signs denoting days, months and years were indicated by them in varying symbols.

The mystery of Teotihuacán and its builders was deepened still further during the International Congress of Americanists held in Mexico City in 1962, when evidence suggesting a possible Chinese influence was presented. Dr. Gordon F. Ekholm submitted striking resemblances between the cylindrical tripod pottery of Teotihuacán and Chinese ceramics of the Han dynasty (206 B.C. to A.D. 220). These resemblances embraced form, color and decorative motifs, as well as the shape of covers and the technique of applying decoration. Dr. Robert von Heine-Geldern discussed possible transoceanic influences on the ancient cultures of America, pointing out provocative similarities between, for example, the Maya architecture of

Several scholars have remarked upon the close similarity between Chinese decorative motifs, such as the example (*left*) and Middle-American motifs, notably the design shown (*right*).

Chichén Itzá and Chinese sculptural reliefs and friezes. Dr. Paul Kirchhoff of the National University of Mexico was of the opinion that the Aztec-Maya ritualistic-divinatory calendar was a Chinese invention; he pointed out that the rhythms, animal symbols, four major divisions and other features of the Mexican calendrical system coincided with that of China.

Dr. Eulalia Guzmán later expressed her opinion:

> It is easy to prove that similar things are born without contact when they occur in the common experience. Everywhere the human mind works in a similar way as the result of this common experience. But the tripod vases of Teotihuacán, in all their exquisite detail, show a highly unusual style, and many elements are behind the Meso-American and Chinese calendars. They are the result of mathematical calculation in relation to astronomical phenomena. The way in which a people advances and builds these things cannot be the result of simple coincidence. Long astronomical observations, religious concepts and complicated mental machinery combine to establish calendrical systems.
>
> Three or four sections of the old Winter Palace in the heart of Peking are the same as those of the Palace of Atetelco at Teotihuacán. Exact parallels are to be seen in the two constructions. The four enclosing and elongated raised foundations that extend around the Atetelco patios are duplicated at Peking. They not only have the same approximate height, but both are approached by wide stairways from the outside, and in each there is a descent from the inside to what is called a sunken patio. This is a misnomer, since the ground surface of the patios in both cases is not lower than the ground of the exterior section. The corner arrangement is also alike in the two constructions. The platforms, or bases, do not meet, but the open space at the corners is occupied by stairways that lead up to the top of the construction and then lead down to the "sunken" patio. The balustrades are decorated with relief sculpture in the manner of the decoration of Tenayuca. These remarkably similar structures were not built at the same time. The Peking Palace dates from the reign of Kublai Khan,

whom Marco Polo visited several centuries later than the date of the Teotihuacán monuments, which Dr. Vaillant places between the fifth and seventh centuries A.D. Since these dramatic resemblances exist, why not, considering the time element, believe that the influence traveled westward from the American continent to Asia? There is some historic support for the assumption that Chinese explorers visited the American continent around the time of Teotihuacán's splendor. Is it unreasonable to suppose that they liked what they saw and that they carried these ideas back to China? The cultural influences may well have traveled from America to the Orient, and not the reverse.

Dr. Guzmán recalled also the style of the architectural reliefs in Peking which reminded her of those of El Tajín.

I was astonished to see from the day of my arrival marked resemblances everywhere to motifs prevalent in our own archaeological discoveries. Every fret I knew from the codices or the Monte Albán jewels I found in Peking, sometimes on the friezes,

Dr. Gordon F. Ekholm has offered as evidence of transoceanic influences a cylindrical Teotihuacán-style tripod vessel (*top*) and a bronze cylindrical-footed Chinese jar from the "Kokka," or late Han, period (*bottom*).

The "sunken" patio of Atetelco, approached at the corners by steps, has been compared by Dr. Eulalia Guzmán to courtyards in the Winter Palace in Peking (*opposite page*).

Ground Plan of a Courtyard in the Winter Palace. *Drawing by Ruben Poblano Cordero.*

1. PLATFORMS.
2. CEREMONIAL CHAMBERS OR WORKROOMS.
3. PASSAGE.
4. STEPS (SOME WITH DECORATIVE CARVINGS).

5A. BALUSTRADES (SOME WITH BAS RELIEFS).

5B. DOUBLE BALUSTRADES.

6. COURTYARD.
7. TWO OR THREE STEPS, FOR PASSING FROM ONE COURTYARD TO ANOTHER.
8. A SEPARATION, OR "RESTING PLACE," BETWEEN STEPS.

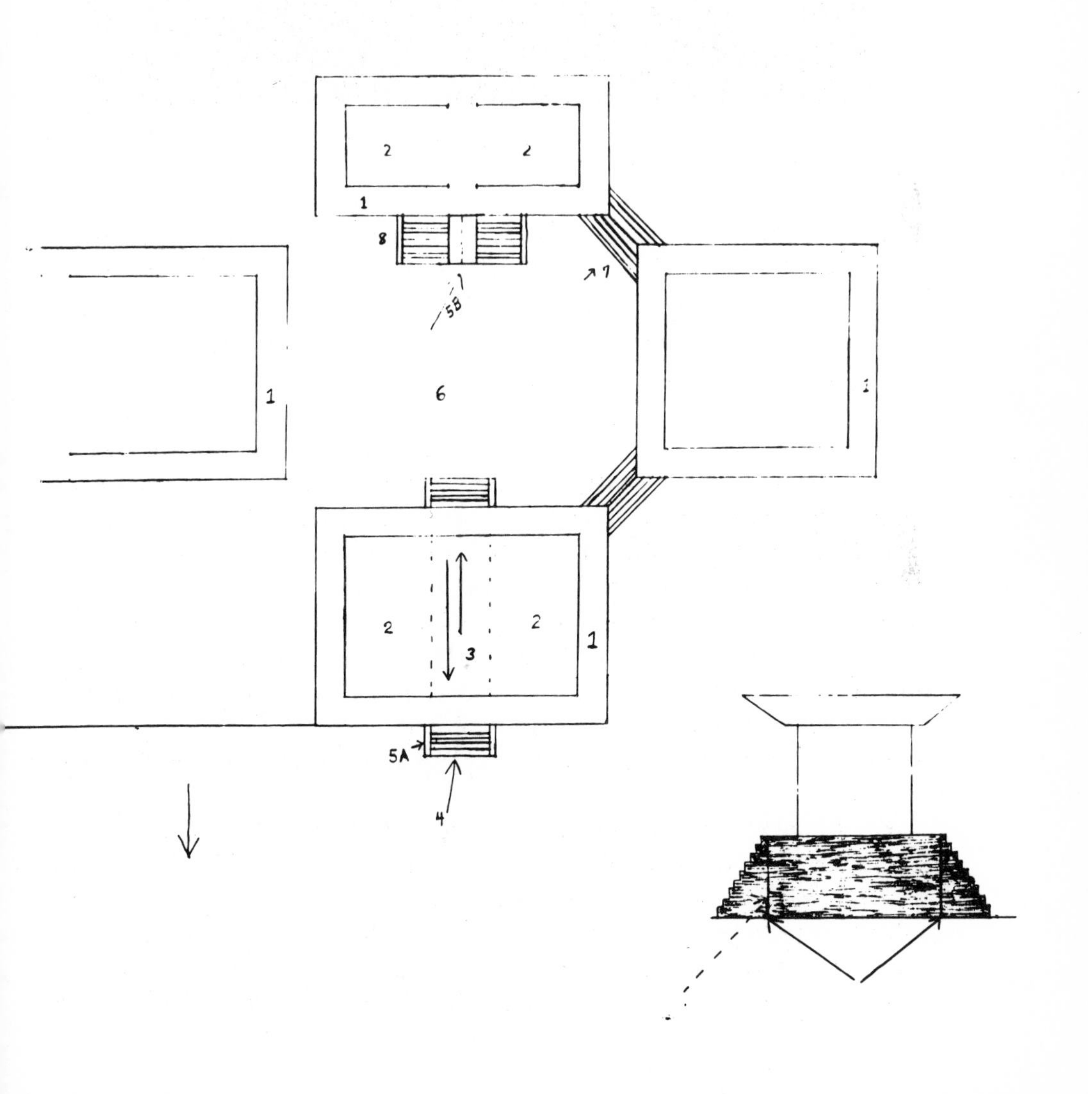

The plump clay dogs of Colima, representative of an almost extinct breed which was fattened for the table, have been compared by Dr. Eulalia Guzmán to similar bronze dogs of ancient Peking.

again in the furniture or on other objects. Then there were the *perros gordos,* or fat dogs, of Colima. I saw several in bronze at the Winter Palace, some courts of which have been converted into museums. These appear to be precisely the same as our own variety.

While up until 1941 the structures of Teotihuacán were regarded by many scholars as an expression of the Toltec culture, it has been shown conclusively that the ancient Toltec capital of **Tollan,** or **Tula,** some 50 miles north of Mexico City, appeared on the architectural horizon after the dispersion of the Teotihuacanos and the abandonment of their ritual city. This erroneous classification stemmed in part from the work of Leopoldo Batres at Teotihuacán. Also, since the Spanish chroniclers often referred to the ancient Toltec capital as a place of grandiose temples and palaces, a veritable "city of marvels," this had led to the drawing of a parallel between the awe-inspiring structures of Teotihuacán and the legendary Tollan.

Dr. Jiménez Moreno demonstrated to the satisfaction of most scholars that the true Toltec capital was Tula, built centuries after Teotihuacán had been deserted and left in ruins following its conquest and burning by the Toltecs, possibly the Toltecs of Tula. Although the claim is still the subject of controversy, excavations and restorations carried out over an eighteen-year-period at Tula by Dr. Jorge Acosta would appear to confirm it. The late Dr. Manuel F. Gamio, however, was among the dissenters, believing that Teotihuacán, a name he suggested was given to the city by the Aztecs, is really ancient Tula, or Tollan.

Although the nomadic Toltec chieftain Mixcóatl, or "Cloud Smoke," the legendary destroyer of the Teotihuacán civilization, was killed in battle, his posthumously born son, Ce Acatl Topiltzin, reared by his grandparents, eventually established himself at Tula, which at that period was in Otomi territory. Tradition holds that this enterprising monarch, after imposing on his Nahuatl-speaking Chichimec subjects the cult of Quetzalcóatl, or the feathered serpent, also assumed the name of the deity. This tradition is supported by a rock carving at Tula depicting Quetzalcóatl and bearing a date corresponding to A.D. 968, which is in agreement with the chronology of events as recorded in the *Codex Chimalpopoca* and the *Anales de Cuauhtitlán.*

To the exodus from Tula in the middle of the tenth century of Ce Acatl Topiltzin, who, some scholars maintain, was deified as Quetzalcóatl, may be traced the rebuilding of Chichén Itzá in Yucatán. Dr. Acosta's work at Tula has verified a connection between the Toltecs of Tula and the city of the "holy and learned Itzás at the mouth of the great well," as evidenced by the striking similarity between Tula's Pyramid of Quetzalcóatl and Chichén Itzá's Temple of the Warriors." The two migrations to Chichén Itzá correspond to the dates given in the ancient Toltec annals. The one in the twelfth century, according to Dr. Acosta, was a natural consequence of the first, since the Toltecs of Tula had an established relationship with the people of Chichén Itzá that harked back two centuries. Thus, as Dr. Sylvanus G. Morley has suggested, the architectural traditions of the so-called First New Empire, influenced by Tula and referred to as "The Maya Renaissance," reappeared in the Second New Empire at the beginning of the thirteenth century.

This rock carving at Tula, dated A.D. 968, supports the theory that an enterprising Toltec chieftain, Ce Acatl Topiltzin, also assumed the name of the Toltecs' principal deity, Quetzalcóatl.

Dr. Acosta's conclusions on Tula may be summarized as follows:

Some investigators believe the Toltec culture developed between Jalisco in the north and Zacatecas in the south, a point of departure for many migrations toward the Central Plateau. Others contend it originated on the coast of Veracruz, in view of characteristics in common with the Huastec, such as marine objects relating to the cult of Quetzalcóatl. Similarities with the culture of the Michoacán region have also been the theme of speculation. However, as the Tarascan culture corresponds to later periods it could not have preceded it but, on the contrary was influenced by it.

Wherever the cradle may be, it is certain that the Toltec culture reached its full development in the middle of the ninth century, and during a short span of 312 years the city of Tula remained unchanged. Throughout this era, under the domination of the Great Priest and King Ce Acatl Topiltzin and his successors, Tula became the highest exponent of culture in Central Mexico and a city of incomparable beauty, the model for Chichén Itzá and the great Tenochtitlán.

The principal god was Quetzalcóatl, whose supremacy lasted until the destruction of the city. Tula was predominantly military, and its strong Toltec armies conquered extensive territory, forming an empire whose frontiers were surpassed only by those of Moctezuma's realm.

By the middle of the twelfth century Toltec domination reached an end. The causes were many. One of them was possibly the extent of the Toltec borders, entrusted to mercenary defenders. Another was the over-all weakness caused by drought, bringing on hunger and discontent. Besides, one must take into account the disastrous internal struggle instigated by the demands —each time more tyrannical—of Huemac, the last king of Tula. Under these difficult conditions it was impossible for the Toltecs successfully to protect their empire. The moment arrived when resistance crumbled and Tula fell to the invaders.

Although Tula was razed by a fire that killed many of its inhabitants, this was not the reason why its culture perished. It continued to flourish in nearby cities where many Toltecs sought refuge. The latter, in time, mixed with the newcomers and formed what is known as "Aztec culture," which was nothing more than a continuation of Tula through Tenochtitlán.

The culture was mainly homogenous and acquired an individual style which was a great aid in establishing the radius of Toltec expansion in Middle America. Naturally, it varies according to region, but the basic characteristics are indisputable. Toltec culture has been repossessed from its detractors, who went so far as to deny its existence. Now we know that it definitely existed and flourished in Central Mexico and, what is still more important, never died. For living through Tenochtitlán, its vestiges remain in our indigenous art.

Foremost among the structures that serve to indicate Tula's former grandeur is the restored Pyramid of Quetzalcóatl, or Tlahuitzcalpantecuhtli. Tula, after centuries of abandonment and isolation, has now taken its place alongside the ruins of Teotihuacán as a major tourist attraction. The Toltec capital was sacked and destroyed in A.D. 1156 by Aztec warriors as they passed through it in their wanderings before settling in the Valley of Anáhuac. Its treasures, which had been accumulating since about A.D. 900, were, of course, dispersed. Most of the principal buildings were demolished and many of the finest sculptures were carried off, to be ulitized in the building of Tenochtitlán. Other pieces were scattered throughout the area; some may be seen imbedded in the walls of nearby houses.

When Dr. Acosta began the restoration of the pyramid he was confronted by "a bump on the ground covered by trees." The structure, which rises to a height of more than 30 feet, was built of a hard stone known as *recinto*. It is of harmonious proportions, enhanced by a portico 178¾ feet long and 48¾ feet wide. The impressive vestibule, originally surrounded by a frescoed wall, now opens on the main plaza. Measuring about 120 feet at each side of its base, the pyramid is divided into five levels, arranged in step formation. With its stately lines, wealth of decoration and striking colored surfaces, it must have one of the most beautiful of ancient American buildings. Originally extending all around the pyramid was a colored benchlike frieze representing a procession of nineteen figures, remarkable for variety of features and attire. Portions of it are still evident at the northeast corner. Some of the figures are priests, others are warriors, some armed with shields and darts, one with a staff. All are shown advancing toward the stairway.

"Virtually all pre-Columbian Meso-American sculpture," Dr. Acosta has observed, "is religious in character. That of the Toltecs, the Aztecs and the Maya glorifies their deities. But at Tula four-fifths of the sculpture represents human beings, not gods, all linked with military might." The bas-relief friezes symbolize the three military orders, the Knights of the Coyote, the Eagle and the Ocelot, or Jaguar.

A reconstruction of Tula, the Toltec capital, which was razed by fire and sacked by Aztec warriors. *Drawing by Gregorio Gutierrez Balderas.* Tula's ball court (*center right*) on which a stone jaguar stands (*center left*) is similar to a court at Xochicalco. Four warrior caryatids which had once served as roof supports for the sanctuary surmounting the Pyramid of Quetzalcóatl (*bottom left*) have been re-installed on the pyramid platform (*bottom right*). Architectonic details of the Tula pyramid have been duplicated at the Temple of the Warriors in Chichén Itzá.

The entrance to the temple that formerly crowned the pyramid was once flanked by two massive columns in the shape of plumed serpents. A final phase of the restoration process was the placement on the pyramid platform of four huge ornately carved columns and four gigantic caryatids originally used as supports for the temple roof. Representing warriors, each figure weighs 8½ tons, measures slightly less than 15 feet in height and is composed of four fitted sections. The pieces of the figures had tumbled from various levels, rolling over a considerable area. They were recovered and with the aid of powerful hoisting cranes were set in place, to comprise one of the most striking sculptural groups known in ancient Mexican art. Representing soldiers, or crusaders, of Quetzalcóatl in the guise of Venus, the evening star, each warrior wears a headdress formed of a wide star-studded band terminating in a feather cluster. Originally the faces were painted and obsidian inlays filled the eye sockets and partly opened mouths. The figures are garbed in short embroidered tunics, topped by elaborate breastplates. On each belt is a clasp on which appears a human face emerging from a disc surrounded by four entwined serpents. The warriors' bracelets and sandals are also adorned with plumed serpents.

An I-shaped ball court, on which a large stone jaguar stands, was recently excavated at Tula. It is similar to a court at Xochicalco.

Because of its central location (some 25 miles south of Cuernavaca) **Xochicalco**, an ancient center of learning, was the site chosen many centuries ago for an assembly of Nahua astronomers. A similar gathering, as evidenced by Altar Q at Copán, took place in the Maya area. To Xochicalco's famed school for priests was sent Ce Acatl Topiltzin, the Toltec leader, by his grandparents, where he distinguished himself for his piety and was made a high priest of the cult of the plumed serpent.

Since these ruins were described in 1785 by Padre José Antonio Alzate, a friend of Benjamin Franklin, Xochicalco has been an enigma. Situated on an isolated hilltop, commanding a superb view of the Valley of Morelos,

The Pyramid of the Plumed Serpent at Xochicalco bears motifs of three ancient American cultures. Here, as at Chichén Itzá, the decorative inclined base of the structures dominates the upper section.

its low, profusely decorated Pyramid of the Plumed Serpent has mocked, Sphinx-like, a succession of scholars who have sought to unravel its secrets. Here are vestiges of several divergent indigenous cultures, each of which left a record upon the sloping sides of the pyramid. On this temple, dedicated to Quetzalcóatl, appear, in harmonious arrangement, typical motifs of the Teotihuacano, Toltec and Maya cultures, beginning the long process of *mestizaje,* or admixture. While some investigators have dated the site about the middle of the eighth century, others believe the site is of tenth-century construction.

The pyramid crowns an intricate complex of structures occupying several adjoining hills, with the main site joined by means of a highway paved with stone slabs, to Coatzin, on which may be seen the remains of several ancient monuments. As many as five terraces faced with stone appear as one approaches the site, rising some 134 feet above the level of the plain. Some of the ruins, excavated by Dr. Eduardo Noguera, have features in common with Zapotec and Maya structures. A ball court is similar to courts at Tula and at Chichén Itzá. In many structures here, as well as in the Temple of the Warriors at Chichén Itzá, the *talud,* or inclined base, dominates the *tablero,* or upper panel. Cornice moldings with an outward sloping plane are also to be found at El Tajín in Veracruz, in the Palace of the Governor, the House of the Turtles and the Nunnery at Uxmal, at Labná and at Sayil.

Xochicalco's ancient pyramid was reconstructed by Leopoldo Batres at the turn of the century. The tails of eight fork-tongued serpents undulate, snail-fashion, across each of the four walls of the pyramid's base to converge on an intricate central ornament. On the west side they are separated by a meticulously cut stairway that leads to a broad platform, on which stand the walls of a small temple. Some archaeologists believe the rectangular shrine was shared by the god Quetzalcóatl and the goddess Xochiquetzalli. Carved friezes of chieftains adorn the façades of the inclined main body. On the second level, warriors in full battle array are depicted. Seated in Oriental fashion, the figures below are shown barefooted and with legs crossed in a Buddha-like pose. Dr. Noguera and other authorities claim they represent priests, their splendid headdresses ornamented with five flowers accompanied by a year-sign. Each carries a bag in one hand. From their mouths emerge scrolls signifying speech. With each figure are glyphs referring to a calendar name, in keeping with the custom of naming a person after his or her birth date. In front of the figures appears a sign said to represent an eclipse: a circle, a cross and a pair of fleshless jaws.

Fork-tongued serpents wind across the base of the pyramid. Shown here is one of the cross-legged figures in a Buddha-like posture.

Dr. Noguera believes that the decoration of the pyramid's west side, which differs from that of the others, is of special significance. He has given the following interpretation of the scene shown to the left of the broad stairway: "Here the sign of *calli,* or house, is placed on an *atadura,* or connecting link, with the numeral 5 beneath. A figure placed behind the glyph evidently binds the two dates since, with an open hand placed over the numeral 1, it connects this date to another glyph, 11 Ozomatli, or monkey, which is pulled by means of a rope." The symbolic meaning, he feels, is a "representation of some adjustment or correction of the calendar," since the Maya-Zapotec system is employed for numbering on one side and that of the Mixtec and Nahuatl-speaking areas on the other. Some traces of color clinging to the reliefs indicate that the pyramid as it originally appeared must have presented a striking effect, in tones of green, vermilion, white, blue and black. With the threat of invasion by the Chichimecs about A.D. 900 the temple was apparently covered with cinnabar, anointed, so to speak, with the red color of death.

Since 1961 Dr. César A. Saenz has brought to light at Xochicalco three ancient stelae which had been erected as isolated monuments and later concealed beneath demolished walls. The entrance to the chamber in which the monoliths had been hidden to prevent their being used to adorn the temples of enemy invaders had been blocked with cut stones and covered with stucco. The three monoliths, each 5 feet high, 12 inches wide and 9 inches thick, are the first stelae containing glyphs found in Central Mexico. Up to the present no stelae have been discovered at Teotihuacán, what was Tenochtitlán or other Central Mexican sites, although undated stelae have been found at Tula. The Xochicalco stelae are beautifully carved with glyphs, numerals of the Maya-Zapotec system, Mixtec-style year signs and other motifs. Two are tinted a mellow rose. On the principal side of the slab designated as #2 is a representation of Tláloc, the Nahua god of rain. On the corresponding sides of slabs #1 and #3 are shown human faces set in the fauces of serpents with split tongues. In the upper part are carved what may be sacrificial instruments or possibly earplugs. The concept is similar to motifs which occur at Tula and Chichén Itzá and it appears to be one of the various representations of Quetzalcóatl.

As his first exploratory step, Dr. Saenz made a trench from east to west in the upper platform of Structure A, which he had studied previously. His excavations had already resulted in the unearthing of the columns of

Three stelae which had been concealed beneath demolished walls appear to supply further evidence of a confluence of cultures at Xochicalco.

a portico and a sunken patio surrounded by buildings. On the east of this construction emerged a temple with a small stairway. There were several rooms on either side of the temple. On the north and south sides of the patio were two large halls. Other dwellings adjoined the pyramid on the south side. Dr. Saenz strengthened the masonry and, in some places, reconstructed it.

When east-west cuts were made in the stucco floor of the temple, he found what appeared to be a square grave, measuring 3½ feet on each side and a little less in depth. The cavity had been covered over with well-cut stones in order to conceal the major portions of the three carefully broken stelae. A few fragments, found on the floor of the temple, had given Dr. Saenz his first clue to their existence. The chamber also contained small stone Teotihuacano figurines, some human bones, obsidian objects such as spear points, a small knife, half a mask of *tecalli,* or Mexican onyx, and beads of jade, shell and turquoise.

The stelae and the stone known as the Xochicalco *lapida,* which he found in 1961, confirm the evidence of a confluence of cultures as evidenced by the carvings adorning the Pyramid of the Plumed Serpent. Not only do the inscriptions on the stelae include Nahua, Zapotec and Teotihuacano glyphs and motifs but also a Maya sign associated with turquoise, water, the color yellow and *maíz: Pop y la Cruz de Kan.* The day sign, represented in a celestial band, bears a striking resemblance to the Zapotec glyph "E." Further study may well assign to Xochicalco an important niche in the cultural pattern of ancient America.

Plumed serpents and fire serpents decorate an ancient pyramid at **Tenayuca** in the outskirts of Tlalnepantla, about six miles west of Mexico City. In any study of the evolutionary phases of Aztec culture, this structure is of unusual interest. Tenayuca, like Tula, has yielded the remains of symbolic or decorative sculpture as well as a profusion of smooth and decorated ceramics, some of which are richly polychromed and of striking originality. It is also a principal source of historical data concerning the Chichimecs, a branch of the Nahuas whose political power and tribal organization constituted an important transition between the two final epochs of Teotihuacán and the Aztecs.

About A.D. 1200 the outlines of coherent history begin to emerge at Tenayuca, originally known as Tenayucan and as Oztopolco, following a legendary past. The region was invaded at the end of the Toltec period during the first quarter of the thirteenth century by the Chichimecs and other tribes, nomads of a relatively unevolved cultural level hailing from the Valley of Mexico. A group of these barbarians, led by the warlord

Xólotl, or "Monster," conquered the remaining bands of Toltecs by using bows and arrows. With the aid of his son Nopaltzin (or "Revered Fruit of the Cactus"), Xólotl established his first capital at Tenayuca.

Although the Chichimecs lived in cave dwellings, Xólotl was sufficiently advanced to order a census taken of his people, the first, it is believed, ever to have been made in Mexico. The epochal event is commemorated in the pueblo of Nepohualco ("The Place of the Count"). In 1246 Xólotl, having extended his rule over the northern part of the Valley of Mexico, forged southward and defeated the Toltec-Culhua of Culhuacán. He selected a Culhua princess as a wife for his son and married his two daughters to two chieftains, Acolnahuacatzin and Tzontecomatl.

Succeeding his father at Tenayuca in 1304, Nopaltzin built the great pyramid with its two parallel stairways. He also introduced the culture of *maíz* at Cuautepec and, emulating the Toltec way of life, ordered his people, who were known as the "People of Dog Lineage," to abandon their caves and to build walled dwellings. The rule of Nopaltzin marked the peak of Chichimec advance, based on arts and crafts borrowed from the subjugated Toltecs, Nopaltzin's son Tlohtzin, or "Hawk," surpassed his father in the adoption of Toltec customs, eventually establishing Nahuatl as the official language. Tlohtzin's son Quinatzin, who succeeded him in 1318, founded the dominion of Texcoco and governed there until 1337. Both father and son left maps of the Tenayuca region.

Meanwhile, for economic as well as political reasons, Tenayuca ceased to be a principal Chichimec city. Throughout years of intertribal strife it was governed at various times by Acolhuas, Tepanecas, Mexicas, Tlahuicas

This drawing of a member of the nomadic tribes which, under the warlord Xólotl, subdued, with bow and arrow, the remaining Toltecs is from the *Mapa Quinatzin*.

and Culhuas. In the opinion of the historian J. Bosque Ceballos Novelo, Tenayuca under the Tepaneca was third in importance after Atzcapotzalco * and Tlacopán because of its strong political influence and large population. Unstable conditions continued at Tenayuca until the time of the Conquest, when it became known as San Bartolo Tenayuca and a son of Moctezuma II, baptized as Rodrigo de Paz Moctezuma, was appointed governor.

During the Colonial period and for almost a century thereafter Tenayuca's pyramid was buried beneath debris. In 1898 the Department of Pre-Hispanic Monuments, then headed by Leopoldo Batres, was beginning a study of the vestiges of Aztec culture in the Valley of Mexico. During the research undertaken at Tenayuca, architectural details characteristic of Aztec culture were found within the pyramid. A survey made in 1925 resulted in systematic exploration and preservation of the ruins. In that year excavations were initiated, after a decade of vigilance over the site as an archaeological zone. Between 1931 and 1957 further research, continued under Ignacio Marquina, revealed, by means of an elaborate system of tunnels, that the pyramidal structure had been gradually expanded to accommodate the superimposition of later structures and their respective

* Some scholars favor Azcapotzalco.

At the time the pyramid built by Xólotl's son Nopaltzin at Tenayuca reached its greatest height, there were 70 steps in its parallel stairways.

double stairways, which were divided by central balustrades and terminated in a dado that changed the slope, or grade.

The practice of covering an original structure in order to increase the height and bulk of a later temple, common enough among Mexico's ancient peoples, is nowhere highlighted with greater dramatic effect than in Tenayuca's six major superimpositions. Each progressively expands the size of the pyramid, from a comparatively small inner core composed of clay and irregular stones from a nearby quarry and river to a ground area of about 4,500 square feet, exclusive of the courtyards, and to a height of about 70 feet. During the fourth successive epoch the pyramidal base was composed of four bodies that reached a height of 58½ feet and a wide stairway bordered by balustrades. While the earlier structures adhered to the same architectonic style, the sixth epoch witnessed impressive innovations, and at its close the pyramid must have resembled the Templo Mayor of Tenochtitlán.

Among the theories advanced by scholars for the periodic remodeling of temples is one which holds that this custom was not prompted by ritualistic observance but by the rise to power of new leaders, with each successive ruler insisting upon a larger and higher structure than his predecessor. The present proportions of Tenayuca's virtually square platform

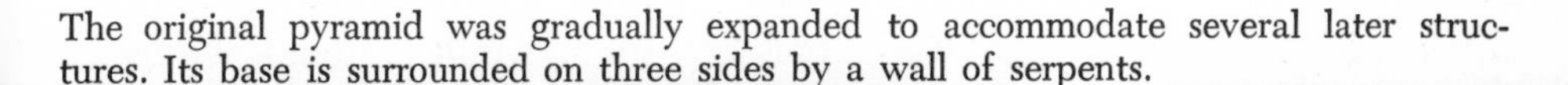

The original pyramid was gradually expanded to accommodate several later structures. Its base is surrounded on three sides by a wall of serpents.

are 221 feet on the eastern and western sides and 208 feet on the north and south, constituting the front and rear façades. The space between the sides of the pyramid and the walls of the balustrade forms a steplike buttress, the culminating addition made at the beginning of the sixteenth century. It is estimated that at the time the structure attained its greatest height there were 70 steps in the double stairway.

Another theory advanced to explain the practice of superimposed construction among the Toltec, Chichimec, Aztec and other peoples of the High Plateau, so strikingly demonstrated at Tenayuca, Teotihuacán and Cholula, holds that the enlargements occurred every 52 years, at the end of a calendrical cycle. According to this view the remodeling of the temples was rooted in a desire to appease the all-powerful deities. For with the completion of a calendar round of 18,890 days, mankind's most perilous hour had struck. It was feared, in fact, that at this point both the sun and the moon might fail to rise again and that in the enveloping darkness terrible demons would descend upon the earth and devour the human race.

Consequently, on the recurrence of the 52-year cycle, the priests, forming a great procession, would regularly assemble on "The Hill of the Star," overlooking the village of Ixtapalapa, south of Lake Texcoco. There they would conduct the ceremony of the kindling of the "New Fire," a rite, according to some accounts, performed upon the breast of a sacrificial victim. Below, the people breathlessly awaited the outcome of a ritual upon which would depend their chances for a sunlit, radiant world or perpetual night. When the flame was sighted on the hilltop there arose a great sigh of relief. Soon messengers of joy, each bearing a torch ignited by the "New Fire," would descend to various temples in the city below amid universal thanksgiving. To symbolize a fresh start and delivery from catastrophe, domestic utensils were customarily broken, old clothes discarded and houses repaired or rebuilt. With such an attitude it would seem logical enough to change also the exterior aspect of their temples as a gesture of gratitude to the deities who had beneficently averted world disaster.

Tenayuca's famous *coatepantli,* or wall of serpents, extending around three sides of the pyramid base, and the coiled *xiuhcóatls,* or fire serpents, set beside small platforms and, from the colors of the painted fragments adhering to the stone, believed to represent winter and spring, were among the spectacular additions dating probably from the fifth period. The *coatepantli* has been compared by Alberto Escalona Ramos to the "avenue of the serpents" of the Khmer Palace at Angkor Wat. Dr. Gordon F. Ekholm in a study of dramatic Asian-American analogies also cited Chichén Itzá's

Unbroken rows of serpents, their bodies touching at midpoint, provide a *coatepantli* (*top*) which has been compared to the "avenue of the serpents" in the Khmer Palace in Angkor Wat. Coiled fire serpents (*bottom*), set beside small platforms, are believed by Dr. Alfonso Caso to have been porters of the sun.

serpent columns and balustrade leading to the Grave of the High Priest, a serpent balustrade in Laos and a bas-relief with such a motif from Borobodur. A serpent balustrade was excavated from the so-called Santa Teresa ruins, underlying present-day Mexico City, just northeast of the Cathedral.

At Tenayuca the serpent bodies, touching one another at midpoint, form unbroken rows. Their heads are of stone and mortar; their tails, or rattles, are represented by three short steps. Imbedded in lateral slopes and decorating the stairway, the number of serpent heads protruding from the pyramid has been estimated by Ignacio Marquina as totaling about 800. A sepulcher at the right of the great structure is adorned with motifs of human skulls and bones in high relief. The use of the colors green, red and black at Tenayuca has been interpreted by some scholars as symbolizing regions of the universe, or day and night or possibly some association with the deities represented in the upper altars.

Dr. Alfonso Caso believes the pyramid to have been a temple of the sun, commemorating the death of the sun. He maintains that the two fire serpents placed on either side of the structure had the function of porters of the sun, or dragons of fire conducting the solar deity during his course. This theory was also held by the late Dr. Hermann Beyer. Dr. Caso has interpreted the altar of skulls as a symbol of the earth, or the tomb of the sun, into which the deity has fallen headlong in a sacrificial death. In the opinion of Enrique Juan Palacios, the dual altars represented an accomplished conceptual unity. The primitive Chichimec god Mixcóatl, a solar deity with warlike attributes, was worshipped here, and the sanctuary on the south side of the pyramid was dedicated to him. Also honored were the

The temple surmounting the pyramid known as Santa Cecilia Azcatitlán has been restored as an ancient place of worship.

goddess of earth, known as Itzpapálotl, and Chicomecóatl, identified with the Aztec goddess of earth and death, Coatlicue. Tonantzin, the mother of the gods, was also venerated at Tenayuca.

Santa Cecilia Azcatitlán, a nearby pyramid surmounted by a small sanctuary, has also been restored and refurnished with accessories appropriate to an ancient place of worship.

The sun was of overwhelming importance to the Aztecs, or, as Professor Ramón Mena called them, the "recent Nahuas" (also designated as the Mexica, the Culhua-Mexica, the Tenocha and the Teo-Chichimecs). They were the last of the various migratory peoples to gain supremacy in Central Mexico. The "People of the Sun" had lived, however, for some time in the Valley of Mexico, spread over the plains around Pachuca. While the alleged route of their wanderings continues to present a challenge to historians, it can be reconciled with the tradition. Scholars have not yet

The "Seven Caves" from which the Aztecs claimed to have emerged were depicted in this drawing from *The Atlas*, a pictorial volume which accompanied Fray Diego Durán's text of *The History of the Indies of New Spain*.

succeeded in establishing, with any degree of certainty, the starting point of the legendary Aztec peregrination or in retracing its course from the place called Chicomoztoc, "The Seven Caves" or "The Seven Lineages," to the equally vague place known variously as Aztlán, Aztatlán and Azcatitlán ("The Place of the Herons" or "Where the Day Dawns").

The epochal exodus of the Aztecs has been indicated symbolically in a post-Conquest pictorial account known variously as the *Tira de la Peregrinación, the Tira del Museo,* and the *Codex Boturini.* Written on bark-fiber paper, primed with a thin coat of sizing and executed on bands, or strips, divided into squares, the *Tira* portrays the Aztecs' legendary point of origin, apparently an island, with a pyramid-temple and dwellings. Standing in a canoe, which he guides with a long oar, a man is shown crossing a body of water. On the mainland, footprints seem to suggest his further wanderings to the north and east. At the new site may be seen a group of dwellings before which are seated their occupants, alongside hieroglyphic symbols of the various tribes they represent. These tribes—all bound by their common language, Nahuatl—are the Malinalca, the Matlatzinca, the Tepaneca, the Tlahuica, the Cuitlahuaca or Chichimecs, the Xochimilca, the Mexica, the Chalca and the Huexotzinca.

In 1930 the anthropogeographers Dr. Carl Sauer and Dr. Donald Brand cited the legendary Aztatlán complex as a narrow strip of plain along the coasts of Sinaloa and northern Nayarit, cut by large streams which flow from the Sierra Madre to the Pacific. Others have pinpointed the controversial spot as San Felipe de Aztatlán, situated on an island in the lake of Mexcaltitlán. The tribes seemed to have no clear memory of the route they had taken before arriving in the Jilotepec-Tula area. That the route followed by their wandering ancestors continued to be of deep concern to the Aztecs is evident in the quest initiated by Moctezuma II, who ordered his priests to locate Aztlán. The best they could do was to trace the tribal migration as far as Tula.

Among the more distant places which it has been possible to identify in any approximate form is Acahualtzinco, between present-day México and Querétaro. There, however, the elusive trail is lost since, as Dr. Jiménez Moreno has suggested, vast prairies extend to the west and north in which no important points of reference exist. The tribe seemed to recollect passing Chichimec tribes, or "nests" of nomads.

In the legendary account of their peregrination, the Aztecs left Aztlán on the counsel of a mystic guide, an idol they called Huitzilopochtli, which they found in a cave. They were directed to continue their wanderings until, on an island in a large lake, they would find an eagle perched upon a cactus in the act of devouring a serpent. This was to be the sign that they had reached their journey's end. Here, it was ordained, they must settle and build so that, in time, they might become the masters of all the land.

Their divinely ordered pilgrimage, according to one version, led through Michoacán and down the west coast of Mexico. After reaching the Isthmus of Tehuantépec they apparently turned northward toward the Central Plateau and the Valley of Mexico. The date of A.D. 1143 emerges from this legend in a reference to Coatepec, near the southern end of the eastern shore of Lake Texcoco. Other sources indicate that the Aztecs halted on the edges of Chapultepec, remaining there from about 1250 to 1300 with the permission of Acolnahuacatzin, ruler of Atzcapotzalco. From this point they apparently wandered for another quarter of a century, always searching for the sign that would mark their ultimate destination. Like the Israelites, who bore the Ark of the Covenant with them on their journey to the Promised Land, the Aztecs bore with them the ashes of their deity Huitzilopochtli, consulting this revered "Holy of Holies" whenever grave problems arose and being answered through the mouths of their priests.

Finally, on the spot where the Metropolitan Cathedral now stands in Mexico City, the sign appeared on what was then a small island. There, under the direction of their high priest Tenoch, the tribe erected their first rude dwellings. In gratitude to their priestly guide they are said to have honored Tenoch by calling the settlement **Tenochtitlán** ("Place of the Tenochas"). This capital, in its prime, awed the *conquistadores,* who first beheld it in 1519, but they had not seen Teotihuacán or even Tula when these cities were at the height of their glory.

Since Tenochtitlán was razed by the Spaniards, little of it remains today save for such vestiges as this terminal of a serpent balustrade from an Aztec temple.

A map of Tenochtitlán in 1519, reportedly drawn for Cortés, was published in Nuremberg in 1524.

1. COYOACÁN.
2. IXTAPALAPA CAUSEWAY.
3. FORT XOLOC.

4, 5. HOUSES AND GARDENS OF MOCTEZUMA IN THE OUTSKIRTS.

6. PLAZA (PRESENT-DAY ZÓCALO).
7. NEW PALACE OF MOCTEZUMA, UNDERLYING THE PRESENT-DAY NATIONAL PALACE.
8. PALACE GARDENS.
9. MENAGERIE.
10. COATEPANTLI, OR "WALL OF SERPENTS," AROUND TEMPLE ENCLOSURE.
11. PALACE OF AXAYÁCATL.
12. PALACE OF MOCTEZUMA I.
13. MARKETPLACE AT TLATELOLCO.
14. NONOALCO CAUSEWAY, LEADING TO TACUBA.
15. CAUSEWAY LEADING TO TENAYUCA.
16. TLACOPÁN CAUSEWAY.
17. CHAPULTEPEC: THE PARK.
18. CHAPULTEPEC: THE SPRINGS.
19. ATLACUIYAYAN (TACUBAYA).
20. QUAYS FOR CANOES PLYING ACROSS THE LAKE TOWARD TEXCOCO AND EASTWARD.
21. DIKE.
22. CAUSEWAY ISSUING FROM THE COATEPANTLI.
23. CANALS WITH WOODEN BRIDGES.
24. AMANALCO LAGOON, WHERE CUAUHTÉMOC WAS TAKEN PRISONER.
25. GREAT IDOL, DECAPITATED BY THE SPANIARDS.
26. TEMPLE, UNDERLYING THE PRESENT-DAY CHURCH OF SAN MIGUEL NONOALCO.
27. TEMPLES TO THE WEST OF THE MARKETPLACE AT TLATELOLCO.
28. HOUSE OF CUAUHTÉMOC.
29. HOUSE NEAR WHICH THE SPANIARDS WERE AMBUSHED.

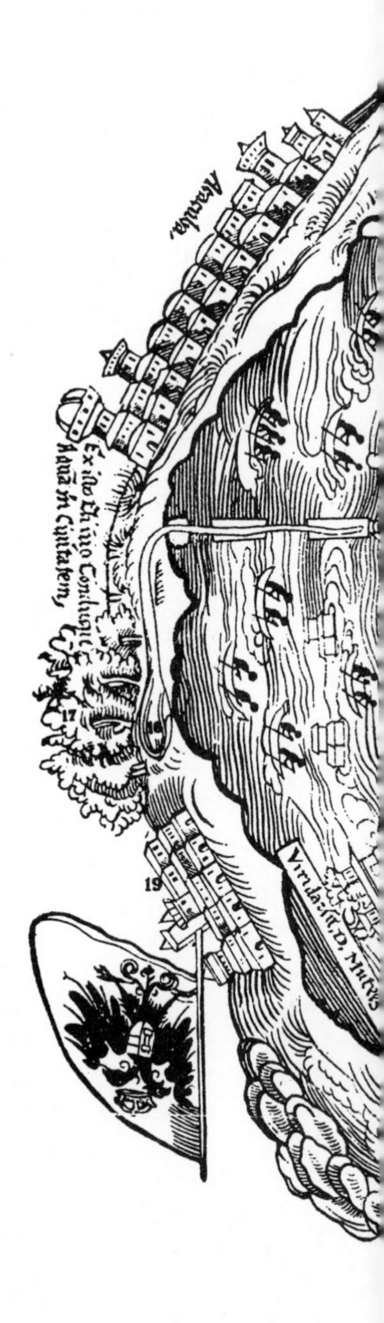

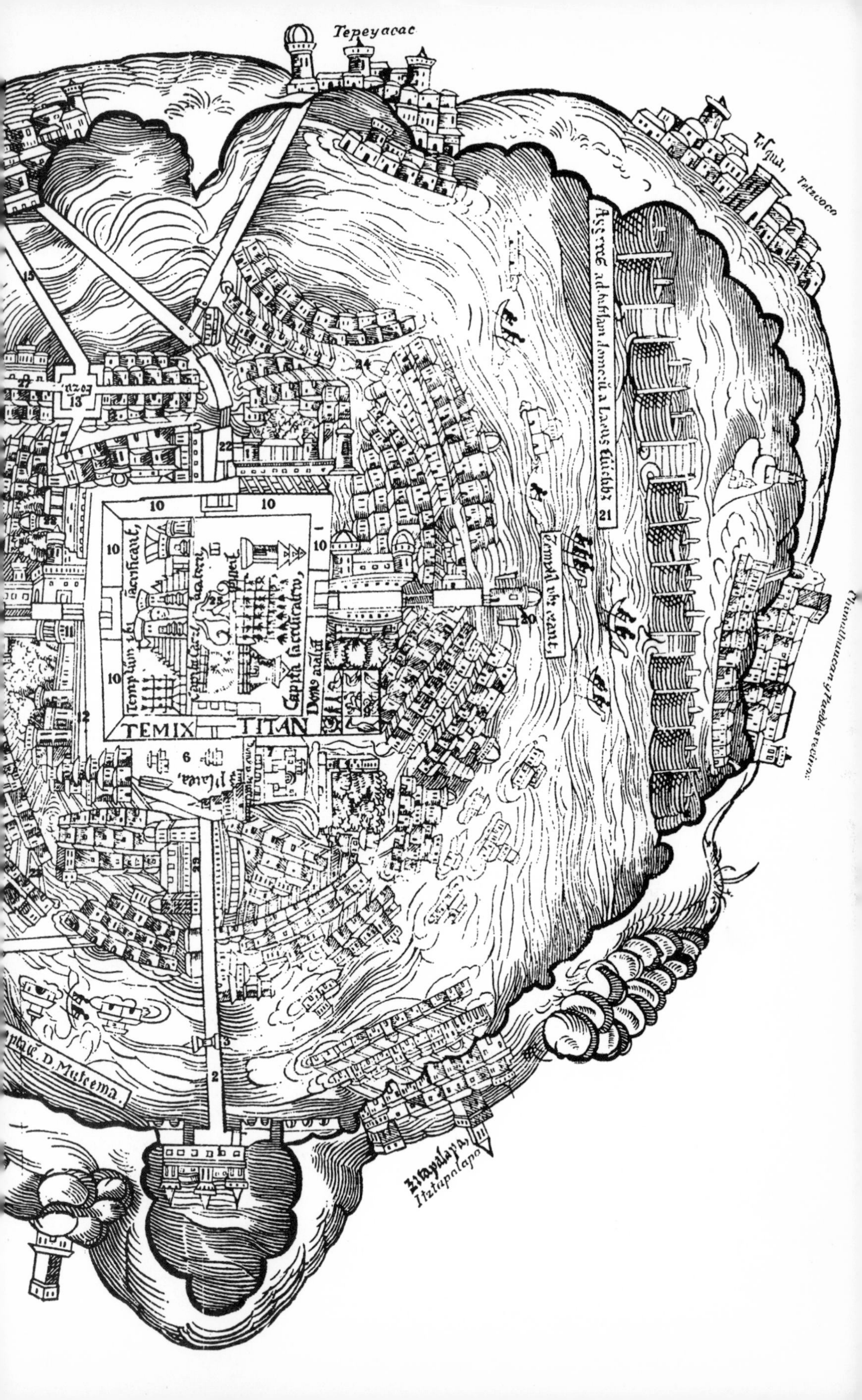

Tepeyacac
Tetzcoco
TEMIX
TITAN
Templum ubi sacrificant,
Capita sacrificatorum,
Plaza,
Itztapalapa
Iztapalapa

CHAPTER IV

The Universe of the Nahuas: Their Concepts of the World and of Time

ONE OF THE MOST revealing features of the ancient culture of the Valley of Mexico was its cosmological vision. The Nahuas pictured the surface of the earth as a great disc situated in the center of the universe and extending in both a horizontal and a vertical direction. Surrounding the earth, they believed, was an immense body of water, extending like a ring on all sides. But neither the earth nor its ring of water were amorphous or undifferentiated, since the universe was divided into four great quadrants. These began at the center, or navel, of the earth and extended to the point where the "celestial waters" that encircled the earth were joined.

Dr. Miguel León-Portilla has pointed out that the four quadrants involve a multitude of symbols. The Nahuas considered themselves as situated "in front of the west, contemplating the progress of the sun." The house of the sun was to be found where it sets "in the country of the color red." To the left of the path of the sun was the south, the direction of the color blue. In front of the region of the house of the sun was the direction, or road, of light, of fertility and life, symbolized by the color white. Finally, at the right of the route of the sun extended the black quadrant of the universe, the direction of the Land of the Dead.

Vertically, above and below this world, or *cem-nahuac,* they believed there were thirteen heavens and nine infernos. The latter were planes, each time deeper, where the dead had to face certain tests, or disciplines, for four years before they could know complete rest. Above extended the skies, which were joined with the waters that surrounded the world, forming a kind of blue vault. This was furrowed with roads at distinct levels, all separated by what the Nahuas described as "celestial crossbeams." In the first five planes were the paths of the moon, the stars, the sun, Venus and the comets. Then there were the skies of various colors and finally the metaphysical beyond, the region of the gods. In the center of all was the abstract Omeyocan, or place of duality, where the dual generating principle and the preserver-of-the-universe principle coexisted.

Dr. León-Portilla has suggested that this image of the unknown might be called a "static" cosmology with, at its center, a dynamic feature. Here primordially the dual principle that dwelt in the highest of all the heavens exercised its sustaining functions, for Ometéotl, acting in the navel of the world, gave foundation to the earth. In Ometéotl (the dual god, Ometecuhtli and Omecíhuatl) were contained both masculine and feminine aspects of the generative being, "moving all that exists." "Its presence reached the waters in the color of the bluebird and, from its enclosure of clouds, it governed the movements of the moon and stars." In Book VI of the *Codex Florentino,* one of the few surviving illustrated records of pre-Hispanic customs, Ometéotl is addressed as "Mother of the gods, father of the gods, the old god lying in the hand of the earth." As the ultimate synthesis of creative energy that gave light to all things, the Lord of time and space, this supreme deity was represented by the masculine symbol of generative force, Ometecuhtli.

The idea of an androgynous supreme deity was carried further by the Nahuas than by other ancient cultures; conception was attributed to the feminine aspect of the synthesis and procreation was the function of the masculine aspect. With regard to creation, it is close to the fundamental concept of the Hindu-Aryan cosmogony. Brahma fell asunder, it was said, into man and wife, and from the striving toward reunion of these two separated parts "worlds were put forth." Each segment of the sundered god sought its complement and counterpart, and thus all life could be regarded as an effort to restore the disturbed equilibrium, or an approach to the primordial unity, pure being.

Stemming from Ometéotl were his sons, the four elements of earth, air, fire and water. Each issued from one of the four directions of the universe to introduce the factors of effort, age, cataclysm, evolution and the spatial orientation of the epochs. In their monumental struggle to prevail, each element tried to direct the life-giving action of the sun. Thus were initiated the great cosmic conflicts symbolized by the feuds between opposing deities.

In the heavens reigned also Ipalnemohuani, or Giver of Life, whose fundamental attributes were designated by various titles, among them Tloque-Nahuaque, or God of the Near and the Immediate, and Moyocoyatzín, or The Lord Who Invented Himself.

The ancient Aztec legends told of a powerful earth-goddess, Coatlicue, the mother of Huitzilopochtli, the Lord of the Universe. A grotesque 5-ton,

6½-foot-high andesite figure of this deity was discovered in 1790, under what had been the main plaza of the Aztec capital, Tenochtitlán, by a pious Spanish churchman who, fearing its demoniacal power, swiftly buried it again. It was rediscovered by Alexander von Humboldt in 1803 and placed on public exhibition. A much-imitated similar figure of Coatlicue was found below the atrium of the Metropolitan Cathedral.

Among the scholars who have penetrated beyond the macabre semblance of Coatlicue is Professor Leo Katz, a painter, educator and authority on pre-Columbian and modern Mexican art. Over the years he has been a champion of the heroic Coatlicue and has made a psychonanalytic study of the image. The French painter and archaeologist Jean Charlot commented that Katz provided "a renewed estimate of Coatlicue." Charlot, long identified with Maya research for the Carnegie Institution, pointed out that he had brought the concept of the great earth-mother and fertility goddess as close to our comprehension as some of the theogonies of the Greeks and Hebrews. The delicately chiseled features, noble brow and physical perfection of the Greek Zeus, the patriarchal bearing of the Old Testament Jehovah are, according to this view, concepts developed from an idealized humanity. Such portrayals of deity would seem to have little in common with the occult rendering of Coatlicue, with ponderous serpents replacing her severed head. Yet while the Greek sculptor of Zeus and the autochthonous American creator of Coatlicue functioned in different aesthetic environments, the ideas that they projected are not so far apart. When traced to their origins, they are strangely alike.

Behind the Aztec concept of this deity, projected more than six centuries ago, lies a highly human story. But, as Professor Katz and other scholars have indicated, mortal attributes seem too weak even to suggest the cosmic power of Coatlicue, who continuously devours the sun as it rises from and sets into the earth, represented by her massive body, the source of food, sustainer of life and messenger of death. Nowhere in the history of art, according to Professor Katz, has a single monument achieved such a complete synthesis of human and abstract universal relations.

According to the ancient legend, on a mountain range called Coatepec close to Tula, once lived a woman known as Coatlicue, the mother of the stars, known as the Centzonhuitznáhuac, among whom was a daughter, Coyolxauhqui, the moon. Each day the mother, a priestess, swept the mountains of Coatepec. Miraculously, she conceived a child. When she was about to give birth, Coyolxauhqui, unaware of the miraculous conception, summoned her brothers and called upon them to kill their mother because she had "dishonored" them. Coatlicue, learning of the plot, was frightened, but the unborn child within her spoke to her and said, "Do not fear. I know what I must do." When her children arrived to destroy her

The Aztec goddess Coatlicue, mother of the "Lord of the Universe," is shown wearing a skirt of dangling serpents.

the man-child Huitzilopochtli was born fully armed with his *chimalli,* or shield, and a single arrow, his face painted like a warrior's. Leaping to the earth, he ordered his sister beaten to death with snakelike torches and her body torn to pieces. Her head, it is related, remains to this day on the Coatepec range. Huitzilopochtli then went forth against his brothers, pursuing them and expelling them from the mountains, in his fury encircling the range four times.

As Professor Katz has interpreted it, "Huitzilopochtli's first act after birth was the destruction of his many older brothers and his plotting sister; they were all blotted out by the rising sun. From the point of view of the subconscious, this presents an interesting analysis of Huitzilopochtli's 'Oedipus complex' in protecting his mother, and the daughter's 'Electra complex' in plotting against her. It is a perfect Freudian background for the surrealist power of this image with its skulls, serpents, cut-off hands and cut-out hearts so strongly reminiscent of early surrealist films." Coatlicue is often represented wearing a skirt of serpents and a necklace of hands and hearts with a pendant skull.

Professor Katz further commented that such motifs remind us that surrealism, the art of the subconscious and of dream-symbolism, is ancient indeed. "The main difference," he maintains, "between new and old here is that modern surrealists are chiefly interested in their own egos and their own complexes, whereas in cases like Coatlicue we are dealing with the age-old struggle to bridge the terrifying gap between the conscious ego of man—the mysterious dream-life of his subconscious on the one hand and the unfathomable cosmic forces on the other."

Padraic Colum has retold in a tale another ancient legend in which it was related how Moctezuma the Conqueror, the grandfather of Moctezuma II, once found a pair of great sandals upon the floor of the Temple of Huitzilopochtli. Accepting this as a sign that the war god would never desert the Aztecs, Moctezuma sent out his priests to bear the sandals to Coatlicue, who dwelt in Aztlán, "The White Place," from which Huitzilopochtli had led the tribes on their long wanderings, guiding their conquests and their building of the great city of Tenochtitlán where they had found a high rock on which grew a cactus with an eagle holding a serpent.

Arriving at Tollan, Moctezuma's messengers were guided by four magicians through gardens where birds of brilliant plumage sang from the branches of fruit-laden trees. When asked why they had come, the ambassadors explained that they were returning to the ancestral palace, bearing to Coatlicue the sandals of her son. As they climbed the mountain to her abode, the feet of the ambassadors sank into the sand, while those of their guides moved swiftly over the surface. When asked why theirs were so heavy and what they ate, the ambassadors replied, "Flesh and *pulque.*" The guides answered that the meat and fermented drink they had consumed prevented their reaching the palace. "Here," the guides said, "we eat only fruits, grains and roots and drink only water, so there is no clog upon us when we walk."

A wind then lifted the ambassadors to Coatlicue's cavern on the mountain peak. When they saw her, they were terrified, for her skirt was of serpents. Coatlicue wept as she looked upon the sandals, for she knew her son would not return to her, for before departing Huitzilopochtli had asked her for two pairs of sandals—one for going and the other for the homeward journey. She thereupon put on a garment of mourning.

When the ambassadors returned to Tenochtitlán they found that the "Old Fire" had been quenched and that a "New Fire" was being lighted upon the breast of a sacrificial victim and a new king—Axayácatl—ruled over the Aztecs.

Coatlicue's son, Huitzilopochtli, was far more terrible in his wrath than Mars, the Roman god of war. His insatiable thirst for blood, legends hold, could be quenched only with living hearts torn from the bodies of human victims in elaborate sacrificial rituals. Often represented in symbols as a hummingbird, it was this guardian of their tribe that the Aztecs worshipped in an enormous pyramid-temple, said to have been some 250 feet high, which stood where the Metropolitan Cathedral of Mexico City rises today.

A mammoth dedication feast given by the Aztec ruler Ahuitzotl in 1487 at the time of its completion and decoration was recounted by Fray Diego Durán. Just as the Roman emperor Marcus Aurelius, in ostentatious ceremonies, received tribute from far-flung provinces, the feast was attended in Tenochtitlán by rulers of neighboring seigniories and their tribute-bearers. Vassal nations were commanded by Ahuitzotl, said Durán, to provide a designated number of victims.

Offerings brought, wrote the chronicler, were "so great in value and quantity that the enemies, guests and strangers were bewildered, amazed." They saw that the Aztecs were masters of the entire world. They realized that the Aztecs had conquered all the nations and that all were their prisoners.

An incredible number of prisoners were sacrificed in Huitzilopochtli's honor, he commented in his *The History of the Indies of New Spain* (*The Aztecs*) (Chapter XIIV, pp. 196-199), translated by Doris Heyden and Fernando Horcasitas.

> All of them [Ahuitzotl, the rulers of Texcoco and Tacuba and the old high priest Tlacaelel] ascended to the summit of the pyramid and each lord, accompanied by priests dressed as gods, went to the place where he was to sacrifice, holding the knife in

The beauty of Tenochtitlán, with its plazas, marketplaces and causeways, astonished the Conquistadores. This restored view shows the central section. The great square originally extended ¼ mile on each side. *Drawing by Gregorio Gutierrez Balderas.*

hand. All the lords of the provinces, all the enemies, were watching from within the bowers which had been built for the occasion. The files of prisoners began to mount the steps, and the four lords, assisted by the priests, who held the wretches by the feet and hands, began to kill. They opened the chests of their victims, pulled out the hearts and offered them to the idols and to the sun. When the sovereigns grew weary, their satanic work was carried on by the priests who represented the gods. The *Chronicle* tells us that this sacrifice lasted four days from dawn to dusk and that, as I have said, 80,400 men from different cities died. All of this seemed incredible to me, but the *Chronicle* has forced me to put it down, and I have found confirmation of it in other written and painted manuscripts. Otherwise I would not dare to write these things, since I would be called a liar. He who translates a history is only obliged to reproduce in a new language what he finds written in the foreign tongue, and this is what I have done.

The amount of time said to have been devoted to the carnage seemed inordinate even to Durán. How could each lord have slain 20,100 men,

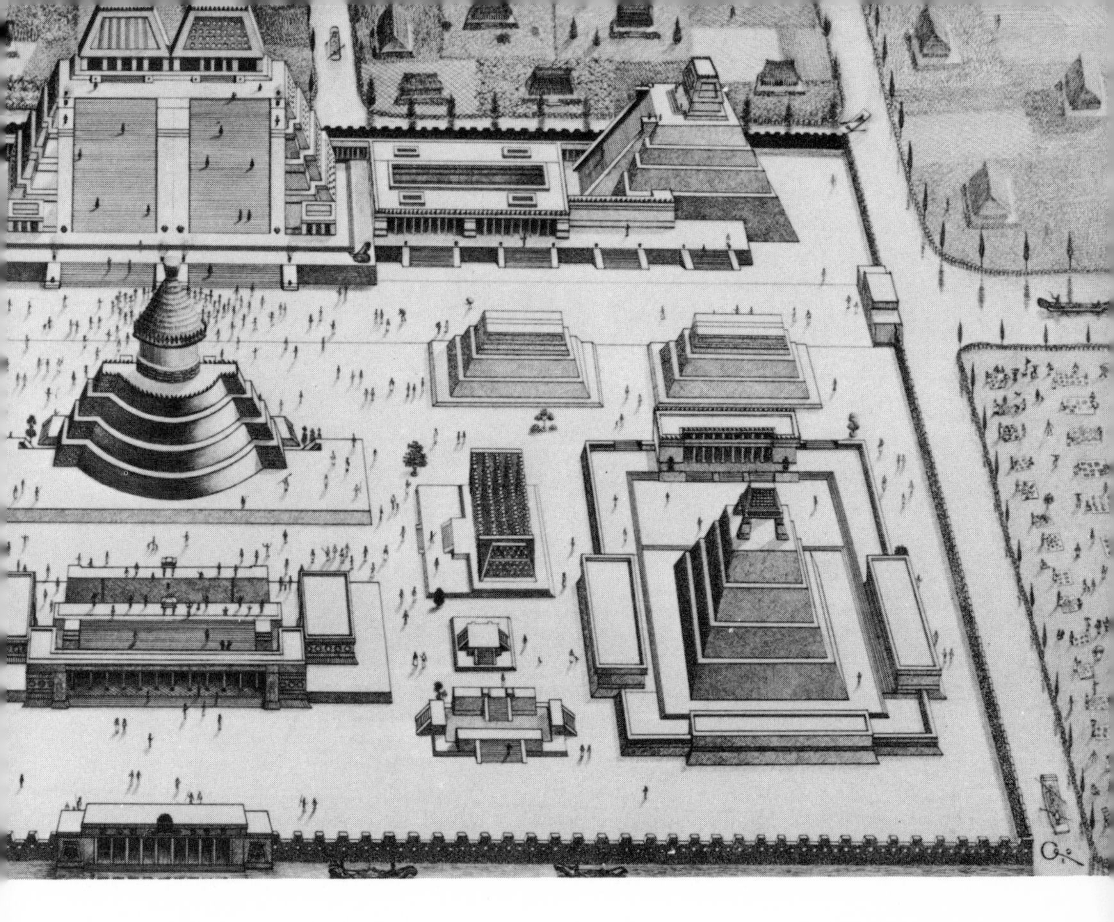

arriving from different cities and proceeding in single file over the two main causeways across the lake? To have carried out this ritual ceremony, each lord would have had to account daily for 5,125 victims apiece and seven men would have had to die every minute, or one every eight seconds. The rites reported would have entailed the casting down of the bodies from the pyramid-temple into the courtyard some 150 feet below. In what huge receptacle could 80,400 sanctified hearts have been deposited? Certainly such a pile of accumulated corpses, whose stench must soon become almost unendurable, would have formed a mound higher than the temple. Bodies of victims were customarily beheaded and the heads placed in a skull-rack. For such an occasion the skull-rack, reportedly constructed of 100 thick tree trunks, would have had to be of skyscraper proportions.

Like many scholars who reject the Durán account as "distorted," Dr. Eulalia Guzmán has pointed out that the friar-chroniclers were often careless in their calculations of numbers, measurements and space and poor judges of human capacity and endurance. Doris Heyden and Fernando Horcasitas remarked of Durán's figure that "The number . . . given . . . has been one of the most controversial subjects in ancient American history. Those who believe this to be a gross exaggeration point out the

This crouching stone jaguar, its back hollowed, may have been a repository for "sanctified" hearts. Masses of victims were reportedly sacrificed by the Aztecs in ceremonies such as the mammoth dedication feast given by the ruler Ahuitzotl to commemorate the completion of the temple of their revered deity, Huitzilopochtli.

problems in disposing of the huge number of corpses and suggest that the Spanish were always prone to exaggerate the number of sacrificial victims as a justification for the Conquest. Those who have defended Durán's statistics have pointed out that a people as dedicated as the Aztecs were to sacrifice, an act which to them was indispensable in keeping the sun and the universe alive, without doubt possessed a system for disposing of the bodies of the victims."

The war god's opposite, the rival deity Quetzalcóatl, presents one of the most intriguing of Mexican legends. This half-hero, half-god, is always represented by the symbol of the plumed serpent, in itself synthesizing the elements of earth, water and air, fundamental constituents of the material universe, since a feathered serpent may creep, glide or fly. Dr. Jésus Amaya Topete, long interested in the influence of the cult of Quetzalcóatl on indigenous art, beliefs and customs, has shown that legends of the "Fair God" are blended with history. He has definitely associated the deity with the historic Topiltzin, who later assumed the title of Quetzalcóatl. This ruler's Toltec appellation was Ce Acatl ("One Reed"). Under Topiltzin-Quetzalcóatl, new tribes, known as the Nonoalca, "The Deaf and Dumb People" and "Those Who Could Not Speak Correctly" came from Tulancingo to Tula, where they erected stately buildings, the columns and walls of which were decorated with magnificent bas-reliefs. Their pottery also showed remarkable grace and originality. According to the legends these people worshipped Topiltzin-Quetzalcóatl's god. It is related that their leader tried to instruct the Toltecs in the humane ways of the One and Supreme Deity and preached the abolition of human sacrifice. The dedicated ruler taught the Toltecs to make other offerings—flowers, butterflies, reptiles, even tortillas. It is believed that as a result of his studies as a youth at Xochicalco, where he might have encountered the cultivated Mixtecs of the Puebla region, he learned the arts of writing, drawing, metalwork and the making of polychromed pottery, which he was able to teach his people. Through such tutelage, it was said, the Toltecs learned to make beautiful ornaments. New and improved methods of agriculture were also introduced. It was even boasted of Topiltzin that he taught his people to make cotton grow in different colors.

In discussing the numerous contributions to Toltec culture made by this wise and public-spirited ruler, Dr. Amaya Topete stated that his admirers among the early chroniclers attributed to him drastic reforms, including an end to bribery, to war, "even to death itself." But Topiltzin-Quetzalcóatl had many enemies, especially among the priests of Tezcatlipoca. According to *Anales de Cuauhtitlán*, a part of the *Codex Chimalpopoca,* three demon gods identified with darkness and disaster, including Quetzalcóatl's avowed enemy-god Tezcatlipoca, came to tempt him. He had no wish to see them, for he knew they wanted him to sanction human sacrifices, which he opposed. When he finally admitted them they endeavored to induce him to drink the intoxicating beverage known as *pulque,* extracted from the *maguey.* He told them he was fasting, but they prevailed upon him to put his finger to the cup and taste the foaming liquid. He finally complied, found he liked the taste and said that he would drink

The legends concerning the banishment of the beneficent deity Quetzalcóatl, shown in the *Codex Borbónico* confronting his arch-enemy Tezcatlipoca, relate his promise that he would eventually return to reclaim his leadership.

it after all. He was then persuaded to drink five cups. In several versions this led to lust. They told him to sing, and Quetzalcóatl, inebriated, sang of his misfortunes and called for his mother Coatlicue. He went to the edge of the sea, into which he stepped, weeping bitterly. According to one legend he was consumed by fire and his heart transformed into a star that shines at dawn. In another legend, after falling into the trap set for him by his enemies, Quetzalcóatl, in tears, went into exile.

It is generally believed that when the just and merciful lawgiver fell victim to intrigues in Tula he fled southward to a place which received the name "Tollan-Chollan" ("Tula of the Fugitives"), and that with him emigrated a group of his disciples. Historians agree, Dr. Amaya Topete has pointed out, that during his stay there the once-small pyramid, or artificial mountain, Tlachihualtepec, grew in height and that from that time the full name of the new sacred city was "Tollan-Chollan-Tlachihualtepec" (apparently Cholula). The ruler is said to have passed twenty years here, departing at the end of this period for Coatzalcoalcos and taking with him four young priests to whom he had taught his doctrines. He is supposed to have sent them back to Cholula but continued on his own journey in the direction of the rising sun, promising that on the date of Ce Acatl, or One Reed, he would return.

The Maya chronicles record that Quetzalcóatl, or Kukulcán, as he was known in the Yucatán area, entered the Maya region between A.D. 987 and 1000. According to Bishop Diego de Landa, the demigod settled first in Mayapán and later in Chichén Itzá. Legend holds that he journeyed to the highlands, where he built a funeral pyre and threw himself upon it, the smoke from the flames turning into birds of gorgeous plumage. Another legend holds that he sailed westward on a raft of entwined serpents. Curiously, in the late 1940's a mummy, reportedly Quetzalcóatl's, was said to have been found "intact" and buried again somewhere near Guatusco, inferring that the mysterious hero died before ever reaching the sea. Durán recorded that he had been informed by an Indian that when Quetzalcóatl went southward after his expulsion from Tula he stopped at Ocuituco, in what is now Morelos, where he made the natives a gift of a thick volume, written in unfamiliar letters. Durán rushed, as he relates, to Ocuituco and begged the Indians to show him the book, only to receive the disappointing news that they had burned it six years earlier for fear that keeping it might bring them misfortune.

The disappearance of many ancient sources may be owing in part to the fact that the autochthonous people of America, whose lives were so violently disrupted by the Conquest, deliberately destroyed or concealed a great part of their past from those who would ferret out every detail.

As Dr. Raúl Noriega, co-editor of *Esplendor de México Antiguo* (*Splendor of Ancient Mexico*), has observed, "The Indian of today still arms himself with dubious response and an inert atttiude before the most simple question about his daily life. For him the racial pact of silence before the white invader is still valid."

Because of such a complex cosmological system a knowledge of astronomy was, of course, essential for members of Anáhuac's priesthood. Religion so impregnated every aspect of life that the priests, as sacred stewards, were called upon to maintain a perfect relation between the astral gods and their worshippers on earth. They had to correlate ritual ceremonies with astronomical events. Theirs was the daily task of watching the movements of sun, moon and planets, charting their mysterious progressions or retrogressions, as well as the clustering of celestial bodies in spectacular groups. Certain deductions drawn from data compiled by them from their close scrutiny of the heavens—astronomical research carried on without benefit of powerful telescopes—enabled them to issue their minatory warnings, to ward off calamities by decreeing sacrifice upon sacrifice, according to some chroniclers, in order to placate their unseen deities. Astronomical knowledge was also utilized to determine the best days for the planting and harvesting of crops and for the casting of horoscopes.

Aztec and Maya astronomers possessed an amazing knowledge of celestial movements that enabled them to transpose to geometric symbols the mathematics of the planetary cycles and thus to determine and to record in chronological outline the sequence of astronomical revolutions and cycles. This calculation, according to Dr. Noriega, was achieved by the astronomer-priests with a perfection unmatched by any culture, ancient or modern. The observations of these early watchers of the skies were frequently reflected in the architecture of their sacred edifices. The Maya, for instance, planned their pyramid-temples in such a way that the sun would illumine the ramparts; at the equinox, or solstice, the shadow cast was level with their bases. One can only speculate on how many millennia of patient and unremitting observation were necessary for the native astronomers to bring their knowledge to such a high level. Whether there was any interchange of higher learning among contemporary peoples who inhabited lands across the sea is one of many questions involving the origin and character of the early cultures of Middle America which may never be answered satisfactorily.

A stone monolith, which weighs approximately 24 tons, with a diameter of 11 feet, has become the object of intensive study by scholars, many of whom are convinced of the importance of what is regarded as the world's most celebrated bas-relief. La Piedra del Sol, or "The Stone of the Sun," has elicited admiration from students of design because of the cohesiveness and harmonious combinations of its diverse elements. Many astronomers, historians, anthropologists and mathematicians concur with Dr. Noriega's belief that it may hold the key to epochal revelations concerning the antiquity of man in the New World and the true measure of his culture. Some feel that La Piedra del Sol may very well be a cosmic Rosetta Stone which may open up the possibility of "capturing the rhythms, duration and repetition of natural phenomena."

Throughout Mexico, in small pueblos as well as in the largest cities, representations of the so-called Aztec calendar stone are, of course, ubiquitous. No tourist who braves the lines of vendors along Avenida Juarez in the Mexican capital can fail to have the grotesque mask of Tonatiuh offered to him in a variety of forms. Craftsmen have, in fact, so overworked the circular design as a motif that its popularity has waned among artisans who pride themselves on exclusive creations in a contemporary mood. But, far from becoming passé, the stone is receiving more attention today than at any period since it was discovered.

In *La Piedra del Sol y 16 Monumentos Astronómicos del México Antiguo con Símbolos y Claves* (*The Stone of the Sun and 16 Astronomical Monuments of Ancient Mexico with Symbols and Keys*), published in 1955, Dr. Noriega argued that the mammoth stone was a "supreme manifestation of cosmographic wisdom and mathematical skill." No less than ten carved stones in the round are known, in some of which special emphasis is placed on cycles of eclipses. Others bear calculations concerning Saturn, Mercury, Venus, and Mars. Curiously enough, none of these repeats the groups of symbols used in the Piedra del Sol.

The dream of establishing the "beginning of time," Dr. Noriega has pointed out, impelled the ancient astronomers to calculate the date and the hour of the so-called "eternal return." Such a concept was born of the constantly observed repetition of phenomena by native astronomers. The succession of days and nights, eclipses and lunations, the transits of the stars and planets, inspired the men of the first advanced cultures of Middle America with the ambition to fix the "great years" of the cosmos, those gigantic periods of time necessary for the recurrence in the firmament of the same stellar and planetary positions and configurations.

The huge Piedra del Sol was unearthed in 1790 during the paving of the plaza below the site of what had been Tenochtitlán's Plaza Mayor. It was placed, through the viceroy's concession, beside one of the towers of the Metropolitan Cathedral. It has been historically established that the monolith, quarried on the mainland and dragged across the causeways to Tenochtitlán as a cooperative project of the allied rulers, was dedicated in 1479 during the reign of Axayácatl (1469–1481), the father of Moctezuma II. It was Axayácatl who consolidated the domain of the Veracruz area, subjugated the Valley of Toluca and successfully pursued the conquest of Guerrero.

The first studies of the stone were made in 1792 by Don Antonio León y Gama, who considered the inscriptions to be a true calendar, with a computation of weeks, months and years and a definition of cosmogonic epochs. In the twentieth century quite another line of research was followed by Dr. Beyer, who held that the stone was merely a votive altar to the sun god and that the signs around the central image of Tonatiuh were sacred decorations appropriate to this deity. Dr. Beyer's interpretation was based on the fact that signs appearing on the stone were in the style of decorations, forming part of the representation of deities who figure in the codices and in various stone glyphs.

After León y Gama the inscriptions interested such scholars as Padre José Antonio Alzate, Alexander von Humboldt, William H. Prescott, Manuel Orozco y Berra, Hubert H. Bancroft and Eduard Seler. Recent investigators include Ramón Mena, Erwin P. Diseldorff, Alfonso Caso, Konrad T. Preuss, Enrique Juan Palacios and José Avilés Solares. The latter two scholars maintain the position that this stone and the "Stone of Tizoc" (made during Tizoc's rule, 1481–1486) were astronomical monuments and not capricious ornaments or simple ensembles of mythical emblems. The "Stone of Tizoc," a great round monolith better known by its misnomer, "The Sacrificial Stone," may or may not have been used in gladiatorial combats. A five-pointed symbol was identified by Eduard Seler and by German scholars working with Sr. Juan Palacios as the equivalent of five Venus-cycles of 584 days each, or a total of 2,920 days, a period equal to eight 365-day calendar years. Dr. Noriega has insisted that the signs are astronomical, religious and chronological symbols that also define identifications or planetary relations in the Maya codices. While he concedes that La Piedra del Sol has a partially calendrical meaning in the second circle and in the symbols of the years 1 Técpatl and 13 Acatl, the other symbols signify, to him, the small and great cycles of the sun and moon, the sun and Venus and the sun and Mars. Since the publication of his study he has found in the *Dresden Codex* ciphers which, he claims, correspond to calculations in this stone and in 24 other ancient astronomical monuments. He has presented four mathematical formulae the results of which, he has stated, coincide with the chronological value of periods of eclipses, transits of Venus across the disc of the sun, planetary cycles and intercycles and great lunar-solar periods.

Reading counterclockwise from the upper right of the great stone are the 20 day-signs. In the band surrounding the jewel-bedecked and thirsty

The "Stone of the Sun," popularly known as the "Aztec calendar stone," was dedicated in 1479 during the reign of Axayácatl. It has been called a "supreme manifestation of cosmographic wisdom and mathematical skill."

sun are symbols of four past "Suns," or epochs: Ocelot, Wind, Rain of Fire and Water. The day signs include Alligator, Wind, House, Lizard, Serpent, Death, Deer, Rabbit, Water, Dog, Monkey, Grass, Reed, Ocelot, Eagle, Vulture, Motion, Stone Knife, Rain and Flower. These are prefixed by the numbers 1 through 13 and then back again to 1. If one begins with 4 Motion (the fifth, or present, "Sun") and counts 5 Stone Knife, 6 Rain, 7 Flower, et cetera, continuing through the earlier "Suns," 4 Ocelot, 4 Wind, 4 Rain of Fire and 4 Water, the signs of the past "Suns" for 585 days, one finds oneself once again at 4 Ocelot. This is the period of the Venus cycle. A timetable of all the planets visible to Aztec astronomers is carved, according to Dr. Noriega, in similar fashion on the stone.

Some lunar-solar periods are alluded to in the Old Testament Book of Daniel and in the Apocalypse. The references in the Book of Daniel are believed to have been compiled in the second and third centuries B.C. Passages which are repeated in Chapter XII, Verse 1, of the Apocalypse begin: "And a great sign appeared in the sky, a woman clothed with the sun, the moon under her feet and, above her head, a diadem of twelve stars." Verse 6 of the Apocalypse relates that "the woman fled into the wilderness, where she had a place prepared by God, so that there 1,260 days might nourish her." In the final lines of Chapter XI, Verse 2, of the Apocalypse, is this prophecy: ". . . and they will trample on the sacred city of 42 months." Since there are 30 days in each of the 42 months mentioned, the total is, again, 1,260 days. From Chapter XI, Verse 3, is the phrase: ". . . and they will foretell during 1,260 days." Dr. Noriega has interpreted these as "cosmic days," or 1,260 years, the duration of a lunar-solar cycle. If this figure is deducted from the third and greatest of the lunar-solar cycles, the cycle of 1,040 years, as given in the Piedra del Sol calculations, is obtained. The Aztec century represented 104 years, while 10 true solar centuries, or 1,040 years, com-

The millstone-shaped "Stone of Tizoc," often called "The Sacrificial Stone," was carved during the reign of Axayácatl's successor (1481–1486).

In the view of Dr. Raúl Noriega, symbols on the "Stone of the Sun" representing various units of time may be coordinated with lunations and synodical revolutions of Venus.

= 365 × 100 = 1,236 LUNATIONS

= 3,650 DAYS = 62.5 SYNODICAL REVOLUTIONS OF VENUS

= 360 × 105

= 37,800 DAYS

= 1,280 LUNATIONS

= 105.5 TROPICAL YEARS

= 66 SYNODICAL REVOLUTIONS OF VENUS

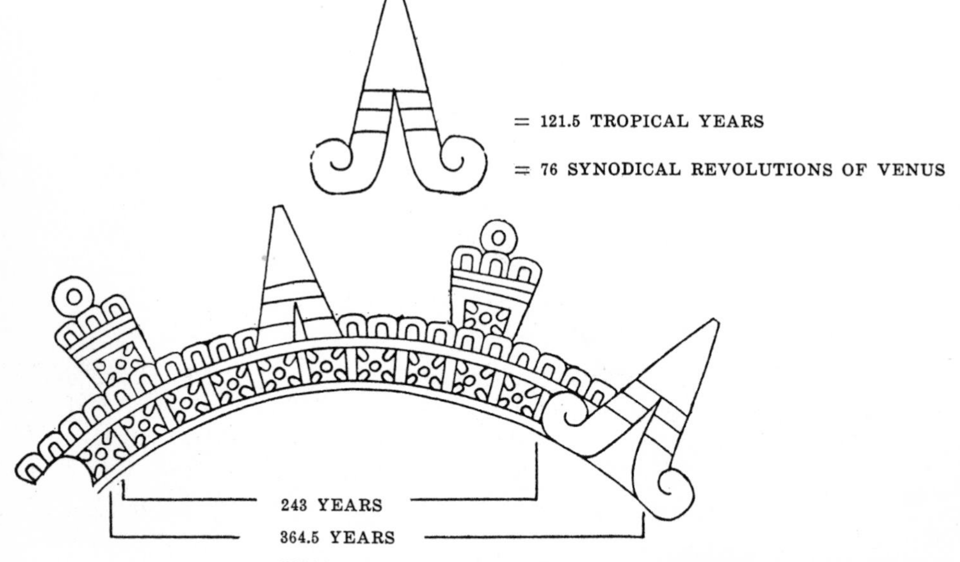

365.25 × 243 + 12 = 88,768 DAYS = 152 SYNODICAL REVOLUTIONS OF VENU[S]

243 = 121.5 + 8 + 105.5 + 8: (+ 121.5 = 364.5 YEARS)

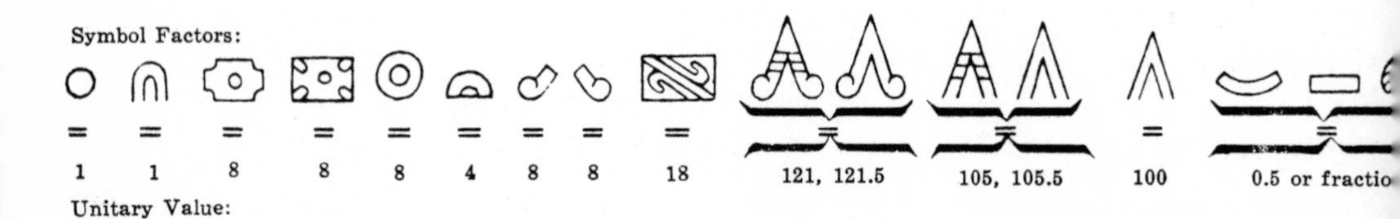

posed a lunar-solar cycle. The concept of 1,040 true solar years, with their 12,863 lunations, is directly related to the Nahua legend of the "Four Suns." The sum of the different epochs assigned to each of the "Suns" is equal to two 1,040-year cycles, a total of 2,080 years. When asked how the wise men of the Middle East arrived at the same mathematical definition of the great lunar-solar cycles as did the astronomers of ancient Anáhuac, Dr. Noriega replied: identical standards in the registry of astronomical calculations and identical mental capacity applied to the compilation of lunar-solar statistics.

The analogies were noted in the seventeenth century by the Swiss astronomer M. Cheseaux, whose interpretive calculations of the Biblical account were cited by Dr. Noriega, including the passage in Chapter VII, Verse 25, of the Book of Daniel: ". . . and in His hand will be put a time and two times, and half a time." According to Cheseaux's calculations, as indicated by Dr. Noriega, a "time" means 360 years, "two times" that number means 720 years, and "half a time" represents 180 years, totaling 1,260 years. The difference between these calculations and those recorded on the "Stone of the Sun" amounts to only .48 of a day. Another page cited in the Book of Daniel is Chapter VIII, Verse 14: "And he told me: 'Till 2,300 days of morning and afternoon . . .' " Since 2,300 true solar years equal 840,051.05 days, and since 28,447 lunations occur in the same period, the difference is only .40 of a day. The basic figure involved in the comparison of Biblical quotations and Aztec inscriptions correspond to the values of the true solar year and the lunar month as used in modern astronomy. These are 365.2421987 days for the year and 29.53058857 days for the month. The 29.5-day lunar cycle was the basis for primitive astronomical records in the opinion of an amateur archaeologist, Alexander Marshack, who interpreted markings on various ancient artifacts. To illustrate his thesis that these ancient markings of dots and lines were Ice Age calendrical notations, he cited an inscribed fragment of "Aurignacian" reindeer bone found in Kulna, Czechoslovakia, some markings on mammoth ivory found in Gontzi in the Ukraine and two series of painted notations from rock walls in Spain. Because, as Mr. Marshack has pointed out, to the ordinary observer "full moon and new moon are not events that occur on precise days the notations sometimes show a month of 30 or 31 days."

According to Dr. Noriega, in everything pertaining to primary astronomical calculations, to the composition of the heavens and to lunar-solar intercycles, the Nahuas and the Maya shared the same knowledge, even though they employed different mathematical symbols. The Maya, he has shown, used numerical symbols of arithmetical expression equivalent to our own even after their ingenuity permitted them, or their predecessors, to invent a system by means of positional mathematics of only three signs—

the dot, or point, the bar and the zero. With these they were able to express any quantity for which modern mathematicians usually use 10 arithmetical symbols. The Nahuas invented or utilized a system by means of which they expressed short and long periods of time by simply repeating ciphers or multiplying them. Among the 13 symbols that have been deciphered by Dr. Noriega are those with the function of expressing a half or other fraction. His research has stressed the fact that the celestial mechanism has provided, over many millennia, points of reference by which to form a mathematical view of the universe. The periodic return of the sun and moon to places at the extremes and center of the east and west horizons; the regular swing of the planets back into the same celestial positions; the eclipses of the sun and moon; the transits of Venus and Mercury across the disc of the sun; and, finally, the rotation of the constellations in unalterable succession, in Dr. Noriega's analysis, gave the early astronomers of Asia, the Middle East and Middle America, the knowledge of a dynamic celestial architecture, precise and harmonious, and governed by numbers of days, years, centuries, even millennia.

Dr. Noriega has called attention to the fact that the ancient Mexicans knew the elapsed time from one transit of Venus to another, while Europeans had to wait for this knowledge until the seventeenth century when Johannes Kepler made the calculations of this phenomena. In acknowledgment of the role of ancient astronomers Dr. Noriega has commented that to date modern astronomy, the direct inheritor of the knowledge of this science, hardly registers its awareness of some four cycles relative to the recurrence of lunar and solar eclipses, while the early American astronomers not only mastered the knowledge of these cycle but discovered no less than 10 more. In regard to solar, lunar and planetary chronological intercycles, of which modern astronomers register 12 at the most, the ancient Mexicans knew at least 40 minor and major intercycles and calculated these in their small and great magnitudes. So exactly did they compute the intercycles of sun, moon and planets, determining when two or more would return to the same relative positions, that twentieth-century mathematicians require up to eight decimal places in order to verify the results.

In the opinion of Dr. Noriega each symbol on the "Stone of the Sun," from the sun-god at the center to the serpentine monsters at the rim, has a function in the measurement of astronomical cycles. Many are aggregates of smaller symbols which, in turn, have significance. Thus, from 29.5, the length in days of a lunation, may be abstracted the symbols for 8, 13, 13.5, 16, 16.5 and 21, all useful in astronomical calculations.

As Dr. Noriega has noted, the chronicler Fray Toribio de Benavente, better known as Motolinia, understood enough of the ancient Indian wisdom to ascertain that the 260-day calendar he found in Middle America was used to measure not only the sun's movements but those of the planets, "or light-giving creatures of the sky." For four centuries, however, this calendar was regarded chiefly as a fortunetelling device which meshed awkwardly with the solar-year count. In three periods of 260 days, Motolinia determined, the ancient Mexcans would expect to see Mars return to the same position with relation to the sun. Saturn made its cycle 11 times in 16 such periods. Five of these counts were long enough for the moon to wax and wane 44 times. The 260-day calendar, known to the Aztecs as the *tonalpohualli* and to the Maya as the *tzolkin*, served as a framework in computing the movement of sun, moon and planets over thousands of years. The number 260 is a multiple of 13 and 20, basic figures in their time-count. Calendars of 260, 360, 364, 365 and 365.2421987 days were employed in computations of solar and lunar eclipses. Since one of the ciphers used was 365.2421987, the true solar year must have been known. Fifty-two years of such precision so nearly equaled 73 cycles of 260 days that, after this lapse of time, the solstices and equinoxes once again bore the same numbers and day-signs. A calendar of 365 days lent itself to Venus-counts, since eight such solar years nearly coincided with five Venus cycles. Multiples of various periods were combined in distinct ways to fix the dates when a certain sequence would repeat itself in connection with the return of a celestial body. Such were the minute calculations evolved over the centuries by men of Anáhuac who, by gazing at the vast heavens, sought to know the unknowable.

According to Dr. Noriega's theory, symbols such as these represent numerical units used by the astronomers of Anáhuac in their calculations.

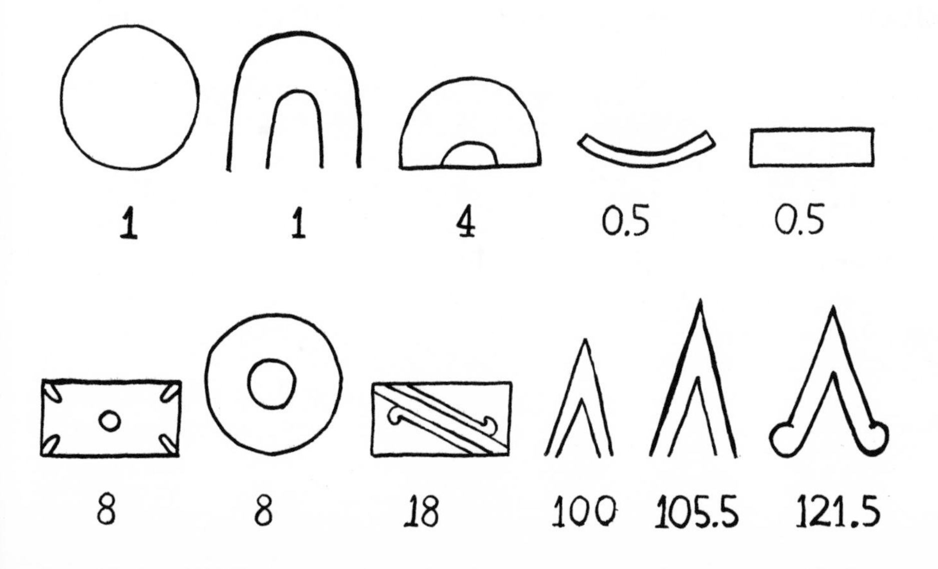

CHAPTER V

Life in Anáhuac

IN ANY STUDY of pre-Conquest life in the Valley of Mexico, dominated for so long by the militaristic ruling caste of Tenochtitlán, the influence exercised by the powerful Aztec rulers and high priests in the determination of collective social patterns can hardly be underrated. The early Aztec rulers bore such names as Acamapichtli (Handful of Reed) (1376–1396); Huitzilhuitl (Hummingbird Feather) (1396–1417); Chimalpopoca (Smoking Shield) (1417–1427); Itzcóatl (Obsidian Snake) (1427–1440); Moctezuma Ilhuicamina (I) (Angry Lord Who Shoots the Sky) (1440–1469); Axayácatl (The Scourge) (1469–1481) and Tizoc (Leg of Chalk). Those who served as "Chief Speaker" in Tenochtitlán from the time Columbus' caravels opened up the Caribbean to Europeans included Ahuitzotl (Water Monster) (1486–1502); Moctezuma Xocoyotzin (II) (Angry Lord, Youngest Son) (1502–1520); Cuitláhuac (Keeper of the Kingdom) (1520) and Cuauhtémoc (Falling Eagle) (1520–1524).

The era immediately preceding the Conquest invites speculation as to the possible effect the more humanistic precepts of Netzahualcóyotl,* the idealistic monarch of Tenochtitlán's neighbor, Texcoco, might have had if they had triumphed over those of his practical Aztec contemporary, the high priest Tlacaelel, who, for several generations, was the actual power behind the throne. He refused to become "Chief Speaker," preferring, instead, to name the rulers of Tenochtitlán. These two extraordinary figures, allies in the defeat of their ancient overlords, the Tepanecas of Atzcapotzalco, supported two highly distinct codes of behavior. As Dr. León-Portilla has pointed out, both recognized the common cultural bond which had been forged by the Toltecs. But while the poet-king

* Some Nahuatl scholars favor Nezahualcóyotl.

Netzahualcóyotl symbolized the hopes of those who desired to continue, or perhaps to revive, the spiritual and aesthetic traditions of Tollan, Tlacalel initiated reforms which had far-reaching repercussions, and his prestige was enhanced by the innumerable military successes and by the impressive grandeur of the Tenocha capital.

Most of the Indian and Colonial chroniclers, as well as later historians, attributed superior wisdom and ability to the Aztecs. Indeed, "The People of the Sun," with their military and political might, their floral wars and alleged human sacrifices, occupy such a dominant place in the annals of pre-Hispanic Mexico that they have, perforce, become the central figures of the Middle-American drama. However, as Dr. León-Portilla has shown, many witnesses and ample documentation attest that another current was also represented by Netzahualcóyotl and the *tlamatini,* or "Followers of Truth," embracing, in ever-increasing numbers, philosophers, musicians, painters, sculptors, architects and astronomers, who hoped to find the meaning of life on an intellectual rather than on a mystico-militaristic plane. Citing a modern parallel, Dr. León-Portilla commented that "in Nazi Germany, alongside the cosmic vision of a mystical-military nature, there could exist philosophical and literary thought, authentically humanist, with ideals completely divergent from those of the Nazi Party."

In ancient Anáhuac the humanistic ideals were represented by the poet-king Netzahualcóyotl; his son Netzahualpilli; Tecayehuatzin, lord of Huexotzingo; and Ayocuan, sage and poet of Huexotzingo; along with many other lords and nobles.

The humanistic attitude in the Nahuatl-speaking world was expressed, according to Dr. León-Portilla, in the lyrics of a song popular at the time of the Conquest:

> Who am I?
> Living thus on wings
> Singing of the flowers?
> I make my songs—
> Butterflies of songs.
> They grow in my soul,
> For the delight of my heart.

A question naturally arises as to the actual extent of the influence such humanists in neighboring Texcoco may have exerted on the life of the Aztecs. Was the "Flower and Song Group" merely an elite of profound thinkers? Certainly the concepts underlying the stern exhortations of Aztec fathers to their children on proper modes of behavior were based on the mystico-military aspects stressed by Tlacaelel, the militarist.

But in the invocations pronounced on life's most solemn occasions—birth, death, marriage, the investiture of a "Chief Speaker," or *tlatoani*—the only deity invoked was Tloque-Nahuaque, "Lord of the Far and Near, invisible like the night, impalpable like the wind." This concept of an omnipresent Supreme Being, whose title "Moyocoyatzín" implied the "Lord Who Invents or Forges Himself Through His Own Thought," was similar to that of the supreme Egyptian deity described as "Master of His Own Transformations." The duality of Moyocoyatzín expressed a metaphysical origin; in its masculine aspect the deity was agent and generator, and in its feminine aspect, that which conceives and gives birth. Moyocoyatzín existed beyond all time and place and represented a mysterious action that could only be conjectured—imperfectly—through poetry, or through "flower and song."

In the Nahuatl culture Macuilxochitl was the god of music, song and dance as well as the patron of social amenities at the courts of the nobles. Indeed, his influence extended to all of life's pleasures, including the delights of love. His temple in Tenochtitlán was located behind the site of the present Metropolitan Cathedral, and offerings made to him were representations of musical instruments. Macuilxochitl often disguised himself as Quetzalcocóchitl, "The Bird That Sings at Dawn." He may be identified by his elaborate dancer's headdress, his feathers and bird's crest. His figure is that of a flayed man, the body painted red. In his mouth is usually a flower and he frequently carries a heart-shaped scepter and a shield adorned with four stones.

Sahagún described the music schools of Tenochtitlán, which included the *Mixcoacalli,* where a wide variety of musical instruments was kept, and the *Cuicacalco,* where songs and dances were taught in the afternoons. Both were in charge of an *ometochtli,* or priest-director of the curriculum and teaching methods. Another priest, known as the *tlapizzatzin,* directed the construction of musical instruments and supervised their maintenance. According to Vicente T. Mendoza's study of musical development in Mexico from early pre-Hispanic periods, *Panorama de la Música Tradicional de México,* (*Survey of Traditional Mexican Music*), native musical expressions which acquired the greatest force and significance were to be found in a belt which had as its axis the 19th parallel. Music enjoyed the highest development and prestige among the theocratic-military organizations of the Aztec, the Maya, the Mixtec, Zapotec and Purepecha or Tarascan proletariat.

Studies of Indian music were also made by the Norwegian anthropologist Carl Lumholtz, author of *El México Desconocido* (*Unknown Mexico*) and by Konrad T. Preuss. The music of the Coras and the Huichols was described in Preuss's *Expedition to Nayarit.* In areas of Mexico where the Spanish culture was firmly implanted, manifestations of Indian music, of course, gradually weakened and finally disappeared, but in isolated regions descendants of the various tribes that peopled the land before Columbus still retain authentic musical traditions. In federally sponsored research projects among Indian groups, investigators have distinguished fifteen distinct groups with their own pure music forms.

In *La Filosofía Nahuatl* (*Nahuatl Philosophy*) Dr. León-Portilla disclosed many little-known facets of the collective personality of the dominant pre-Columbian Nahuatl-speaking peoples who inhabited the Valley of Mexico. His analysis traces the complex interrelations of motives, ideas, aspirations and beliefs to the very mainspring of their ancient cultures, providing a logical approach to a true appreciation of Toltec and Aztec art and architecture. In the foreword to the volume Dr. Angel M. Garibay, director of the Seminary of Nahuatl Culture, University of Mexico, points out that his research dealt with a cultural phenomenon in Mexico which had not received sufficient attention. He contends that while some, because of prejudice, ignorance or disdain, might be inclined to scoff at a title such as *Nahuatl Philosophy*, the same persons will go into ecstasies over pre-Columbian monuments, relegating to the realm of legend and fantasy the concepts of the ancient culture that produced these structural miracles. Such a position, in which one refuses to credit the ancient American races with the intellectual powers and the spiritual awareness associated with Western civilizations, is all the more surprising, he points out, since it is only natural to concede that any civilization capable of executing La Piedra del Sol or of designing and building such constructions as the various pyramids of Mexico should certainly be able to connect thoughts and give expression to emotion. But the autochthonous American peoples are often either denied this mental capacity or are ignored on grounds such as, "We have no way of knowing what they really thought or felt, what ideals controlled their acts or directed their progress during the millennia in which their cultures flourished."

The ancient Nahuas, as Dr. León-Portilla has explained, were people of diverse cultural activities and, at the beginning of the sixteenth century, included the Aztecs and the people of Texcoco, Cholula, and Tlaxcala, who had established themselves at different periods in or near the Valley of Mexico. All shared a common heritage not only of the ideas and traditions but of the extraordinary creative spirit of the Teotihuacanos and the Toltecs. By the time of the Conquest, in fact, there were so many manifestations of art and culture in the great centers such as Texcoco and Tenochtitlán that the Conquerors, rude soldiers for the most part, were struck with amazement. The narratives of Hernán Cortés and Bernal Díaz del Castillo reveal their incredulity upon contemplating the gardens and palaces of Tenochtitlán, with its impressive plaza and buildings of quarried stone, the thriving marketplace of Tlatelolco,* and also the rigidly circumscribed code of the Indians.

But other less obvious aspects of the cultural life of the Nahuas escaped the notice of the Conquerors; it remained for the first Franciscan missionaries in New Spain to observe and record them. Impelled by an eagerness to learn more of their Indian converts, the scholarly friars often penetrated further into the strange and wonderful manifestations they beheld, some of them even comprehending the masterwork of the genius of the Indian: his chronology and his cosmology. With a deeper understanding of the native concepts of time and of the universe, these dedicated men were able, at last, to get some idea of the great cosmological myths and of the precepts by which the Aztecs lived.

Questioning the older Indians, the friars set down, as they understood them, Nahuatl discourses and classical recitations, songs that bade the people honor the gods, ancient verdicts given by judges, the sayings and refrains learned from teachers in the *calmécac,* or school for the sons of nobles, and the *telpuchcalli,* a predominantly military school for the sons of the common people. Among the outstanding early chroniclers were Olmedo, Motolinia, Durán and Mendieta, but it is especially owing to the efforts of Sahagún, who collected hundreds of folios of the data gathered by the first friars who came to New Spain, that the story of the Nahuas can be traced in such detail. He also solicited from his Indian informants opinions interpreting the legends and traditions, which served as a base for his "encyclopedia" of Nahuatl lore and wisdom.

A glimpse of the proscriptions and traditions directly affecting the life of the people of Anáhuac, which anthropologists found differed but little from the daily life of the Maya, was presented by Dr. Walter Krickeberg in *Culturas Antiguas de México* (*Ancient Cultures of Mexico*). Using Sahagún's Nahuatl section, he showed that the social structure was based on a family group headed by the father. Upon marriage a woman left her own *capulli,* or clan, with its elected administrative functionary, for that of her husband. A widow with children usually married the brother of her late husband, so that he could take the place of the children's father. Only sons had the right of inheritance. Where there were no sons, the brother of the husband inherited. Only women were punished for adultery.

The practice of intertribal marriage, preserved since the beginning of clan organization, was considered a tradition-hallowed custom. Marriage to blood relatives was forbidden, as were marriages between child and stepparent, daughter-in-law and father-in-law, et cetera. Among Mixtec princes, however, marriage between brother and sister was as frequent as with the

* Some Nahuatl scholars favor Tlaltelolco.

Incas of Peru or the pharaohs of Egypt. Betrothals were arranged by families involved, usually by elderly women. The consent of both families was necessary; if a young man resided in a house of bachelors, permission from the director, or governor, was required.

As part of the wedding ceremony the bride was borne upon the shoulders of an older woman, followed by a retinue carrying torches, to the home of the bridegroom. The couple then sat upon a *petate,* or woven fiber mat, before the sacred hearth, tying together symbolically the ends of their clothing. After eating and drinking together, they were duly instructed by an elderly man and woman on their marital duties. But before being permitted to live together as man and wife they had to wait four more days, which were dedicated to religious ritual.

For reasons of economy, only members of the upper classes were allowed the luxury of several wives or concubines. The latter were often the daughters of *macehuallis,* or ordinary men, who considered it an honor to have their daughters in the household of the ruler or of nobles. They were regarded as distinct from professional prostitutes. According to Sahagún's Aztec sources, prostitution, or *ahuianime,* was widespread in the large cities of the Valley of Mexico. The friar was told that prostitutes "walked, obscenely painted and dressed, and with coarse faces, near the lake, in the streets and markets, without any home." The Indians also mentioned professional procurers and *cuiloni,* "who imitate women and speak like them."

In the *Codex Mendoza* is a description of a marriage ceremony and the nurture of a child. The newborn infant was tied in a cradle made of a rectangular board provided with a projection to guard the baby's head, similar to that used by North American Indians. On the day of birth or the following, depending on the omens, the infant was named by the midwife. While reciting prayers she bathed the infant in a washstand placed on a mat in the courtyard of the parental home. Meanwhile, three youths announced the child's name by crying it through the streets. The umbilical cord, in the case of a boy, was buried with miniature arms and tools near a battlefield. For a girl it was buried with domestic utensils near a hearthstone. The name of the child was taken from the calendar date corresponding to the day of name, from some physical peculiarity or from a special event occurring on that date. Boys received names of animals and girls of flowers, with the intent of obtaining the favor of some deity or guardian spirit. The Mixtecs used names from the calendar, then gave the child an additional name on its seventh birthday. A famous Mixtec prince was called "Eight Stag Jaguar Claw," a princess of the same house, "Thirteen Lizard Turquoise Butterfly." After the Conquest the second name became more important than the first. The calendar names of the Aztec kings, for the most part, have been forgotten.

Children were exhorted to diligence and disciplined sharply. The wise counsel of their fathers was intended to keep them from idleness and vice. Gossip, gambling, drunkenness and theft were considered among the worst faults. Offenders were "cleansed" by means of sticks and stones, cold water and nettles. They were placed before a mirror—for self-examination—and given bright torches of *ocote,* or pine, for clearer vision and better self-understanding. Punishments might include beating with sticks, inflicting deep scratches with cactus thorns, forced inhalation of chile smoke or confinement in dark rooms.

The diet of the people was frugal and their tasks numerous. Boys from the age of thirteen were encouraged to work, ordered to fish or to cut reed grass. Girls helped in the preparation of food, spinning and weaving until marriage at sixteen or eighteen. Boys of the higher social classes pursued their education after the age of fifteen in schools for soldiers or for priests whose divine patrons were, respectively, Tezcatlipoca, "First Warrior," and Quetzalcóatl, "First Priest." A *telpuchcalli* probably existed in each clan. Military service and public works such as road-building were obliga-

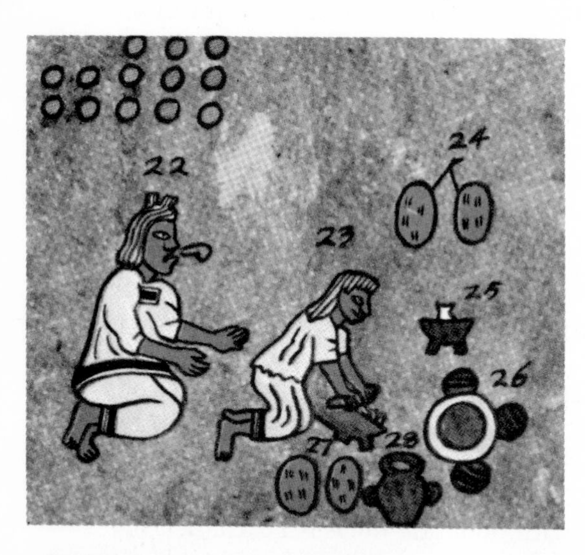

Such daily activities as preparing *maíz* for tortillas and fishing to augment a frugal diet were depicted in the *Codex Mendoza,* reproduced in *Medicina Precortesiana.*

tory for all ordinary men. The *calmécac,* situated close to a temple, was reserved for those who were being trained for the priesthood or for high administrative posts. Students of both seminary and military schools served in the temples, helped the workers in the fields, built homes and listened to court sessions. Some went to war in the capacity of squires. Often a student was obliged to remain in the training institution until marriage at twenty or twenty-two, at which time he would be given a banquet and showered with gifts.

In the ordering of life there was a veritable galaxy of Nahua deities, some identified with birth, some with death and others with sickness. Their worship created an unending complex of symbolism and complicated rites. Horoscopes were cast for newborn infants by the priests in accordance with the different combinations of the ritual two hundred and eighty-day calendar, the *tonalpohualli.* Several deities were associated with medicine. Foremost was Quetzalcóatl, the morning star, god of creation, giver of life and of wisdom. Others included Xipe Tótec, "Our Flayed Lord," the god of the spring, flowers and skin ailments, and Xólotl, the brother of Quetzalcóatl and "Star of Venus," the god of sickness and of abortions.

Honored by the people of Anáhuac were Xipe Tótec (*left*), and Tlazoltéotl (*right*), known as the "eater of filth," to whom sins were confessed, shown in the act of giving birth to the god of *maíz.* This representation of the goddess (original in the Robert Woods Bliss Collection, National Gallery of Art, Washington, D.C.), was reproduced in *Medicina Precortesiana.*

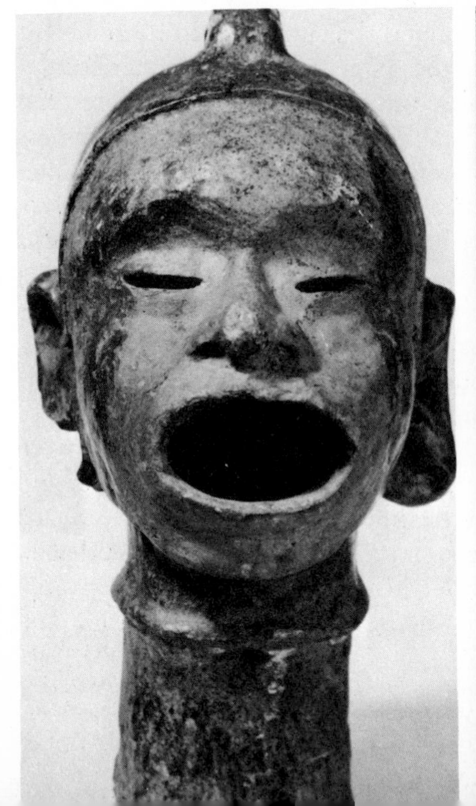

Xochiquetzalli was the goddess of pregnancy and the protector of unborn children. Xoaltecuhtli was the god of dreams and Ixtlilton, "Little Black Face," the god of children, health and cures. Amímitl was associated with dysentery. Tezcatlipoca was identified with sickness and cures. Tlahuizcalpantecuhtli was the god of medicinal herbs. Primarily an earth goddess, Tlazoltéotl, "Eater of Filth," alone among the female deities had a moral significance, since, in eating refuse, she was believed to consume the sins of mankind, leaving them pure. Sickness and death were associated with gods who lived in supernatural regions. Tlalocan, the "Paradise of the South," was the abode of Tláloc, who was identified with dropsy. Mictlantecuhtli, the god of death, dwelt in Mictlán, the underground world.

Dr. Daniel Rubín de la Borbolla, director of the Museum of Popular Arts and Industries and the Museum of the National University of Mexico and author of *La Medicina en México Antiguo* (*Medicine in Ancient Mexico*), prepared an exhibit on ancient medicine. Placed by Dr. Mario González Ulloa in the Hall of Fame of the International College of Surgeons in Chicago, it shows the profound understanding in pre-Columbian times of natural laws as they affected the "ills that flesh is heir to," together with eloquent testimony concerning various treatments administered by indigenous practitioners of the art of healing. The display includes ceramics, sculpture, pictographs from various codices, charts and ancient surgical instruments.

Dr. Rubín de la Borbolla has traced a connection between the priest and the *curandero,* or medicine man, among the Aztecs and other ancient Indian peoples. His study reveals that the ancient Indians diagnosed and treated many ailments such as arthritis, intestinal ulcers, gastrointestinal upsets, respiratory ailments, syphilis, malaria, typhus, mountain dizziness and other maladies. For disorders of the digestive system the oft-prescribed purgatives, emetics and antidysenterics included *capullin* bark, cacao, almonds, yellow tomatoes and an herb known as *iztauhyatl.* For hepatitis the juice of the prickly pear, or *noxtli,* was used.

Native surgery, of course, suffered from lack of asepsis. Operations were performed, however. The Indians were most advanced in trepanning. The perforation of the cranium was practiced throughout all America perhaps as early as 2000 B.C. It was common among the various peoples of Mexico and of the Andean plateau, although different techniques were used. In Mexico the operation was performed with *puzones,* or drills, and later with boring instruments which facilitated cutting of bone. Sharp blades were made from obsidian. Trepanning was often recommended in cases of sunken skull fracture in order to reduce pressure. From the archaeological evidence of patients who underwent such an operation and lived for a long while afterward, it may be concluded that some trepanations were successful.

Cushions of cotton were employed in the mending of fractures, sutures were fashioned from human hair and splints from *tejamanil,* a native wood. Ligatures were devised and pain alleviated by the use of a large variety of plants, fungi and analgesic fruits. Cases of insanity were divided into two types: *tlahuililocayotl,* or passive, and *xolopiyotl,* aggressive. It was believed that nervous maladies had their origin in the abuse of a ritual plant known as *toloatzin,* the modern jimson weed. There were medical specialists, some of whom flayed victims with extraordinary skill in ritualistic ceremonies, bloodletters, dentists, oculists and interpreters of horoscopes.

Dr. León-Portilla stressed the distinction made between the true physician and the pseudo physician. In *La Filosofía Nahuatl* he contended that the pre-Columbian "wise men" tried to comprehend, as did Heraclitus and Aristotle, the temporal origin of the world and its fundamental position in space. To this end they "forged a series of concepts of rich symbolism that were each time more purified and rationalized." He believed they could distinguish between that which was true or "scientific," and that which did not go beyond mere magico-religious credulity, citing a passage from the *Codex Matritense* de la Academía. This description was supplied to Sahagún by his Indian informants:

> The true physician is a wise man (*tlamatini*) who gives life. He is a skilled experimenter with herbs, the stones, the trees, the roots. He proves his remedies. He examines, experiments, alleviates sickness. He massages; he correctly adjusts bones. He prescribes physics; he makes his patients feel well; he gives them beverages; he bleeds, operates, stitches, makes them react; covers their wounds with ashes.
>
> The false physician laughs at the people. He plays a joke on them. He provokes indigestion, aggravates ailments. He has his secrets and guards them. He is a wizard who possesses seeds and knows poisonous herbs. He is a sorcerer, who claims to foretell the future with rope devices. With his seeds and herbs he worsens the condition of the sick and he kills with his medicines.

Two books dealing with the treatment of human maladies in the pre-Hispanic era have contributed to a better knowledge of early Mexican medicine. One, *The Art of Dental Mutilations* by Dr. Samuel Fastlich, dental surgeon of the National University of Mexico, and Dr. Javier Romero is concerned with the ancient indigenous practice of filing the teeth and encrusting them with jade, marcasite and other stones. The volume, with a preface by Dr. Alfonso Caso, also contains information on mouth disorders, which appear to have been common among ancient peoples, judging from the profusion of remedies. Nahuatl words relative to stomatitis, or inflammation of the mouth, and gingivitis, or inflammation of the gums, may be found in the Motolinia *Vocabulario,* a sixteenth-century Spanish-Nahuatl dictionary. *The Art of Dental Mutilations* is illustrated with drawings by the late Miguel Covarrubias and with photographs of archaeological material, including examples of ancient surgical instruments.

The other book, *Medicina Precortesiana* (*Pre-Cortesian Medicine*), by Dr. Marc Jost, a graduate of the Sorbonne and a member of the Faculty of Medicine of the University of Paris, was published by the Grupo Roussel, S. A. of Mexico. The author, after analyzing hundreds of murals, pictographs from codices and sculpture reflecting the treatment of diseases and injuries, was convinced that the native peoples had acquired good scientific principles. In his introduction Dr. Rubín de la Borbolla stated that it represented the first systematic combination in this field of archaeological material and historic information with authentic examples of indigenous art. He is of the opinion that pre-Cortesian medicine, so rich in empirical therapeutics, passed through phases similar to those of other civilizations and that it had a fruitful influence on sixteenth-century Europe and on the *mestizo* population of America. Most of the plates illustrating the work are copies by Mexican painters of pictographs from Sahagún's *Historia de las Cosas de Nueva España.* The material for this great source-book of indigenous culture was conveyed through pictographs, executed by pupils at the Academía de Santa Cruz de Santiago de

Epilepsy was known and treated, as were a number of maladies and ailments, by physicians of Anáhuac. This drawing from the *Manuscript of Sotuta* was reproduced in *Medicina Precortesiana.*

Tlatelolco, where Sahagún taught Latin. Here, in line with the liberal policy of the early period of Spanish colonization, native boys were educated. A course in Indian medicine was included. The Spaniards believed New World remedies were more effective in the treatment of native diseases than those of Europe.

Among the favored treatments discussed in Dr. Jost's compilation is one dealing with fractures. Illustrated with a pictograph from Sahagún's work, the remedy reads: "Fractures of the leg bones are cured with the powder of a root called *acocotli* and that of the prickly pear. These should be placed on the fractured leg, which then should be wrapped, bound with linen or other cloth. Four splints should next be placed around the bandage and the whole strongly tied with cord." The treatment also called for bloodletting from the veins between the large and fourth toe, "so that the wound will not become infected." The splints were to be worn for twenty days. After that time a poultice of *ocotzotl* with powder from the root of the *maguey* was to be applied. "After a little while, when the injured one is feeling better, he may bathe the leg."

The resources of pre-Columbian physicians were greatly enriched by the vast gardens of Anáhuac, with their many varieties of medicinal herbs, hailed by both Cortés and Bernal Díaz as "without equal in the entire world." One of the most beautiful, described by Cortés, was located on the shores of Lake Texcoco, adjoining a house in Ixtapalapa. It was visited by Dr. Francisco Hernández who, as court physician to Philip II of Spain, had been sent to the New World as *Proto-medico* of the Indies to investigate the commercial and medical values of the native remedies, already famous in Europe. He spent seven years studying plants in various parts of Mexico and returned to Spain in 1577, leaving behind copies of his manuscript. This first work dealing with native materia medica was published in Mexico in 1615, its Nahuatl-Latin text having been translated into Spanish. Dr. Hernández also visited the famous tropical garden of Huaxtepec, inherited by Emperor Moctezuma from his namesake and predecessor. He mentioned finding two medicinal trees there, brazilwood and *yolozochil,* the latter used from prehistoric times as a heart stimulant and known to the Mexicans as *manitas* because of its resemblance to tiny withered hands. Because the garden of Huaxtepec furnished a large supply of herb medicines, a hospital was founded at the site shortly after the Conquest.

Although Dr. Hernández's book listed some 1,200 medicinal plants for which the Aztecs had Nahuatl names, the richest source of our knowledge of ancient medicine is derived from an illustrated herbal known as the *Badianus Manuscript* or *de la Cruz-Badiano Aztec Herbal.* Compiled in Nahuatl by Martín de la Cruz, a teacher of native medicine, it was trans-

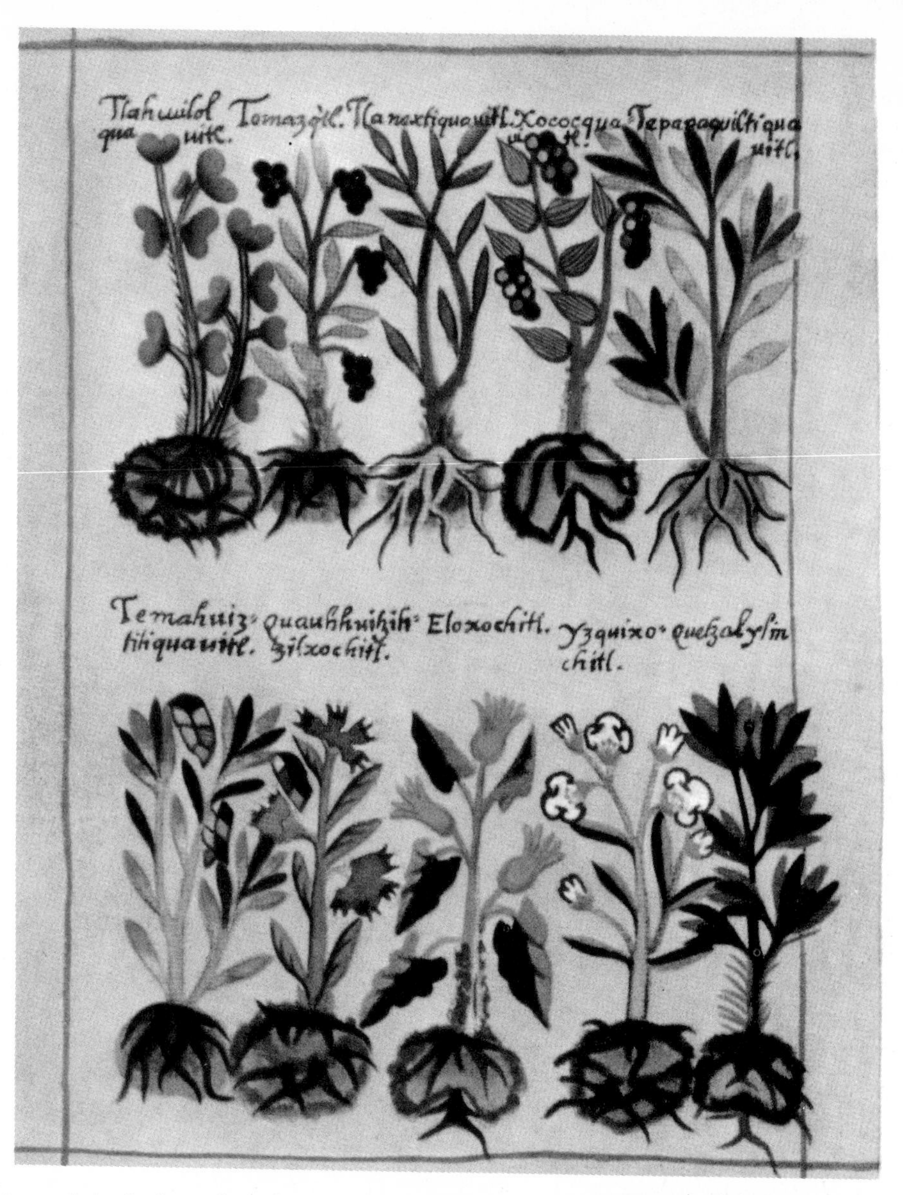

Many of the herbs and medicinal plants grown in Anáhuac's famous tropical garden of Huaxtepec were illustrated in the pictorial volume known as the *Badianus Manuscript* or *de la Cruz-Badiano Aztec Herbal* and reproduced in *Medicina Precortesiana.*

lated in 1552 by Juan Badiano, a reader in Latin, of Xochimilco. Both Indian scholars had been trained at the Academía Santa Cruz de Santiago de Tlatelolco. The manuscript, also known as the *Codex Barberini,* discovered in the Barberini Library of the Vatican by Carl Russell Fish and made public in 1911 through his work on manuscripts in Italian archives, had been dedicated to Don Francisco de Mendoza, son of the first Spanish viceroy to

Mexico. It was profusely illustrated in vivid colors and richly bound in red velvet with metal clasps.

In 1939 an English edition of the old herbal was made possible by the Maya Society, headed by Dr. William Gates, who had been associated with the Motul dictionary project sponsored by Governor Felipe Carrillo Puerto of Yucatán. An edition containing a facsimile color reproduction of each page of the original was issued by the Johns Hopkins Press in 1940. In preparing it for publication, Mrs. Emily Walcott Emmart sought to provide a literal rendering of the text, supplemented by footnotes concerning the historical background of the manuscript and other material drawn from the botanical and historical literature of the sixteenth century.

Included in the book were 118 remedies for various ailments, ranging from broken bones to hiccups. For a fractured head the following treatment was prescribed: "Herbs that spring up in the summer, wet with dew, ground up in the blood of a punctured vein and white of egg, with emerald, pearl, crystal and the bezoar stone of the *huatzin* bird and little earthworms are to be smeared on the fractured head. When there is no blood found, burned frogs will serve." One who had the hiccups was advised to grind in water and cook the stalk of the herb *cahuatli,* the leaves of the herb *mexixquitl,* the frond of the herb *tlatlanquaye,* the bark of a red pine and grass. The remedy also called for the mixing of these, after cooking, with white honey. The brew was to be taken "in moderate portions." The last stage of the cure consisted in warming the chest with a wad of cotton impregnated with the fumes of white incense and smearing it with warmed juice of the leaves of cypress and two other herbs of pungent odor, first ground in water. A wound was apparently treated by instilling into it the juice of the bark of the *ylin* tree, the root of the *tlalhaohuehuetl* shrub, wax and the yolk of an egg. Dr. Jost has pointed out that the embryonic juices in the yolk of an egg contain citopoyetinas, a factor in the regeneration of tissue.

The belief that fragrant flower perfumes and pungent incense were a protection against unseen evils as well as disease is exhibited in a cure known as "A Help for One Crossing a River or Lake," which reads: "Whoever wishes to cross a river or a lake in safety is to wet his chest with the liquid of the herbs *yauhtli* and *tepepapaloquitlitl,* crushed in water. In his hand, moreover, he is to carry a beryl, both the head and viscera of a sea-snail, a sardonyx and the eyes of a large fish enclosed in the mouth." As Mrs. Emmart has shown, the head and viscera of the sea-snail suggested a symbolic association with Quetzalcóatl, the god of the wind; carrying the snail indicated its use as an amulet, a means of protection against wind and storm.

Travel was frequent in Anáhuac, and traders, or *pochtecas,* had need of a snail talisman and the protection of their patron, Yacatecutli. Aztec traders had to conduct commerce with other areas by land and sea to obtain goods for such market centers as Tenochtitlán and its twin city, Tlatelolco. Decades before the arrival of the Spaniards, natives of the eastern coast, the Totonacs and the Maya in particular, were known as skilled navigators and conducted a flourishing "merchant marine." The early mariners had a compass that pointed east and used for their sails palm leaves and *tule,* a reed or bulrush. Jésus Bracamontes Aviño, a naval archaeologist and director of the Naval Museum, has built several models of their vessels, ranging from simple floating rafts, known as *rama* or *tronco flotante,* to canoes of advanced construction. While a pictograph in a native codex shows a craft with an upward-curving prow and stern, the mobile canoes were generally long, narrow and shallow, with standing oarsmen providing power. In the *trajineras,* or barges, of the garboard stroke type, planing was laid next to the keel. In 1516 Aztec barges appeared on Lake Texcoco in a great procession, the "Petitioning of the Water," led by the *tlatoani,* or chieftains, whose own sumptuous barges were decorated with life-sized sculptured figures.

According to Sr. Bracamontes Aviño, Aztec traders made regular trips from such points of interchange as Xicalango ("Where the Language Changes") on the Gulf of Mexico and Xoconusco on the Pacific Coast. En route to Nito in the Honduras Gulf they touched at Chetumal on the southern part of the Yucatán Peninsula. The regular coastal trade route, developed by 1500, lay between the present Veracruz coast on the Gulf of Mexico and the mouth of the San Juan, the river which today defines the boundaries of Nicaragua and Costa Rica, possibly extending, according to Sr. Bracamontes Aviño, as far as Laguna Chirique in Panama. Potonchon, Sealak, Catoche and Bacalar were points which attracted large numbers of merchants.

In his *Atlas of the Mexican Conquest,* the achievements of early mariners who explored Mexican waters and, like Columbus, encountered these early native craft, were chronicled by Dr. Amaya Topete. Each of forty maps is accompanied by an account of the principal episodes in connection with overland penetrations and voyages of discovery. The earliest voyage of exploration appears to have been that of Juan de Solis, who set out from Santo Domingo in 1506. When he had sailed in the expedition of Amerigo Vespucci in 1498 he had come close to Yucatán. In 1506, with Vicente Yañez Pinzon as his pilot, he sailed northward along the coast until he reached the Bay of Chetumal. Upon their return to Spain in 1508, Pinzon was authorized by Ferdinand the Catholic to discover and conquer the islands and mainland of the West Indies, while de Solis was made second in command. They failed to locate any pearl fisheries or gold mines in Yucatán, and de Solis was later killed by Indians while he was exploring the banks of the Río de la Plata in Uruguay.

Peter Martyr, an early chronicler of events in New Spain, wrote of the effect on the unfortunate Indians of the ruthless quest by the Spaniards for riches: "Our men's insatiable desire for gold so oppressed these poor wretches with extreme labor and toil, whereas before they lived pleasantly and at liberty, given only to play and pastimes, as dancing, fishing, fowling and hunting for little conies, that many of them perished for very anguish of mind, the which (their unaccustomed labors) are things of themselves sufficient to engender new disease. . . . But it shall suffice to have spoken thus of the pestiferous hunger for gold. . . . The ravenous hunger for gold hath greatly hindered our men from tillage of the soil."

It was "tillage of the soil" that led Dr. Herbert J. Spinden to trace the probable sources of Moctezuma's fabled gold. The clearing of land for large-scale cultivation of bananas and other tropical fruits brought to light ancient trade routes that had been hidden for centuries by impenetrable forests and that once linked the ancient civilizations of Mexico, Central and South America. Over them were carried gold, pearls and precious stones from South America and the Isthmus of Panama to the distant heights of the Mexican Plateau. A route from San Juan in Nicaragua and another from the Isthmus of Panama, Veragua Province, were identified by the archaeologist S. K. Lothrop, who believed the latter site to be the headquarters of the most enterprising group of exporters of gold and jewelry in the New World: they traded by sea with the *pochtecas* of the Valley of Mexico, a distance of more than 2,500 miles.

Dr. Spinden's identification of a hitherto-unknown culture zone in the forests of eastern and northern Nicaragua connected these southern gold fields with the lavish court of the Aztec rulers. Since the days of the Conquest, the source of Moctezuma's vast wealth has baffled treasure-seeker and historian alike; tradition and rumor, as recorded by the early Spanish chroniclers, pointed to lands "beyond the Maya region." Such stories and his own research among the ruins of the rich archaeological area on the American mainland lying between the Tropic of Cancer and the Equator convinced Dr. Spinden of the existence of a well-defined route by which pre-Hispanic peoples had carried on a flourishing commerce. He found some evidence to support his theory in the Maya monuments of Chichén Itzá. Journeying through the tropical jungles of the so-called "Mosquito Coast" of the Caribbean to eastern Honduras and northern Nicaragua, he found vestiges of an ancient culture of a high order. His discovery not only filled in the gap of the line of ancient civilizations that extended down the Central American coast from the Yucatán Peninsula to the border of Costa Rica and verified the persistent reports of a traffic in gold and gems centuries before the Conquest, but also fixed the date of the "Metal Age" in America.

In attempting to locate the sources of the treasure of the Aztecs in Costa Rica, Panama and Colombia, archaeologists were long confronted by the same savage tribes encountered by Columbus on the coast during his fourth voyage in 1502. His descriptions indicated that these tribes—the Jiquaque, Poya and Mosquito—would have been incapable of taking part in any sustained trade relations. It is Dr. Spinden's belief that the people who built the palisaded towns, produced the advanced art and developed the *maíz* worship of which he found ample evidence, were either destroyed or displaced by barbarous immigrants from the South American forests shortly before the coming of the "Great Admiral."

Whatever the fate of the original inhabitants, there is clear indication, he believes, that they were involved with the gold trade, first between the Toltecs and the Maya, and later between the Aztecs and Zapotecs on the one hand and the people of the Costa Rica region on the other. In the culture zone known as the "new Chontal area" gold ornaments of unmistakably Costa Rican origin have been found which compare favorably with the finest specimens of the medieval goldsmith's art. Among the many objects brought to light and considered as archaeological proof of trade are several hundred pounds of tiny copper bells of Maya manufacture. If the savage tribes of the "new Chontal area" had not, in the days of the Conquerors, blocked the way to the Colombian gold fields, it is possible that Mexican history would have recorded a less tragic story. The failure of the Spaniards to satisfy their lust for the precious metal in Mexico, and their constant suspicion that the Indians were keeping secret the location of rich deposits, gave rise to cruel reprisal and consequent reciprocal hatred.

The earliest use of metal on the North American continent has been dated, by Dr. Spinden, between A.D. 700 and 800, after the abandonment of the Old Maya Empire. During the closing years of this brilliant Maya period, for the first six centuries of the Christian era when the Maya culture flourished in what are now Chiapas and Tabasco, the Petén and Izabal districts of Guatemala and the adjoining western part of Honduras, there was a migration northward into the Yucatán Peninsula. In this area was begun the monumental building of the New Period, with the cities of Chichén Itzá, Uxmal and Mayapán as the crowning achievements. It was this later Maya civilization that knew the use of metal. Copper, gold and silver, although entirely absent from the remarkable ruins of the Old Period—Tikal, Copán, Palenque and Quiriguá—have been found in abundance in the ruins of Yucatán. Quantities of beautiful metal objects—gold jewelry of rare workmanship, copper bells, silver discs and other ornaments—have been reclaimed in dredging operations at the Sacred Well of Chichén Itzá.

There were no gold mines in Yucatán, and only a few regions in the whole territory that fell under Aztec control are recorded in the tribute-roll of Moctezuma as sources of gold.

At the peak of the traffic between the Colombian gold fields and the capital of Anáhuac the old trade route, according to Dr. Spinden, touched at Chichén Itzá only by way of a wide detour. The road started in the land of the Zenu on the coast of the Gulf of Darien and branched out into the territory of the Quimbaya, called the finest goldsmiths of ancient America. Skirting the eastern edge of the Isthmus of Panama, it ran through the territory of Talamanca in Costa Rica and the heart of the "new Chontal area," entering the Maya region at Quiriguá and passing the city of Tayasal, which had been founded by the Itzás when conditions in Chichén Itzá under Toltec oppression became intolerable for the "holy and learned men."

At about this period the route also penetrated Mazateca territory. Cortés encountered the Mazateca in the heart of the Yucatán Peninsula when he followed the route into Guatemala in 1526. In Dr. Spinden's opinion this tribe was one of several whose real home was the "new Chontal area." Bernal Díaz, who accompanied Cortés on this expedition, described the palisaded villages of the Mazateca and the houses built along the route to Yucatán for the accommodation of traders. These towns, with their walls and moats, correspond to the ruins unearthed by Dr. Spinden. Today the Mazateca are located several hundred miles farther northwest. It has been proved that their language, and that of the Otomis as well, is related to the language of the cultured tribes living south of the Nicaraguan lakes and sometimes referred to collectively as the Chorotegas.

From Tayasal the ancient trade route continued in a northwesterly direction through Zapotec and Mixtec country, with an important station at Teotitlán del Camino in northern Oaxaca near the boundary of what are now Veracruz and Puebla. The height of the gold trade marked the maximum of splendor for the Zapotecs and the Mixtecs. The former, borrowing much from the Maya, attained a high degree of civilization. They excelled in gold work, leaving unparalleled examples of gold jewelry.

Before the Otomis overthrew the Toltecs in the Valley of Mexico, the trade route, it is believed, terminated at Tula. The last capital of the Toltecs, Tula's power was completely broken in A.D. 1070. Near it, on the ancient route, was Teotihuacán, where stood the lofty Pyramid of the Sun and the Temple of Quetzalcóatl, the deity to whom the Toltecs attributed the origin of the goldsmith's art. Toltec craftsmanship flourished in Atzcapotzalco long after the Conquest, and Bernal Díaz remarked that its goldsmiths compelled admiration from the most skilled in Spain. Sahagún wrote that some of them, called "beaters," "worked in gold with the hammer, pounding it to make it thin like paper." Others, called *tlaltaliani*, "fuse the gold, or anything else in it, or silver. These are the true artisans, who are also called by another name, 'Tulteca.' They are divided into two classes because each one works the gold according to his own manner." There are references in various Spanish chronicles and in Aztec codices to processes used by the Aztecs to make gold leaf and to model and cast jewelry and other objects of gold and silver, an inheritance from Toltec artisans.

According to Moctezuma's account, his gold was obtained from "three places in Mexico," but investigations of these sources apparently did not satisfy a succession of Spanish rulers. As late as September 6, 1536, María, queen of Charles V, sent a royal cedula to the governor of Nicaragua, commanding him to undertake the discovery of the great stream draining into the Nicaraguan lake. The queen directed the "present or future governor of the province of Nicaragua" to explore the river flowing into the North Sea, for she was informed, she said, that "this is a very large river, like the Guadalquivir that flows by Seville, and that at the outlet of the North Sea it was reported that there are many people and that it is very rich in gold and that from thence was carried to Yucatán the gold possessed by Moctezuma."

Dealers in gold, silver and precious stones were plentiful in the Aztec capital and in its rival city, Tlatelolco. They displayed their wares in great markets, or *tianguis*. Such markets existed elsewhere in the Valley of Mexico on a smaller scale. In pre-Columbian times the native skill of the craftsman or artisan was the chief factor behind the extensive commerce of Anáhuac and its markets, which served as outlets for the rich and varied products of the fertile soil, as well as a multiplicity of objects made by skilled hands.

Barter was the means of exchange, and values were established by the desirability and rarity of the merchandise. Money, as an exchange medium of fixed value, did not exist. As a substitute, in the adjustment of small transactions, the people of Anáhuac used grains of cacao which, easily transportable, could be converted into chocolate, a favorite beverage. When larger amounts were required in negotiations, feather quills filled with gold dust, often arranged like the blades of a fan and adorned with jewels and hammered copper, served the purpose.

In the markets one section was usually given over to fruits and vegetables, stacked in symmetrical mounds on woven straw mats. In other sections might be displayed cotton garments, carefully folded or hung so as to show their patterns. Among the tools were farming implements, rows of obsidian blades, domestic utensils of various types, awls, bone needles and hatchets of copper. The stalls of the feather vendors were ablaze with the green plumes of the quetzal bird. Here, too, were hung multihued feather cloaks, examples of the rare skill and patient labor of Aztec craftsmen. Dealers in jewels and ornaments displayed their precious wares—jade, obsidian, moonstone, opal and crystal, highly polished and carved in artistic designs for personal adornment.

For centuries Tlatelolco boasted the most prosperous commerce of the whole Plateau. It was described by Cortés as a "place of many plazas containing great markets, one twice the size of Salamanca, enclosed by arcades where daily there were 60,000 people buying and selling all the kinds of merchandise found in the land." The chronicler Bernal Díaz was also impressed. "When we arrived at the great market-place called Tlatelolco," he recalled, "we were astonished at the number of people and quantity of merchandise and at the good order and control maintained, for we had never seen such a sight before. Each kind of merchandise was kept separate in its own place. Let us begin with the dealers in gold, silver and precious stones, feathers, mantles and embroidered goods. Then there were Indian slaves, both men and women, and they brought them along

All kinds of merchandise, from feather cloaks to bread "with a cheese flavor," were to be found in the great marketplace of Tlatelolco, depicted in a fresco by Diego Rivera.

tied to long poles, with collars around their necks so they could not escape, but others they let walk freely. Next there were traders who sold great pieces of cotton, cloth and articles of twisted thread, and those who sold cacao. In this way, one could see every type of merchandise to be found in all of New Spain. There were those who sold *henequen* cloth, ropes and sandals and sweet roasted roots from this plant. In another place there were skins of tigers and lions, of otters and jackals, deer and other animals like badgers and mountain cats, some tanned and some crude, and other merchandise."

He enumerated many commodities—beans, sage and other herbs, vegetables, fowl, rabbits, deer and young dogs. The vendors of fruit and cooked foods and those who sold pottery "made in a thousand different forms, from great *ollas* to little jugs," were described, as were a variety of wooden articles, ointments, paper and "reeds scented with liquid amber and full of tobacco." The list of objects for sale included salt, stone knives, bread "with a cheese flavor," brass and copper axes and gourds and "wooden jars that are gaily painted." He could not, he said, tell of all the things that were sold because they were "so numerous and because the great market with its porticos was so crowded with people that one would not have been able to see and investigate everything in two days."

In a letter to Charles V, Cortés told the king he had also seen "various kinds of honey and honeycombs of the bees and canes of *maíz* which are as yellow and as sweet as sugar." He also mentioned "honey from some plants which are called *maguey* . . . from these plants sugar and wine are made which are also sold." The most generally accepted theory regarding the derivation of the word *pulque* traces it to *poliqui*, meaning "decomposed" in Nahuatl. The Spaniards corrupted *poliqui* to *pulcre* and later to *pulque*. The word *maguey* is of Spanish origin; the Aztecs called the plant *metl*.

Just as ancient peoples on the shores of the Mediterranean, in India and in southern Africa used the saps of various trees and plants and the juices of fruits as libations to their gods, so the Aztecs and other tribes of the Central Plateau extracted the sap of the *metl*, or *maguey*. It develops perfectly between 6,315 and 8,775 feet above sea level in the area now comprising Hidalgo, Tlaxcala, México and Puebla. The preferred variety of this plant is *Maguey manso*, known also as *Maguey pulquero* or *Agave atroverins*. Before its liquid can be extracted a plant must be from four to six years old. The fibrous roots and thick shoots can resist prolonged drought. *Maguey pulquero* flowers only once and dies soon afterward; just before the end it sends up a long stalk topped by flowers. Propagation is usually from shoots, or *mecuates*. The plants can thrive in poor, dry soil and can store reserve water.

One theory advanced for the ceremonial role of *pulque* in pre-Conquest Mexico holds that it may have started with the discovery that the *maguey* plant offers a means of quenching thirst. Although climatic conditions in Mexico are believed to have been somewhat milder several centuries ago, there were doubtless extremely dry areas in the northern and central deserts. The importance of thirst-quenching plants was not, however, limited to arid regions. According to Martín del Campo, "It is *pulque* that is the fundamental drink of the inhabitants of enormous stetches of land where there is no drinkable water, and it is plain that pulque is to be preferred to contaminated water." It is also considered by some authorities to be a valuable natural source of vitamins and minerals.

According to an old legend told to Sahagún, a woman, Mayahuel, later regarded as a goddess and the mother of Centzon Totochtin, the patron of Tepozteco, invented *pulque* and knew how the *maguey* should be pierced in order to extract the honey. In the apparently pre-Columbian *Borgia Codex*, which originated in Puebla or possibly Tlaxcala, Mayahuel is a prominent figure, dressed in white, the color of *pulque*. The *Cospi Codex*, in the University of Bologna collection, pictures the goddess with *maguey* flowers in her hair. Patécatl, a *pulque* god shown in the *Borgia Codex*, is credited with discovering how to supplement the honey from the *maguey* to aid in the fermentation process. His name, like that of his associate deities, was taken from the locality in which he was worshipped. Several place-names survive to identify the first makers of *pulque* with a mountainous place called Chichinahuia. Because this drink was topped with foam, the snow-capped peak was also called Popocatepetl, meaning "Foamy Mountain," not, as is popularly supposed, "Smoking Mountain."

Excessive drinking of *pulque* was controlled, if not eliminated, by a taboo on the "fifth cup." This was reserved for priests, in whom it induced an ecstatic reaction, often causing them to dance. Even a fourth cup was frowned upon, since it might result in drunkenness, a punishable offense in Tenochtitlán except in privileged cases (the sick, the aged or celebrants at certain festivities).

The *Codex Magliabecchi*, probably painted between 1562 and 1601, has several representations of *pulque* deities, including Mayahuel and Atlacoaya. Eduard Seler noted that the face of a *pulque* god was usually painted in two colors, one half in red and the other in black or dark brown with yellow spots. This decorative scheme also characterized representations of Tláloc and Quetzalcóatl. *Pulque* deities were further distinguished by a crescent-shaped ornament worn directly under the nose. The discovery of the *pulque*-producing *maguey* was an event of extraordinary significance to the Nahuas. The *Tira de la Peregrinación* leaves no doubt that the plant sought by the Aztecs near Chalco was the *maguey*. The discovery was apparently made in Coatitlan during the Aztecs' twenty-year stay there. In a pictograph a figure is shown in the act of drawing off the sap with an *acoctl*, or tube. The date of the planting of a *maguey* crop is given as A.D. 1224 and that of the first manufacture of *pulque* as A.D. 1239.

In *El Maguey y El Pulque* Oswald Goncalves de Lima pointed out that, for the Aztecs, *pulque* was a nutritive drink, their divine *ánnarása,* a medicine and a ritual intoxicant related to their complex pantheon and with cosmological links that paralleled, in some respects, the various ancient traditions of the Old World. Sahagún referred to *pulque* as "the medicine drink, the ritual liquor, the white wine, the *temoatl*, the sacred wine of the conquered warriors who are to be immolated." Their *octli,* he said, was the "drink of the brave and the wise until the downfall of their civilization." *Octli* was drunk as a ceremonial liquor at harvest festivals and as a stimulant in the gladiatorial combats in which prisoners-of-war engaged. After the prisoners received their small shields and wooden clubs topped with feathers and their bodies were painted for the encounter, they were given "*pulque* of the gods" to drink. But with the flight of the gods from Anáhuac *pulque* lost its sacred character and its ritualistic dignity. In time, many shrines of the old agrarian deities, once worshipped as symbols of death and rebirth, vanished or were reduced to rubble.

Two of the *pulque* deities, Mayahuel and Patécatl, recognizable by the crescent-shaped ornaments worn under the nose, were pictured in the *Codex Magliabecchi.*

CHAPTER VI

Rivals and Vassals of Tenochtitlán: Xochimilco, Tlatelolco, Texcoco, Malinalco, Tlaxcala, Tepoztlán and Cholula

In what was known as the Valley of Anáhuac several ancient sites contain vestiges of once-flourishing city states, some of them rivals of now-obliterated Tenochtitlán. Many were reduced to the stage of mere vassals by the Aztecs. Some resisted, adopting various defensive strategies, but nearly all were listed in their tribute rolls.

Archaeological sites in or near Mexico City include Xochimilco, its floating gardens a reminder of the tiny island foothold gained by the Aztecs, who began as mercenaries for their neighbors and by wars and confederation transformed their marshy hamlet into a dazzling seat of empire within a few hundred years; Tenochtitlán's twin-city, Tlatelolco, with its unrivaled marketplace; and Texcoco, a seigniory famed for a poet-king's benevolent rule.

At some distance from Mexico City are other ancient sites: Malinalco, subdued by the Aztecs in 1476; Tlaxcala, which provided Cortés with many warriors; Tepoztlán, which honored the *pulque* gods; and Cholula, which accorded special homage to Quetzalcóatl, the "fair god."

Today the spade and pick are penetrating the rich archaeological zone of **Xochimilco,** the site of the circular calendar stone known as Cuauh Tochtli, or Six Rabbits. Xochimilco ("The Place Where Flowers Grow") has long been a prime tourist attraction because of its canals which date back to the era when *chinampas*, or "floating gardens," were established on Lake Xochimilco, under Acatonalli, elected as a tribal ruler in 1256, long before the Aztecs reached the Valley of Mexico.

Professor José Farías Galindo of Xochimilco, who has prepared a history of the region, cited various sources, including Joseph Marius Alexis, the *Codex Aubin* (1574), the *Codex Xolotl*, de Alva Ixtlilxóchitl, the *Anales de Chimalpahín*, Fray Diego Durán and Juan de Torquemada, to support his theory that the Xochimilcas were actually the first of the seven Nahua tribes to arrive in Anáhuac. They entered it, he believes, from the northwest, having passed through Ahuilazco, near Tula, in what is now Hidalgo. It is said that their first settlement, "The Place Where Our God Is," was at Tochimilco in Puebla. Afterward they settled in various places in what is now Morelos, including Tepoztlán, Tlacotenco (now called Santa Ana), Acalpixcan and several other pueblos. According to Professor Farías Galindo, the tribes arrived at the site of Xochimilco A.D. 989, having come there by order of their priest Huetzalin, whom they had chosen in Tula. Their roundabout route took them to Tepetlapan and Coapan, but in 1196, he believes, they settled down at Cuauhilama, or Vieja del Bosque, the site now known as Acalpixcan (Nahuatl for "Where Canoes Are Taken Care of"). They believed this was the central point in the mountains around the lake. To maintain life in this rugged elevated region they struggled constantly to increase their arable land. Here they cleared space for their temples and constructed a great highway from stone slabs.

Among the deities to whom temples were dedicated were Chicomecóatl, or Chantico, goddess of hearth-fire and fecundity, usually represented with a large open mouth and "grumbling teeth." Durán remarked that she was the particular goddess of the Xochimilcas, although she was also worshipped by the Mexicas and the Acolhuas of Texcoco. Also worshipped at Cuauhilama were Cihuacóatl, or Quilaztli, an earth goddess and patroness of women who died in childbirth; Amímitl and Atláhuac, goddesses of floating gardens and canals; Tetzáhuitl, known also as Tetzáuhpilli or Tetzauhquitzin, god of rain and of farmers; Centéotl, god of corn and of sowing; Xochiquetzalli, goddess of domestic labor, the harvest, the "New Fire" and flowers; her mate Xochipilli, god of beauty and the patron of dancing, games and love; Macuilcalli, god of virgins; Chiconahuizcuintli, god of the aged; and Nahualpilli, god of the young.

In their early years, according to Professor Farías Galindo, the Xochimilcas were governed by a warrior chief known as Tlatócatl. Great religious festivals were held in Cuauhilama to celebrate the ascent of Acatonalli to the throne in 1256. From the time of the priest Huetzalin to Acatonalli all Xochimilca noblemen were elevated to sovereignty through great personal merit. "When they deviated from strict self-discipline," Professor Farías Galindo has stated, "they immediately ceased to rule and many times were judged by the council of old men." Acatonalli, facing a severe food shortage, consulted his venerable guides and assumed the

At Xochimilco, famed for its scholars and *chinampas*, or floating gardens (*top left*), was found the calendar stone known as Cuauh Tochtli, or "Six Rabbits" (*right*).

responsibility of acquiring land along the lake. Nine years after his accession he could proudly display several thriving *chinampas*. This rapid agricultural development aroused the envy of powerful neighbors, in particular the inhabitants of Culhuacán, Coyohuacan, Atzcapotzalco and Tenochtitlán, as well as the allies of the Tlahuica. Some of the ensuing wars lasted for as long as two hundred years. As vassals of Tenochtitlán and Atzcapotzalco, the Xochimilcas were required to give support both in wars of conquest and in the "floral" battles involving numbers of prisoners-of-war selected as combatants. Defying their overlords, the Xochimilcas joined the forces of Cortés.

Between 1256 and the Conquest 22 lords reigned in Xochimilco. Their last king, Apochquiyauhtzin, served for 22 years as a Colonial cacique and was baptized as Martín Cerón de Alvarado. The "wise men" of Xochimilco trained several noble students who became famed for their achievements. Xochimilcan scholars included Martín de la Cruz, the author of a volume on native herbs, and Juan Badiano, who translated the work into Latin.

In August 1894 the antiquarian-lawyer Nicolas Islas Bustamante visited the Acalpixcan zone near Xochimilco and photographed its carved rocks. Dr. Hermann Beyer published his findings in 1924. Many of the petroglyphs may be seen today. In the direction of Acalpixcan's cemetery, vestiges of an ancient highway indicate a circular route marked by various resting-places. On the left the road leads to Cihuacóatl, an enormous rock which was dynamited at its base. What has been preserved of the petroglyph depicts two serpents, a left arm, a leg and a foot. On a rock protected by an iron grating is a carving representing Huetzalin on a pyramid, with an incense burner in his hands. Cipactli is the carving of an alligator representing the Origin of Life, a day name, light, night or darkness. On another rock are the *báculo,* or staff, of Quetzalcóatl, Xonecuilli and Citlalcueitl, the "Lady of the Starry Street," or Citlaltónac, "Milky Way." Because of the skull in the center pierced by a flint knife the Xochimilcas call it "The Song to Death." The carving known as "The Knight of the Jaguar" was badly damaged by the Conquerors and by fungus. Itzpapálotl, or "Obsidian Knife Butterfly," represents a stellar or agricultural goddess. Another carving which has survived the ravages of time is that of a jaguar, which symbolized war and the strength of the Xochimilcas. A sculptured calendar of a year corresponding to A.D. 1287 was, according to Professor José Avilés Solares, the inspiration for the great Aztec calendar stone executed during the last half of the fifteenth century.

To the northwest may be seen the foundations of what may once have been priests' quarters, consisting of three adjoining rooms. About 33 yards to the north is a "solar eye," a stone map of Nahualapa indicating the ancient highway. The road ends 219 yards to the east. Here are pyramidal steps and, at the side, "eyes of water," or springs. On the path is another stone map delineated in dots instead of in lines, a technique practiced by native artisans. In the opinion of Carmen Cook de Leonard, the archaeologist Florencia Muller and the geologist Maldonado Koerdell, this stone map is of greater archaeological significance than the Yucatecan *maqueta* indicating the territory between Chichén Itzá and Kabáh.

Toward the south is a large esplanade ending in what may have been an observatory. Traces of a stucco may be seen on a shrine known as El Adoratorio. Professor Farías Galindo believes that the monument known as the Great Astrigal, indicated by a detour from the highway and some remnants of platforms, was probably erected by the Xochimilcas in honor of their particular goddess.

At the far end of the cemetery next to the path are two petroglyphs. Las Flores, which is very well carved (Xochimilcan artisans were noted for their stonework), represents Cocoxóchitl, or Dahlia. Yoloxóchitl, or Magnolia, symbolizes the four corners of the universe, with the earth in the

Xochimilcan artisans, noted for their stonework, carved at Acalpixcan symbols of a butterfly and a jaguar (*top*) as well as a profile representation of the priest Huetzalin holding an incense burner (*bottom*). Several other petroglyphs and stone maps of the area have been found at this site.

center. The little hill of Tetítlan is the site of a petroglyph known as La Primavera, depicting Xochipilli, which is gradually being destroyed by fungus.

A pyramidal mound facing south is known as El Huacal, or Huetlalcueye, distinguished by three crosses which have been placed above it. Other remains include stone maps of Nativitas Zacapan; sculptured slabs representing the Nemonteni, or the five unlucky days at the end of the year; the skull of Miccahuilhuitl; a representation of Coatlicue; a representation of La Malinche; and a figure of a Huastec warrior.

According to legend, **Tlatelolco** dates back to the shadowy era when Nahuatl-speaking tribes halted their long wanderings at the sign of a cactus on which perched an eagle with a snake in its beak. Tenochitlán was split, so a story runs, by priestly edict into four quarters at the center of which stood the main temple. Dissatisfied with the section assigned to them, the Tlatelolcas soon moved to a higher location, separated from

Tenochtitlán by a stretch of water known as "The Place of the Mound." Archaeologists have uncovered evidence indicating that the site, presently occupied by the Lagunilla Market, the Church of Santiago de Tlatelolco, a railroad yard and a military prison, may have been inhabited as early as A.D. 1100, some centuries before the founding of Tenochtitlán.

A bitter rivalry existed between the twin cities; Tenochtitlán envied Tlatelolco for its splendid temples and palaces and the wealth and commercial prestige derived from its vast market. Tlatelolco was also famed for its guild of traveling merchants. Membership in the *pochtecatini* was granted to outsiders only by royal permission. The *pochteca* had their own judges and enjoyed the privileges of high social rank. As Durán observed, "One way to gain fame and wealth was to deal in merchandise and buying and selling. Thus Indian merchants who also possessed land and slaves to sacrifice to their god were numbered among the magnates of the land." The *pochteca* sometimes acted as infiltrators, giving full reports of the areas they visited. It is said of them that they "purposely stirred up trouble in unconquered provinces so that their emperor could become personally insulted."

Tenochtitlán's long-smoldering jealousy of Tlatelolco's prosperity culminated in a great civil war. Hostilities broke out after the death, in 1472, of the celebrated poet-king of Texcoco. Netzahualcóyotl had, in previous disputes, proved an effective mediator between the rivals. The showdown for economic supremacy was hastened by the arrogance of the Aztec ruler Itzcóatl's successor, Moctezuma Ilhuicamina, who was inordinately greedy for tribute and, according to some sources, sacrificial prisoners. Relations reached a crucial point when Tlatelolco's military leader Moquihuix,* known as "The Drunkard," won the battle of Cotastla. To celebrate the victory the Tlatelolcas wanted to build a larger pyramid than that of Tenochtitlán. This rivalry was aggravated by a crisis at the domestic level, a subject dramatized by Salvador Novo in *La Guerra de las Gordas* (*The War of the Fat Ones*). Moquihuix had married Chalchiuenenetzin, or "Jade Doll," the sister of Axayácatl, who succeeded Moctezuma Ilhuicamina in 1469. Apparently Moquihuix found his wife "too thin" and otherwise unattractive and compelled her to "sleep in the kitchen on a worn *petate*." Chalchiuenenetzin reported her humiliation to her powerful brother, revealing, at the same time, the extent of fortifications of Tlatelolco and the resources and troops at the command of her estranged husband.

Axayácatl led his forces into the principal square of Tlatelolco, where he confronted Moquihuix. In a desperate defense of the city "The Drunkard" organized battalions of women and even children, who sought to impede the advance of the invaders by showering them with garbage, of which

* Some scholars favor Moquihuixtli.

The battle between the forces of Tenochtitlán and Tlatelolco, in which Moquihuix was defeated, is pictured in *The Atlas*.

there was an almost inexhaustible supply from the market stalls. An ancient codex portrays the Tenocha victor placing the head of the enemy general on a pole; at the bottom of the pyramid steps may be seen the remains of the vanquished Moquihuix.

After Tlatelolco's defeat in 1509 a military governor was appointed, heavy tribute was exacted and the great pyramid leveled. But local enterprise soon rebuilt it and when the Spaniards saw the imposing temple in 1520 they admired the "magnificent structure." Tlatelolco's ceremonial center has been identified as the ultimate bastion of defense against the Spaniards in which the remnant of the Aztec forces met defeat.

The archaeological zone is on the northern outskirts of Mexico City. As excavations were carried on to install utility conduits, to widen streets or to make other general improvements, residents of the area realized that their homes had been built over a once-important site. Fragments of pottery, obsidian arrowheads, broken knives, razors and even monolithic sculpture turned up as relics of past occupancy. Recent excavations by the National Institute of Anthropology and History in the Square of Santiago have created a spectacular showpiece in a historical center within the ultramodern Nonoalco-Tlatelolco housing development. Enclosed in this enormous urban project are the ruins of the ancient metropolis, the remains of the house in which Cuauhtémoc ruled briefly and a Franciscan monastery, now a museum. Here Sahagún compiled his exhaustive work on the life and customs of Anáhuac.

Enclosed within an ultramodern housing development is an area known as the Plaza of the Three Cultures, which contains the remains of Tlatelolco's ceremonial center, part of a house in which Cuauhtémoc ruled briefly and a monastery in which Sahagún completed his definitive work on the customs of Anáhuac.

By 1945 preliminary exploration had revealed the existence of temple walls and the steps of a large pyramid. Extensive excavations, undertaken in 1960, resulted in the uncovering of three sides of a pyramidal complex, the Templo Mayor, and the process of restoration was begun. As in the case of Teotihuacán, the project presented a minimum of technical difficulties. After various penetrations around the central group of buildings, the sloping, stuccoed walls, floors and stairs of the pyramid were located. Extending from southeast to northeast, the structure is divided into sections inclining from north to south. The walls are of basalt and fragments of reddish *tezontle*, secured with mud covered with a thin stucco. For the greater part of their length the platforms are protected with a binder, as are the red stone slabs supporting the stairways. Adjoining the pyramid are traces of small platforms and dwellings. Two flights of stairs and the wall of what may have constituted the priests' quarters are now being restored. Around the pyramidal base extends a paling approximately 2 feet deep, with a projection of 6½ feet.

Among the first edifices to emerge from the excavations were a circular temple dedicated to Tláloc and a quadrangular structure dedicated to Quetzalcóatl which were demolished to make way for the housing project. Both temples were remarkably well preserved, considering, as Professor Farías Galindo has pointed out in a detailed study of the area, "the quantity of rocky material and mud which they contained." The site, a lake bed, had been drained and refilled to a height of 13 feet.

Also found were two small altars forming a circle, believed to have been built on pilework intermingled with offerings and the skeletons of men, women and children. The debris found with the altars would seem to indicate that the pier piles might include even the remains of priests, kings and noted warriors. Imbedded within the construction were the remains of dogs, *maíz*, calabashes, bulrushes and other organic matter. The excavations also revealed fifteen sepulchers and a large ossarium. About a yard below the last of the four steps of the altar of this charnel house were found the remains of a chieftain, or high priest, the feet of the personage crossed at the lower step, as though he were sustaining the weight of the altar. The body had been divided into five parts and the face painted with red hematite. At the right was a small ceremonial censer and at the left a bow and staff. Beneath the body had been placed a funerary lamp of turquoise-blue, encircled by heavy green and red lines, and a bed of reeds. Beside it had been placed a flute. Also found nearby were the remains of a dog, an animal associated with death. Not far from the interment were offerings of small jars and polychromed plates. Other objects included a *pulque* cup, an incense burner adorned with an eagle's head and green and white clay figurines.

The seigniory of **Texcoco** ("The Place of the Large Rocks"), which once rivaled that of the Tenochas, suffered the same fate as many of the other small realms, which either ceased to exist as autonomous domains or were reduced to ruins under the military might of a succession of conquerors. One by one, the once-brilliant seigniories bordering on Lake Texcoco, extending from Coatlinchan on the north to beyond Chapultepec on the southwest, were extinguished.

The earliest chapters of the Texcocan story contain some blurred pages, a number of which are missing. A mysterious relic of early artisans who carved in rock remained for many centuries, save for erosion, near Coatlinchan ("In the House of the Serpent"). A huge unfinished figure, more than 23 feet high, nearly 15 feet wide, about 13 feet thick and weighing 180 tons, lay imbedded in a gully. Believed to be a representation of Tláloc, the rain god, or, in the view of some scholars, of the goddess of the waters, the monolith is said to have once stood erect, crowning the hill of Tláloc.

When an attempt was made to dislodge the half-buried figure in order to move it to the new anthropological museum in Chapultepec Park, the people of the pueblo of Coatlinchan protested. Cases of dynamite used to blast it from its millennial resting-place unaccountably disappeared. Hoisting cranes and machinery needed to place it on a 92-wheel trailer-truck were badly damaged by irate townsfolk. While a local spokesman denied that the inhabitants of Coatlinchan still regarded Tláloc with

The huge monolith of Tláloc, the rain god, is shown before its removal from a gully in Coatlinchan in the area which was once Texcoco (*left*), to its present location at the entrance to the National Museum of Anthropology in Chapultepec Park (*right*).

the awe of their ancestors he explained that the deity, whose name signifies "Wine of the Earth" or "That Which the Earth Drinks," derived from the words *tlalli,* meaning earth, and *octli,* wine, is an inextricable part of the local legend. The pueblo's opposition was finally overcome. In return for the surrender of the monolith, Coatlinchan was awarded a direct road from Texcoco, as well as a new school, improved irrigation facilities and jobs for its unemployed.

Archaeologists have found it difficult to identify Texcoco's original hegemony. The earliest references indicate that it was peopled by various tribes whose languages and dialects represented many of the approximately 165 spoken in pre-Columbian Mexico. It is known that the Chichimecs established a capital in this region under Xólotl at Tenayuca. About the middle of the thirteenth century several groups arrived in the Valley of Mexico in quest of lands. One of these, the Acolhuas, had abandoned their original settlement at the fall of Tula, returning, during this period, to seek Xólotl's protection. The Chichimec chieftain bestowed two of his daughters on Acolhuan tribal leaders and gave three chieftains small lakeside domains. Acolnahuacatzin, head of the Tepaneca tribe, was allotted a region around Atzcapotzalco, "The Ant Hill of the People." This site, northwest of Mexico City, was an ancient one, having been occupied perhaps as early as 3000 to 1500 B.C. A stratigraphical survey made in 1913 by the late Dr. Manuel F. Gamio and Franz Boas for the International School of

Archaeology established the existence of three distinct cultural levels: Pre-Classic, Toltec and Aztec.

The Tepanecs, who appeared in the Valley about A.D. 1230, found Atzcapotzalco a place of importance. It had played a prominent role at the end of the epoch of Teotihuacán III by A.D. 900 or earlier, when the greater part of the famed "City of the Gods" was destroyed and its culture shifted to the region north of the present Mexican capital. After the fall of Tula Atzcapotzalco again became the destination of uprooted people. It attained its greatest military and political power under Tezozomoc, described as a clever and perverse ruler. The son of the Tepanec leader Acolhuacatzin and Cuitlaxochitzin, a daughter of Xólotl, Tezozomoc is said to have been born in Atzcapotzalco in 1320 and to have died there, at the age of 106, in 1426. As a result of his daring and intrigues, he pushed his dominion far beyond the frontiers he had inherited. He fomented internal discord in Culhuacán, already in a state of decadence because of a shortage of agricultural lands. This situation had driven many Culhuas into Texcoco, where they integrated their ancient skills with those of the Texcocans.

Among Tezozomoc's conquests was the influential seigniory of Xaltocan, which was founded in 1230 and included the islands and eastern shore of Lake Xaltocan. Soon Xaltocan began to dominate the northern part of the Valley of Toluca, its territorial acquisitions finally embracing the zone inhabited by the Mazahua ("Those Who Have Deer"), a people related to the Otomi ("Bird Hunters or Trappers"). Tezozomoc waged war against the Texcocan ruler Ixtlilxóchitl. Feigning a desire for peace, he had treacherously advanced upon the unoffending seigniory. Hoping to spare his people unnecessary bloodshed, the young Texcocan monarch fled with his ten-year-old son Netzahualcóyotl, seeking shelter in the forests of Mount Tláloc. Pursued by Tezozomoc's soldiers, he bade his followers look after their own safety and quickly concealed his son among the leafy branches of a giant tree. For a few moments he was able to hold off his pursuers with a sharp-edged club, but he was soon slain by enemy lances. The body of the king was left to the wild beasts, while his royal garments, insignia and jewels were appropriated.

From his treetop refuge Netzahualcóyotl witnessed the scene, climbing down that night to watch over his father's remains until the arrival of loyal adherents. He was saved from Tezozomoc's cruelty through the devotion of an old tutor, who hid him safely in the mountains, often fleeing with him from place to place. Tezozomoc, bent upon wiping out the line of Ixtlilxóchitl, relentlessly pursued the young prince and placed a price upon his head. On one occasion a guard, by changing clothes with the royal youth, freed him from a captive's cage, where he was scheduled to be cut to pieces in the public plaza.

At the death of Tezozomoc, his son Maxtla assumed power in Atzcapotzalco, later killing the rightful heir, his older brother Quetzalayatzin. Maxtla's two-year reign was marked by the assassination of Chimalpopoca of Tenochtitlán. The people of Tenochtitlán then elected as their ruler Itzcóatl, who headed a revolt aimed at releasing the Tenochas from Tepanecan power.

Netzahualcóyotl, deeply conscious of his heritage and endowed with a compassionate nature, dreamed of a unity that would transcend his native Texcoco to include adjacent domains. He hoped to assure peace by forming a triple alliance, which would be composed of Texcoco, Tenochtitlán and Tlacopán (modern Tacuba). Maxtla's crimes sparked his decision. He soon induced his father's old generals to raise an army and succeeded in winning the support of Huexotzingo, whose warriors crossed the mountains to capture Tenayuca, After a siege Atzcapotzalco fell, and with its destruction in 1428, Tepanec power in the Valley of Mexico was ended. The date marked the real beginning of the Aztec empire. Itzcóatl's successor, Moctezuma Ilhuicamina, continued and intensified his ambitious policies.

The confederation envisioned by Netzahualcóyotl, as Dr. Jiménez Moreno has pointed out, had antecedents in earlier alliances. The system was perfected with each regrouping until it reached the Tenochas, who, following the example of the enterprising but ruthless Tezozomoc, continued the integration of pre-Hispanic domains of the Central Plateau and other parts of Middle America. Because of its superior military organization Tenochtitlán soon became supreme in the triple alliance, encroaching not only on the sovereignty of Tlacopán, which never functioned as a equal member, but even on that of Texcoco.

Netzahualcóyotl's reign marked the apex of Nahuatl intellectual development. A lover of peace, he believed in one omnipotent god, ruler of a heavenly realm from which corruption and death were eternally excluded. As a monument to his faith he built a great temple in pyramidal form, each of the first nine levels representing a paradise. The tenth, with a gem-encrusted roof, was dedicated to the nameless deity, unsullied by any mortal attribute. In an era when human sacrifice and idolatry were allegedly prevalent, Netzahualcóyotl refused to permit the image of any god in his temple, and its altars were never stained with the blood of sacrificed victims. Fragrant flowers and *ozocol*, an aromatic incense made from pine-wood resin, were the only offerings made there.

Within a short period after he assumed power in 1418 Netzahualcóyotl, with his marvelous energy and rare intelligence, led his people to a true renaissance. A devoted patron of science, art and industry, he gave a new impetus to creative efforts in many forms. Science, especially astronomy, and the study of history, painting and sculpture flourished under the auspices of his illustrious "Academy of Music." In periodic competitions the learned men of the kingdom acted as jurors in judging poetry. Prizes were awarded for merit, but bad works sometimes met with a death penalty. Netzahualcóyotl was Texcoco's leading poet, as well as a brilliant orator, a wise judge and mediator. His speeches and some of his epics have survived through the translations of de Alva Ixtlilxóchitl.

Among Netzahualcóyotl's notable public works were a long dike in Lake Texcoco and an aqueduct from Chapultepec to Tenochtitlán which he helped Moctezuma Ilhuicamina to build. The scientific methods of agriculture that he introduced brought prosperity to his realm. With his death in 1472 the Texcocan "Golden Age" came to a close. In one of his own verses the monarch had observed, "If there are bounds to pleasure, the saddest life must also have its end," and in his *Lamentations* he had remarked, "All things on earth have their end." Nowhere, perhaps, were his melancholy reflections upon the transient character of mundane glories realized more drastically than in his own capital of which hardly a trace remains. The waters of Lake Texcoco have been practically eliminated by the shrinkage of four centuries and later drainage. The scattered stones of a few structures at Los Melones at the entrance to the present town of Texcoco as well as the ruins of Netzahualcóyotl's palace at Texcotzingo, where aqueducts, baths and stairways were cut from a rocky hillside, are all that now bear witness to Texcoco's vanished splendor.

Legends trace the origin of the cultural branch of the Nahuas who built the monolithic structures of **Malinalco** ("Intricate or Crooked Place" or "The Place of the Herb *Malinali*") near Tenancingo in a small valley south of Toluca to their emergence, along with the Aztecs, from the "Seven Caves." Although they, like the Aztecs, emphasized the art of war and glorified the warrior, the people of Malinalco were conquered in 1476 by Axayácatl. A quarter of a century later Ahuitzotl's stone-carvers began inscribing the unmistakable signs of Tenochtitlán upon the rock. A policy of drawing Malinalco more tightly into the Aztec sphere was continued under the second Moctezuma and halted only by the Spanish Conquest. The structures and sculptured motifs of Malinalco are distinctly Aztec.

Malinalco, with a spectacular view of the snow-shrouded peak of Nevado de Toluca, has been likened to the rock-cut temples of Ellora on the sun-baked mountain slopes of Hyderabad in southern India and also to Petra, the rose-colored city carved from rock cliffs near the Wadi el Araba south of the Dead Sea. Dr. George C. Vaillant declared that the excavations in the Malinalco cliffs thrust the monolithic temples of Abu Simbel on the west bank of the Nile "into the limbo of provincial opera-

At Malinalco, its structures hewn from rock, a headless jaguar crouches at the right of the stairway leading to the Cuauhcalli, or "House of the Eagles."

house scenery." The site was explored between 1936 and 1939 by José García Payón for the National Institute of Anthropology and History.

A controversial feature of *Cuacuauhtinchan,* or "Eagle's Nest," as Malinalco's archaeological zone is called, is the *temalacatl,* on which a gladiatorial rite may have been enacted. Although now little more than the remains of a platform, it shows vestiges of a cement floor. There are indications that it was similar to the one which formed part of the great sacred precinct of Tenochtitlán, as reconstructed by Ignacio Marquina. It was probably once covered with stucco and decorated with bas-reliefs and paintings.

Malinalco's chief temple, the *Cuauhcalli,* or "House of the Eagles," served as headquarters for two military groups, the Knights of the Eagle and the Knights of the Jaguar. A headless jaguar crouches at the right of the broad stairway of the truncated structure, now covered at its first elevation with a conical thatched roof, which was erected to protect the treasures of the sanctuary. To the right of the entrance, which is in the form of the open mouth of a monster with fangs and a forked tongue, is the head of a serpent. Inside the temple are three pieces of sculpture, each of which represents a sacred animal. All have been cut from the rock of the semicircular bench abutting the circular wall. On the east and west are so-

Through an entrance in the form of the open mouth of a monster (*top*) the circular sanctuary may be seen. In it are eagles and a jaguar, all carved from rock (*bottom*).

called "flayed" eagles, while another eagle may be seen in the center of the circle. On the north is a jaguar, its body gracefully extended, suggesting that it may have served as a throne. The broad tail feathers of the eagles and the long slender tail of the jaguar curve upward and rest partly flush against the wall. Behind and to the right of the eagle near the center of the circle is a hole 12 inches wide and 13 inches deep. According to some investigators this circular opening may have been the receptacle in which the hearts of sacrificed warriors were deposited.

Warriors in full battle array and a captive are depicted on a fading mural found at Malinalco.

Malinalco's finest mural, now almost obliterated, depicts soldiers in procession, with full insignia, spears and shields. In their midst may be seen a captive warrior in red stripes, destined, according to the earlier interpreters, for a sacrificial ceremony in which he would become a messenger to the sun. The solar messenger was customarily a warrior from the ranks of the enemy who had been trained since childhood as a warrior. It is claimed that the purpose of the *Xochiyaoyotl,* or "floral wars," held periodically between Tenochtitlán, Texcoco and Tlacopán on one side and Tlaxcala, Cholula and Huexotzingo on the other, was to procure prisoners for the ritual sacrifice. Acatzingo, a pueblo near Malinalco, is believed to have been the scene of these conflicts, as indicated by a rock bearing a semidestroyed hieroglyph. The Aztecs, as the people of Huitzilopochtli, the "chosen ones" of the "Lord of the Universe," allegedly considered themselves to be charged with providing the deity with sanguinary nourishment. For this reason, making war became a form of worship, since it was a means of providing human blood which, according to Aztec lore, the god regarded as the most precious and dynamic of all sustenance. Unlike wars of conquest, the sacred "floral wars" were waged with no aim to acquire new territories or to impose tribute on conquered people.

A wooden *huehuetl,* or vertical drum, found in Malinalco bears a bas-relief on which may be seen a figure with the skin and plumage of an eagle. The ascending eagle is an aspect of Huitzilopochtli, the incarnation of the sun. On it is carved a hieroglyph of the day Nahui Ollin (4 Earthquake or Movement). This, the chroniclers claim, was associated with the ritual of the messenger of the sun. In his *Historia de las Cosas de Nueva España* Sahagún provided a description of this ceremony. A year before his day of doom, the handsomest and most courageous prisoner-of-war was selected by the priests for the sacrificial role. During this period he was treated with the greatest consideration and trained in the ways of royalty. He passed the hours in a garden, receiving the homage due Huitzilopochtli. But twenty days before the sacrifice the general adulation and the priestly attentions increased. Four lovely maidens attired as goddesses became his companions, and his hours were filled with music and dancing. The day of the prisoner's death was one of special jubilation. Bidding farewell to his tearful consorts, he led a procession in his honor. Followed by a brilliant retinue and accompanied by the priests who had attended him throughout the year, he advanced toward a small temple. Following the priests up the temple steps, he broke, as he ascended, the flute he had played during his months of preparation for this fateful hour.

The climax of the ceremony, as practiced in Tenochtitlán, was described by Sahagún. The messenger, having passed into a circular temple through an entrance resembling the fanged jaws of serpent, would have saluted a gorgeous sun disc flashing from the wall, reciting his mission, now and then directing his gaze upward to include the real sun in his address to the deity. Presently, in the course of the ceremony, four priests came forward to strip the youth of the staff, shield and "sacred bundle" he carried. Then they lifted him by his hands and feet and placed him in a sacrificial basin in the shape of a flayed eagle, such as that in Malinalco's *Cuauhcalli,* or in a stone receptacle known as a *cuauhxcalli.* A high priest then instructed the messenger to deliver the message from the people to the palace of the sun and, knife in hand, performed the final rite. After the heart of the warrior had been extracted and exhibited to the sun it was placed in a repository. The staff, shield and small bundle were lashed like trophies to the solar disc. Instead of being flung to the ground, as in the case of an ordinary sacrifice, the body of the messenger was carried reverently down the steps. The head was usually impaled in a skull-rack. The messenger, thus freed from earthly shackles, was believed to enter upon a blissful existence. Joining the warriors who had preceded him, he was destined to spend his mornings throughout eternity greeting the sun with joyous cries and the roll of drums. Accompanying the messenger to the zenith was a hummingbird, which would sip the nectar from every flower and, after four years, would return to earth.

In 1962 and 1963 Malinalco's structure, known as Monument II, was explored under the direction of Dr. César A. Saenz. The work was carried on with great difficulty, partly because of the corrosive effects of time and vandalism, first by the Spaniards and then by local inhabitants, who carried away sculptured stones for the construction of colonial and modern edifices. The stairway and balustrades of this building as well as sections of semicircular structures were restored. Quantities of ceramics, ranging in period from the Pre-Classic to the Aztec, were recovered.

Huitzilopochtli was often worshipped as Tepeyóllotl, the jaguar god, at neighboring Chalma and honored in Malinalco rites as Oztéotl, god of the caves. The natives of the province of Ocuila paid him homage in a cavern among the mountain peaks. Even today throngs kneel and pray before the so-called "Sacred Image" of Chalma. A heavy wooden cross, venerated in the Cathedral of San Miguel de Chalma, was borne to the site in 1540 by two Augustinian monks, Nicolas de Perea and Sebastian de Tolentino, to replace a representation of the god of the caves. *Oztéotl* has been interpreted by Cecilio A. Robelo, editor of a dictionary of Nahuatl mythology, as "heart of the god of the mountains." The Nahuas regarded the mountains as an inexhaustible vase, eternally refilled with water, and liable to crack and flood the earth. The fact that from mountains emerged springs from which rivers were born gave rise, he believes, to this concept and probably accounted for the placing of images in caves. As the "Eighth Lord of Night" the deity is also regarded as the master of the echo, since in nocturnal silence the reverberating sounds became the voices of the night.

The pyramid of **Calixtlahuaca** ("Place Where There Are Houses on the Prairie") was erected by the Matlatzinca, neighbors of the Malinalca. This structure, about 40 miles from Mexico City and 5 miles north of Toluca, was dedicated to the wind god, Ehécatl, an aspect of Quetzalcóatl. The Matlatzinca ("Those Who Have Little Nets") were culturally related to the Aztecs but had Otomi linguistic ties. Although their precise provenance has not been established, their legends record a splitting-off from the Aztecs during the peregrination from the "Seven Caves" to the Valley of Anáhuac. Some archaeologists regard the Matlatzinca as the original inhabitants of Tula who, like the Toltecs, were once driven from the site. Toltec names, the use of the Toltec calendar and many architectural similarities, as well as this temple to the wind god, have led José García Payón and others to associate the Matlatzinca culture with Toltec influence, however it may have been derived. It has been pointed out that the old name of Toluca was Tollucan; like Tula, it means "Place of the Bulrushes."

The circular pyramid of Calixtlahuaca was dedicated to the wind god Ehécatl, an aspect of Quetzalcóatl.

At the pyramidal site of **Teopanzalco** ("Place Where the Old Temple Stands"), within the boundaries of Cuernavaca, Morelos, is a structure of the Aztec period with two stairways, each leading to its own temple. Recently excavated and partly reconstructed is a temple to Quetzalcóatl, which may be reached by a stairway on the east side. It is 16 yards in diameter and 3 yards in height.

The famed Tlaxcalan wall, built after years of repeated warfare in order to make the territory of **Tlaxcala** impenetrable, offered no real obstacle to the Conquistadores. After a few fierce battles the Spaniards found the oft-besieged Tlaxcalans their ready allies in overthrowing long-hated Tenochtitlán.

The early history of the Tlaxcala region was marked by many retreats and repulses before its frontiers were more or less defined. The area is believed to have been inhabited by the Olmec-Xicalanca about 1350, probably a Chocho-Popoloca or a Mixtec-speaking group, to whom some investigators have attributed the building of Teotihuacán and Tula, and later by a strong migratory nucleus of Teo-Chichimecs, who arrived from the Valley of Pahauhtlan in what is now Puebla. Their presence brought about a war with the incumbents and a battle was fought in the foothills of Cerro de Peteticpac. The newcomers took possession of the heights, Chicometepetl and Contla, and from this position advanced in full strength, defeating the Olmec-Xicalanca, who were obliged to flee toward Zacatlán, Otallan and Huehuetocan.

The outstanding figure of the region to emerge from this period was the warrior Culhuatuhtli, claiming descent from the Nahuatl-speaking Culhuas through Acamapichtli, a Culhua who became the ruler of Tenochtitlán in 1376, as well as the priest Teoyohuamiqui and the tutelary war god Camaxtli. Culhuatuhtli defeated the Texcocans, but since Texcoco was not his sole goal he led his army eastward to Cholula. Remaining here for a while without meeting resistance, he then proceeded to Contla. When peace was attained the Teo-Chichimecs instituted their system of command, a loosely federated form of government derived from the Culhua-Coatlinchán culture. While each dominion in the territory that became Tlaxcala was autonomous and selected its own administrative policies, such a confederation functioned as an effective unit in time of war, when the chieftains would meet in council and appoint a supreme commander.

While the Tlaxcalan tribes were occupied in the organization of their several dominions they were attacked by the Huexotzincas, allied with other tribes. Fighting in the cultivated fields of Zahuapan, they defeated the invaders, obliging them to flee. After this victory the frontiers were marked out and fortresses and watchtowers built. To the northeast was erected a massive wall, 9 feet high, 20 feet thick and 10 feet wide, extending for two miles along the Otomi-Totonac-Tlaxcala frontier. This was built as far as the place known as La Laguna, or Hacienda La Mancera, where Cortés entered Tlaxcala. In the era preceding the Conquest Tlaxcala had been involved in an almost continuous state of siege, often resulting in a scarcity of necessities. Its location was perilous, since it was surrounded on all sides by hostile neighbors.

The first of the four dominions set up by the Tlaxcalan tribes was located on the slope of Matlalcueye in Tepecticpan. The second, established further down the slope was known as Ocotelulco and was assigned to the traveling merchants. Quiahuiztlan was reserved for judges. To the east was Tizatlán in which the ceremonial center was erected.

Tizatlán ("The Place of the Chalk") was originally inhabited by artisans. At that time the ceremonial center served an area of more than 2,230 square miles; the present state of Tlaxcala measures only a little more than two-thirds of this area. According to Motolinia, Tizatlán was founded by a group of artists, pottery makers and those who were dedicated to music and the dance. The ancient heritage of fine craftsmanship has survived in the Apizaco canes and in the ceramic, carding and weaving industries of Contla and other nearby pueblos. The population of Tizatlán was distributed into several sections, thus forming seven *calpulli,* or landowning kinship groups.

The ruins of San Esteban Tizatlán on the heights of San Martin Texmelucan are not far from Tlaxcala, the state capital. Excavation of the ruins, discovered in 1924, was begun in 1927. The first discovery included a

The broad platform of San Esteban Tizatlán is divided into two sections. Large fired bricks were used in its construction.

large monolith representing Tezcatlipoca and several *teponaztlis,* or horizontal drums, made of stone or wood and used in religious ceremonies. A quantity of pottery was also found, a few examples of which are exhibited at the entrance of the archaeological zone. Workmen also uncovered an imposing stairway leading to a broad platform divided in two sections. The construction, notable for its use of large fired bricks, supports two low altars, the sides of which are adorned with well-preserved frescoes. They are now contained in glass display cases and some of their original brilliance has faded. Depicted in magnificent array are personifications of gods of earth, fire, water and death, each deity carrying the resplendent insignia of his or her particular function. Vivid turquoise-blue, bright coral and yellow predominate in exquisite color combinations. Professor Farías Galindo has described the frescoes in detail:

> On the west altar are two personages, Tezcatlipoca and Xiuhtecuhtli. The body of the former is covered with black and yellow stripes. He wears a high warrior's headdress of fine plumes from which extrude locks of hair. His nose ornament is a blue square which reaches to his mouth. On his temples are "smoking mirrors," symbols of war, and he wears another, indicating fire and water, in place of his left foot. Adorning his chest is a circular gold plate representing the planet Venus, to which four little silver bells are attached. At his waist is a *cuecoxtechimalli,* or rosette, from which dangle tiny balls and heron feathers. He wears a *maxtli,* or short apron. In one hand he holds a bag of *copal* (incense) or possibly seeds, and in the other a *chimalli,* or shield. This is the best-preserved figure among the frescoes.
>
> Next to Tezcatlipoca is Tlahuizcalpantecuhtli, or Quetzalcóatl's duality. His face is yellow, with a black stripe down the middle. His body is entirely black and he wears a *tlahuitzolli,* or enormous crown, as a crest. On each side of his figure may be seen four flint knives painted in red and white. His anklets and bracelets are of tigerskin and he carries two banners, one yellow and black, the other yellow and blue, symbolizing light and war. At the right side appears the date III Ollin and behind is a *xiuhcóatl,* or fire serpent.
>
> Richly attired and surrounded by all the animals that have any relation to her, follows the goddess Matlalcueitl, second wife of Tláloc, the Tlaxcalan patron of fertility and waters. In the center is her duality, swimming naked and surrounded by many fishes. Above the frescoes are three old bearded men and a fero-

One of the deities portrayed in the frescoes adorning two low altars at Tizatlán is Tezcatlipoca. The smoking mirrors on his temples are symbols of war.

cious eagle. Shells and snails are scattered toward the blue head of Tláloc, god of rain and benefactor of agriculture.

Last in line is Mictlantecuhtli, the gloomy god of the dead, whose crest is a huge skull. At his waist is seen the *cuexoctechimalli* in green. On his upper jaw is nailed a flint knife, and in his right hand he carries the *pantayahualli,* or sacrificial banner. His body is covered with a blue cloak, thinly striped with red at the back. The skull is topped by a crest of feathers, divided by a long yellow line, terminating with the bells of Venus. He wears a short apron and *cactli,* or sandals, in blue and green. Before him are spread hearts, skulls and a hand, motifs which are repeated on both sides of the same altar, together with ants, jaguars, a duck, snail-shells, skulls, shields and autosacrificial thorns. The whole is completed with quadrilaterals and Greek-style frets in cross forms, painted with the colors of the deities to which such ornaments belong. Here, too, is the face of Xipe Tótec, the lord of spring and of artisans, surrounded by emeralds.

It has been suggested that the altars of Tizatlán, long and wide enough to accommodate a human body, served as couches for forms of autoimmolation and for self-inflicted torture, common among pre-Columbian religious cults.

Six other archaeological zones in Tlaxcala have been located, although none has yet been adequately explored. Some 52 mounds await exploration in Xochitecatitlan, the seat of the Olmec-Xicalanca, the first inhabitants of the territory of Cuatlanga. Others include Calpulpan, of Teotihuacano origin; Contla, with its large temples of Petla; Teotlalpan, generally believed to have been founded by Otomi families; and Papalotlan, close to the Puebla boundary, settled by the earlier Teo-Chichimecs.

At the time of the Conquest, Tlaxcala's federated judicial and economic power were represented by four lords, who exchanged their responsibilities as quartermasters, tax-collectors and tribute-dispensers for roles as senators when Tlaxcala became a republic. Before a sumptuous altar of gold leaf in Tlaxcala were celebrated the first Christian marriage ceremonies in the New World, while at a huge stone baptismal font the lords of the four dominions were duly baptized, receiving new Spanish names in ceremonies attended by their Spanish soldier-godfathers.

The *Lienzo de Tlaxcala,* a pictorial account of the Tlaxcalans' part in the Conquest, painted about 1552, probably for Viceroy Luis de Velasco, emphasizes their significant role. By royal decree Tlaxcala received the title of "Very Noble City."

Unlike the "Very Noble City" of Tlaxcala, commended by the Spanish crown for its collaboration with Cortés's forces, **Tepoztlán,** 76 miles south of Mexico City and 12½ miles northwest of Cuernavaca, was set afire by the Spaniards when its inhabitants refused to surrender. Prior to the Conquest it had been dominated by the Aztecs. Among the tribute items rendered by it to Tenochtitlán's rulers were unique animal-form vessels made to hold the thick, potent, fermented juice of the *maguey, pulque.* A slab bearing a glyph of the first Moctezuma's successor, Axayácatl, was found embedded in a Tepoztlán temple wall.

The picturesque site of the Tepozteco pyramid, with its temple to Ometecuhtli in his guise as the god of *pulque,* rises above Tepoztlán and commands magnificent panoramas of the Valley of Mexico and the Valley of Morelos. Tepoztécatl was one of several deities honored by the Tlahuica, a Nahuatl-speaking tribe which emerged, along with the Aztecs, from the mythical "Seven Caves." The patron of Tepozteco was also known as Centzon Totochtin, or "400 Rabbits," alluding, according to the anthropologist Eduard Seler, to the many *pulque* gods and the multifarious forms of drunkenness. The summit occupied by the temple is known as Tlahiltepec, or "The Hill That Sheds Light." Ruins of ancient structures on surrounding crags indicate that the region was settled by Pre-Classic peoples long before the building of the Tepozteco pyramid or even those of Classic Teotihuacán.

The structure at Tepoztlán known as "The House of the Tepozteco" was dedicated to the *pulque* god Centzon Totochtin, or "400 Rabbits."

The massive, well-preserved pyramid on a knoll, popularly known as "The House of the Tepozteco," first came to notice at the International Congress of Americanists held in 1895 in Mexico City through a detailed study of the monuments presented by Francisco M. Rodríguez. His descriptions and maps show that the top of a towering crag was leveled to form a platform about 30 feet high, reached by a rear stairway. The structure, with walls 6 feet thick, is composed of two bodies. A narrow passage runs between the two stories and a partly destroyed stairway, flanked by broad ramps, provides an entrance on the western side. The ruins of a shrine where offerings were made to the *pulque* deities occupies a small square area at the foot of the stairway. Polychromed motifs and some figures identified as images of the sun originally adorned two stuccoed pillars at the entrance to the temple's two-chambered inner sanctum. On the western side reportedly once stood a statue of Tepoztécatl which, according to tradition, was destroyed in the sixteenth century by order of Fray Domingo de la Asunción.

Today the steeples and spires of **Cholula** rise above the plain like trees of a forest and the blue- and gold-tiled church of San Francisco Acatepec attracts thousands of tourists, but many others come to Cholula, an ancient center of Quetzalcóatl worship, to visit its ancient pyramid. Today, as in remote antiquity, the "artificial mountain dominates the city, even though, as William H. Prescott pointed out more than a century ago, the original outlines were slowly effaced and the growth of shrubs and wild flowers, mantling its surface, gave it the appearance "of one of those symmetrical elevations thrown up by the caprice of Nature rather than by the industry of man." As one approaches the city, this truncated mound, now surmounted by the Church of Nuestra Señora de los Remedios, is visible for miles. Much of the material that once faced the pyramid was used for the building of this church in the early nineteenth century. The once-impressive stairway was used to obtain stone for the ramparts.

The huge mound underwent continuous modification through the centuries. The *Codex Telleriano-Remensis,* a mid-sixteenth-century pictorial manuscript with a Spanish commentary, mentions that at the site were erected "round temples without any corners" in honor of Quetzalcóatl, regarded as the creator of the world, the "Lord of the Wind." Joseph de Acosta and Durán described circular buildings dedicated to the cult of Quetzalcóatl as practiced at Cholula. Juan de Torquemada depicted the temple of Quetzalcóatl at Cholula as "circular in form and very sumptuous." Motolinia referred to a temple in Cholula which was built in a large court on a square foundation "capped with a high circular wall and covered with its spire." Some 30 years later Fray Gerónimo de Mendieta mentioned temples of this type in Cholula, Tlaxcala and Huexotzingo. Quetzalcóatl temples at Calera and at Zempoala suggest a similar construction. A round temple in Tenochtitlán dedicated to the god of the air was described by Fray Bartolomé de las Casas. Since the "air goes all around

Much of the material used to face the pyramid of Cholula, an ancient center of Quetzalcóatl worship, was used to build the church which now surmounts it.

The enormous truncated mound, once topped by a sumptuous temple dedicated to Quetzalcóatl, is shown as seen by a traveler to "Sciolula" in the early 1800's.

the sky," the Indians explained to him, the temple also had to be round. Its entrance was fashioned to resemble the mouth of a great serpent, he recounted, and painted "in the manner that, in our Castile, it is customary to paint the mouth of hell—the fangs twisted, horrible—and, to the Spaniards, on entering by that door it seemed that their flesh crept."

Cholula's great landmark, measuring about 1,400 feet on each of its four laterals, with irregularities on two of the sides owing to the removal of some structural material, covers 42 acres, making it the world's largest such monument in terms of cubic content. Its total height has now been reduced to about 210 feet. Excavations were begun in 1931 under the direction of José Reygadas Vertiz, who found that it was composed of a series of superimposed structures. Labor of the most delicate and exacting kind was required in excavation, since archaeologists hoped to be able to explore the interior without destroying the exterior. The general plan of excavation decided upon was to follow the walls and ramparts of the construction in order to reach stairways and platforms at different levels. When a portion of a stairway was discovered, a tunnel was dug horizontally along its identified base. Then another tunnel was driven upward until the main dimensions were ascertained. Using the same techniques, walls and other structural features were measured.

The work at Cholula progressed with difficulty. The process of deterioration had gone unchecked for centuries, and the adobe bricks that

Excavations and tunneling revealed seven superimpositions, as shown in this partial scale model of the pyramid.

had originally faced the huge pile had been forced apart. Much of the structure was hidden under a layer of debris. When the project came under the supervision of the National Institute of Anthropology and History, Ignacio Marquina followed Reygadas Vertiz' plan, but elaborated upon it by boring two tunnels that crossed the pyramid from north to south and from east to west. By 1951 the principal superimpositions had been revealed and a plaster model had been constructed on a scale large enough to show how the more ancient edifices had been covered. The model, together with a number of ceramic objects found at various stages, is now on exhibition in a museum at the foot of the pyramid.

The mound may be entered through a small opening on the eastern side. One traverses narrow stairways and a bewildering maze of dark labyrinthine passages that cross and recross one another, with here or there a patch of frescoed wall adorned with butterflies and insects in earth tones or colored yellow, white or black. The tunneling revealed seven separate constructions, the first of which, according to Marquina, was probably the result of an even earlier superimposition. The original mound was almost square, with its east and west sides 367¼ feet long and its south and north sides 347¾ feet long. The pyramid as it now stands, he believes, was in constant use from the Pre-Classic period to about A.D. 1200. The first structures reached only half the present height and formed the enormous base for later larger pyramids.

Historians differ on the reasons for its construction. Although it may not have been built originally to honor Quetzalcóatl, in its later superimpositions, at least, it was the scene of rites identified with this deity. As William H. Prescott described it, "On the summit stood a sumptuous temple in which was the image of the mystic deity, 'god of the air,' with ebon features, unlike the fair complexion which he bore upon earth, wearing a mitre on his head waving with *plumes of fire*, with a resplendent collar of gold around his neck, pendants of mosaic turquoise in his ears, a jeweled sceptre in one hand, and a shield curiously painted, the emblem of his rule over the winds, in the other. The sanctity of the place, hallowed by hoary tradition, and the magnificence of the temple and its services, made it an object of veneration throughout the land, and pilgrims from the furthest corners of Anáhuac came to offer up their devotions at the shrine of Quetzalcóatl."

According to the *Relaciones* of Gabriel Rojas, a *corregidor* of Cholula, a temple on a grandiose scale still existed here up to the time of the Conquest. The chronicler recalled it as "immense, with a chapel on top in which was enshrined an idol known as 'Nine Times Rain.' " Whether or not it was the temple that attracted the throngs, Cholula was, for a time at least, a powerful city. According to R. H. K. Marett, it was a "refuge of culture in a barbaric age," where the old Toltec arts and crafts were revived. Despite the political ascendancy of the Aztecs, Cholula's pottery was conceded to be the finest in the land. No match, however, for the steadily growing Aztec might, Cholula was eventually compelled to render tribute and to supply warriors on demand to Tenochtitlán. The priesthood, however, managed to retain its prestige. The two chief priests of Cholula bore the name "Quetzalcóatl" as a part of their title, and the high priest of Quetzalcóatl ranked below only the high priests of Huitzilopochtli and Tláloc. While here the "god of the air" was accorded homage over the "god of war," tradition holds that the demon gods forced Quetzalcóatl to drink a fatal "cup of banishment." Cholula's potion was indeed bitter during the Conquest, when Cortés reportedly massacred thousands of its inhabitants in a single day. Such slaughter only strengthened the popular belief in the Conqueror's supernatural identity, since the people of Anáhuac were allegedly inured to sacrifice that the gods might thrive.

A relic of Cholula's past which is being studied today is the *Lienzo de Cholula*. Dr. Amaya Topete, a Nahuatl scholar and the author of several books on Mexican history, believes that it was painted in the period of Don Gabriel Marcelino Chichimectatecuhtli, a grandson of the last king of Cholula. As part of their political strategy the Spaniards often maintained in power chieftains of subdued principalities as well as their successors.

Members of the Marcelino family continued to receive the post of Indian governor.

Working with the Nahuatl scholar Byron McAfee, Dr. Amaya Topete has deciphered many of the representations of events. Pictured are houses, churches, hills, rivers, people and animals, along with dismembered limbs of supposedly sacrificed victims. A small figure in Spanish attire is identified by a reference as Cortés. Inscriptions, mostly in Nahuatl, explain the various images. There are references to ancient rulers and to those who built the "artificial mountain." There is a mention of the last king, Quetzalcóatzin, "whom the enemies came to kill," as well as a reference to his widowed queen. She was friendly to the Conquerors and with her children was baptized on August 3, 1521, receiving the name of Doña María. This was just ten days before the fall of Tenochtitlán.

Cholula, famed for the quality of its pottery (*top left*) during the ascendancy of the Aztecs, was termed by R. H. K. Marett a "refuge of culture in a barbaric age." This fresco of a butterfly (*bottom*) was found in the course of excavations.

CHAPTER VII

The Fair God's Return: Prophecy, Plunder and Pilgrimage

ACCORDING TO THE LEGENDS, an uncanny series of coincidences linked the Aztecs' "Fair God" Quetzalcóatl and the destinies of Hernán Cortés, Moctezuma II, and Cuauhtémoc. The incredible rapidity of the Spanish Conquest was entwined with the Aztec belief that Quetzalcóatl would one day return to Anáhuac, from which centuries earlier he had departed. In any event, Cortés's landing on the shores of the Gulf of Mexico had for the powerful Aztecs, masters of their world, unimaginable consequences. Instead of overlords they became almost overnight a conquered people, no longer able to exact from vassal states tribute and prisoners.

By tradition the return of Quetzalcóatl was predicted for a One Reed year, and the landing of Cortés at Veracruz in such a year constituted a precise fulfillment, with amazing fidelity, of an ancient prophecy. Such an event had been foretold by the Aztec priests. According to their divinations the returning "Fair God" would be white-skinned, would have a black beard and would be garbed in black. Had not Quetzalcóatl, before embarking for the "Land of the Sun" assured his handful of faithful followers that he would return to reestablish his rule in a One Reed year? It would be, he had warned, a "time of tribulation for the people."

Naturally, the return of Quetzalcóatl was fearfully awaited. By Aztec reckoning One Reed years occurred at irregular intervals. Two were recorded a little more than a century apart, one corresponding to A.D. 1363 and another to A.D. 1467. When Quetzalcóatl did not return in either one of these, anticipation centered on the next—corresponding to A.D. 1519. Moctezuma II, described in the *Codex Mendoza* as "a learned astrologer, a philosopher and skilled in all the arts," concluded that since

Quetzalcóatl had gone eastward on his raft of entwined serpents he would probably return from the east, arriving somewhere on the shores of the Gulf. The dilemma facing the Aztec ruler and his advisers was how the returning avenger should be received when he came.

A strange portent was a sight Moctezuma beheld when he fell into a trance while studying the head of a water bird. As related by Sahagún, the emperor had looked into a magic mirror on the bird's head and had seen the reflection of an unfavorable constellation. Peering more closely, he had perceived "reeds like men approaching, armed for war and mounted on deer." Companions to whom he had confided his dread vision later passed on his words to the chronicler, adding that Moctezuma had told them, on that occasion, that he had foreseen the return of Quetzalcóatl.

From the time of this strange vision a close watch had been kept along the Gulf. Rumors had reached Tenochtitlán of the landing of strange men at Champotón and Tabasco. Perhaps news of Columbus's voyages, during which he had encountered a Maya craft, had also reached the ears of the Aztec ruler. Francisco Hernández de Cordoba's exploratory foray in the fall in 1517 was followed by the expedition of Juan de Grijalva in 1518. When his fleet was sighted messengers hurried to Moctezuma with

Strange portents of the imminent return of Quetzalcóatl, as shown in the *Codex Magliabecchi* (*left*), alarmed the Aztec ruler Moctezuma II, described as "a learned astrologer, a philosopher and skilled in all the arts" (*right*).

the news. One described the galleons as "hills moving in the sea." The bearer of such bad tidings was killed instantly, but other watchers were sent. The new observers reported in greater detail, since they had seen "strange men" descend from "two big towers and enter canoes to fish in the sea." The visitors, who remained a fortnight, were described as white-skinned, bearded and long-haired. Their leader somehow managed to convey that other men like himself would return the following year.

Moctezuma was by now convinced that Quetzalcóatl's prophecy would soon be fulfilled. He had received other warnings that doom was imminent. A curious light had appeared in the northern sky. There was an earthquake. The magicians he consulted in order to interpret such portents confirmed his worst fears. After remaining dormant for decades the volcano Popocatépetl had suddenly become active, and the streets of the Aztec capital were flooded with boiling water. Several other signs of impending disaster that filled Moctezuma with increasing consternation were reported by chroniclers. The emperor's sister Papantzin fell into a coma, which was taken as death. She awakened from it in her grave, and when brought back to the palace reported a vision in which she had seen strange men swarming over the country, leaving devastation in their wake. A fire partially destroyed the temple of the sun god. All these alarming events were construed as precursors of even greater calamity.

And, in the very One Reed year that Quetzalcóatl was expected to return, Hernán Cortés arrived on the shores of the Gulf. It was a Nine Wind day, or, as the Spaniards reckoned it, Holy Thursday, April 21, 1519. (Mme Laurette Séjourné, in *Burning Water*, placed the month of Cortés's arrival as February and the date of his appearance in Moctezuma's capital as eight months thereafter.)

Cortés's skin, like the "Fair God's," was white, his beard sable. Moreover, he wore a velvet cap resembling the one that Quetzalcóatl was reputed to wear. And since he went ashore from San Juan Ulloa on Good Friday he was dressed in black, thus conforming to the sombre attire attributed to Quetzalcóatl. In fact, according to some chroniclers, the aura of presumed divinity surrounding Cortés in the eyes of Moctezuma and his frightened counselors was a significant factor in the speed of the Spanish Conquest, opening doors that might otherwise have remained closed to any foreign invader. Other historians believe that Cortés himself invented the legendary connection and aided and abetted the spreading of such a notion. In any case, it has been claimed that when Cortés arrived in Mexico both ruler and priests believed—and were fatalistically reconciled to their terrible conviction—that the bearded conqueror was indeed the reincarnation of their revered deity.

As recorded in a biography of Cortés by his chaplain, Francisco López de Gómara, Hernán Cortés was born in 1485 in Estremadura, Spain. At the age of fourteen he was sent by his parents to Salamanca to the home of an uncle, Francisco Nuñez de Valera. At the end of two years he returned to Medellin, without having learned "anything of value," and to the disappointment of his parents, who had hoped he would become a lawyer.

Gómara described the young Cortés as "rowdy, mischievous and wayward, a lover of arms." It is clear that he possessed an extraordinary sagacity and a remarkable capacity to achieve his own ends. He was a shrewd judge of character and of situations and knew how to turn both to his advantage. Such qualities served him well from the time he first arrived in the Antilles, where he won the favor of the Colonial governor Nicolas de Ovando. Later, Diego Velásquez made him his secretary and gave him Indians to work lands he had been granted in Cuba.

On his return to Cuba in 1518 Juan de Grijalva reported to Governor Velásquez the riches of the land he had visited, producing, in support of his words, gifts of gold received from the friendly and hospitable natives. They had also described to Grijalva the great city of Tenochtitlán and the power of its ruler, Moctezuma.

Cortés, his cupidity inflamed by what he believed to be the fabulous wealth waiting there for the taking, by artful tales and falsehoods soon succeeded in having himself named as captain-general of the fleet which the governor decided to send to the new lands. Although Cortés had been told by Velásquez that he might lead a third expedition, his voyage was not actually authorized; when he set sail in February of 1519 the governor had already decided to replace him. Cortés proceeded, in any event, with a fleet of 11 vessels, 17 horses, 10 cannon and 600 men. Had he but known it, his adversaries were to outnumber his small army by more than 350 to 1. But superior forces did not daunt the Conqueror. William H. Prescott summed up his amazing military achievements as the leader of a "handful of adventurers, indifferently armed and equipped." He called their exploit unparalleled—"that they should have landed on the shores of a powerful empire inhabited by a fierce and warlike race, and in defiance of the reiterated prohibitions of its sovereign, have forced their way into the interior, without knowledge of the language or of the land, without chart or compass, without any idea of the difficulties they were to encounter, totally uncertain whether the next step might bring them on a hostile nation, or on a desert, feeling their way along in the dark, as it were." He commented further, in admiration of their intrepid campaign, that, "though nearly overwhelmed by their first encounter with the inhabitants, they still pressed on to the capital of the empire, and, having reached it, threw themselves unhesitatingly into the midst of their enemies; that, so far from being daunted by the extraordinary spectacle there exhibited of power and civilization, they were but the more confirmed in their original design," seizing the monarch and executing his ministers before the eyes of his subjects. Having been driven from the capital, they regrouped their forces and, with "consummate policy and daring, succeeded in overturning the capital and establishing their sway over the country."

On reaching the island of Cozumel, when Cortés's company first rebelled, their leader rekindled their enthusiasm with promises of great and fertile lands that would make them exceedingly wealthy. Arriving in Tabasco, Cortés apparently sought gold from the lords of that region, but finding no gold or silver there, concluded that it was not the place for him. But upon reaching Veracruz, where he received ambassadors from the Confederation of the Valley of Mexico, Cortés was confident that he was truly in a rich land. His reply to the emissaries, bringing among other gifts a wicker basket filled with gold ornaments, sent by Moctezuma, who sought to placate the dreaded stranger and keep him at a safe distance, was blunt: "We suffer from a malady of the heart that only gold can cure." He entreated the messenger to return with a gilt helmet full of the gleaming "remedy."

His ability to get the best of a bargain, often through deceit, was illustrated again and again, perhaps never more lucratively than when he eventually secured from the Crown in recognition of his services a decree creating him the "Marqués del Valle de Oaxaca," with a rank second only to that of a duke. He considered his domain, reportedly rich in mineral wealth, to embrace a vast area, appropriating to himself *encomiendas* (land grants) in the Valley of Mexico, in the Valley of Toluca, in Mi-

Cortés's arrival in Veracruz with ships, horses and dogs was pictured in *The Atlas.* The Conqueror is shown with La Malinche, his mistress and interpreter, and an ambassador sent by Moctezuma.

choacán, in Colima (more than 35 towns), in Puebla, the Huastec area and what is today Guerrero.

As early as his nineteenth year the young Cortés was apparently a *burlador de maridos* (a "mocker of husbands") and was considered a bold youth in Hispaniola. In Cuba he was obliged to take as his first wife Catalina Juarez Marcaida by her godfather, Governor Velásquez, but continued to have relations with other women, among them his cousin, Leonor Pizarro, by whom he had a daughter. His second wife, the Marquesa, bore him several children. In Mexico he took as his mistress his Indian interpreter, Doña Marina, or La Malinche, as well as her niece. In a judicial inquiry, a trial to which royal officers might be subjected at the expiration of their terms or at the sovereign's pleasure, held in January 1529, many of Cortés's former companions related what they knew of the crimes and petty deceits practiced by the Marqués del Valle both upon his own countrymen and upon the natives from the time he founded the Villa Rica de Veracruz. In the course of this *Juicio de Residencia* his

This portrait of Cortés (*left*), which hangs in the Jésus Nazareno Hospital in Mexico City, painted more than a century after his death, is considered to be a copy, both in features and armor, of a portrait of Charles V. La Malinche (*right*), a native of Tabasco who had been sold as a slave, was given to Cortés. She proved invaluable to him in achieving so rapidly the conquest of Mexico.

former companions accused him of being a "bad Christian," with "unscrupulous licentiousness" being enumerated among his vices.

From the day he embarked upon the dunes of the beach of San Juan Ulloa he wasted no time in pursuing his objective, advancing from this small island to the mainland and moving north along the coast, transporting men and equipment to Villa Rica de Veracruz, and continuing to Zempoala in the Totonac region, his goal always Tenochtitlán. To achieve this his force had to zigzag its way across the countryside. Cortés went from Jalapa to Xico in the southwest, then, circling the mountain of Perote, pressed north to Xalacingo, Tziutlán and Tlatlaqui before descending to Tlaxcala, where he fought the Indians who became his chief allies. After concluding a pact with them Cortés was ready to advance on

Cortés, confident he would gain in the Aztec capital the gold he sought, wasted little time in proceeding from San Juan Ulloa to his goal, Tenochtitlán, aided in his advance by native escorts.

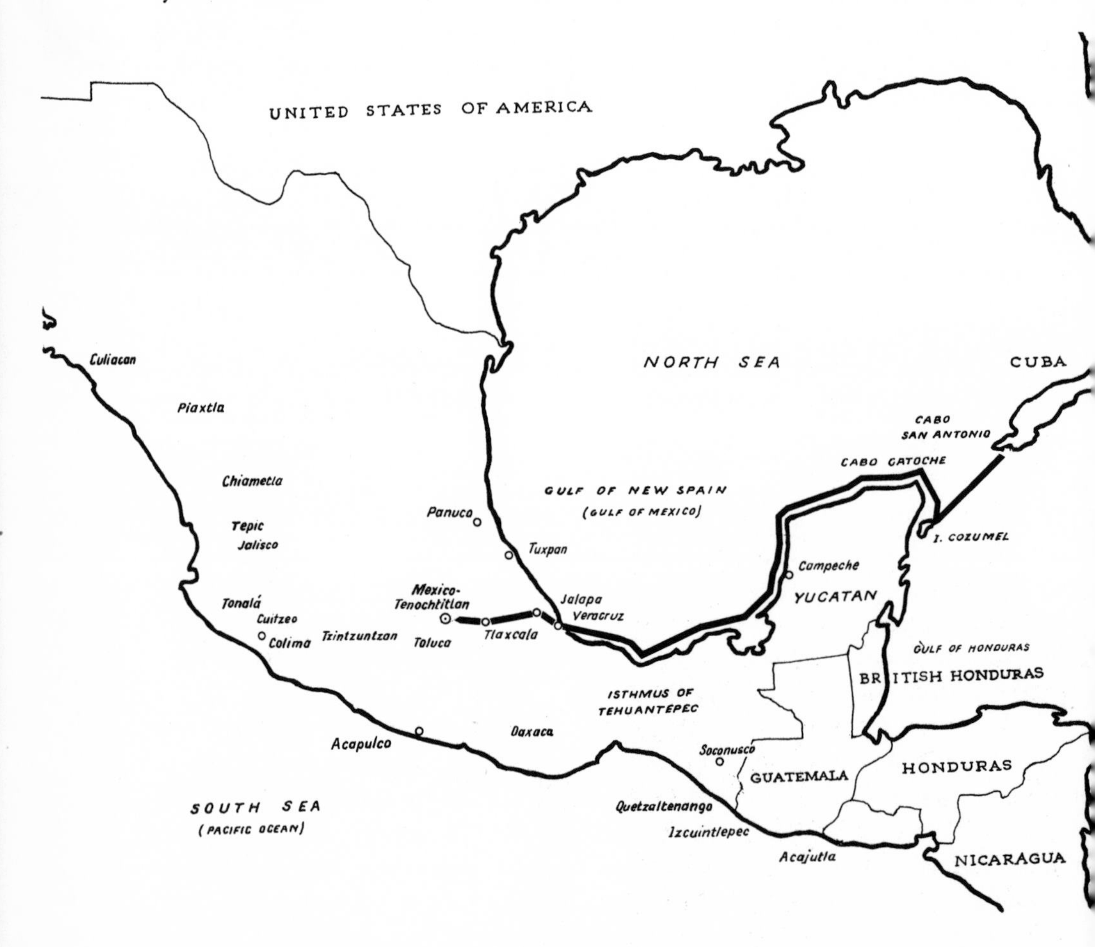

Moctezuma's capital. Here, he was confident, lay the fount of untold riches, to which he must gain access by one scheme or another.

The Indian escorts who had come with him from Zempoala warned him, saying, "Lord, do not go through Cholula, because the people of that place are great traitors, and Moctezuma has his war garrison there." The Aztec ambassadors, however, insisted that he take the level road to Cholula, pointing out that there they would learn the emperor's wishes. Yicotencatl the Elder of Tlaxcala told Cortés that his people had been wronged by the Cholulans and that members of Moctezuma's garrison at Cholula had stormed Tlaxcala at night. According to Bernal Díaz, Cortés was urged to take the road leading through Huexotzingo, since the principal lords of that city were relatives and would guarantee his safe passage. But such counsel was of no avail, for Cortés determined to go to Cholula, which he had heard was a "great city, well towered with high buildings and splendid temples, built on a vast plain." From afar, it "looked very much like Valladolid of Castilla la Vieja."

When the march started, Cortés sent messengers to Cholula, asking the lords of the city to present themselves to him. They apparently declined the honor, pleading sickness, and sent in their stead two or three persons of no great authority. Bernal Díaz believed that this affront predisposed Cortés against them. Explaining the attitude of the Cholulans, the chronicler observed that the lords of Cholula regarded the Tlaxcalans as their enemies and for this reason refused Cortés's invitation to visit him in Tlaxcala. A few days earlier some Tlaxcalans accompanying Pedro de Alvarado and Bernardino Vásquez de Tapia had been attacked by country folk and the Spaniards had been saved only by two detachments sent at full speed from the Cholula garrison to escort them as far as Guaquachula.

No untoward incidents, however, occurred when Cortés with his men and a great army of Tlaxcalans entered Cholula, although there were signs of unrest. In a letter to Charles V, Cortés told the Spanish king that during the three days he spent in Cholula the supplies he received "went from bad to worse" and that the lords and nobles of the city seldom came near him. Francisco de Aguilar, a *conquistador* who became a Dominican friar, reported that the Spaniards and their Indian allies received no food for five days and that Cortés ordered his men to kill the 2,000 slaves who supplied them with wood and water.

According to Cortés, La Malinche informed him that she had learned from the wife of a Cholulan chieftain that a great concentration of Moctezuma's troops had been sent from Tenochtitlán to attack him. Cortés immediately ordered 30 Cholulan lords to be brought before him and placed in custody. It is said that the subsequent mass slaughter took place in the inner court of a building occupied briefly by Cortés which still stands in Cholula. Bernal Díaz claimed that the Templo Mayor was the scene of the massacre. Sahagún wrote that Cortés summoned the entire population —nobles, chieftains and people—and when they were all assembled in the temple courtyard, ordered all exits closed. At his prearranged signal the Spaniards goaded their horses into the crowd, trampling the people to death. A soldier who had been an eyewitness recalled that about 5,000 Cholulans were killed, followed by the plunder and burning of the principal houses and temples. The booty, it was said, consisted of "much gold, precious stones, cloth and feather garments, because Cholula was the richest city in the land, all of its inhabitants being merchants." According to the historian de Alva Ixtlilxóchitl, based on the testimony of Vásquez de Tapia, the number of the slain reached 20,000, and in the estimate of Fray Bartolomé de las Casas, the total numbered 30,000. Cortés, who later boasted that more than 3,000 had been killed in two hours, had described the city to the king as being of "considerable size, having up to 20,000 houses in the main centers and as many in the suburbs."

The Cholula massacre, an incident that rivaled Ahuitzotl's allegedly bloody feast, was only one of a variety of ruthless tactics devised by the lad who had failed to learn "anything of value" at Salamanca. Met inside Tenochtitlán by leaders of the Confederation of the Valley of Mexico, the Spaniards were escorted to Axayácatl's palace. No sooner were they lodged there than Cortés, who had placed armed men at the street entrance, shot off a cannon to terrify the populace. Then, bolting the doors, he informed his hosts that they were his prisoners and demanded to be led to the royal treasure room. He promised the officials their freedom in exchange for four hostages apiece. But when each produced his closest relatives they were also declared prisoners.

While encountering some resistance in his efforts to subdue the Aztecs, Cortés persisted, despite sundry threats to his authority and a bitter struggle for entrenchment in Tenochtitlán. Ground lost there had to be regained—at high cost. When Governor Velásquez sent a force from Cuba to arrest him, the crafty Cortés left the capital at once and managed to capture Pánfilo de Nárvaez, the man dispatched to put him in chains, and succeeded in persuading the new forces to join his own. But while Cortés, who had brazenly placed Moctezuma under "house arrest," fought to maintain official supremacy, his lieutenant Pedro de Alvarado was responsible for a deterioration of relations with the Aztecs in Tenochtitlán. This crisis precipitated the famous "Noche Triste," or "Night of Sorrow" in which hundreds of Spaniards and thousands of their Indian allies perished. Aztec reprisals increased after Pedro de Alvarado attacked some nobles peacefully gathered for a religious ritual. Moctezuma died after having been stoned when he was taken to a rooftop and asked to address the people in behalf of the invaders. His successor, Cuitláhuac, who became briefly the leader of native resistance, had been released by the Spaniards in an effort to expedite the reopening of food supplies to them.

In the forced flight from Tenochtitlán on the night of June 30, 1520 (Lopez de Gómara reported it as the night of July 1), about half of Cortés's army was destroyed and nearly all of his soldiers were wounded. Many in the rearguard divisions who were unable to escape were later killed as prisoners of war. Cortés himself was wounded in the retreat but finally succeeded in reaching a haven in Tlaxcala. For some weeks he and his men slowly recuperated from the effects of the disaster. Then, aided by his Tlaxcalan allies, he conquered Tepeaca, Itzocan, Quauhquechollan and other neighboring towns. After he had sufficiently reorganized his forces he marched, on December 28, 1520, toward Texcoco. In addition to the remnants of his own army he had with him 25,000 native warriors. In less than a year Tenochtitlán would be taken, street by street.

Some historians consider the ultimate surrender of Cuauhtémoc, the last Aztec commander-in-chief, on August 13, 1521, in a Tenochtitlán lagoon, to have been a direct consequence of an ingenious stratagem devised by Cortés: the building of a fleet of brigantines.

Cortés's daring naval maneuvers on Lake Texcoco, according to C. Harvey Gardiner, author of *Naval Power in the Conquest of Mexico,* was unparalleled, since no similar victorious naval engagement concluded a war and ended a civilization. "One sees," he remarked, "in kaleidoscopic panorama, the sweep of naval history from ancient Salamis to Korea, ships under sail and oar—ramming, boarding, fleet action, task-force operations, blockade, liaison duty, Marine-like raids by naval landing parties, close support of land operations and psychological warfare. Like Salamis, which was fought for the control of the eastern Mediterranean, the battle of Tenochtitlán also involved the mastery of a world."

When Cortés became convinced of the support a fleet could give him in confronting a skillful, well-equipped enemy, he immediately launched a "crash" shipbuilding program. *The General Archives of the Indies* contains the following account of an order he had given to the master shipbuilder Martín López: "Proceed to the city of Tlaxcala with your tools and everything necessary and search for a place where you can cut much wild oak, evergreen oak and pine, and fashion it into the pieces required to build 13 brigantines." The project proceeded slowly, with setbacks owing to labor problems and discontent. There were several instances of sabotage, including an attempt to burn the shipyard. Years later, in 1534, López complained that in Tlaxcala he had been obliged to provide all the skilled carpenters and other laborers with "wine, vinegar, oil, cheese and other provisions" at his own expense as well as with supplies of all kinds, maintaining them as well as himself, "because if at any time the Marqués gave them something taken from the Indians it was a case of giving them something one day and nothing for twenty, so that they practically had to maintain themselves."

But the vessels were finally put together at the edge of the Zahuapan River, near Tlaxcala and then dismantled for transporting to Lake Texcoco. The route over which the prefabricated brigantines were borne cannot be identified, but the historian José María Luis Mora has concluded that they reached their objective via the plains of Apam, where, some historians contend, the battle really took place. During the reassembling of the fleet, Texcoco was the center of intensive naval activity, especially since two projects had to be undertaken simultaneously. There was not only the assembly of the ships but also the task of completing a canal following an Indian irrigation ditch into Lake Texcoco from the banks of the narrow, shallow stream where the shipyard for the final assembly was located, a relatively inaccessible site quite a distance from the shore. The building of the canal reportedly occupied 40,000 Texcocans, laboring incessantly in relays of 8,000 men each, over a period of seven weeks. López de Gómara reported that the caulking had been made of human fat. Before the canal could be used, a series of twelve dams, it was said, had to be built in order to impound the waters. No evidence of such a canal exists today, but as late as the nineteenth century it was claimed that traces of it were still visible.

There had been previous waterborne clashes. The old chronicles abound with such phrases as "The native spies came, some in canoes by water," or, "We had a skirmish with some powerful Mexican squadrons which had come in more than 1,000 canoes," or, "More than 2,000 canoes, carrying over 20,000 Mexicans had come to Chalco," or, "We saw an infinite number of canoes on the water, with countless warriors in them." The Indian craft, according to Motolinia and Abbé Francisco Clavijero, author of *Historia Antigua de México,* were flat-bottomed and without keels, a bit narrower at the bow than the stern, and hollowed out of a single tree.

An account of the launching of the brigantines was given by F. Cervantes de Salazar in *Crónica de la Nueva España.* The event, which reportedly took place on April 28, 1521, was commemorated centuries later by the erection of a memorial shaft on the supposed site in 1938. This memorial, however, gives the date as April 5. Fray Olmedo celebrated mass at the water's edge and blessed the ships before a throng of Spaniards and their Indian allies. Cries of excitement mingled with the roar of guns. When the moment of the dedication of the fleet arrived, the rough veteran of many campaigns, according to de Salazar, "shed tears of gratitude," confident that the fleet held the key to victory. The daring amphibious assault permitted the encirclement and blockade of the Aztec capital.

The brigantines built at Cortés's order (*left*) were, according to some chroniclers, a powerful resource for the Conquistadores. The Aztec canoes (*right*), illustrated in the *Lienzo de Tlaxcala,* were flat-bottomed and without keels.

With his scant resources the realistic Cortés could hardly expect to conquer the powerful Aztecs by arms, yet he began to tighten the knot still further. At Cortés's instructions Cristóbal de Olid was sent to Chapultepec, where he cut off Tenochtitlán's water supply by breaking the city's pipes at the spring. There were, of course, some setbacks. When a group of Spaniards incautiously advanced, 62 of them were captured. At one point Cortés's Indian allies lost heart and many defected. Nearly all the men from Tlaxcala, Cholula, Huexotzingo, Chalco and Tlalmanalco departed, leaving only 200 of the original contingent of 25,000, although Cortés numbered the force at 50,000. Two weeks later a majority of the deserters returned, almost all of them from Tlaxcala, many from Huexotzingo and a very few from Cholula. With La Malinche as his interpreter, Cortés addressed them, expressing his forgiveness of their action because of "their ignorance of Spanish laws and rules." He embraced the chieftains, even those who went back to their respective lands. According to de Alva Ixtlilxóchitl, the Tlaxcalans, in passing through Texcoco, sacked and ruined it, saying the Spaniards had urged them to do so.

López de Gómara gave a detailed account of the three-month siege which culminated in the capture of the Aztec leader by the captain of a brigantine. Cortés was reportedly reluctant at first to destroy such a beautiful city but later determined to raze every house, filling the canals with the debris. According to Durán, Cuauhtémoc boarded a small canoe and, covering himself with a mat, was rowed out of the city by a single retainer. Some of Cortés's men spotted him from their brigantine and he was taken prisoner. At his command the remnant of Aztec forces yielded. Cortés himself reported the capture to Charles V.

After the Spaniards seized and razed the city they established their own capital on the site. The gold they found, estimated to have been worth $15,000,000, represented only a small part of the fabled Aztec treasure. Cortés and his men had been tantalized with a glimpse of Moctezuma's gold. Francisco de Aguilar described the royal treasure vault: "A very small low door that was stopped up in a secret treasure-chamber and recently covered with plaster should not be so without mystery and it was ordered to be opened." The Spaniards found "a spacious room, in the middle of which was a heap of gold, jewels and precious stones as high as a man. So high was it that one was not seen on the other side, which pile, if we wish to know about it according to history, was not a thing acquired by Moctezuma, nor a thing that he might be able to profit by, because it was the treasure that all the kings, his forefathers, went on leaving and which the king who came in was not able to profit by; and so, on the death of the king, the same day that he died, all the treasure that he left of gold, stones, feathers and arms, and finally, all his wardrobe, was put into that room with much care as a sacred thing . . . as a treasure of the city and for the grandeur of it." Yet questioning and torture of the captured Cuauhtémoc failed to reveal the whereabouts of the gold hoard the Spaniards were positive had been hidden.

The conquering forces continued their swath of destruction and domination in outlying areas and looked toward the western ocean. Cortés, consolidating his gains, envisioned a burgeoning commerce on the boundless waters of the Pacific. He realized that as a land bridge Mexico could serve as a link to the coveted spices of the Indies, that it was in fact the road to the Indies sought even before Columbus by Prince Henry the Navigator of Portugal. By 1530 Acapulco knew the movement and excitement of a great port. Along with Marquesa, it became the point of entry and departure for a vast trade, much of it based on the demand for the epicurean delights of the New World. The enterprise of Spanish mariners soon made possible a globe-encircling course, from Madrid to Havana to Veracruz, from which, after cargoes were borne overland, ships crossed the Pacific to the Philippines and beyond.

When native resistance was finally overcome there remained as booty the lands and peoples, and in the name of the King of Spain both were split among the victors. The fate of the Cholulans, for instance, who survived the massacre was an especially sorry one. Some were taken to distant lands in expeditions or as colonizers. Jorge de Alvarado, brother of the fair-haired Pedro de Alvarado, nicknamed *El Tonatiuh,* or "The Sun," was sent with some 200 Cholulans to settle in Guatemala by his father-in-law, Governor Alonzo de Estrada. The Texcocan ruler Ixtlilxóchitl, who for his services to the Spaniards had been awarded Cholula and two provinces, declined the gift, replying that since these had been the property of Cortés's ancestors it was only proper that he should enjoy them, a further indication of the conviction that the Conqueror was indeed Quetzalcóatl, returning to seek redress. The settlers in Puebla de los Angeles charged that they had not been granted, as promised, the people of Cholula, Tlaxcala and other regions, for their personal service. Some of the Cholulans came to Cortés, complaining that while they had rendered assistance to the Spaniards, the promises that had been made to them had not been kept. Cortés took the delegation to Castile, where he assured the king that their complaints were well founded since he, as a representative of the Crown, had promised that they would not be deprived of their kingdom.

But despite titles and ceremonials in Colonial *cabildos,* or municipal councils (in Cholula the old Spanish custom of carrying a golden mace in public processions was copied), the Cholulans and other Indians of Mexico remained in virtual slavery, a result of the survival of the *encomienda* system which, although officially outlawed, sanctioned a veritable indenture system for the benefit of European settlers who came in the wake of the "hills moving in the sea."

For her scholarly reevaluation of the role of the white invaders, and of Cortés in particular, La Sociedad Mexicana de Geografía y Estadistica (The Mexican Society of Geography and Statistics), Mexico's oldest scientific body, bestowed its biennial gold medal in 1959 for the first time upon a woman. The recipient of the society's honor was Dr. Eulalia Guzmán, an archaeologist, educator and pioneer leader in the campaign against illiteracy. She had made a comprehensive study of Cortés's "Five Letters" to Charles V in a book announced as *Clarifications and Rectifications of the Invasion of Anáhuac.*

The Conqueror cherished the hope that his astutely prepared explanations would clear him of various charges made by his rivals, but when he returned to Spain, expecting a victor's welcome, he found that royal favor had turned against him and he spent his last years a disappointed and neglected man. Dr. Guzmán analyzed minutely the personality, character, methods, talents and exploits of the Conqueror, reexamining the available evidence and shattering the overly romantic legend woven around his figure. There were other reevaluations, with contemporary scientific analyses by experts contrasting with earlier descriptions of Cortés. Bernal Díaz's assertion that Cortés was of "good stature" was refuted in 1946 by Mexican anthropologists who examined the remains of Cortés. Since 1833, at the order of Lucas Alamán, who had hidden them during the War of Independence, they had been immured in the chapel of the Hospital Jésus Nazareno, which had been founded and endowed by Cortés as "Our Lady of the Conception." At the instigation of Dr. Daniel Rubín de la Borbolla two separate examinations were made by Dr. Eusebio Dávalos Hurtado and Dr. Javier Romero of the National Institute of Anthropology and History; both concluded that Cortés was of less than medium height. Díaz stated that as Cortés grew older he became stout and developed a large paunch. He also stated that the Conqueror was somewhat bowlegged. This was borne out by the fibulae of his skeleton, which show a deviation from the axis toward one side. While Díaz attributed to Cortés a "great chest," the anthropologists revealed that he had a funnel-shaped thorax. Díaz observed that if Cortés had had a "larger countenance he would have been of better appearance." His allusion to a smaller-than-normal countenance becomes clear in the light of reports by medical specialists who found that Cortés had an atrophied lower jawbone. His cranium was small and reduced in its transversal measurements. Evidence of degenerative symptoms corresponding to dwarfishness was found in the bones, a condition diagnosed as congenital syphilis of the osseous system.

Dr. Guzmán's study challenged those who had revered the name of Cortés as a symbol of valor, ability and inspired leadership and as a heroic destroyer of ships that would have made his escape possible in the case of defeat in a strange land. She studied the principal chronicles of the Conquest written by eyewitnesses and by those who were informed by eyewitnesses and compared them with Cortés's own version of the same events.

The interpretation of Cortés by Orozco in his fresco of 1922 in the National Preparatory School is based on the traditional source for the likeness of the Conqueror, the portrait of Charles V. A detail from a mural entitled "Cortés and the Tribute-Bearers," in the National Palace, painted by Diego Rivera in the late 1940's, shows the features of the Conqueror rendered in a realistic manner (*opposite page*), based on the analysis of his remains by various specialists, who declared that he was, in fact, syphilitic.

She noted points of agreement, contradictory statements and certain omissions in the Cortés accounts. She was able to examine official copies of Cortés's five letters to the Spanish king and noted many errors in transcription. Comparing the originals with the copies, she was struck by the frequent faulty rendering of place-names. Cortés would often correct his earlier spellings as he acquired greater familiarity with the country. Díaz and other chroniclers of the Conquest often made similar errors.

Defining the historian's proper function as a "search for truth rather than arguments," Dr. Guzmán has declared that some instances of "honest error," as well as deliberate deceit or distortion attributable to partisanship, may have contributed to incorrect evaluations by later scholars. Considered judgments would be difficult to form in the light of partial, contradictory, vague, malicious or infantile accounts. Early Spanish writers, she pointed out, engaged in what amounted to a veritable "conspiracy of silence" concerning some aspects, such as human sacrifice, of the indigenous culture they encountered in the New World.

Among the common causes of "honest error" brought to light in the course of Dr. Guzmán's research were poor translations or misrepresentations of Nahuatl words or symbols. She found that the word "offering," for example, was frequently translated as "sacrifice." In several instances she traced the word through comparative texts and discovered that it had been given different meanings. Where a chronicler might describe the "sacrifice" of thousands during a religious festival in Tenochtitlán he might, in the next paragraph, tell how the ashes of the "sacrificed ones" were collected in small baskets immediately after the ritual. If human beings were actually "sacrificed" in great numbers, the remains of such a holocaust could hardly have been disposed of so swiftly. Other chroniclers, however, described paper banners on which images of human beings were painted. Obviously, such paper effigies could be quickly reduced to ashes and gathered up in small receptacles. Thus a confusing reference to annual Aztec sacrifices of children emerged with the puzzling statement that "the same children were presented for sacrifice again next year by their parents," doubtless indicating ceremonies of dedication or religious offerings. Mme Laurette Séjourné, however, refers in *Burning Water* to actual sacrifices of children to Tláloc. She quotes Fray de Sahagún's statement that ". . . the parents of the victims submitted to these practices, shedding many tears and with great sorrow in their hearts." Dr. Guzmán cited the common symbolic representation of the Virgin Mary as the "Mother of Sorrows" with seven swords literally piercing her heart, commenting that a misinterpretation of symbols by early Spanish historians might also have constituted a source of "honest error." Cortés stated that he had never seen a ritualistic sacrifice and that the only human sacrifices he had witnessed during his stay in Tenochtitlán had been the normal execution of prisoners of war during the siege.

In the course of her research Dr. Guzmán studied the letters of Cortés and the various accounts of Bernal Díaz, of Cortés's biographer Francisco López de Gómara and of the native historian de Alva Ixtlilxóchitl in order to establish the routes taken by the Conqueror in his marches from Zempoala to Tenochtitlán and from Tenochtitlán to Honduras. The versions of Cortés and Bernal Díaz she found often in flat contradiction. Finally, she compared the itineraries in order to place in plain sight both the discrepancies and the coincidences. In checking comparative sources against the statements made by Cortés, she kept in mind the fact that he might have distorted the truth for several reasons. Most of the statements derogatory to the Indians made by Cortés were, in Dr. Guzmán's view, deliberate, long-range calculations in the furtherance of his own ends. She concluded that his uncanny power to deceive was so great that it might be said he achieved the Conquest on this talent alone, through his favorite technique and main resource of creating surprise by swift action.

The primary motivation in Cortés's frequent distorted version of events was, she believes, to cover up his treason to Governor Diego Velásquez and his defiance of the piracy laws, which made him subject to the death penalty. As to the alleged destruction of his Cuban fleet before ordering the march inland, she feels there is a grave question both as to the details of this act and as to his motives. Each of the three versions or explanations of the disposition of the fleet entrusted to Cortés—burning, beaching or scuttling off the coast of New Spain—has its proponents. In his letter to Charles V dated October 30, 1520, Cortés himself claimed that the vessels were beached. C. Harvey Gardiner, a student of naval tactics, believes that the story of the burning of the fleet was purely a literary invention of the sixteenth century, set forth "to magnify the heroic proportions of Hernán Cortés." In any event, Dr. Guzmán maintains that the "burning" or "sinking" of the fleet was far from a heroic act. She points out that it was necessary for Cortés to get rid of the illegally held vessels, the property of Governor Velásquez and Cuban investors. One obvious way out of the dilemma was the destruction of the evidence of his guilt. She is of the opinion that he was prompted solely by the law of self-preservation and not by any noble determination to win or lose all and that it was not a courageous gesture of readiness to face the consequences of defeat. If he valued life he could not afford to keep the ships in his custody without recompensing their rightful owners for their just share of the profits from the Mexican enterprise. The issue may one day be resolved by underwater dredging in the coastal waters off Veracruz, where the ships of Cortés were allegedly burned or foundered, with "frogmen" and underwater archaeologists adding a conclusive chapter to the saga of the Conquest.

Dr. Guzmán has pointed out that Cortés was deeply concerned with pleasing the Emperor and casting the best possible light on his own accomplishments or blunders. Cortés claimed, that, for instance, it was at Moctezuma's urgent plea that he allowed him to go up on the roof of his palace to "calm his restless subjects" and that, while he was there, a stone was thrown which mortally wounded him and caused his death three days later. Dr. Guzmán maintains that this version is pure fiction, as she likewise characterizes the "voluntary" donation of the realm of Anáhuac to the Spanish king. She concludes, in fact, that "Mexico still belongs to the Indians," since it could not have been legally ceded to the Spanish Crown. As she indicates, Moctezuma was not empowered to make peace on his own nor could he force his cochieftains to accept any treaty. Certainly he could not have compelled them, she asserts, to cede the realm of Anáhuac to any hypothetical *Señor,* nor could he have ceded the lands of other city-states, all members of the Confederation of the Valley of Mexico. It was on the basis of this "voluntary" donation that the Spanish Crown always designated Moctezuma as the "last king of New Spain," thus ignoring the claims of all other allied and independent peoples, as well as Cuitláhuac, Moctezuma's immediate successor, who died a victim of smallpox, and his ultimate successor, the valorous young Cuauhtémoc, his nephew and son-in-law. There was no hereditary throne. Those whom the Spaniards called "kings" or "emperors" were leaders chosen by an electoral council from the heads of the ruling family. Before Moctezuma's death, under suspicious circumstances, the thirty titular lords who composed the Confederation were seized and killed so that no witness to Moctezuma's alleged "voluntary" donation of Anáhuac remained inconveniently alive.

The memory of Cuauhtémoc, despite Cortés's efforts to becloud the circumstances of his death in remote Honduras, has remained undimmed and Dr. Guzmán has been an influential figure in the movement to identify his place of burial. His character presents a marked contrast to that of the artful Cortés, and his tragic story, like the legend of the wise and gentle Quetzalcóatl, has become a part of his country's spiritual heritage. No incident, perhaps, in all of Mexico's history has so profoundly impressed itself upon the national consciousness as an example of supreme courage and devotion to duty as has the torture and death of "Falling Eagle," who sought a guarantee for his people from the Conqueror and ultimately paid for his surrender with his own life.

Cortés, after plundering Tenochtitlán, branded the faces of its inhabitants with hot irons and attempted to force Cuauhtémoc to divulge the location of the Aztec treasure. Even though fire was applied to the soles of the young ruler's feet, which had been rubbed with oil, neither he nor his fellow-sufferer, a chieftain from Tacuba, would reveal it. His noble reply to his companion's agonized complaint has become a classic rejoinder in the Mexican tradition: "Am I perchance reclining on a bed of roses?" López de Gómara, who recounted the incident in his biography of Cortés, praised Cuauhtémoc's bravery and courage. Durán described him as a "courageous young man of an invincible spirit."

In the *residencia* proceedings held in 1529 regarding Cortés's conduct the torturer of Cuauhtémoc defended himself by saying that "he had kept all the treasure of Moctezuma for himself." Bernal Díaz, whose account of Cuauhtémoc's tragic defeat revealed the Aztec leader as an unfaltering protector of his people to the very end, claimed that the "treasure" had been stolen by Indian allies from Texcoco, Huexotzingo, Tlaxcala and Cholula and that the Spanish *teules,* or "white gods," who had manned the brigantines when Cortés besieged Tenochtitlán, had amassed their goodly share.

Cortés did spare Cuauhtémoc for four years after the fall of Tenochtitlán but took him with him, as he customarily did when he rode through the capital, on a long and, as it turned out, needless journey to Honduras to demonstrate his refusal to countenance any threat to his supremacy. One of Cortés's subordinates, Cristóbal de Olid, had dared to set up an independent domain. Enroute to Honduras it was suggested to Cortés that Cuauhtémoc and others had conspired to kill him. Reprisal after each of these incidents was swiftly forthcoming. Cortés did not know when he started out if Francisco de las Casas, whom he had quickly dispatched as his deputy to Honduras, had carried out his orders, nor that, in fact, his rival was dead. He may have feared that any sign of weakness might encourage further rebellion.

López de Gómara gave a detailed account of the expedition and the events which led to the hanging of those lords who, on the word of Mexicalcinco, the "informer" later known as Cristóbal, had plotted against Cortés. Those ordered by Cortés to accompany him on the long march also included Coanacoxtzin of Texcoco, Tetlepanquetzal, also known as Tetlepanquetzatzin, of Tacuba (Tlacopán), Ocuitzin of Atzcapotzalco, Xihuacoa and Tlacatlec, also known as Cihuacóatl Tlacotzin.

The account of F. Alvarado Tezozomoc, the *Crónica Mexicayotl*, translated by Adrián León from Nahuatl into Spanish, named the "conspirators" and "the real traitor." According to the sequence of events as narrated by Tezozomoc, in the year 7 House (1525 of the Christian calendar) men from Tlatelolco and Michoacán denounced Cuauhtémoc and the others who had been taken to Hueymollan by Cortés. The charges were made that Cuauhtémoc of Tenochtitlán and Tetlepanquetzatzin of Tlacopán wished to rise again against the Spanish. The real traitor was apparently Cotztemetzi of Tlatelolco. When Cortés learned of the denunciation he had Cuauhtémoc, Tetlepanquetzatzin and Cihuacóatl Tlacotzin baptized. Their baptismal names became Don Fernando Cuauhtemoctzin, Don Pedro Tetlepanquetzatzin and Don Juan Velasquez Tlacotzin. Immediately afterward they were sentenced and hanged on a *ceiba* tree.

Durán summarized the arduous journey to Las Hibueras in this manner: "It seems that after a few days' journey he [Cuauhtémoc] was accused of rebelling against the Spaniards and of trying to assassinate them. Several witnesses appeared to denounce him and Cortés had the Aztec ruler hanged. In this way perished the great Cuauhtémoc, who had ruled over Mexico three or four years. That he might not depart this world alone, the other chieftains whom Cortés had brought along were executed also. Some died a natural death, others were hanged or run down by hounds and still others died in different ways. Some Spaniards who attempted to kill Cortés and steal his ship were also hanged."

Dr. Guzmán, in her re-evaluation of Cortés, quoted the opinion of Spanish historians of the sixteenth century that it had become too great a burden for Cortés to guard his princely prisoner and that the presence of the former "Chief Speaker" had become insupportable.

Cortés gave his own version of the expedition in a letter to Charles V. On October 12, 1525, he said, he left Tenochtitlán for Las Hibueras on the east coast of Honduras, ostensibly to punish Cristóbal de Olid for his disloyalty. The Conqueror deemed it imperative, he explained, to take along with him a number of native chieftains to guarantee that their respective towns would remain submissive. Accompanying the expedition were two Franciscan friars, Fray Juan de Tecto and Fray Juan de Ayora, who had come from Spain in 1523. Both were countrymen and personal friends of the king. Bernal Díaz called them "great theologians." The former had been master of theology in the University of Paris, confessor to Charles V himself; the latter was guardian of the Franciscan monastery of Ghent.

From Coatzalcoalcos, where the force was joined by nearly all the Spaniards to be found there, the march apparently became extremely difficult because of the size of the expedition and its impedimenta. Cortés carried objects that would make an ostentatious display—plates of silver and gold—and included in his entourage musicians, jugglers and for his own table even a pair of hogs, in care of their keepers. Following the coast of Tabasco, the marchers crossed rivers, swamps, lakes and estuaries for which the Indians had to build bridges so that not only the men but the horses might cross. They were also required to serve as a defense guard, to carry and store equipment, to find provisions and to build huts for the captains and chieftains each night they camped in an uninhabited place. Before arriving at the mouth of the Grijalva the expedition abandoned the coast and, seeking drier land, ascended by a southern route and then straightened out toward the east. Roads had to be opened in the forests and marshes could be traversed only with great difficulty.

Then, exhausted by weariness and hunger, they crossed the Usumacinta and reached the realm of Acallán. According to a narrative of 1528, *Unos Anales Históricos de la Nación Mexicana* (*Some Historical Annals of the Mexican Nation*), written by Tlatelolco scribes, the long retinue arrived on February 26, 1525, in a village that de Alva Ixtlilxóchitl called Teotilac. On the following day, the chieftains of Itzamkanac, the capital of Acallán, came to salute the great "Chief Speaker" and to present to him gifts consisting of eight baskets of jewels, gold and precious stones and fine feather garments. They remained with Cuauhtémoc the rest of the day, conversing and dancing, departing at nightfall for their own city.

De Alva Ixtlilxóchitl and others testified that hardly had the lords of Acallán departed than a spy whom Cortés had placed among the Indians denounced the conversations of Cuauhtémoc with the other chieftains that day. Without further ado the Spanish soldiers entered the camp where Cuauhtémoc and his companions slept, placed them in chains and brought them into the presence of Cortés, who ordered them to be hanged from a *ceiba* tree. According to Bernal Díaz, when Cuauhtémoc was about to be hanged he reproached Cortés in this fashion: "Oh, Malintzin, for days I have understood that you would give me this death, and I have known of your false promises. You are killing me without the justice that God demands of you. But why did you not tell me so when I surrendered my person to you in my city of Mexico?"

De Alva Ixtlilxóchitl, who stated that Cortés resented Cuauhtémoc's reception by the chieftains of Acallán "with great reverence and rich gifts," further related that on the return of the spy to Tenochtitlán he was questioned by Ixtlilxóchitl, lord of Texcoco, about the denunciation. The spy assured the ruler that he had denounced no one but that Cortés had ordered him to describe the chieftains who had been talking with Cuauhtémoc and that he had described nine among them. The native historian, recounting the inquiry made by his ancestor, said that Cuauhtémoc was killed on Shrove Tuesday "three hours before dawn." The tradition in the town of Cuauhtémoc's birth holds that the hour was "one o'clock in the morning, when everyone was sleeping. Juan de Torquemada declared, "This day, Shrove Tuesday, they were seen hanging at dawn." Cortés, Bernal Díaz and Ixtlilxóchitl, the lord of Texcoco and the brother of Coanacoxtzin, concurred. Chimalpahín, a sixteenth-century Indian chronicler, said simply that "they tied the feet of Cuauhtémoc to a tree." The *Mapa de Tepechpan*, an early post-Hispanic Nahuatl manuscript, shows the figure of Cuauhtémoc hanging by the feet, with his mutilated neck almost on the ground.

Dr. Guzmán, in her study of the Ixcateopan tradition, reported that two aged brothers from a neighboring village, Pipincatla, had told her of a version passed down from an ancestor who had been a companion of the young prince: "Cuauhtémoc was hanged by the feet; then he was set afire from below and, the flames rising around the head of the victim, he died." She remarked also on the fear and caution with which Torquemada recorded the event in his history, stating merely that "they hanged him at dawn." A document written at the end of the Colonial epoch referred to "the most horrible crime" and further stated that "his martyrdom had no equal."

Fray Mariano Cuevas, S.J., in Chapter I of the first volume of his *Historia de la Iglesia en México* (*History of the Church in Mexico*), referred to the deaths of Fray Juan de Tecto and Fray Juan de Ayora, neither of whom returned from the Las Hibueras expedition, and noted that one of them protested vigorously before Cortés "the barbarous death that he gave to Cuauhtémoc." Describing to Charles V the fate of his friend and confessor, Fray Pedro de Gante wrote that Fray Juan de Tecto had died amid the trials and vicissitudes of the Honduras expedition. The circumspect Torquemada reported merely that the friar died of hunger while seeking shelter under a tree. The Ixcateopan tradition has it that Cortés hanged the friar who defended Cuauhtémoc because he did not wish him to reveal what the young ruler had discussed with him. According to the version, Cortés also resented the friar's plea that the oak cross which he had brought from Spain might remain near him to the last. A plate of the *Codex Rios*, painted between 1566 and 1589, in which Cuauhtémoc and a companion are shown hanging from a tree, also shows a friar, a crucifix in his hand, dangling from a nearby gallows.

Dr. Guzmán noted that Cortés in his version of the events did not mention the pueblo specifically by name, while Bernal Díaz referred to it as "an uninhabited place." "Cortés always combined the small and the large," Dr. Guzmán observed, "in order to avoid the truth." It was precisely to the "uninhabited pueblo," she contends, that he took Cuauhtémoc "to torture and kill him." In an unpopulated place "he could well commit the crime in the way he wished, at night, when the people slept, and without time for any investigation."

The Chontal tradition holds that three days after the death of Cuauhtémoc a group of thirty warriors, deserting from the ranks, rescued the body of their beloved young lord. Covering it with fragrant leaves and wrapping it in fine garments, they bore it in an epic march toward the west until they reached Zompancuauhuitl (later called Ixcateopan). There, with the pomp and ceremony befitting Cuauhtémoc's royal status, they buried him in the palace of his maternal ancestors, probably first burning the corpse, as was the custom in the case of Mexican rulers.

The funeral route, according to tradition, had traversed the area which now includes Chiapas, Oaxaca and Guerrero. It had led through jungles and over mountains in an odyssey that today would be considered incredibly exhausting if not impossible. But when one considers the love that the marchers had for their dead emperor and the stamina and discipline of the warriors, their feat is entirely plausible. Traveling by night, they could rest by day in friendly towns where local guides could help them reach the next stage in their mournful journey.

According to age-yellowed records and Chontal tradition Cuauhtémoc was born in Zompancuauhuitl on February 23, 1501, the son of the Aztec prince Ahuitzotl, whose father, "King" Ahuitzotl, had pushed the Aztec empire to its farthest boundaries. Cuauhtémoc's mother, the Chontal princess Cuayahtitlalli, was the daughter of the lord of Zompancuahuitl and of Queen Atl (a Nahuatl name signifying "Mist of the Sun"). A descendant of the royal families of Tenochtitlán and Texcoco, one of her paternal ancestors was the poet-king Netzahualcóyotl.

Cuauhtémoc's ancestry was recorded by José Francisco who, in his *Arco Iris de Paz* (*Rainbow of Peace*), written in 1768, gave details of his youth and education. The chronicler related that the Aztec prince studied in the *calmécac,* or school for young nobles, at the side of the sons of the royal families of Texcoco. On his return to Zompancuauhuitl he probably served as an assistant military commander, since an army had been formed against the Spanish invasion which had been launched in Moctezuma's realm. When only twenty-one he had to assume the official responsibility for Anáhuac after the death of both Moctezuma and Cuitláhuac. His story forms one of the most enduring and moving chapters in all of Mexican history.

Dr. Guzmán, who has compared the various chroniclers' references to Cuauhtémoc's last days, was particularly interested in the local tradition that he was buried in the town known today as Ixcateopan. Here legend and tradition, documentary evidence and scientific deduction blend to keep the Mexican people poignantly aware of Cuauhtémoc's nobility. Is the gallant Cuauhtémoc actually buried in the ancient town of his maternal ancestors? The question has aroused endless controversy and has rekindled embers of racial bitterness. Historians and politicians may still dispute the authenticity of the Ixcateopan tomb, but there is no question concerning the homage given the brilliant young *tlatoani.*

The centuries seem to dissolve in this old Chontal town set in the Momostli and Enmedio mountain ranges that run through northeast Guerrero as the visitor listens to oratory delivered during the annual ceremonies honoring Cuauhtémoc's memory. Delegations from distant pueblos reverently place wreaths before the main altar of the parish church. The townsfolk display a fervent civic consciousness, and schoolchildren present patriotic programs reflecting the conviction that their pueblo is indeed the "Sanctuary" of the *Patria.* "Cuauhtémoc" banners adorn the low adobe houses on either side of the steep, cobbled streets, and posters above the city gates proclaim the local faith in this cherished Chontal tradition.

Near Ixcateopan are deep, luxuriant canyons—El Salitre, Río Oscuro and Barranca Honda. The lush vegetation of the surrounding countryside is kept perpetually green by springs, some of them giving rise to the San Pedro, Atengo and San Miguel, which form the Río de los Sabinos, emptying into the Río Balsas. As the Ixcateopan visitor drives along the narrow mountain road, carved out in places from perpendicular walls that drop into vast canyons, the presence of *El Joven Abuelo de la Patria* ("The Young Grandfather of the Fatherland") seems to fill the region with his benign presence and to evoke the poet Kubli's lines:

> With an eye to the summit and with steady pulse
> against thy flesh—a living reef—
> The people train their fairest flowers
> and take honey from the thorn of the cactus.

A genealogical inquiry prompted the first official investigations. The tradition of the tragic journey had long been entrenched in the memories of descendants of the family of Chimalpopoca. Members of the family, particularly Sr. Salvador Rodríguez Juarez of the eleventh generation, wished to know if the ancestral records, some of them recopied during the course of the centuries, were genuine and lent support to the oral tradition that had been handed down from father to son in Ixcateopan. The exact whereabouts of the presumed tomb had evidently been deliberately concealed by the town's elders. The civic secret remained relatively safe for many years because of Ixcateopan's complete isolation; the tortuous road from Iguala was opened only in the mid-1930's.

Sr. Rodríguez Juarez brought to the parish priest of Ixcateopan, Fray David Salgado Estrada, documents alleging that Motolinia had ordered the remains of Cuauhtémoc removed from the *teocalli* to the parish church. Referring to the reburial, Motolinia, who arrived in Ixcateopan in December 1529, stated, "Crowds were present at the interment of their Señor King Cuauhtémoc. His remains were buried and not burned as were the others, this already having been done. Everyone of this land assisted at the act and peace descended upon Ixcateopan, formerly Zompancuahuitl, on December 20, 1529. I confirm the act of burial about which I write and bless you in the name of the Lord." His reference to the changing of the town's name to Ixcateopan is significant, for the name derives from five Nahuatl words, the combined meaning of which is "Here Lies Your Señor Beneath the Church." In keeping with the evangelizing spirit of the epoch Motolinia added to Ixcateopan the name "Santa Maria de la Asunción."

Fray Salgado knew that an old record book in the archives contained a strange entry: "A pope, a king or an emperor reposes beneath our main altar." He was also aware that in 1568 an inquisitorial process was instituted against the *corregidor* Diego Díaz del Castillo, a *mestizo* son of Bernal Díaz. Diego Díaz del Castillo was accused of hearing confessions of the Indians by the old vicar Fray Francisco Moya, who complained further that the magistrate would not permit him to make certain church repairs. The two points, according to the scholar Dr. Amaya Topete, are significant when considered together. He has suggested that the wily *corregidor* might well have conceived the idea of receiving confessions without ecclesiastical sanction in order to learn the truth about the hidden relic and, fearing that workmen might uncover it, prohibited repairs to the church.

On February 2, 1949, the priest announced from the pulpit: "This church is for me a venerated crypt, holding the remains of our last Aztec emperor. And I say to you, and let my words be carried by the four winds to all the world, that in truth, our last emperor is here interred."

On February 18, 1949, Dr. Guzmán arrived in Ixcateopan. As a recognized expert on sixteenth-century script, which she had studied for many years in the libraries and museums of Europe, she was asked by the National Institute of Anthropology and History to determine whether, in her opinion, the documents in the possession of the Rodríguez Juarez family could be regarded as authentic. After seven months of preliminary investigation the decision was made, on September 18th, to excavate the main altar of the church. For more than a week Dr. Guzmán directed the work of the excavators who were digging beneath the 25-ton altar, through various layers of construction and adobe to the living rock. Removing several tons of stones and earth, they reached a depth of 6 feet. On September 26th their efforts were rewarded by the discovery of a hardened clay pit under which, beneath two flat stones, was found a small crypt containing charred human bones, 39 beads, two rings, a plaque in the form of a lance

Documents owned by a family of Ixcateopan declare that Fray Toribio de Benavente, known as Motolinia, ordered the remains of Cuauhtémoc re-interred in Ixcateopan's parish church in 1529.

point and a rectangular plaque which covered the bottom of the crypt. An oval plaque of native copper bore a chiseled Latin cross and the inscription: "1525–1529 *Rey e S. Coatemo.*"

Dr. Guzmán promptly designated the bones as those of Cuauhtémoc. A decade later, Senator Carlos Celis, in an address celebrating the tenth anniversary of the discovery, referred to the controversial bones, which had been placed in a crystal casket and to the various acrimonious disputes that had flared around them. He proclaimed "the final closing of the tomb of the calumniators."

While the discovery tallied with the oral tradition of Ixcateopan, four members of a committee of investigation sponsored by the National Institute of Anthropology and History contended that the crypt below the altar was not a tomb but an ossuary containing eleven bones of an unknown man or men. Anatomists of the University of Mexico Medical School and the Military Medical School pointed out that group burials were common among ancient Indian peoples and that possibly Motolinia himself had arranged the mingling of the remains, since their use as talismans or emblems of hatred could inspire an uprising against the Spaniards.

The oval copper plaque found below the altar of the parish church in 1949 bore a chiseled Latin cross and the inscription "*1525–1529 Rey e S. Coatemo.*"

Dr. Silvio Zavala, director of the National Museum of History, arrived with a group of scientists on October 9, 1949; in less than a week a statement was issued by the group that there was insufficient evidence to prove that the remains were those of Cuauhtémoc. Dr. Guzmán and Guerrero authorities termed their conclusion "too hasty," claiming that with a possible exception or two the investigators were opposed to the exaltation of a native hero. A commission known as "The Investigators of the Bank of Mexico," composed of prominent specialists and headed by Dr. Alfonso Quiros Quaron, visited Ixcateopan. This commission, four and a half months later, declared the discovery to be authentic.

Among the aspects studied were the antiquity of the church; this was investigated by Dr. Alexander V. Wuttenaw, an authority on Colonial architecture. Dr. Luis Chavez Orozco delved into Ixcateopan's tradition. Estabislao Ramírez, an engineer and mathematician, calculated the age of the oxidized layer formed on the oval copper plaque. Using the formula of N. Cabrera and N. F. Mott of the University of Bristol, and taking into consideration that oxidation was effected in two periods, they estimated the age of the second oxidized layer at no less than 387 years. A prominent Mexican engineer, José Antonio Cuevas, stated that it would have taken at least 300 years, according to the rate of soil consolidation, to effect the deformation and settlement of the fill of the crypt and the superimposed structures at the site. He drew attention to the fact that beneath the pyramidal rock pile a clay paste covered the jagged edges of the slate and the stones inserted to fill the gap at the top of the crypt. This, he maintained, had not been disturbed at any point.

Dr. Isaac Ochoterna, in the histological abscission of a fragment of tibia, found copper ions and minute crystals of copper salts. Ferric oxide was also found in the dry earth massed within the skull. Spectroscopic examination of this earth and that lining three sides of the sepulcher revealed the presence of copper and iron in proportions similar to those deposited in the bones. This test supported the conclusions of Urdinivia, whose radiological, chemical and spectrographical analysis of the bones showed both copper and iron, the first in very small quantities and the second in larger proportions. Finally, the blackish earth, or *limonita,* that almost filled the crypt and covered the osseous remains, was partially integrated with mixtures of iron. Examination of the teeth of the principal skeleton by the odontologist Dr. Félix del Paso resulted in the following observations: "Examination of the radiological images was reduced essentially to the jawbones and existing teeth, in synthesis the results indicating that the porous tissue of this part of the skeleton, the characteristics of size, form and calcification revealed a young adult without abnormalities. The characteristics of construction, form, proportion and process of development of the anatomical parts studied show that the principal skeleton was that of a male person of from twenty-five to thirty years and that in life the person had all of his teeth and that in the lower jaw they were well aligned and in normal occlusion." The odontologist Dr. Fermín Reygada declared, "The maxillia correspond in structure and uniformity of superficial aspect to the major group of bones and belong to one single person, thereby eliminating the possibility that the skeleton is that of a person of the feminine sex." The age range of twenty-one to twenty-five years was confirmed by Dr. A. R. Atkinson, whose opinion coincided with that of Dr. Reygada.

The dissension among the investigating groups led to the appointment of another known as *La Gran Comisión,* which included, among others, Dr. Alfonso Caso, the late Dr. Manuel F. Gamio and Dr. Jiménez Moreno. Their study resulted in two separate reports, one supporting and one denying the authenticity of the tomb. The Ministry of Education refused to accept either verdict and asked the experts to continue their research.

Ixcateopan was eventually named the final resting-place of "Falling Eagle." On December 29, 1955, following the first "civic caravan" to the site, the name of Cuauhtémoc was inscribed in letters of gold on the central wall of the Salon of Sessions of Mexico's Chamber of Deputies. Since that time pilgrimages to the Sanctuary have set out from the capital every September 26th at dawn.

The polemics between the experts flared once again in August of 1956 when a tangential investigation was launched. Professor Antonio Pompa y Pompa was asked to explore southeastern Mexico to verify his claim that the grave of the Aztec prince actually lay in this region rather than in the mountains of Guerrero. His investigation, which was centered in the zone of Laguna de Términos near the ruins of Itzamkanac in the Petén district of Guatemala, failed to produce any evidence of Cuauhtémoc's tomb.

The "barbarous death" Cortés gave Cuauhtémoc was to tarnish further the Marqués's name. The peoples of Mexico, like Moctezuma, had reason to dread the "reeds like men approaching, armed for war and mounted on deer." The new "fair god," when he came, laid claim to their land and all they possessed—and was insatiable in his demand for that gleaming remedy that alone could cure his consuming "malady of the heart."

Part Two

OTHER PRE-HISPANIC CULTURES

CHAPTER VIII

Northern Mexico: Casas Grandes-Paquimé

NORTHERN MEXICO HAS YIELDED in **Casas Grandes-Paquimé** in northwestern Chihuahua a significant discovery. Situated less than a mile from Nuevo Casas Grandes and covering an area of 103,782 acres, this complex of multiple dwellings lies so close to the Mexico-United States border that it is likely to become a major tourist objective. Both nations have collaborated in its excavation, Dr. Charles C. Di Peso representing the Amerind Foundation and Professor Eduardo Contreras the National Institute of Anthropology and History.

Paquimé's remarkable communal houses have been compared with several sites in the southwestern United States such as Casa Grande near the Gila River in Arizona, Mesa Verde in southern Colorado and Pueblo Bonito in Chaco Canyon in New Mexico. Its occupants seem to have enjoyed an advanced way of life, a superior knowledge of architectural principles and a mastery of the materials used. The construction is of such grandiose dimensions that investigators have formulated the hypothesis that this fortress-city was once the metropolis of a state. The idea has gained support as new explorations in the archaeological zone have unearthed nearly a thousand small archaeological sites with similar features. Apart from the five-story multifamily "apartment houses" which give the city its unique aspect, Paquimé has been shown to be an imposing ceremonial center. Its monuments border a great central plaza and are distributed in such a way that the ensemble presents a most harmonious and impressive effect. Within the enormous structural complex are two I-shaped ball courts with the same general plan and function as those of Xochicalco and Tula. Part of one of the courts was swept into a canyon. Obvious Toltec influences are present in the four circular platforms placed symmetrically around a central cruciform construction in the heart of the ceremonial area. Investigation proves it to be an aesthetic entity with elements hitherto unknown among ancient American cultures. A quantity of ceramics of exquisite craftsmanship and distinctive design demonstrate the high cultural level attained by the inhabitants. Metal objects, such as a copper pendant in the form of a turtle, are indicative of a link between Paquimé and Toltec northward expansion.

An outstanding feature of Paquimé's multifamily dwellings, designed both for security and comfort, was an efficient drainage system. Drainage canals composed of stone slabs run beneath buildings connected by a series of patios. Perfectly calculated levels were maintained to assure the discharge of water into a nearby river and to prevent any obstruction of the conduits. Potable water was supplied by a canal fed by a spring several miles away. In one of the patios was discovered an inside *noria,* or draw well, that once could supply water for those living within the fortress during periods when it was perilous to go beyond its walls. The entrance to the well was reached by a narrow stairway; as an additional precautionary measure, the entrance itself was camouflaged by a room approximately 49 feet below the surface. There is evidence at Paquimé to suggest that

Toltec influences have been discerned at Casas Grandes-Paquimé by the presence of four circular platforms placed around a central cruciform construction. A ball court may be seen at right.

its inhabitants constantly feared surprise attacks by hostile tribes. One of the indications of the precautions taken is the system of doorways that connected the rooms and led to stairs serving the upper stories. The low narrow openings made it necessary for anyone entering to bend almost double in order to pass through, and only one person could be admitted at a time. Access to the rooms was always from inside the patios; there were no exterior stairways. Another security measure may be seen in the relation between Paquimé and an observation tower five miles from the site. The lookout, on a hilltop called Cerro de Moctezuma, was believed to have been manned by a guard permanently stationed there to warn, by means of signals, of the approach of an enemy tribe. In the mid-sixteenth century the Spaniards found a people they called "Sumas"—a tribal name which may have been derived from or abbreviated from Moctezuma—in possession of the tower region.

The ample provisions for comfort made by Paquimé's communal dwellers is evidenced by the remains of an extensive heating system. No room in the great complex, judging from the number and varieties of clay stoves, was without its protection from the winter cold. Further warmth was furnished by wooden beds raised a few feet off the floor and equipped for easy ascent with adobe steps at one end. To accommodate the side rails of the beds, slots were cut in the adobe walls of the sleeping chambers. Although the walls of the dwellings were of clay, superior casting techniques ensured their durability. Moreover, their thickness was proportionate to their elevation. Those of the lower floors usually measured 3¾ feet, whereas 1⅔ to 2 feet were allowed for the walls of the upper stories. The finish on walls and floors is of a superior quality. The smooth hard floors give the appearance, as Professor Contreras observes, of having been made of cement. The walls are perfectly in plumb and the clay so skillfully handled that one might mistake it for the finest stucco. In some rooms the walls show as many as eight coats of paint. In others the walls seem to have been polished. Pine wood, known as *tazcata,* was used for pillars, beams and rooms. Heavy logs were transported for this purpose from distant forests.

Traces of fire and ruthless destruction indicate that this citadel of Mexico's northernmost culture probably fell to Opata invaders from the west. The Opatas, a branch of the Piman family of North American Indians, occupied a territory that straddled the present United States-Mexico boundary. A subdivision of the Uto-Aztec linguistic stock, they called themselves the "Village People." Possessing lands extending from the west boundary of Chihuahua to the Río San Miguel in Sonora, their chief centers were located along the Río Yaqui in Sonora.

Excavations have revealed an efficient system both for draining water and obtaining it, including a canal made of stone slabs and a concealed draw well (*top*). Access to the rooms was always from inside the patios (*bottom*) as a precaution against hostile tribes.

This Pre-Classic clay figure from Jalisco has been called a *magueyero*. A product of western Mexico, it may represent a step in the process of making *pulque* from the maguey, a plant which retains water and which thrives in poor, dry soil.

CHAPTER IX

Western Mexico: The Coast Peoples and the Tarascans

THE ARCHAEOLOGICAL PATTERN of western Mexico, as Dr. Herbert J. Spinden has pointed out, is largely woven by the wanderings of displaced peoples. The territory now occupied by Michoacán, Nayarit, Colima and Jalisco and, to some extent, Guanajuato, Guerrero, Sinaloa and Zacatecas, was, from early pre-Hispanic times, an axis of great movements of tribes, languages and cultural ideas. A program designed to establish the interrelationships of New World cultures has been inaugurated in Jalisco, Michoacán and Guerrero by the Institute of Andean Research. H. B. Nicholson and Jack Smith, who directed archaeological reconnaissance and test excavations, reported that results obtained to date include the demarcation of twelve phases, extending from the hunting and gathering phase of the Ajureado culture of about 11,000 years ago through the Spanish Conquest.

This vast western area was also a crossroads in a later era. During the Toltec period, while the Aztecs and other groups began moving south, probably to follow up and consolidate a commerce in gold, pearls and emeralds, a counterpart carried Nicaraguan tribes and arts northward. The origins and routes of dissemination of remarkable techniques, including "negative painting" on pottery, have been traced to the region between the river basins of the Balsas and the Lerma-Santiago. From what is now Arizona to Argentina, the native art of lacquerwork was dependent upon the supply of a native plant yielding the insoluble gum used with the *aije*, or plant mite, for affixing a surface to gourds and *ollas*. Certain cults, such as that of Xipe Tótec, god of spring and fertility, appeared in central Mexico, for instance, after a long well-documented past in the cultural complex of peoples of the Oaxaca area to the south.

According to one theory, the northward movement of tribes to the rich lands of western Mexico began possibly as far back as 5000 B.C. With the breaking up of the continental ice cap, the migration from Asia was facilitated and population increased in the Equatorial zones of America. Apparently, migrants moved north from the regions which are today Colombia, Peru and Ecuador. The Jalisco anthropologist José Corona Núñez has surmised that the displaced peoples must have traveled on large rafts, following the contours of the Pacific Coast until they succeeded in discovering adequate space in which to reestablish themselves. Probably finding the great deltas where the Lerma-Santiago and the Balsas enter the sea, they followed these rivers to higher elevations. In the rich Lerma-Santiago delta region they engaged in agriculture and pottery-making, pursuits that had long occupied the older inhabitants with whom they intermingled.

Those who followed the course of the Lerma-Santiago are believed to have inhabited what are now Nayarit, Colima and Jalisco before migrating to the highlands of the Central Plateau. Professor Corona Núñez is of the opinion that after a while the restless newcomers divided, one group branching out toward Jalisco, Colima and Michoacán to settle down at Chupícuaro. The others, pressing on to the Valley of Mexico, probably mingled with the descendants of the Tepexpán man and a primitive tribe of Olmecs, who had reached the same territory earlier by following the course of the Río Balsas through what is now Guerrero. Olmec influence existed in Guerrero over a long early period, and it is claimed that this early group became the founders of the Pre-Classic culture.

Throughout much of the region on the Pacific side of the 100th meridian bluish-gray and sea-green jadeite and other stones from the Mezcala River basin were utilized to produce highly simplified head and body forms, in the Mezcala style resembling somewhat the *hachas* of the Totonacs and used as cutting tools, as well as face panels with perforated eyes and mouths. To the north, the district between Taxco and Sultepec has yielded examples of highly stylized profiles, with exaggerated, projecting noses.

At two sites in Jalisco near Ciudad Guzmán (formerly known as Zapotlán El Grande) rock paintings in red, white and black have been found that are believed to date from a period prior to the Pre-Classic. These, together with a number of petroglyphs carved on rocky walls in Nayarit and Jalisco, are the sole evidence of human life during this earlier period thus far to appear. The carvings discovered near Huajicotl are in the form of concentric circles, which are said to represent symbols of water, air and fire.

Although fossil remains of extinct animals—mammoth, horse, bison and camel—have been unearthed on the shores of Lake Chapala and the Sayula

The Pre-Classic figure (*top left*) was found in Colima. The other (*top right*) was found in Chupícuaro. Highly simplified forms were used in the head (*bottom left*) and standing figure (*bottom right*). Such pieces were often carved from jadeite and other stones found in the Mezcala River basin.

Petroglyphs have been found in Jalisco, the provenance of this incense burner of volcanic stone.

and Zacoalco valleys, nothing has been found to date to link them with man's activity in the area. Little precise data exist concerning the period from 200 B.C. to A.D. 400 in western Mexico. But with the dawn of the Classic period and throughout the succeeding 500 years the culture of the entire western region shows the consistent development of a definitive character. Professor Corona Núñez has pointed out that stirrup-shaped handles similar to some of those found on pottery of South America may be seen on *ollas* of western Mexico, and the bottle-shaped tombs dug out of sandstone here dramatically recall those of the ancient homeland in Colombia, Peru and Ecuador. Similarly, on the mountain peaks of Nayarit, *maíz* was sown on great terraces, a system of cultivation evolved through necessity in the Andean highlands and evidently carried to western Mexico as an Equatorial-zone heritage.

In the ceramic art of Nayarit, Jalisco and particularly Colima no aspect of daily or domestic life seems to have been overlooked by the skilled potters. The small figures of yellow clay which give a vivid picture of the activities of people of the Pre-Classic period are highly valued today. Included among prize examples of figurines are a water-carrier, a pipe-smoker, a *pulque*-drinker, parents with their children, dancers, acrobats and musicians. Representations of hunchbacks and persons suffering from various deformities and ailments occur in profusion, including those afflicted with spinal curvatures, aged men with thin legs and arms, and hollow-eyed, flat-chested women. A notable example from Nayarit shows twenty women arm in arm, encircling a pair of dancers who face each other, clasping hands. In another group male and female dancers alternate in a circle around a drum player and musician or singer. A third notable piece depicts a ball game, with the spectators seated on the steps of temples at the ends of a ball court. All three examples are exhibited in the Museum of Archaeology of Western Mexico in Guadalajara.

The ceramic art of the Classic period in Nayarit features standing or seated warriors, some helmeted and wearing armor and others carrying stout clubs. Ballplayers wear broad belts and gauntlets which allow the fingers freedom for pitching the ball. Musicians are shown beating turtle shells or drums. A single crouching dog or several dogs in a semicircle are familiar themes in Nayarit's zoomorphic yellow clay pottery; human figures and dogs in circular dance formations are also represented. The Classic horizon in Colima produced remarkable zoomorphic and anthropomorphic pottery in a brilliant black clay of fine quality. Among the best known sub-

This group of joined figures, one of many examples of the potter's art which provide a glimpse of the daily life of the early peoples of western Mexico, is in the collection of the National Museum of Anthropology.

The musicians and acrobats, or performers (*above*), as well as the ball players and tiers of spectators (*left*) are in the Anáhuacalli collection bequeathed by Diego Rivera to the nation. The seated figure (*right*) is from Colima.

Included among the clay figures of Colima and Nayarit are many scenes of domesticity as well as representations of aged persons and others suffering from deformities or disease.

Vessels of red and black clay from western Mexico also show a variety of human and zoomorphic forms, among them a parrot and a pair of dancing dogs.

jects in this category are the hollow effigies of fat dogs and the celebrated dancing dogs. Other vessels realistically portray turtles, coiled snakes, parrots, armadillos and spiders.

"Nowhere, not even in China, the classic land of ceramics," the late Paul Westheim observed in *La Escultura de México Antiguo* (*The Sculpture of Ancient Mexico*), "has the creative fantasy of man invented so many vessel forms as ancient Mexico." In virtually every one of the great Middle-American cultures at their peak development, excellence of design and imaginative ornamentation characterized not only the votive bowls, with their multiplicity of painted or relief representations of gods, symbolic animals in plastic projections of metaphysical experiences and talismans against misfortune and death, but also characterized the modest utensils that bore images of man and aspects of life which reflected a remarkably close observation of the forces of nature.

An ancient Post-Classic round monument, which may have been built as a temple to Quetzalcóatl, has been uncovered in the ceremonial center at **Ixtlán** in Nayarit, recently excavated under the direction of Professor Eduardo Contreras. The structure, measuring 98 feet in diameter and 13 feet in height, has slightly sloping walls that are topped by a wall with a series of crosslike perforations. One of the four stairways leading to the top still shows a handrail marked with crosses. Two pyramidal bases, one facing north, the other south, each with central steps, stand within the court. Indications are that these bases supported small temples with porticos framed by columns.

Crosslike perforations have been found in a wall and a handrail of a structure excavated at Ixtlán, which may have been a temple dedicated to Quetzalcóatl.

One of the few peoples of central western Mexico who resisted subjugation by the powerful Aztecs of the Central Plateau were the Tarascans, who once occupied the greater part of what are now Michoacán, Colima and Jalisco, with political power centered within Michoacán. One group was known as the "lake people" and the other "the people of the Sierras," who were reputed to be the founders of the Tarascan kingdom. Each had a different dialect.

As George Kubler has pointed out in *The Art and Architecture of Ancient America,* the term "Tarascan" has been applied rather indiscriminately to practically all of the ancient products of western Mexico. "Today," he has stated, "the Tarascan civilization is believed not to antedate the tenth century." Two phases of the lake region are known archaeologically, he maintains, the earlier antedating perhaps the Toltec horizon and represented by T-shaped mounds ending in a round section. These burial platforms are known as the *yácatas* of Tzintzuntzan. He cites as products of the post-Toltec phase of Tarascan expansion Chac-Mool (reclining) figures, elaborate lapidary work in turquoise and obsidian and the lost-wax process used to cast objects in gold, silver and copper.

According to their own legends, the Tarascans also emerged from the "Seven Caves" but, instead of entering the Valley of Mexico along with their traveling companions, remained in the area around Lake Pátzcuaro. Since the Tarascan tongue is a language distinct from Nahuatl, anthropologists have generally discounted the legend of a common origin with the ancient Nahuas. A more likely explanation is that they lived for a time in Michoacán in close proximity to Nahuatl-speaking tribes of Mixtec origin.

By the time of the arrival of the Spaniards the Tarascans constituted one of the most powerful of the domains, with the court of their capital rivaling in splendor that of Moctezuma's. They ranked foremost among ancient Mexico's producers of distinctive articles of superior craftsmanship, fashioning from copper, obsidian, gold and silver, works of singular charm. Their expressive figurines were modeled from a paste extracted from the pliable substance of *maíz*-pith, and their colorful *jícaras,* or gourds, were brightly varnished. Their radiant featherwork, made possible by the multicolored plumage of their gorgeous regional birds, was unsurpassed. The lyricism that characterized Tarascan creativity was also reflected in the poetic imagery of their place names, such as Uruapan, which means "The Place Where the Trees Always Bear Fruit."

The story of an early Tarascan "strong man" known as Hireticátame, or "Corpulent King," is told in the chronicle, *Relación de Michoacán.* This leader made various conquests of those Tarascans who had settled on the shores of Lake Pátzcuaro. Following his murder, he was succeeded by his son Sicuirancha, who was absent from the area at the time of his father's death. Sicuirancha established himself in the region known today as Quiroga, and kings of this dynasty ruled for many years. The ruins of the royal palace may be seen on Lake Zirahuén.

Pavacume, a Tarascan chief, established amicable relations with the lake-dwellers and secured the unity of his realm by marrying the daughter of a Jaracuaro fisherman. From this union was born the real founder of the realm, Tariacuari, who unified many of the tribes of the territory. For some time invaders and islanders lived in harmony, but rivalry developed between Tariacuari and the sons of his uncle, and the final years of his life were filled with defeats. In his quest for power he engaged in many nefarious enterprises, including treason against his own son, Curatame. Upon his death his sons and second cousins completed the conquest of the large region around Pátzcuaro ("Smoky Place"), which was divided into three sections. His nephew Tangaxoan fell heir to Tzintzuntzan, and in a short time the rule of Ihuatzio, with its royal palace, passed to Tangaxoan's descendants.

A series of five structures, each with a round nucleus, stretching from east to west along the top of a low eminence near the pueblo of **Tzintzuntzan** ("The Place of the Hummingbirds") in Michoacán, have become a popular objective for tourist groups and students of Tarascan culture. In *Las Yácatas de Tzintzuntzan,* Dr. Nicolas León expressed the belief that the monuments were temples and, at times, places of defense or fortification. The space occupied by the mound at Tzintzuntzan, with its distinctive mode of construction, measures 466 feet in length and 95 feet in width. The artificial terraces, platforms and sloping bodies have almost disappeared, but it is possible to reconstruct Tzintzuntzan's original impressive appearance from the remaining sections of the circular-type pyramids. The *yácatas,* like the structures at nearby Ihuatzio, were made with a filling of loose flagstones without mortar and held in place by walls of stone blocks. The exterior coating of *xanamu,* rock from volcanic lava hand-cut in uniform dimensions, had, as a binding material, a mixture of clay and river pebbles. Large surface areas were carved in deep relief. On the east side of the great Tzintzuntzan mound rose a monumental stairway. A singular and attractive architectural feature of the complex is the gradual narrowing of small stairways as they run from the ground to the top of the various circular units.

In the mid-1930's President Lázaro Cárdenas, eager to shed new light on the pre-Conquest history of his native Michoacán, commissioned Dr. Alfonso Caso and Dr. Daniel Rubín de la Borbolla to select a promising Tarascan site for research. Their choice was Tzintzuntzan. After months of

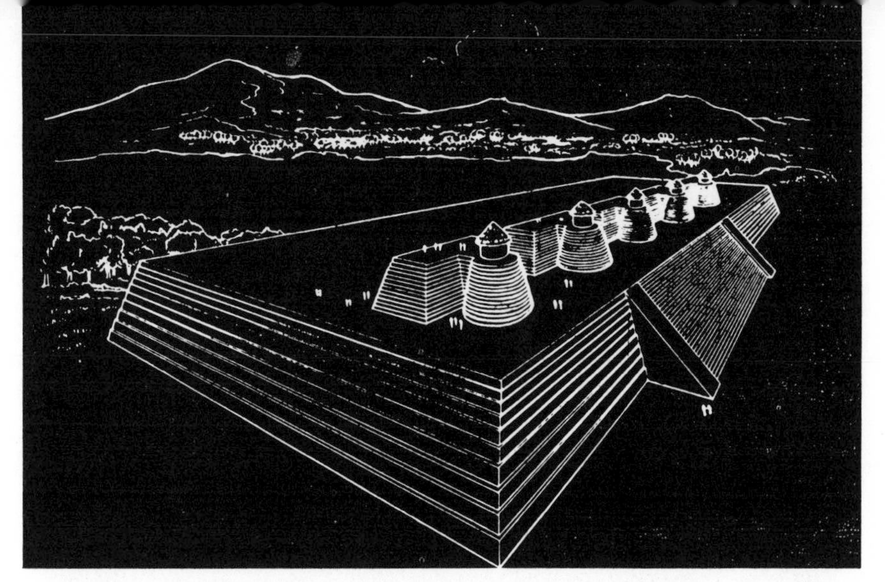

The five circular structures, or *yácatas,* which once stood on the great mound of Tzintzuntzan, are reconstructed as they appeared about A.D. 1500.

exploration they were able to verify many of the claims made as to its ancient splendor as presented in *Crónica de Michoacán* by Pablo de la Purísima Concepción Beaumont. Along with Carl Lumholtz, Dr. Caso and Dr. Rubín de la Borbolla believed that the small *yácatas* were sepulchers, since they found human bones among the debris, and that the large T-shaped *yácatas,* with arms extending 50 feet in length and 12 feet in height, were centers of religious ritual. Their efforts resulted in the discovery of the interment sites of members of the royal household. On one side of the central round pyramid they found the tombs of the "Bearer of the Golden Pincers" and the "Keeper of the King's Lip Plug." On the side reserved for the women they found the burial place of weaving women and cooks. The tomb of the kings was too deeply imbedded in the mass of dislodged rock and rubble filling for any attempt to locate it in less than the equivalent of a long-range, costly excavation project. Nor were the archaeologists able to verify the theory of Charles Hartford, a British investigator, who, in 1878, with official permission, had undertaken to cut through the massive masonry on the slope of a hill known as Caurato in the belief that a concealed doorway gave access to the center of a *yácata,* "wherein was a great room filled with fabulous royal riches," while adjoining, as the *Crónica* described it, was "a subterranean road to Ihuatzio."

Around 1480 Axayácatl, after conquering the Valley of Toluca, launched an attack against the Tarascans. But on the two occasions that they met, the Tenochas, surprisingly, suffered their most overwhelming defeats, owing not only to the relentless fighting spirit of the Tarascans but also in part to their copper weapons. Later their king Zuangua successfully resisted an invasion by Ahuitzotl, regarded as the outstanding con-

Excavation of the *yácatas* of Tzintzuntzan has revealed an inner construction of loose flagstones held in place without mortar by walls of stone blocks.

queror among the Aztec rulers of Anáhuac. They remained an independent entity until they met the common fate after refusing to unite with the Aztecs against the Spaniards.

But even Cortés, in his first expeditions, failed to conquer Michoacán. It was not until July of 1522 that Spanish forces, under the leadership of Cristóbal de Olid, entered Tajinaroa and later, after bitter fighting, Tzintzuntzan capitulated. At the time of the Conquest, Tangaxoan II, or Tangaxoan Zincicha, known as "Old Shoe," occupied the Tarascan throne. He was a weak and cruel ruler, but his cruelties were mild when compared with those of Nuño de Guzmán, who, in the spring of 1530, achieved the final subjugation of the Tarascans after torturing and executing their ruler on the banks of the Río Lerma, when he failed to produce the additional gold demanded. The Spanish conqueror of Nueva Galicia then penetrated the realm of Tonallan, in the immediate environs of the present capital of Jalisco, and continued his victorious advance to Nayarit and then to Sinaloa, founding en route the cities of Culiacan—in 1531—and Guadalajara—in 1532.

CHAPTER X

The Valley of Oaxaca: Monte Albán, Mitla, Yagul, Zaachila and Giengola

In the Valley of Oaxaca in southwestern Mexico lies the imposing site of **Monte Albán.** In this area may also be found several other ancient sites that provide eloquent testimony to the individual and combined achievements of the Zapotec and Mixtec cultures. Such sites as Mitla, Zaachila, Yagul and Giengola are now under extensive exploration by the National Institute of Anthropology and History in collaboration with the University of the Americas and other research organizations.

Like some cyclopean symbol, Monte Albán, representing the remains of five distinct epochs ranging from the eighth century B.C. to the sixteenth century A.D., dominates the sawed-off top of the "White Mountain" and the hills of Tecolote and Azompa. Six miles west of Oaxaca City, Monte Albán's more than 150 tombs, underground passages, large plazas, I-shaped ball court and truncated pyramids rising in groups form a perfectly distributed architectonic system occupying an area a mile long and a quarter of a mile wide.

The site commands a far-flung panorama that permits surveillance of all possible approaches, which suggests that it may have been originally a defensive stronghold. Four platforms enclose the enormous courtyard that crowns the highest of the hills. The southern platform affords an unbroken view of the entire complex and supports two temples facing north and south. Both are surrounded by mounds upon which are the foundations of smaller structures. All the principal edifices are placed at regular and corresponding intervals above the great platforms.

Conflicting theories are held on the antiquity and identity of the founders of Monte Albán, "Holy City of the Zapotecs," who with the Mixtecs were one of the two major linguistic groups of Oaxaca. Constantly emerging also are varying appraisals of their character. According to Ritchie Calder, author of *The World Man Created,* Monte Albán's huge ritual center "testifies through its massive structures—the runnels of whose altars are discolored by the dark stains of sacrificial blood—to the power and arrogance of the priestly cult, which left an aura of brutality around the stones themselves. The priests," he goes on, "not only tore out the hearts of their victims—the finest of youths, exercised to the acme of physical perfection—but the heart of the country as well." In his drab picture of the region he noted that the Valley of Oaxaca, "once possessing a fertility as legendary as the Garden of Eden," is today desolate, presenting a melancholy prospect of "bald hills and valleys gashed with gully erosion." As does the French archaeologist M. Paul Rivet, Calder attributes the ravaged countryside to the heedless fanaticism of the priests who, like the pyramid-builders of Egypt, used thousands of people as slaves in the construction of their temples. The Zapotec burden-bearers, he contends, not only carried massive blocks of stone up steep hillsides but were ordered to furnish, by destroying the forests, prodigious quantities of lime to build their gigantic temples. Heavy rains completed the process of devastation by washing away the unprotected topsoil, leaving a barren terrain.

Yet no pre-Columbian culture has received more lavish praise than Monte Albán in this paean by the German journalist Egon Edwin Kisch, quoted by C. W. Ceram in *Gods, Graves and Scholars:*

> Is there any other spot on earth so completely shrouded in darkness and so mute in the face of all our questions? Which feeling is paramount in us, enchantment or bewilderment? Is it the spatial complex, the outlines of which suggest a prospect of infinity? Or is it the pyramids, which look like stately stairways leading on and up into the inner reaches of heaven? Or is it the temple court which—thanks to our powers of imagination—is filled with many thousands of Indians in impetuous prayer? Or is it the observatory, with peepholes let into the masonry walls which provide a line of sight along the azimuth of the meridian? Or is it the spectacle of a stadium such as Europe has never built from ancient Roman days to the twentieth century, one hundred and twenty steeply rising tiers of stone seats?
>
> Or is it the system of arranging hundreds of tombs so that no grave disturbs its neighbor, with consequent avoidance of a cemetery effect? Could it be the gay mosaics, the frescoes with their figures, scenes, symbols, and hieroglyphs? Or the vessels of clay, sacrificial bowls of noble sweep, urns of geometric rec-

tilinearity, four-footed, and within each of the feet a little bell that tinkles for help if an intruder threatens to make off with it?

The story of Monte Albán has long offered a challenging enigma to archaeologists because of the various waves of peoples who converged upon the Valley of Oaxaca both from the north and the south. "Even today," Dr. Ignacio Bernal has commented, "we really know nothing of the beginning. So far nothing has been uncovered in the Oaxaca Valley to show the existence there of an early man, of a pre-sedentary or a pre-agricultural people." No evidence exists that mammoth-hunting man, vestiges of whom have been found in the Central Plateau, ever inhabited this region.

Lacking, at present, any trace of the earliest primitive cultures, usually dated between 20,000 and 1000 B.C., some details of the substance of Oaxaca's first advanced civilization are nevertheless gradually being accumulated. During recent years archaeological research of the periods after the seventh and eighth centuries B.C. has been greatly facilitated by the sorting and classifying of examples of ceramic art found in abundance in the region. Dr. Bernal and Dr. Caso, authorities on the Zapotec and Mixtec civilizations, have been able to fix approximate time-markers to determine the eras which preceded and followed the Classic Zapotec style in evidence at Monte Albán.

The site of Monte Albán represents the remains of five epochs, with construction ranging from the eighth century B.C. to the sixteenth century A.D.

The name *danzantes* has been given to nearly life-sized figures carved simply on large slabs. These are believed to date from the earliest period of habitation at Monte Albán.

The initial stage, characterized by megalithic architecture, has been designated as Monte Albán I. Huge boulders were used by its builders. Dr. Bernal has named the *danzante* complex as the most characteristic trait of this stage, dominant not only throughout the Valley of Oaxaca but in numerous sites in the Mixtec and Pacific areas. Manifestations are not confined to the celebrated near-life-sized figures of what have been called *danzantes,* or dancers, with outflung arms and legs, carved simply like line drawings on large slabs.

During the first two periods the social order was well advanced, judging from the facts that the people built with dressed stone, had acquired the art of bar and dot numeration, and had developed a calendrical system that was inscribed on stone monuments and by means of which a small group of priests presumably exercised a rigid control over the daily lives of the masses.

The earliest temples built upon the pyramids at Monte Albán have vertical walls instead of the sloping variety adopted in later periods. The plain rectangular tombs have flat roofs and are lined with stone. The gray pottery is highly polished and engraved with distinctive linear markings or carved with the symbols of two deities, one of which is represented by an Olmec jaguar mask. Many of the pottery vessels are shaped like men but more often are in the form of animals—ducks, rabbits, tigers, eagles, bats—suggesting the belief that the destiny of each individual was linked to that of an animal.

The late Pablo Martínez del Río maintained that the Pre-Classic, or Proto-Classic, period coincided with an ancient epoch in Mesopotamia when, during a theocratic regime, the cuneiform script was evolved. He has compared the pyramids of Mexico to the Babylonian ziggurats, temple-towers with outside stairways, which were conceived as mountains; the word "mountain," he has pointed out, was charged with religious significance.

The Monte Albán II culture can be identified at some twenty sites in the Oaxaca Valley. In Dr. Bernal's view, this knowledge and these skills were evidently acquired from a group of Chiapas highlands migrants, who brought with them many innovations—four-legged vessels, clay cylinders with an open lip for holding other vessels, pottery finished in different colors over a thin coating of stucco. While there was no fundamental changes in the writing and calendrical systems, certain refinements appeared in the art of Monte Albán II. The erect clay figures and the huge urns were of

Stone seats rise in a steep tier from an I-shaped ball court at Monte Albán. Many structures have been excavated in this vast complex, its outlines suggesting a "prospect of infinity."

finer quality than those of Monte Albán I. The old low-relief *danzantes* showed improved workmanship and apparently recorded conquests, as seen on Building J known as the Observatory. Glyphs depicted victories of Monte Albán chieftains over other peoples.

Later, about the time of the beginning of the Christian era, the Monte Albán II and Monte Albán III cultures seemed to fuse into a single type. Although there is evidence of a new influence, believed to be from Central Mexico or the Valley of Puebla, the same type of hieroglyphic inscriptions remained in use in the Monte Albán area. The impact of Teotihuacán —rapidly becoming at this period the great metropolis of Middle America— and its modes, concepts and techniques, was to crystallize all previous influences into one superior culture. At this juncture, during the first or second century B.C., emerged the culture known as Monte Albán III. Marking the dawn of the Classic period and corresponding to the era of highest development of the Maya civilization at various sites in southeastern Mexico, it is the first point at which the Zapotecs may be positively identified. Dr. Bernal has cautioned against the use of the word "Zapotec" to designate the dwellers on the "White Mountain" prior to the era known as Monte Albán III-A, the period of finest flowering. He believes that the cultural descendants of the III-A period are undoubtedly the Zapotecs encountered by the Spaniards in the sixteenth century, whose descendants form a part of the present population of the area.

The architecture of the Classic period of Monte Albán is distinguished

A wall painting depicting a procession was found in the structure known as Tomb #105. It is believed to date from the era marking the greatest splendor of the arts at Monte Albán, about A.D. 500.

by a *talud,* or sloping wall base, and a *tablero,* a perpendicular plane above it, derived directly from the architectural style of Teotihuacán. The carving is extremely stylized and, while variously interpreted, the decorative theme is always a serpent. By this stage tombs had become even more elaborate, with antechambers and niches. The inverted-V roofs, made with inclined stones, of Monte Albán II were now superseded by flat stone-slab roofs. Often they were adorned with huge frescoes covering the entire interior. The Zapotec tombs are the most elaborate burial chambers discovered to date in the Americas.

In terms of ceramics, Monte Albán III is marked chiefly by its funerary urns on which a number of gods, including female deities, are represented. Molds were employed during Monte Albán III-B and thereafter. Wall paintings and paneled frieze façades are typical of the larger tombs of the later Monte Albán III period, notably tombs #104 and #105, both dated at about A.D. 500. In this period occurred the most brilliant expansion of Zapotec architecture. Dr. Bernal believes that Monte Albán, as it may be seen today, is the result of the culture of this period. "If we bear in mind," he has pointed out, "that nine-tenths of the city is still buried, and if we remember that the colored paint has disappeared, the Monte Albán of today will give us an approximate picture of what it was, say, about the year 850 or 900."

As in Central Mexico the Classic period was marked at Monte Albán by a flowering of the arts and by the rigid administrative control exercised by the priesthood. The greatest splendor of the Golden Age was reached probably about A.D. 500, after some four centuries of masterly creation in stone and stucco, in lavish carving, in painting of decorative symbolic forms on the walls of temples and palaces and of hieroglyphic inscriptions on stelae.

The sudden collapse, about the beginning of the tenth century A.D., of the Classic culture in Teotihuacán and also in the great Maya cities had inevitable, if indirect, repercussions in Oaxaca. Although Monte Albán was not burned and sacked, as was Teotihuacán, it ceased to be a capital and political center. Little by little the grandiose buildings and temples began to crumble because there was no one to repair them. Various cities soon divided its power as a religious center, but none was strong enough to usurp its place. Before the decline set in, however, Zapotec influence extended over territories that had previously looked to the Teotihuacán culture. Through Tehuacán in Puebla the Monte Albán III-B influence had spread northward to Cholula and Huexotzingo. Mariano Fernandez de Echeverria y Veytia, a learned eighteenth-century interpreter of Pre-Columbian culture, spoke of Zapotecs who occupied towns south of the present capital of Puebla, a claim verified by Dr. Bernal, who traced Monte-Albán-III-B period ceramics to that locale. During the epoch known as Monte Albán IV, of which very little is known, the nearby sites of Zaachila and Mitla were established or enlarged.

During the period designated as "Monte Albán III," the Zapotecs built elaborate burial chambers. On their funerary urns and censers, such as those shown, various gods, including female deities, were represented.

The epoch known as Monte Albán V lasted until the Spanish Conquest. This era is today the focal point of intensive archaeological research and is noteworthy as the period of the famous cache of jewels found in Tomb #7 by Dr. Caso in the early 1930's. Many of the tombs of this later era were reused by the Mixtecs. Excavations have, as yet, revealed no evidence of new construction. The changes to be noted are chiefly those of technical and aesthetic decadence rather than of style. The ceramics are coarser, and rough stone was evidently used for building instead of the carefully carved blocks of the previous era.

Dr. Bernal would prefer to substitute the term "Mixtec period" for the phase known as "Monte Albán V," attributing the Tomb #7 jewels to the Mixtecs since, as he claims, the culture of this epoch was imported or produced locally by people who came from the northern, or Mixtec, area. Although the old Zapotec culture survived, the industrious newcomers settled down in various Zapotec sites. The famous cache yielded examples of exquisite bone carvings unsurpassed in ancient America. Vases and other vessels of translucent local onyx, or *tecalli,* of superior workmanship, objects of gold, jade, alabaster, pearl, coral, mosaic and rock crystal, are included in this priceless collection which, following a legal battle for possession between the state and federal governments, is now housed in a small regional museum in Oaxaca City. Lost-wax casting, repoussé technique, filigree plating and soldering were all practiced in the area with great skill as early as A.D. 1000, although some of these processes, notably the lost-wax process, attributed to Benvenuto Cellini (1500–1571) appeared in Europe centuries later. Of the more than 170 tombs and nearly 1,000 burials studied at Monte Albán, only a single metal object attributable to the Zapotecs was found, although many metal objects of Zapotec origin have been unearthed in other regions.

Only a little more than 18 miles southeast of Monte Albán are the gemlike, elegantly adorned palaces of **Mitla** ("Where Arrows Are to Be Found") variously attributed to the Zapotecs and the Mixtecs. Its ruins have been described as a "group of exquisite miniatures." Mosaic Grecian-style frets and diverse geometrical motifs cover the façades of the various units, symmetrically placed around an almost square courtyard. Four units —Grupo de Adobe, Grupo del Arroyo, Grupo del Norte and Grupo del Sur— have been studied thus far. Some of the buildings apparently date from as far back as the late Classic period. A fifth group is formed by a series of columns, among which rises one known as "The Column of Death." Popular superstition holds that a man may foretell how many years remain to him by leaning against it and measuring with his fingers the space between its top and his head, each finger indicating a year of life. A small mural painted on a lintel over a doorway is in the same style as the Mixtec codices.

The earliest lengthy description of the ruins, which cover an area of 1,640 feet from north to south and 948 feet from east to west, was given by the Dominican friar Francisco de Burgoa in his four-volume *Historia Geografica,* published in Mexico in 1674. The designs of the geometrical motifs, duplicated on the walls of subterranean tombs, are unsurpassed for their ornamental effectiveness, lyrical precision and subtle integration with the architecture. In *Cruciform Structures Near Mitla,* published by the American Museum of Natural History, Dr. Marshall H. Saville, for many years director of the Museum of the American Indian, Heye Foundation, commented: "The massiveness of the construction and simple and chaste ornamentation place these great Mitla tombs in a class unapproached by any other known burial chambers in ancient America. As noted by Holmes, the geometric fretwork mosaics differ from the great façades of the Yucatán buildings in subject matter rather than in kind, for the decorated surfaces there, although depicting animal forms, are mosaics in the sense that they are made up of separate hewn or carved stones set in mortar to form ornamental designs."

Clues as to the respective roles of Mitla and of Monte Albán in the development of the great Oaxaca Valley cultures have been sought since 1954 at **Yagul,** located between the two celebrated sites. Here students, working under the direction of Dr. John Paddock, excavated for seven years as part of an anthropological field-study course. In 1960 the project

The structure known as "The Hall of the Mosaics," at Mitla, is noted for its more than 150 panels of mosaic and carving, based upon key fret and spiral fret patterns.

was directed by Dr. Bernal and since then the nearby site of Cabillito Blanco has also been studied. Since the present-day village of Mitla lies above the ancient residential area, researchers have been prevented from gathering there an adequate sampling of pottery, and at Monte Albán the massive Classic-period complex of structures which were built over those of the Pre-Classic complex, has made a thorough study of the lower levels at times impractical. Thus few vestiges of the Post-Classic have been found in this area which might illumine the culture flourishing at Monte Albán immediately preceding the Spanish Conquest, in the period during which the ritual center was little more than a Mixtec burial-ground. At Yagul, however, there are houses and tombs dating from the late phase, and pottery is in relatively abundant supply. Some Yagul tombs already investigated were found to contain offerings identified by Dr. Caso as Mixtec. Others, recently opened, reveal remains of both Zapotec and Mixtec occupations, corresponding to Monte Albán periods III and V.

Current discoveries elsewhere have suggested new possibilities regarding interrelationships between the Zapotecs and Mixtecs and the building of new Mixtec cities above the older Zapotec centers in various parts of the Oaxaca Valley. Hope for unraveling the tangled web of the Oaxaca story has been fostered at **Zaachila,** or Lachizaa ("Place of the Oldest Things"), where Mixtec culture flourished about A.D. 1200. Although government archaeologists made several attempts to survey this site, the Indians of the region, jealously guarding their brilliant past, would permit no outsider to approach within exploring distance. During repeated efforts made by research parties the natives resorted to violence, using sticks and stones against intruders to prevent any examination of the vestiges of their ancient culture. However, in 1962 an expedition from the National Institute of Anthropology and History, which included a restoration technician, Jorge Angulo, was allowed to begin work. The first tomb, unearthed early in February, revealed Zapotec and Mixtec remains side by side.

The initial 1962 excavations at the old Mixtecan capital uncovered the tomb of what may have been a ruler of Zaachila. Below a flight of steps was a small room with access to an antechamber covered by two enormous slabs. In the tomb were stuccos, vases and other decorative material depicting human and animal figures, all of Mixtec origin. The sepulcher, consisting of six lateral niches, three on either side, was given the name "Ocelots," since representations of these animals dominated the wall. In the niches were objects of indisputable artistic merit, some even of marvelous quality: offerings of animal-form vases, some with jaguar, or ocelot, heads; 35 small bowls decorated with drawings of animals and plants; six polished tripod decanters; three funerary urns, one adorned with the

eye of an ocelot, another with a human foot and the third carrying at the edge of its opening a green and yellow parrot. An adjacent niche yielded a beautiful *tecalli* vase; two obsidian earplugs; a *bezote,* or lip plug, of stone believed to possess medicinal properties; three turquoise mosaic masks; a feathered rabbit carved on bone; a few *malacates,* or spindle whorls; a *huehuetl,* or vertical drum; fragments of cloth and leather and bits of red and green paint in containers.

In the opinion of Angulo, who described a figure executed in shell and turquoise in a piece 10⅘ inches square as "the most precious I have encountered," the Mixtec culture "has been sadly undervalued. Embracing characteristics that remove it from the commercial, it has been interpreted mainly as a late occupant of established ceremonial centers or as merely complementary to decadent cultures. Here, at Zaachila, the Mixtec culture is shown to be the possessor of long experience as well as of new blood that came to rejuvenate and perhaps to modify advanced cultures like the Zapotec. Zaachila demonstrates that the Mixtecs must not be given a second place or a precise dating."

At Yagul, an ancient walled fortress which lies between Monte Albán and Mitla, houses and tombs from the Post-Classic period have been excavated, and pottery is in relatively abundant supply.

Architecturally, Tomb #1 in Zaachila, built between A.D. 700 and 1050—a period corresponding to the dispersal of the Teotihuacanos and the arrival in the region of the Mixtecs—is of the Monte Albán III type, with long, planed, unbroken surfaces. But Mixtec elements are not lacking. Among these is the famed, simply designed Grecian fret, enclosed in rectangles which give it the aspect of a decorative frieze. The tonal values are unique and its balance is perfect.

Eleven burials—all of males—eight in the antechamber and three in the central hallway—were found. Angulo concluded that the tomb, which measures 19½ x 3 feet, was later reused for additional burials, as was the case in the niches. Near the interments were found clay *apaztles,* or sieves, for washing the lime out of corn before grinding it, a fine turquoise disc and a decorative figure lacking a left leg and foot. Other objects brought to light included six four-legged vessels, gold filigree beads that had once formed a necklace and a *caracol,* or snail, carved in stone, bone and jade. There was also a collection of coyote and human teeth, the latter marked by the customary dental mutilation. The upper part of each niche was adorned with modeled figures representing owls, symbols of night and darkness; two *mizquiztlis,* or corpses, face to face; and two personages bearing calendrical glyphs, 7 Flower and 9 Flower. At the rear of the entrance is a man-turtle in a ventral position holding flints in its hands. Wearing an elaborate serpent headdress, it is covered by a turtlelike shell that permits the free use of the extremities. In Tomb #11 there are three lateral niches containing human and animal bones, indicating that the latter may represent a secondary burial. The south recess contained only a well-finished copper hatchet with a wooden handle. At the back were found two human skeletons with ear and lip plugs.

This figure, wearing a serpent headdress, its torso covered by a turtle shell, was found on a rear wall of a tomb in Zaachila.

Some of the problems facing scholars who are endeavoring to reconstruct the history of southwestern Mexico include the diversity of physical, linguistic and ethnic group elements. In this territory are tropical coasts, a great valley of temperate climate and elevated sierras in which may be found occasional small valleys with a rather cold climate. Under these variable conditions live and have lived numerous indigenous groups whose differentiated characteristics and cultures cannot properly be considered as a unit. Today some fourteen languages, aside from various dialects, are spoken in Oaxaca, with the result that frequently there is lack of communication among the more isolated peoples. Recent studies affording an ethnographic as well as linguistic base have shown that the distribution of the cultures was distinct in both the prehistory and the early history of the area.

A civilization designated by Dr. John Paddock of the University of the Americas as the "Nuine" ("The Hot Lands") culture flourished, he believes, some 1,500 years ago in the Mixteca zone of Oaxaca, reaching its peak in southern Puebla and northern Oaxaca between A.D. 500 and 1000. Dr. Paddock has cited distinct styles of pottery and stonework.

Legend and documented record are subtly interwoven as warp and woof in the fabric of the Mixtec story. According to their legends, the Mixtecs, "People of the Clouds," were born from two trees growing on the banks of the Achiutla River. One of their leaders, seeking land to colonize, shot arrows at the sun, assuming the solar orb to be the owner of the land. When the reddened disc sank behind the horizon the Mixtec leader believed his arrow had reached its mark and thus declared himself to be the rightful owner. Yacuno, one of the major Mixtec capitals, later known as Tlilantongo,* was supposedly founded at the site. In tracing the three dynasties of Tlilantongo the Mixtecs represented Tamoanchan, humanity's native country, as a split tree trunk from which a man is seen emerging. The Mixtec genesis is depicted in the fourteenth-century *Codex Vindobonensis,* or *Vienna Codex,* given to Cortés by Moctezuma II. This tree, as interpreted by Mme Séjourné, is "a kind of cosmic pillar, the split from which the individual emerges shows birth to be a separation, a theft; and that unity and movement are reestablished only if the incarnate particle can rise upward again to God."

According to one version, Mitla was founded about the twelfth century by Pezeloa, a Zapotec high priest, and subsequently became the seat of his religion. A sumptuous temple was erected in honor of the principal deity, Yostaltepetl. In one of the four sections of the city was located the temple, in another the sepulcher of the high priest Huijatou, "One Who Sees All," and his ministers. A third section served as the tomb of the kings of Teotzapotlan, the Aztec name for Zaachila. The fourth, with an entrance that was always closed, gave access to a dismal cave, said to be a hundred

* Some scholars favor Tilantongo.

leagues in length, in which were thrown the bodies of sacrificial victims and of warriors killed in action. The existence of dark underground passages flanked by numerous tombs supports the theory of those historians who identify Mitla as Lyobaa, the "Place of the Dead."

In his work on Oaxaca, de Burgoa described the tombs of Mitla:

> They built, in a frame, this opulent house and pantheon, above and below. The chambers beneath the earth, that were closed, were equal in size and in artistry to those around the spacious patio. It is not known from what quarry were cut the stone pillars of such size that two men could not reach around them with their outstretched arms. Without pedestals, these cylindrical shafts, of a single piece, 15 feet in height and a foot and a half in width, so well matched and smooth that one must admire them, follow one another in order to sustain the roofs. The slabs are so perfectly matched and adjusted that without mortar or any kind of adhesive agent they appear to be continuous or to have had the joinings removed.

This city of the Mixtecs was apparently later peopled by tribes who arrived in the region about the middle of the fourteenth century from the north, after occupying sites in Veracruz and the Central Mexican Valley. Abandoning the latter area under the pressure of Aztec power, they descended from the mountains and overthrew the Zapotecs in various places in Oaxaca during the Late Classic and Post-Classic periods. During the long struggle for supremacy, Zapotec culture deteriorated, while that of Mitla, under a Toltec-influenced regime, attained a refined magnificence hitherto unknown in Middle America. Not only was a unique architectural style developed but a polychrome technique utilized in the abundant ceramic production. The art of the Mixtec goldsmith and worker in other metals demonstrated an incomparable originality and technical ingenuity. Remarkable skill and rare taste were also displayed in miniature bone carving and in feather mosaic work.

The creativity of the Mixtec artisans who fashioned rare treasures such as those found in Monte Albán's Tomb #7 was praised by Egon Erwin Kisch, quoted in *Gods, Graves and Scholars* by C. W. Ceram:

> Who would have ever imagined "savages" could polish rock-crystal with such precision technique, or assemble necklaces in twenty rows made of 854 chiseled and mathematically equal constituent parts of gold and precious stones? A brooch shows a

> knight of death that Lucas Cranach himself could not have made more apocalyptic. Garters that are like the ones worn by the Knights of the Garter. Ear-rings seemingly woven from tears and thorns. Headdresses—tiaras worthy of a pope or popes. Plaited rings to set off the fingernails. Bracelets and arm-bands with fat embossments, cloak-pins, and clasps made of jade, turquoise, pearls, amber, coral, obsidian, jaguar-teeth, bones and mussel shells. A gold mask, over the cheeks and nose of which is sculptured a trophy made of human skin. Fans fashioned from the feathers of the quetzal bird—what Byzantine empress, what Hindu maharani, what American multimillionairess ever in her whole life owned such a lovely trinket as many of these Indians keep beside them even in the grave?

The Mixtec Golden Age lasted for five centuries, and during some of this period Mixtec cities were dominated by the Aztecs. Archaeologists learned something of the later fate of Mitla by their excavations at Zaachila, long considered a possible key to discovering more about the Zapotecs and Mixtecs. The site was the capital of the Zapotec empire at the height of its influence, about A.D. 1200, embracing most of Oaxaca, northeast as far as Tehuacán in Puebla and northwest to Ometepec in Guerrero. Acknowledging its dominance were Monte Albán and cities in the Valley of Tlacolula—Mitla, Zimatlan, Etla and Huitzo. It is believed that a Mixtec invasion forced the Zapotecs out of these centers. Led by Cocijoeza, they apparently retreated to the southeast and established a new capital near the present city of Tehuantépec on the Isthmus. Their old capital, Zaachila, however, remained for them a sacred spot.

Under Cocijoeza, Zapotec and Mixtec relations showed a fraternal trend when he called upon the Mixtecs, with whom he had formed an alliance, to help fend off an attack from Ahuitzotl of Anáhuac. Ahuitzotl, determined to avenge the ambush of a group of Tenochtitlán merchants journeying south over the old trade route, marched upon Oaxaca, slaying many of its inhabitants. He conquered Mitla in 1494. The assistance that Cocijoeza received from the Mixtecs enabled him to resist the long siege of the Aztec forces by retreating to a fortress city, **Giengola,** on the side of a mountain 1,300 feet above sea level. Giengola still shows vestiges of the double walls that surrounded it, 10 feet in height and 6 feet in width. Its great plaza, 300 feet long, was reached by a flight of 300 stone steps. A complex of ruins on the edge of a cliff is believed to be the remains of Cocijoeza's palace, with its circular platforms and a rambling complex of stairways, terraces, spacious rooms, pools and gardens from which may be glimpsed Tehuantépec.

With the Mixtecs, who were eager to avenge the conquest of Mitla, Cocijoeza marched upon Tehuantépec, a member of the great Tenochtitlán federation. Following the defeat of the Aztec forces Ahuitzotl offered his daughter Pelaxila in marriage to the Zapotec monarch. Dissatisfied with the terms of the truce the wily Aztec sent the princess to learn from the Zapotec sovereign the most propitious hour in which to renew the invasion attempt. Her beauty, it was said, led Cocijoeza to believe she was a spirit; a mole on her hand convinced him she was divinely human. They fell in love and the princess revealed her father's plans to her husband. In a master stroke of diplomatic strategy Cocijoeza dispatched the Zapotec army in full battle array to meet Ahuitzotl at the border and, with every mark of courtesy and expression of good will, to escort him clear across Zapotec territory. The couple was blessed with a son, Cocijopij, who, at the time of the Conquest, ruled Tehuantépec. Although Cocijopij professed Christianity, taking the name of Juan Cortés, in baptism, he continued to worship his ancient deities and for his fidelity to the gods of his fathers was tortured and finally executed.

The history of the Mixtecs has been traced back beyond A.D. 692 largely through research undertaken more than three decades ago by Dr. Caso. One source of information of the early eras is the *Codex Nuttall*, or *Codex Zouche*, so named by its discovery in the late nineteenth century by Mrs. Zelia Nuttall in the library of Lord Zouche of Harynworth in England. Painted about 1360, this codex is regarded as a Mixtec genealogical record and has served to confirm Dr. Caso's dynastic lists of Mixtec rulers. Dr. C. A. Burland of the British Museum has placed the great Mixtec hero 8 Deer or Ocelot Claw, Lord of Tlilantongo, in the first half of the eleventh century A.D. Excavations at Tlilantongo have brought to light the oldest known types of Mixtec pottery. This codex gives details of the leader's birth, marriage, service as a junior priest and elevation to Lord of Tlilantongo. Included also is the story of his conquests in the mountains, where several chieftains surrendered to him, and his victory in what appears to have been a civil war, or attack upon Tlilantongo. "Following this event," according to Professor Burland, "the triumphant chief commenced another campaign in which the list of captured towns indicates that his path of conquest led from the mountains across the plains and finally to the Pacific. The story ends with the ceremonial death by sacrifice of 8 Deer's elder brother, 10 Movement. It does not include the death of 8 Deer himself at the age of fifty-two." The codex also confirms events recorded in the *Codex Vindobonensis*, such as the disastrous defeat suffered by the Mixtecs in 1495 at the hands of the Aztecs.

There are scant references to the Oaxaca region during the Conquest period. Aside from general works such as those of Antonio de Herrera and

Juan de Torquemada, there are few accounts of the Conquest in this area. The sixteenth-century chroniclers did not seem particularly interested in recording aspects of Oaxacan history and traditions. Neither de Alva Ixtlilxóchitl nor F. Alvarado Tezozomoc made any newsworthy contribution to the Oaxaca story. A few accounts were left by friars interested in linguistics, among them Juan de Cordova, Fray Francisco de Alvarado and Antonio de los Reyes.

In succeeding centuries, foremost among the early visitors to Mitla was Guillermo Dupaix, who explored the site in 1806. His *Antiquités Mexicanes* (*Mexican Antiquities*) was published in 1834. The German artist Eduard A. E. Muhlenpfordt, accompanied by Juan Bautista Carriedo, visited Mitla in 1830. Part of the results of their collaboration was published in 1851, and when later completed by Antonio Peñafiel, appeared in 1890 as *Monumentos del Arte Mexicano Antiguo* (*Monuments of Ancient Mexican Art*), with the Muhlenpfordt plates. Désiré Charnay and Adolphe F. Bandelier visited Mitla in the nineteenth century. Visiting Mexico for the first time in 1888, Eduard Seler published several works by the turn of the century on various aspects of ancient cultures of Oaxaca; not only descriptive, they introduced a scientific method for the study of antiquities.

CHAPTER XI

Northern and Central Veracruz: The Huastec and the Totonacs

A PROLIFIC PRODUCER of art treasures that reached distant regions of Middle America in the course of trade, the Huastec culture, centered in what are now southern San Luis Potosí and northern Veracruz, was roughly contemporary with that of the great highland cities—Tenochtitlán, Texcoco, Tula and Atzcapotzalco—and with that of Zempoala, the Totonac center. The Huastec capital was the enormous city of **Tamuín** ("Place of Bonfires"), situated in northern Veracruz near the coast. Since this populous tribe, while undoubtedly once part of the Maya, appears to have little in common with the Maya of Yucatán and Guatemala, some anthropologists have explained the difference as the result of an early splitting of the original dwellers of the Veracruz coastal region. The Totonacs occupied the area between the Huastec and the Yucatán-Guatemala territory.

Although Tamuín was brought to public attention in 1939 by Joaquin Meade, whose report on his explorations appeared that year in the record of the Congress of Americanists, it was not until 1962 that any systematic exploration of the site was undertaken. This work is currently being conducted by a French archaeological mission headed by Dr. Guy Stresser-Pean of the Musée d'Homme of Paris with the cooperation of the National Institute of Anthropology and History. Dr. Stresser-Pean began his work in the Huastec area in 1936 as an ethnologist. He later specialized in physical anthropology and linguistics, later adding archaeological research to his ethnological research. His explorations of Tamuín have revealed that the ruins of the ceremonial center near the Tamuín River and the town of Tamuín, to which he has given the name "Tantoc" ("Dark Place"), were not those of a true pyramid. Joaquin Meade believed that Tamuín's highest mound concealed a pyramid taller than the Pyramid of the Sun at

The stone head (*left*) was found in Hidalgo, the profile head of a warrior (*right*) at Tantoc, near Tamuín.

Teotihuacán and that, in type, it resembled the towering structures of Tikal in Guatemala. As in the case of Netzahualcóyotl's "Hanging Garden," a high hill had been terraced on one side, that nearest the center quadrangle, making it a natural elevation 165 feet high.

Among the objects excavated were the stone head in profile of a warrior, an exceptionally fine Totonac piece that had reached the site via commerce, and a stele showing a figure in deep relief standing in a niche. During the first two seasons, the Tantoc plaza with its mounds was excavated. One mound, 20 feet high, with a stairway facing on the plaza, marked the ceremonial center. Vestiges of walls enclosing the structures, stucco floors, sections of pebble and adobe walls and the remains of shell and other offerings were also found.

Beyond Tamuín, in the middle of the San Luis Potosí-Huastec region, rises the solitary "Consolation" pyramid. Its graded bodies and sculpture have been classified as Maya. Here also is a group of smaller pyramids with names that begin with "Tan" or "Tam." The "Tzintzin" or "Tubub" (signifying "Bird of Stone") complex occupies the hill of Tamtzan, or Tanchan, near the pueblo of San Francisco Tancuayalab, known also as Cuyalab el Viejo, "The Place of the Staff of Command."

To the north stretch the plains of Tamuín and the Tanchipa range. According to some authorities this is the center of some ancient Huastec, and possibly Maya, ruins. On this hill is a true truncated pyramid measuring 66 feet in height, 197 feet in length along its two laterals, and 66 feet in width, with a sanctuary measuring 7 by 13 feet crowning its top. In place

A monster-faced deity known as the "Diving God" is represented in this Huastec stone sculpture from Tuxpan, Veracruz.

of the usual stairway are two ramps, broken by an esplanade. At a distance of 82 feet are three altars, placed in an east-west direction. The floors are coated with red and yellow stucco, and the cornices are covered with stucco. The pyramid-temples, known as *cues* (derived from the Maya *ku* meaning "sanctuary"), are obviously associated with the worship of Kukulcán. Some, as H. E. D. Pollock pointed out in his study of circular structures in Middle America, in which he quoted Eduard Seler, are steep cones with a circular base and truncated top, and others are low pyramids with a quadratic base.

The Huastec are noted for their life-size dual representations in stone of gods such as the "diving god" or priests, often showing both aspects of life and death. An outstanding work which never fails to elicit admiration is a representation of the young Quetzalcóatl as the evening star, bearing on his back his son, personifying the sunset, into the Kingdom of the Dead. Although the monumental stone sculpture is well known, few are acquainted with the so-called Huastec "minor arts," which include a wide variety of exquisite jewelry and other objects of personal adornment, among them breastplates, earrings and pendants fashioned from shell and mother-of-pearl. The shell of the sea snail, which could be found in virtually inexhaustible supply along the shores of the Gulf of Mexico, not only provided artisans with a unique material for shellwork but also suggested patterns for their carvings. Many of their designs were based on mythological scenes, described by Professor Salvador Toscano, in his *Arte Precolombino*

While noted for their monumental stone sculpture, Huastec artisans also worked in shell and mother-of-pearl, fashioning a variety of breastplates, pendants and jewelry.

de México y de la America Central (*Pre-Columbian Art of Mexico and Central Mexico*) as "codices in shell." Two deities, Mixcóatl and Tlazoltéotl, may be shown standing on a base of entwined serpents and a Quetzalcóatl figure frequently appears in various pieces wearing a pectoral in the form of the shell of a sea snail and earrings made of a spiral shell.

South of the Huastec area lay the territory of the Totonacs. In the northern section was the noted city of the Zempoalans. From Jalapa's lofty eminence on Cerro Macuiltepac, with its vast panoramas of far-off *tierra caliente* jungles and Orizaba's eternally snow-capped summit, the road to **Zempoala,** known also as Cempoalla and Cempoallan ("Twenty Waters"), slopes gradually down for a 48-mile stretch to the Gulf Coast. Passing Tamarindo, with its profusion of semi-tropical flowers, one sees suddenly stark pyramids and platforms, in striking contrast to the radiant luxuriance of the approach.

Zempoala's archaeological zone occupies a rectangular area of three square miles in the *hacienda* of Agostadero between the Actopan and the San Carlos Chachalacas rivers. With changes taking place in the course of the San Carlos Chachalacas, sections of the ancient city have been isolated and modern streets have invaded the ceremonial center. Originally the city was divided into ten precincts, or enclosures, each containing religious edifices dedicated to administrative or military uses. Thick walls, covered with stucco, separated the various units, which were surrounded by dwellings built upon platforms or embankments. Water was supplied by subterranean pipes, and adjacent farmlands were irrigated by canals.

The precinct of Zempoala's Templo Mayor is occupied by the Great Temple on the north and the Pyramid of the Sun on the east. The latter is also known as Las Chimeneas because of a series of semicircular pillars suggesting a row of chimneys on a rooftop. Its foundation measures 78 feet at the front and 72 feet at the sides. Originally the pyramid was composed of seven slightly inclined bodies, the lower one covered in order to build the lateral platforms. The stairway, 30 feet wide, has nearly vertical balustrades. The columns were formerly adorned by bas-relief stucco designs representing a lizard.

In the adjoining precinct is a building called Las Caritas because of the many small clay heads adorning its walls. Its stairway is flanked by broad balustrades and, like the Great Temple, it faces east. The first of its two superimposed platforms measures 66 feet across, 48 feet at the sides and nearly 10 feet in height. A niche opens at the rear of the structure. In another precinct is an edifice known as that of El Dios del Aire, or "The God of the Air," which is one of the few extant circular temples associated with the cult of Quetzalcóatl as god of the wind. A large unexplored area,

Las Anonas, with vestiges of numerous walls, platforms and pyramids, stretches beyond the Quetzalcóatl temple.

The first archaeological research at Zempoala was undertaken by the Scientific Exploring Commission in 1891–1892 after identification of the site by means of a description of the route taken by the Conquistadores on their march to the Valley of Mexico. Jésus Galindo y Villa, a member of the commission, published a monograph containing a general plan and the dimensions of the remaining monuments. A decade later, Jesse Walter Fewkes, an archaeologist of the Smithsonian Institution, made a study of the ruins, publishing his findings in the Smithsonian annals. Since 1939, explorations have been carried out under García Payón's supervision.

Conquered in 1461 by the Confederation of the Valley of Mexico during the respective reigns of Moctezuma Ilhuicamina over the Aztecs and Netzahualcóyotl over the Texcocans, Zempoala appears to have been subject to Texcoco. That this Totonac territory was for some time outside Aztec jurisdiction seemed evident to Dr. Eulalia Guzmán, who pointed out in her study of Cortés that López de Gómara placed the Huitzilapan, or La Antigua, River three leagues north of the lands of Moctezuma. Francisco Antonio Lorenzana referred to Zempoala as being two leagues from Antigua —formerly Huitzilapan—which was the second site founded by Cortés. Juan Bautista Pomar and de Alva Ixtlilxóchitl repeatedly affirmed that the seigniories of the coast, from the Pánuco River to the boundaries of Chalchiuhcueyecan, were subject to Texcoco.

A reconstructed view of Las Chimineas at Zempoala, so named for its chimney-like formations, was drawn by José M. Velasco in 1891.

The Spaniards were impressed by the city. The first descriptions written by Bernal Díaz, Cortés and Las Casas, later synthesized by Torquemada, give the following picture:

> When the Spaniards entered Zempoala and saw such a splendid city—so new and attractive—with houses made of adobe and others of lime and *cantera* [a local stone], the streets filled with people who came out to see them, they corroborated the choice of the name, *Nueva España,* that Grijalva had given to the land. Zempoala at that time had a very large population with great buildings, finished with fine wood construction, and each house had its own orchard and irrigation system. Altogether, this garden place seemed like a delightful paradise, not only because it was so verdant and cool, but laden with fruit as well. A market was held every day of all the salable products, to which the many persons present did justice. . . . The Spaniards saw that the Zempoalans lived under a well-organized political order and that all held their Lord Ruler in high veneration. Our men admired them because of these things and because, unlike other Indians of the islands, the Zempoalans did not go around nude.

Cortés, in a letter to Charles V, stated that he left Zempoala for Tenochtitlán, accompanied by the principal chieftains and an army of warriors and *tamemes,* or baggage-bearers. López de Gómara stated that Cortés left Zempoala on August 16, 1519, with some 1,300 Zempoalans. According to Bernal Díaz, who noted that Cortés carried with him 40 chieftains, it was at Zempoala that the decision was made to go through Tlaxcalan territory.

In April and May of 1520 Zempoala figured in the rivalry between Cortés and Pánfilo de Narváez, which interrupted Cortés's first sojourn in Tenochtitlán. According to one version, members of a delegation sent by Cortés to Charles V disobeyed their leader's express orders by landing at Cuba, apparently because Francisco de Montejo wished to visit property he owned there. At any rate, in Cuba the emissaries freely discussed their exploits and the marvels they had encountered. This news soon reached the ears of Governor Velásquez, who, taking advantage of his friendship with Juan Rodríguez de Fonseca, then in charge of the *Consejo de Indias* (The Council of the Indies), an important governmental body in Spain, obtained authorization to wrest command from Cortés and take him prisoner. Organizing a force of 19 ships, 1,400 soldiers, 20 cannons, 80 horses, 70 infantrymen and 90 crossbowmen, Velásquez placed them under the command of Pánfilo de Narváez. On March 2, 1520, the expedition left Guaniguanico and in the following month disembarked and encamped at Zempoala.

After some fruitless negotiations with him, Cortés ordered the Chinantecs, neighbors of the Zapotecs, who were famous for their long lances, to make 250 pikes with copper points with which to face Narváez's cavalrymen. He then set out with 70 men for Zempoala, enlarging his force with groups he met along the road. At Cholula he was joined by Juan Velásquez de León with 120 men and, upon reaching the coast, by a contingent of 76 foot soldiers commanded by Gonzalo de Sandoval.

Encamped on the banks of the San Carlos Chachalacas, Cortés renewed negotiations with Narváez, but since each demanded complete submission of the other, no compromise resulted. Deciding to attack, Cortés ordered Velásquez de León to go to his rival's quarters with some soldiers who happened to have friends and relatives among the Narváez forces on the pretext of visiting with them. Cortés's real purpose, however, was to distract the enemy's attention while preparing an attack, which began during a heavy rain. Pizarro, Sandoval and Velásquez de León were chosen as captains of three groups of 70 men each, while Cortés reserved for himself the remaining force of 20 picked men. Sandoval was ordered to attack the Great Temple, which Narváez had transformed into a fortress, with part of his artillery at its base. A cannon had been mounted atop the structure.

The leader of the "punitive expedition" did not expect that Cortés, with his inferior equipment, would dare attack. When he learned through the Zempoalan chieftain Chicomactl that Cortés was approaching, he commanded that "every hand be raised against the enemy in a war of blood and fire." He then went forth to meet Cortés but, because of the heavy downpour, decided to return to his camp, leaving two sentinels at listening posts where the enemy was expected. Disregarding the storm, Cortés moved cautiously toward the pyramid and seized one of the sentinels. The other escaped and cried out in alarm, but his voice was drowned out by the thunder. Too late, Narváez saw the followers of Cortés ascending his pyramid stronghold.

Some historians have challenged the account by Bernal Díaz concerning the arrival of Narváez, pointing out many discrepancies in his narrative. They have called attention to reports of bribery and treason in which even the friars participated and have concluded that there was neither an actual nor a simulated battle. Dr. Eulalia Guzmán has maintained that the *Lienzo de Tlaxcala* confirms the reports of intrigue and bribery and of the circulation of gold ingots by Cortés in the enemy's camp via Fray Olmedo. López de Gómara contrasted the inept actions of Narváez with those of Cortés. In the commotion, he asserted, a pike thrust cost Narváez an eye. Narváez's men were apparently able to fire only one gun, the touchholes of which had been plugged with wax to keep out the heavy rain. This, according to López de Gómara, provided a basis for a claim of subornation of the gunner and others. According to the *Lienzo de Tlaxcala,* Cortés apprehended Narváez when the "avenger of Velásquez" was unarmed, and furthermore the capture was effected not at Zempoala but at Huitzilapan, where, pretending to tender offers of peace, Cortés went to salute Narváez.

The Totonacs of the Gulf Coast were identified by name for the first time in the annals of New Spain when a delegation of five Zempoalans came to inspect Cortés's entourage. According to Bernal Díaz, the embassy from Zempoala was delayed in reaching San Juan Ulloa through fear of the Aztecs. He referred to certain Aztec tax collectors who were first imprisoned at Cortés's suggestion but later secretly set free by Cortés. The Aztecs were transported four leagues by boat in order to place them beyond Zempoala and beyond the reach of the Totonacs. Although evidently it had been under Texcocan domination Bernal Díaz said the city had recently been conquered by the Aztecs. In any case, the incident suggests political differences and nominal Aztec control over both areas. Cortés later sent four Totonacs on the first treasure ship to reach Seville from Mexico. The treasure included bells, jewels, feather ornaments and "books such as the Indians use."

According to Torquemada, who headed the Franciscan mission at Zacatlán in the Sierra de Puebla in 1600, the Totonacs, whose name signifies "People Who Came from Where the Sun Rises," emerged from the famous "Seven Caves" in company with the Xalpaneca, leaving the Chichimecs within the cavern. The Totonacs claimed to have remained at Teotihuacán long enough to construct the Pyramids of the Sun and Moon, continuing thereafter to Atenamitic, said to be the site of the historic Zacatlán.

Very little trace of the early Totonacs remains today. Some of their clay figurines and stone carvings have survived, and native and Spanish chroniclers left various accounts of their culture. Las Casas commented on the equable Totonac temperament, relying on the report of an eyewitness who lived among the Totonacs in the years immediately following the Conquest. "In all that time," the friar wrote, "he never saw an ugly or unjust thing which they did to one another, nor offense nor wrangle, nor affront of words nor deeds, but that all lived in great peace, calmness and concordance, humble and amiable with one another, taking care in nothing but to keep their laws and to occupy themselves in the arts and practice of their religion."

While the indigenous peoples of ancient Mexico have been described as *la raza triste* (the sad race), a characterization that might apply to those Indian communities where centuries of exploitation and impoverishment have left their melancholy imprint, nowhere is such a generalization more strikingly refuted than in the singular art form native to the Central Veracruz region, Remojadas in particular. That sadness was not an inevitable quality of the pre-Columbian inhabitants of Middle America is also demonstrated in the youth-songs of the *tlamatini,* or "Followers of Truth," the disciples of the humanistic philosophy of Netzahualcóyotl, the poet-king of Texcoco. The art of sculpture has perhaps found no happier expression in Middle America than the small clay heads known as the "little smiling faces." Modeled, for the most part, with exquisite delicacy, these form a complete registry of the human capacity for gladness—embracing amusement, humor, mirth, pleasure and unutterable bliss. According to Alfonso Medellín Zenil, director of the Jalapa Archaeological Museum, the appealing small heads of Remojadas represent deities of music, dance and happiness. Whether or not such deities found a place in the Totonac pantheon, these figurines undeniably possess an individuality that endows them with a quality of sheer delight not to be found elsewhere in pre-Columbian or other ancient art. Like a rainbow the radiant trajectory touches every degree of joyous expression, from explosive jocundity to indescribable rapture. The consummate artistry of the Remojadas sculptors

The sculptors of Remojadas were adept in capturing in the clay heads known as "the little smiling faces" (*left*) the human capacity for happiness. A finely modeled clay head from Veracruz is shown (*right*).

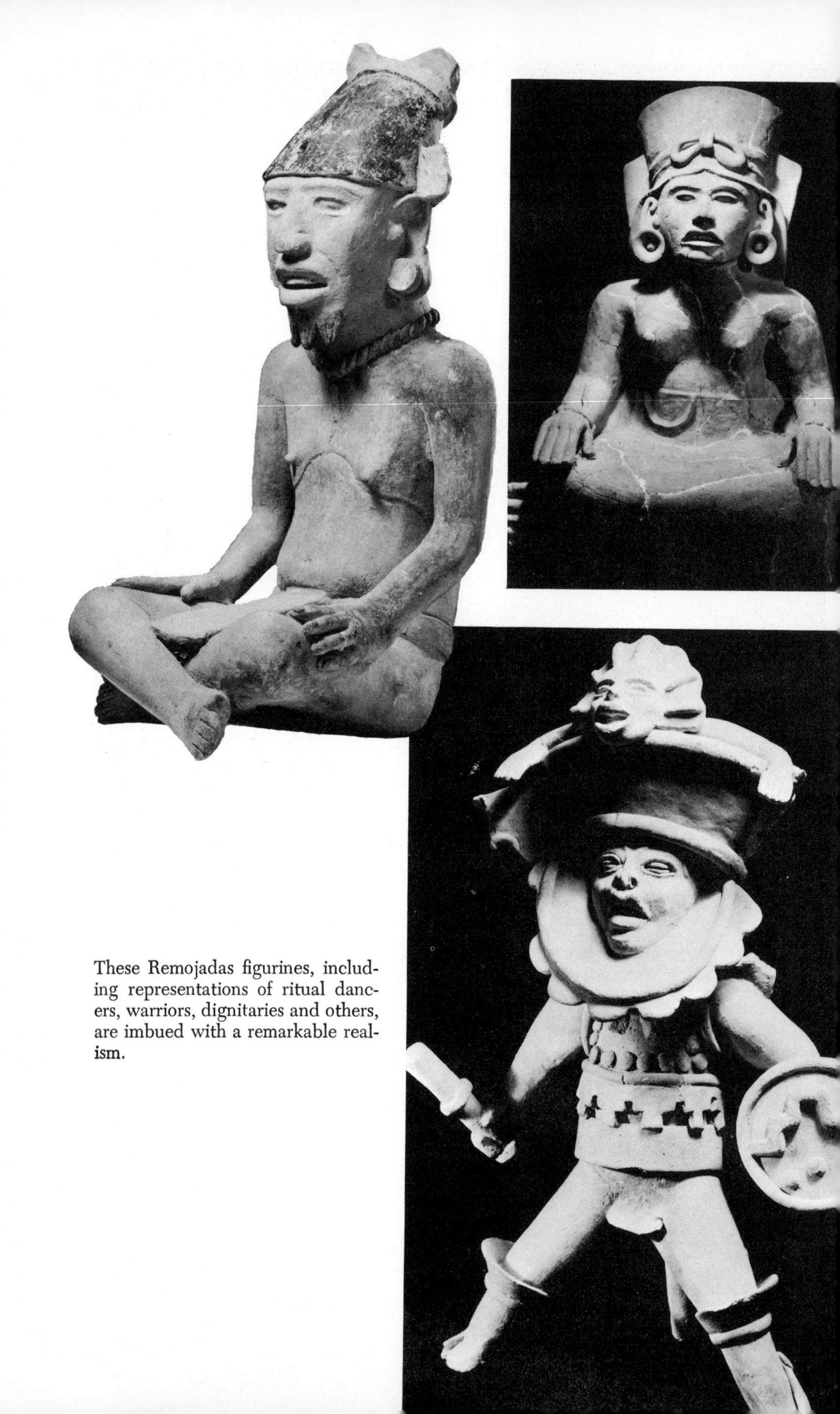

These Remojadas figurines, including representations of ritual dancers, warriors, dignitaries and others, are imbued with a remarkable realism.

captured even the tremulous suggestion of a quivering lip or eyelid. In their life masks they mobilized all the endearing character lines of the human countenance, all the creases impressed by the passing years. The result is a flawless projection of man's inner response to beauty, charm and goodness.

In explaining the phenomenon of the cheerful heads, Sr. Medellín Zenil has commented that, in Remojadas, generations of sensitive people, lovers of their traditional art, existed peacefully and tranquilly before the crushing avalanche of conquest. They honored deities similar to those of the tribes that surrounded them, deities often terrible in their power to destroy or exact vengeance. The proximity of these influences indicates that spiritually, at least, the people of Remojadas were not isolated. Yet, despite the fact that on all sides they were exposed to an art of mysticism, taking an abstract or metaphysically symbolic form often with animals deified, the sculptors retained their profound and exclusive concern with humanity and continued to produce objects imbued with a remarkable realism.

The art of Remojadas is, however, only a single aspect of the multifaceted aesthetic expression of Central Veracruz, an area known in the sixteenth century as Totonacapan, embracing a large strip along the Gulf Coast from a little north of the Cazones to nearly the Río de la Antigua on the south. The important culture zone penetrated as far west as Tulancingo in Hidalgo. According to the native legends of Tlacolulan, near Jalapa, the original Totonacs emerged from the sea. As they increased in numbers they founded thirteen settlements "within a range of six leagues." The legends referred to a first settlement "four leagues beyond Zacatlán." Juan de Torquemada marveled at the reports that ten generations of chieftains ruled for eighty years but said the reports were authentic. During the reign of the second leader the Chichimecs arrived in the land hungry and poor. They were fed and treated with great kindness by the Totonacs, and amicable relations between the two peoples were maintained for many decades. But upon the death of the eighth chieftain his two sons ruled jointly and strife developed. The Chichimecs, taking advantage of internal dissension, then seized control and occupied a dominant position until the arrival of the ambassadors of Moctezuma I in southern Totonacapan. Various campaigns by the Aztecs continued until the northern section yielded to Moctezuma II.

Leading authorities on Mexico's remote past agree that the Classic Veracruz center **El Tajín,** near Papantla and some 11½ miles south of the Poza Rica oil center, played a vital role in Middle-American civilization. In the opinion of Dr. Caso, the origins of El Tajín may be traced to the Olmec-La Venta orbit, which he has hailed as the progenitor of the Maya, Teotihuacan, Zapotec and other major native cultures. In the opinion of the German archaeologist Walter Krickeberg, whose work, *Los Totonaca,* was published in 1933 before the Olmec-La Venta area had been excavated, the Maya culture, rather than that of the Olmec-La Venta, was the true cultural substratum along the Gulf Coast. Dr. Jiménez Moreno maintains that the La Venta culture underlies both Teotihuacán and El Tajín, or that Tajín culture, derived from La Venta, was an influence at Teotihuacán; but he points out that there is no proof that the builders of El Tajín were related linguistically to the modern Totonacs, who were, perhaps, rather recent intruders. José García Payón, in charge of excavations at El Tajín during the 1950's, believes a definite connection exists between El Tajín and Teotihuacán and suggests that El Tajín artisans were present during the building of Teotihuacán, either as a dominant group or as a slave element.

The main site of El Tajín was abandoned about A.D. 1200, probably because of wars and destruction by fire. As Isabel Kelly and Angel Palerm pointed out in their study, *The Tajín Totonac,* published by the Smithsonian Institution, Institute of Social Anthropology, in 1952, the arrival of the supposedly Otomi and Teo-Chichimec invaders accords surprisingly well with the probable dates of 1180–1230 for the destruction of ancient El Tajín.

Near El Tajín was the Tula-affiliated center of Teayo, once believed to be an Aztec site but now shown to have had an earlier Toltec influence. In the years following the collapse of Tula and the end of Toltec supremacy there, mass migrations were common; in many cases the newcomers dislodged the original inhabitants of a community or imposed their own cultural patterns.

El Tajín, situated in a narrow valley, spreads over the summits and slopes of several hills, enclosing it on three sides. The main structures of the ceremonial center of the ruined city cover about 150 acres. More than a hundred earth-covered mounds in the archaeological zone still await exploration. The name, signifying "The Place of Much Smoke, Incense, Thunder and Lightning," was given by the Totonacs to the region because of the bolts of lightning which frequently struck its Pyramid of the Niches.

The 365 niches of the Pyramid of the Niches at El Tajín have been variously interpreted as ornamental devices, as symbols of the 365 days of the solar year, or as receptacles for urns or sculpture. The stairway, its balustrade adorned with stone meanders, appears to have been an afterthought.

This extraordinary structure and others remained hidden for centuries in a dense tropical jungle until parts of it were cleared for vanilla plantations. First publicized in the *Gazeta de México,* El Tajín and El Tajín Chico remained in an abandoned state until 1934 when excavations were begun under government supervision.

Persistent research has established a few facts concerning the later history of the culture that produced its splendor. The earliest construction period, attributed by Covarrubias to the "Olmecs proper," designated as the Paleo-Olmecs, has been fixed within the fifth and sixth centuries; the second, during which the Pyramid of the Niches was built, falls between the sixth and seventh centuries; the third extended from the seventh to the twelfth century. In the twelfth century, or possibly in the early decades of the thirteenth, the architecture of El Tajín underwent marked stylistic changes. In this period the characteristic niches, which are to be found only here and at nearby Yohualichan and Cuetzalan, and friezes decorated with intricate fretwork were superseded by Toltec-influenced bas-reliefs and plane surfaces.

The 365 niches of the pyramid, doubtlessly representing the number of days in the solar year, have been the subject of controversy. Some authorities claim that their function was to hold funerary urns or sculpture; García Payón maintains that the niches, with red centers framed in turquoise blue and constituting the structure's chief ornamental feature, were never intended to contain objects of any kind. Their significance, he believes, is purely mystical. The interplay of light and darkness may suggest life and death. In any event, the effect created by an architectural device based on chiaroscuro achieves a striking contrast between luminosity and shadow.

The ceremonial center forming the nucleus of the ruined city is divided into two sections. One, known as El Tajín, lies between two creeks; the other, El Tajín Chico (Little Tajín), rests upon an elevation that, as in the case of Monte Albán in Oaxaca, was leveled off to form a broad terrace. Radiating from the Plaza del Arroyo, the heart of El Tajín proper, are shrub-covered mounds. Beyond these, on the four sides of the Plaza, are important temples.

On the west is the famous Pyramid of the Niches. Including the base of the crowning sanctuary, this unique monument is more than 44 feet high and rises on a square base measuring 108 feet on each side. All of its six stories are of the same elevation, approximately 9 feet. Each covers a smaller area than the level beneath in order to leave a parapet on which one could walk around the entire structure. Probably the most original use of stairways in pre-Columbian art may be seen in this building. Independent of the pyramid itself, the function of the stairway seems to be more that of a ladder casually placed against a wall. While decorative, it was apparently conceived as a "necessary evil," an afterthought rather than a part of the overall architectural plan. The cornices, niches and other ornamental elements lie behind the stairway, and some of the niches are built into it. The balustrade is adorned with stone meanders and occasionally with a motif suggesting a human vertebrae.

On the south of the Plaza del Arroyo and facing north is Structure II; to the north and east are Structures III and IV, both in the process of excavation. Behind Structure III is another great plaza, with a ball court at its center. At the same distance from the Pyramid of Niches, although separated by mounds, is another ball court, its end walls profusely decorated with low-relief panels, on one of which is depicted a real or symbolic human sacrifice.

The elaborately carved sections of huge cylindrical columns (*top*) recall, in their ruined state, the remains of the fallen columns of the Temple of Zeus at Olympia. The relief (*right*) on the wall of a ball court at El Tajín depicts a ritual sacrifice or an agricultural symbol.

A number of structures and platforms, most of them still unidentified, make up the extensive architectural complex of El Tajín Chico. The largest building of this section, known as the Edificio de las Columnas (Building of the Columns), is outstanding not only because of its superior dimensions (with its annexes, its surface area encompasses 39,984 square yards) but also because of its daring design and decoration. The central unit, rectangular in plan and containing several chambers around an open hall, crowns the summit of the artificial mound and commands a superb view of the whole archaeological zone. The structure rises 150 feet above the plaza. On the west, platforms support a construction which awaits excavation. The southern annex is also known as "The Building of the Tunnels" because of two ascending passageways that lead to a shrine above.

Enormous blocks of concrete originally supporting the roof of the portico on the terrace still lie on the platform. In their fallen state the huge elaborately carved, cylindrical sections recall a similar spectacle of crumbling grandeur: the remains of the fallen columns of the Phidian Temple of Zeus at Olympia, toppled by an earthquake in the sixth century A.D. There are other suggestions of ancient Hellas in this tropical New World city, now in a state of ruin owing to the methods of its builders and to the exuberant vegetation and heavy rains.

The stepped meander and the interlaced design of the Greek-type fret, either as a large isolated motif or as a frieze within a border as at Mitla, are dominant decorative features at El Tajín Chico. Entire façades of the central complex are covered with carved symbols in the form of a Greek cross, with the ends of the arms bent, giving rise to the popular designation, "Hall of the Swastikas."

The low-relief sculpture of a remarkable delicacy adorning many of the buildings is regarded as among the finest expressions of ancient Ameri-

The façades of the central complex at El Tajín Chico are covered with swastika-like symbols.

can art. But during El Tajín's third, or decadent, period the delicacy of the figure-carving was lost and the reliefs show rounded instead of angular edges. Profile carving in high and low relief, with both sides of the stone utilized for double imagery, attained a state of perfection at El Tajín unknown to the ancient Egyptians. The so-called "hatchet" and "palmate" stones, found in abundance in this region and in far-flung areas as trade items, constitute other characteristic Veracruz art forms in a different vein from the smiling heads of Remojadas. Faces of the dead are depicted on some of the "hatchets," and many designs represent deities symbolized as animals. Another distinctive form is the so-called stone "yoke," first believed to have been used around the neck of sacrificial victims. Examples of sculpture have been found in which ball players are shown wearing these "yokes" as ritual girdles with palmate stones tucked into them. A controversy developed during the 35th International Congress of Americanists over the use and significance of these highly carved horseshoe-shaped stones. The Mexican archaeologist Antonio Castro Leal was of the opinion that the "yokes" were fashioned to guard and support the heads of the dead. Dr. Rafael Girard of Guatemala has pointed out that the form is a ritualistic symbol which occurs in the design of altars not only in the Central Veracruz region but in the Quiché-Maya area of Guatemala and in other areas, including the Pre-Classic sites of Copilco and Cuicuilco.

Typical Classic Veracruz stone carvings include stone yokes and hachas, or hatchet stones, such as the profile head (*left*) and stylized heron (*right*).

CHAPTER XII

Southern Veracruz: The Olmec-La Venta

THE ORIGINS OF THE Olmec-La Venta culture remain one of the most baffling enigmas of Mexican archaeology, since the Southern Veracruz region, where its major vestiges are to be found, was occupied at various times by different peoples. *Olmec,* from *olli,* or "rubber," means "People of the Rubber Country;" thus any of the racial groups who inhabited this area, famous even in pre-Columbian days for its production of rubber, could be designated by this title. A controversy arose over the assignation of a date in remote antiquity by the late Miguel Covarrubias to the monolithic Olmec heads and sculpture of **La Venta** and **Tres Zapotes.** Archaeologists now agree that the works are between 2,000 and 3,000 years old, and Carbon-14 tests, as recorded by Philip Drucker of the Smithsonian Institution, in his *Ceramic Stratigraphy of La Venta,* support the view that this culture flourished between 800 and 500 B.C.

La Venta man was restricted to a relatively small domain. While the ancient Maya culture embraced a large territory, encompassing parts of what are now Yucatán, Campeche, Tabasco and Veracruz, as well extending into San Salvador, Honduras, Belize and Guatemala, the archaeological record indicates that the mysterious people of La Venta dominated only a narrow triangular strip extending through the Isthmus southward to Salina Cruz on the Pacific Coast, a distance of about 140 miles, thence northward to a point in the hills beyond Santiago Tuxtla, the present Tres Zapotes.

Marshland and tangled mangrove roots envelop the isolated site of this forgotten civilization, centered on a small island in the Tonalá River, which marks the boundaries of Veracruz and Tabasco. For many years all that remained of the ancient culture among the giant ferns in the silent, deserted jungle were some monolithic heads of black basalt and some stone altars sculptured in deep relief. Except for one head, which had evidently been discovered in 1858 and taken to Tres Zapotes, the huge stones were still imbedded where they were found in the 1930's and "rediscovered" in 1940–1941 by oil prospectors. Excavations at the site were begun in 1942 by Dr. Matthew W. Stirling, Philip Drucker and Waldo Wedel of the Smithsonian Institution. Dr. Stirling also examined the Tres Zapotes head. The huge stone blocks from which these heads had been fashioned had apparently been transported over mountains and through marshes from a quarry more than 60 miles away. The heads, several altars and stelae were transported on petroleum barges to the La Venta Museum Park in Villahermosa. One head is now owned by the Hermitage in Leningrad. Another is on exhibition at the National Museum of Anthropology in Mexico City. A 9-foot 16-ton basalt head which for centuries had lain half-buried in a 10-foot hole at San Lorenzo Tenochtitlán, about 40 miles from Minatilán, has been loaned by the University of Veracruz to various international exhibits. An Atlantean figure has reportedly been found also at this site.

The heads and bas-relief figures show a distinctly rounded cranial formation, broad forehead and regular features, with a small nose and full, well-modeled lips. The eyes of one of the heads are carved in such a way that they look inward like those of a person absorbed in meditation. The close-fitting helmets, which may have been worn by players in an ancient ball game, resemble the protective headgear worn by modern football players, while suggesting also the traditional head covering worn by Buddha figures, although without the classic bead circlet. They differ from the wooden helmet or warrior's cap of puma or jaguar skin used by the Maya, who appeared later in the area. There is no trace of the skull deformation commonly practiced by the broad-headed Maya, who deliberately changed the shape of infants' heads in order to produce, in maturity, a receding forehead that formed a straight line with the nose. Such deformation was probably practiced by the Maya in order to differentiate themselves from neighboring tribes.

One cannot help but be impressed by the similarity of the sculpture and bas-reliefs of the La Venta zone and those of famous shrines of Ceylon and the rock-carvings in the Ajanta caves of India. Perhaps the most striking ancient American resemblance to a traditional Buddhist figure appears in deep relief on the horizontal façade of what may have been a large altar stone. The carved figure, variously described as a deity, priest or king, is seated in the familiar posture of Lord Gautama Buddha, as the "Light of Asia" is shown in innumerable images throughout the Buddhist sphere. The facial expression, the cast of features and the attitude of detachment subtly combine to present a unique type that bears little similarity

A 20-ton altar with a Buddha-like figure carved in deep relief in a niche (*top*) was brought from La Venta to Villahermosa. The Olmec stone head (*bottom*) has slanting eyes and a down-turned "jaguar" mouth.

Shown (*top*) is one of the monolithic heads of La Venta, with broad forehead and full lips, which was later transported by barge to Villahermosa. The 27-ton stele (*bottom*) at Villahermosa shows in relief a warrior with a high headdress, carrying a weapon or implement.

to that of any other race of ancient America. Citing such analogies, Dr. Paul Kirchhoff presented various arguments during the International Congress of Americanists in 1962 in his claim that an early contact existed between India and the peoples of Middle America.

The theory that the Olmec culture was ancestral to that of the Maya gains support from dated stelae and altars showing human figures emerging from a niche. This device was commonly used by the Maya. An altar nicknamed "The Quintuplets" includes five childlike caryatids. Olmec artisans also carved a number of small figurines with a combination of jaguar- and baby-faced features. Some baby-faced figures with slit eyes and snarling mouths were found at Los Bocas in Puebla as well as at Tlatilco and Tlapacoya.

A monumental seated figure has been found at Los Idolos, Misantla, which, according to Alfonso Medellín Zenil of the University of Veracruz, shows the influence of the late Post-Classic Totonac horizon, which can be dated anywhere between the eighth century A.D. to just before the Conquest. Made of dark gray basalt and weighing 5 tons, it is 5 feet high and more than 5 feet at its greatest width.

This massive-shouldered headless figure was found at Los Idolos, Misantla.

CHAPTER XIII

Chiapas: The Central Depression and Frailesca Area

SINCE 1955 THE New World Archaeological Foundation, a department of Brigham Young University, Provo, Utah, has conducted extensive investigations in Chiapas, a region especially significant to archaeologists because of possible ancestral links to the Zapotec and Maya cultures. Working under a permit granted by the National Institute of Anthropology and History and with the cooperation of municipal and state authorities, the Foundation has, as its stated aim, the unearthing of evidence bearing on the origins of New World cultures as set forth in the *Book of Mormon* discussions of the era between 300 B.C. and A.D. 400. The study has been carried out under the direction of leading American, Canadian, French and Mexican archaeologists, including Dr. Richard S. MacNeish, Frederick A. Peterson, Gareth W. Lowe, Pierre Agrinier and Carlos Navarrete. A statement by the directors of the Book of Mormon Research Project was issued in May 1962, showing that sufficient progress had been made to justify further excavations in the Central Depression at **Chiapa de Corzo.**

Embracing an area of 9,000 square miles, the Central Depression parallels the Sierra Madre range, which lies to the west and southwest. There are mountains on its northern limits, on the east rise the Chiapas highlands and on the southeast is the Cuchumatanes range of Guatemala. As preliminary exploration of more than 200 archaeological sites in this area has indicated, the Central Depression was heavily populated an entire millennium before the Christian era by people who were contemporary with the Assyrians and, later, the Phoenicians. Hailed as a crossroads of history, the site of Chiapa de Corzo, formerly overlooked, has yielded abundant vestiges of a very early phase. The initial five years of excavation and consolidation of the ruins, situated within the boundaries of the town of Chiapa, mentioned by Bernal Díaz, have brought to light several distinct periods of construction as well as proof of continuous occupation. Some 85 mounds are scattered over an area of 4 square miles.

Dr. Peterson, former field director for the Foundation, has commented on the great antiquity of the site: "It is evident that the Maya and other advanced civilizations of Middle America began quite late. There must have been a first formative culture on which these civilizations, including Teotihuacán and La Venta, were based." In recent years archaeologists have concentrated on the Olmec as the probable "mother culture," but numerous Carbon-14 dates obtained at Chiapa and other sites point to an early homogeneous culture extending from the Valley of Mexico to central Peru. Testing has indicated that the bottom cultural layer at Chiapa de Corzo could be dated about 1300 B.C. A Carbon-14 date of 6500 B.C. has been obtained from a site in central Chiapas. Some of the architectural remains of Chiapa de Corzo—unadorned, stone-faced pyramids with broad stairways and numerous platforms differing radically from those of the neighboring Maya area—can be dated about 550 B.C.

The ancient site has yielded tombs containing unique objects. In the interment chamber of Tomb No. I, dating from the dawn of the Christian era, a meticulously cut ceremonial lance fitted with a prismatic obsidian blade and the apparently cruiciform shank studded with 56 shark teeth, was found close to the remains of a lavishly adorned individual. Against the south wall, among stone offerings and funerary pottery, were found four carved human femurs. Pierre Agrinier, who discovered them, commented, "I am certain that religious considerations determined the material used in the making of the representations of deity and motivated the artist who carved them . . . those properties that held psychological and spiritual values appropriate to the message he had sought to convey. . . . As the Chiapa bones were surely important ritual objects, there was ample justification for the selection, by the artist or his overlord, of human bones."

From the millions of potsherds, painstakingly collected in hundreds of baskets which occupy an entire floor of the Regional Museum of Tuxtla Gutierrez, Bruce W. Warren, a ceramics expert, has been able to establish some salient facts about the development of the peoples who inhabited Chiapa de Corzo in its earliest epochs. The shards represent some fourteen different cultural phases. Many of the clay vessels found at the site appear to have come from zones hundreds of miles away. Some pieces eloquently document Olmec influence and are believed to have emanated from La Venta. In the opinion of Dr. Caso a number of the Chiapa de Corzo ceramics predate Monte Albán. There are, at any rate, evidences of extensive trade relations with the great Zapotec capital. Far-flung commerce is also indicated by the marked similarity of the oldest pottery to that produced on the northern coasts of Peru. Supporting the theory of early trading by means of a direct sea route are pieces which show a remarkable affinity with the initial phases of the little-known La Victoria culture on the Pacific Coast of Guatemala. Archaeologists are still endeavoring to find conclusive evidence of the relationship of the origin of this ancient culture to the later Maya civilization which occupied much of southern Mexico and northern Central America.

The apparent antiquity of the Chiapa de Corzo site was a major consideration in its selection as a study area by the New World Archaeological Foundation. As defined by a spokesman for the Church of Latter Day Saints, the *Book of Mormon* is a history of the first colonization of America by the Jaredites, who were said to have come to the New World from Mesopotamia, following the confusion of tongues among the heaven-defying builders of the Tower of Babel. The Jaredites were believed to have been destroyed by bloody civil wars and supplanted by a new race sprung from Lehi. According to the *Book of Mormon* a second wave came directly from Jerusalem about 600 B.C., often referred to as "The Lost Tribes of Israel," the descendants of whom purportedly people North and South America. According to the Mormon record Lehi was succeeded by the youngest of his four sons, Nephi, whom "the Lord has appointed ruler." His three brothers and their followers, the Laminites, rebelled against him. In punishment, it is claimed, they were condemned to have dark skins and became the ancestors of the American Indians. The fair-skinned Nephites flourished in their rich lands, according to the narrative, and built an advanced civilization but were continually at war with the Laminites. Also according to the *Book of Mormon,* Christ is believed to have appeared to the Nephites at the time of the Crucifixion, giving them power to found a church and establish a priesthood.

According to the tenets of the Mormon faith these events were recorded in a book written upon golden plates and announced to Joseph Smith by a "celestial messenger" on September 21, 1823, in Palmyra, New York. Smith claimed he received, after four years of probation, a volume 8 by 7 inches, with a thickness of 6 inches. Some of the plates were partly sealed, it is claimed, but the rest were covered with small engraved characters in a script called "Reformed Egyptian." The messenger, it is claimed, left two stones resembling spectacles used by seers in ancient times to aid in the translation. Joseph Smith was said to have been assisted in his task by Oliver Cowdery and others who claimed to have seen the plates. When the work was finished the plates were supposedly returned. The first edition of the *Book of Mormon* appeared in 1830.

Up to 1959 some twenty ancient sites of the Frailesca subregion, in which Dominican friars had established *haciendas* during the Colonial period, had been visited by various scientists affiliated with the New World Archaeological Foundation, during several winter seasons, since torrential rains in the nearby mountains at other times prevented almost all automobile travel. According to Thomas S. Ferguson, work is proceeding throughout the area under the auspices of the Foundation with the objective of "making archaeology a vehicle for the communication of high spiritual and social values."

At Izapa in Chiapas, near the Pacific Ocean and the Guatemala border, with the exploration directed by Gareth Lowe, Thomas Lee and Eduardo Martínez, have been found stelae carved with human figures which, in Ferguson's opinion, are "without doubt the most exciting early stone sculpture yet encountered in the New World." Discovered at the perimeter of what is known as the "Tree of Life" plaza in association with matter given a Carbon-14 date of from 200 to 100 B.C., they fall, in time and style, between the earlier Olmec and later Maya cultures. Dr. Matthew Stirling discovered a stele here about 1940 which he reported as "Stele 5" in *Stone*

The Izapa stele known as "The Stone of the Beheaded One" (*left*) is shown in detail (*right*). In the foreground may be seen a decapitated body and severed head, in the background a serpent-topped palanquin carried by two bearers.

Monuments of Southern Mexico, a publication of the Smithsonian Institution. This, according to Dr. M. Wells Jakeman, in a paper published by the Archaeological Society of Brigham Young University, portrays in sculptured stone a scene described on page 13 of the *Book of Mormon.* While it still remains in the plaza, which is to be maintained as a national monument and archaeological park, other stelae (1, 21 and 50 and the round altar of Stele L) have been removed to the new National Museum of Anthropology. Stele 2 is now held to be the oldest dated object in the Americas, earlier by five years than the famous Stele C of Tres Zapotes. Facing the plaza are mounds containing temple platforms dating back to 700 B.C. One pyramid, now partially excavated, has received a dating of 1500 B.C., which would make it the earliest known pyramid of the New World.

Recent excavations conducted by the New World Archaeological Foundation in the Santa Marta cave northwest of Chiapa de Corzo beyond Ocozocoautla have resulted in the identification of the site as having been inhabited by people of an ancient preceramic culture. This research was directed by Dr. Richard S. MacNeish and Frederick A. Peterson. Explorations to date indicate that the cave may have been occupied by five distinct groups. The earliest of these is believed to have arrived between 7000 and 3500 B.C. This remote era is known as the "Santa Marta phase." Differences in coloration of the soil and other natural factors indicate, they claim, that in this era the climate was perhaps drier than it is now. During the occupancy of the cave by the fourth group the climate became less dry but became much drier by the time of the fifth group.

Judging from the quantity and thickness of occupational deposits, the groups, which were of varying sizes, were not sedentary peoples. The subsistence activities of the earlier arrivals are indicated by bones of deer and peccary, large projectile points and sharpened flakes and blades. That the cave dwellers may have roasted meat over coals is suggested by the presence of carbon patches and occasional fire-cracked rock. A profusion of burned and cracked shells shows that they probably collected shellfish. While they may have had an incipient agriculture, there is no evidence that *maíz* was known. Their technology was directed chiefly to the chipping and flaking of flint for cutting, drilling and scraping tools and to the grinding from boulders of rude *metates* and *manos*. There is a hint of religious ritual and probably a belief in an afterlife in the discovery of a single multiple-burial place.

Vestiges of later cultures, designated as the "Cotorra phase," reveal a different way of life. These have been dated, by means of Carbon-14 tests, from 1500 to 1100 B.C. There is an abundance of corncobs. The scarcity of scrapers suggests that clothing may have been fashioned by the weaving of cloth rather than by the working of skins. Obsidian was more prevalent at this stage. Pottery-making—as evidenced by a large number of modeled clay vessels shaped into bowls with flaring lips and cylindrical, flat-bottomed jars often decorated with red, brown or yellowish paint—appeared as a new facet of technology. It was to continue in a remarkably long sequence.

Part Three

"THE HILLS OF MAYAB": THE MAYA CITIES

CHAPTER XIV

The Maya Riddle

IN THE CENTURIES since Hernán Cortés invited his men to follow him onward from Cozumel, perhaps to "wear the crown of victory" or "finding, with him, their tombs in the hills of Mayab," numerous books in many languages have been published on the ancient Maya and their remarkable culture. But what volumes remain to be written on this almost inexhaustible subject!

Still largely unrecorded, for instance, are the step-by-step processes over millennia of agricultural experimentation that resulted in a profusion of plants which made possible the flowering of an amazingly rich civilization and one which first produced more than half of the major crops now grown by American farmers. Hundreds of vegetables, herbs, fruits, berries and medicinal plants were discovered and domesticated by the Maya of Yucatán and Central America or their predecessors. Dr. MacNeish has, of course, documented many of the earliest agricultural phases. The list of products from Middle America which have added to the world's table fare include the turkey, corn (the Indian *maíz*), sweet potato, pineapple, tomato, pepper, squash, pumpkin and cacao as well as various beans and fruits such as the avocado, chirimoya and papaya. Other products which have enriched world economy include cotton, tobacco, rubber, vanilla and other spices, cochineal and various dye woods.

What volumes could be written also on the remarkable cultural level attained in the intricate hieroglyphics of Maya scholars, the detailed illustrations of the codices, the precise astronomical observations that enabled them to make long-range calculations and predictions. The concern of the Maya savants with cosmic phenomena and with the passage of time is revealed in their familiarity with changing celestial patterns and the progression of stars and planets through the heavens. Their grasp of mathematics and their use of a positional system of numbers based on a concept of zero, in use a thousand years earlier than the system, in many ways more cumbersome, utilized in western Europe, has been hailed as one of the greatest intellectual achievements.

Modern builders have admired the ancient structures of the Maya, many of which are equipped with subterranean drainage channels, as well as their plazas, paved with a fine lime cement. They built sumptuous tombs to receive the remains of their revered rulers and priests and adorned their temples with mural painting, relief carving and sculpture unsurpassed, in the opinion of art authorities, for pure decorative effect. Maya artists were expert in their ability to fill a given space with the "inevitable design," while their functional architecture, which achieved an aesthetic and ideological integration, has inspired contemporary builders and city planners.

In the quest for answers to such provocative questions as the origins of the Maya, the coastal waters of Yucatán are currently being explored for vestiges of submerged cities. The Quintana Roo shores, for instance, have been found to be honeycombed with caves. Some of these contain ancient shrines and subterranean passages, leading, it is believed, to temples and lookouts on the cliffs above.

The theme of a disastrous flood as well as a cataclysm may be found in the Maya legends. According to de Landa, their supreme deity was Hunab-ku, the father of Itzamna. "Among the multitude of gods which this people adored," de Landa related, "they worshipped four, each of whom was called Bacab. They said there were four brothers whom God (Hunab-ku), when he created the world, placed at the four points of it, to hold up the sky so that it should not fall." The Bacabs, apparently, did survive the great deluge which reportedly destroyed all previous worlds.

In *Yucatan Adventure* Leonard Clark told the story of his trek with Hal Hennesy into remote areas of the Yucatán Peninsula, including a territory in which no white men had ever before set foot. As Clark speculated at Uxmal on those who had been fascinated by the Maya before him, he recalled all that he had read previously which might provide clues. According to T. A. Willard, Teobert Maler believed Atlantis lay near or beneath Uxmal. From the top of "The House of the Magician," it was said, he used to stare toward the southeast, hoping to see in the sky its "white-stoned" reflection. Le Plongeon had named one of the westward-facing buildings "The Temple of the Sacred Mysteries" and had deciphered a certain inscription as "This edifice commemorates the continent of Moo—the Lands of the West—that land of Kui—the birthplace of our

Sacred Mysteries." "That night," Clark recalled, "I began wondering if Maler with his Atlantis theory, Churchward with his Mu, Le Plongeon with his Lost Lands of Kui and Moo, from whence all knowledge was sent throughout the world, and including Dr. Morley, and his knowable facts purely localized, were not all correct in the general sense, and that the Maya *Uxben,* the very Motherland—those Lands in the West; the central one of the Three Lands—did not lie unknown and unsuspected in the lower middle of this Peninsula and between the Old and the New Empires."

Clark had noted that in the Maya *Codex Tro-Cortesianus* it was stated that the land had long ago been torn asunder in tremendous upheavals. He and Hennesy discovered that the lands of the interior, a vast desolation of empty trackless wastes, yet a country that had once supported a population of 25,000,000, were, in fact, markedly uneven. Frequently the ridges had been utilized as part of the architectural design in building great pyramidal structures, now largely in ruins, their stones wrenched apart by the roots of tropical trees. Site after nameless forgotten site was discovered by the two adventurers; in some instances they found walls decorated with Maya or pre-Maya sculpture still standing. Today explorations in this inner region are being undertaken under the supervision of the National Institute of Anthropology and History. The story of the Yucatán Peninsula, now compounded largely of legend and a complex of theories, may someday be reappraised in accordance with the results of scientifically organized research.

An ancient and aesthetically productive Maya culture flourished at Tikal, which may have been the oldest Maya site, in the northern Petén district of Guatemala, evidenced, according to Dr. Morley, by the "Leyden Plate," found in 1864 at Puerto Barrios. A carved jade pendant, 8½ inches long and 3 inches wide, it is believed to have been made at Tikal in the third quarter of the eighth *baktun,* or eighth cycle of 144,000 days. This date of 8:14:1:3:12 corresponds to a date of A.D. 320 according to the calendrical correlation commonly known as the "Thompson correlation," which was worked out over a period of years by J. Eric S. Thompson, J. T. Goodman and Juan Martínez Hernández. An early monument known as Stele #9 of Uaxactún was found in the northern Petén area. Its inscribed date of 8:14:10:13:15 corresponds to a date of A.D. 328. According to Wolfgang Cordan's *Secret of the Forest,* George Guillemin, a Swiss archaeologist, found a stele with a date of 8:12:14:8:15 at Tikal in 1959.

One cannot help but speculate not only upon the origins but also upon the strange circumstances that caused the brilliant Maya civilization to disintegrate at the very height of its maturity. No documents exist that might illuminate the true causes of this phenomenon, and to date no comprehensive analysis has been made. Many diverse theories and hypotheses have been advanced by modern scholars as possible explanations, including a shortage of water, depletion of the soil, epidemics, yellow fever, earthquakes, uprisings against the ruling classes, an invasion from the north, et cetera. But the riddle has remained unsolved.

The carved jade pendant known as the "Leyden Plate" is believed to have been made at Tikal, possibly the oldest of the Maya sites.

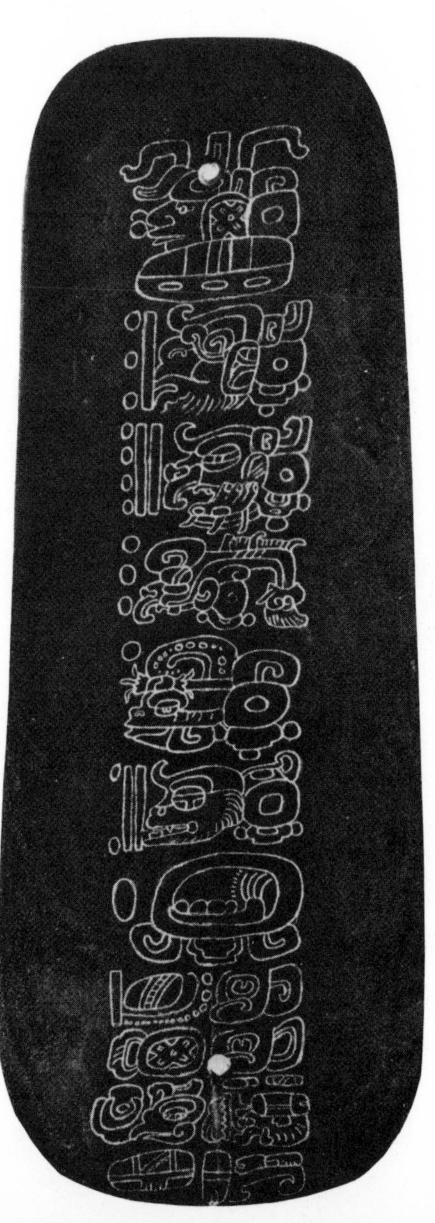

Certainly some of the wells are dry in the rainless seasons, and many subterranean rivers which provided the source of their water may have dried up long ago. On the exhaustion-of-the-soil theory, Dr. A. V. Kidder, Sr. has maintained that such an explanation is not valid in the case of the abandonment of Copán in Honduras, which is situated in an extremely fertile and well-watered valley. Dr. Morley has expressed a similar view with regard to the Quiriguá archaeological zone of eastern Guatemala: "The waters of the Montaguá inundate the valley and continuously enrich its soil with successive deposits of alluvial matter. An abundant supply of water and great humidity, combined with the richness of the alluvial mud and the unremitting heat of the tropical sun, have made the Quiriguá region one of the most fertile in Central America."

J. Eric S. Thompson and others have pointed out that soil-depletion would not satisfactorily account for the sudden desertion of monumental centers that had been occupied long before the earliest inscribed dates. Pre-Classic-type sculpture of Copán, for example, relates this site to a Pre-Classic culture of Miraflores in southwestern Guatemala and to the culture

Copán, the site of a gathering of astronomers, is noted for its carved altar and "Hieroglyphic Stairway." Although situated in a fertile, well-watered valley, it was, for unknown reasons, abandoned by the Maya.

of the Pacific region, which preceded the Classic horizon. Both Angel Palerm and Eric R. Wolf have noted that the period during which the Maya cities flourished seems too long and the abandonment too sudden to make the theory of cultural extinction because of the impoverishment of the soil completely acceptable. The causes of the decadence of the Classic Maya civilization may, they feel, be more complex and not directly or even principally attributable to agriculture.

According to Dr. Rafael Girard, no mass interments have been found throughout the Classic period which would justify the theory that epidemics of catastrophic proportions occurred in the region. Moreover, malaria and yellow fever are generally considered diseases which were not indigenous to America. Over the centuries no earthquake has been severe enough to destroy the Maya structures so solidly erected atop high pyramids. Earthquakes of great intensity have seldom been known to affect the lower lands of the Atlantic Basin, where most of the major Maya sites are located.

Alfred Kidder II, associate director of the University Museum, University of Pennsylvania, traces the abrupt collapse of the Maya culture and the end of the Classic period to intolerable strain caused by priestly despotism. His father had been the first to advance the theory of a social revolt.

It is, of course, unlikely that a similar massive revolt would recur in numerous small autonomous states distributed over a territory encompassing some 378 by 126 miles. Moreover, the stability of the Maya communities was contingent upon the maintenance of intimate links between the priestly rulers and the people. Only the rulers, representing the gods upon whom all life depended, could, according to the Maya beliefs, maintain the necessary contact with the benevolent and harmful forces of nature or provoke divine punishment for infractions of the rigid moral code. The people depended upon their spiritual directors and the directors' powers depended upon their ability to control the people. As Dr. Girard has shown, the Maya community was characterized by a unity and interdependence within a social structure that constituted a "magic" totality. On the maintenance of such a unity, in his view, rested the continued existence of the Maya as a coherent social unit. He has based his conclusions on the attitudes of the present-day Maya, who are detached not only from contemporary western mores but from the way of life of other indigenous people of Mexico and from the *mestizo* population. The Maya community, which he calls a "living whole," has been compared by him to a serpent whose head is the priest and whose body is the people. This concept is eloquently expressed in the word *Hor-Chan* in Chortí, a Maya language, for the sacerdotal title. *Hor* signifies head, or chief; *Chan*, serpent. *Chan* may also be taken to mean the self-determination of the Maya, who called themselves "The People of the Serpent." Within the frame of their concept of allegiance, a popular revolt against the priestly ruling class would signify the destruction of the whole social structure.

Some scholars, citing both archaeological and ethnological evidence, have maintained that the centers of the once-great Classic Maya civilization which flourished in Guatemala and Honduras and what is now Chiapas, were probably destroyed by foreign invasion. Advocates of this theory have emphasized the fact that the non-Yucatecan Classic Maya centers were never totally abandoned. In the southeastern part of this area today, on both sides of the north-central Guatemalan-Honduran border, some 30,000 members of a large indigenous group known as the Chortí continues to speak their native language. Within this region, particularly in valleys and plains of easy access, are many towns bearing Pipil-Nahuan place names, while in the more isolated mountainous areas the place names are Maya. The Pipil were Nahuatl-speaking migrants from Central Mexico who began to come into the area at the close of the Classic period. Anthropologists have found that the entire territory is saturated with their influence, evidence that two distinct types, the Chortí and the Pipil, coexisted in the southern Maya area during the Post-Classic period. The Pipil earthworks, in contrast to those of the Chortí, are of a low elevation and, like the Pipil ceramics and stone utensils, of such poor appearance that they have offered little incentive to investigators.

Significant archaeological testimony indicates that the Pipil occupation of the ceremonial center of Copán took place at the beginning of the Post-Classic period, probably with the collapse of the Classic period in the southern Maya area. The presence of the Pipil in Copán is attested by the mounds that may be seen in the airport field near the central part of the site known as the "Acropolis" and by Pipil-type ceramics. The name *Copán* is of Pipil origin and signifies "bridge." The discovery of a clay head of the Pipil type on the top of Pyramid 36 by S. K. Lothrop suggests that not only did these people inhabit and name Copán but also used a Maya temple for their own religious rites.

A similar incident was reported at Comalcalco by Dr. Herbert J. Spinden. This site was the last northwestern outpost of the Maya area to be invaded by the Pipil. Above Maya stratification he found the remains of Post-Classic-type ceramics that have now been identified as Pipil. According to Dr. A. V. Kidder, Sr., it seems probable that the Pipil culture of the southern coast of Guatemala was contemporary with or antecedent to the final years of the Classic period of the Petén region. The last Maya *katun* (a 7,200-day or approximately 20-year period) definitely to be commemorated by the dedication of a corresponding monument in several sites ended on a date corresponding to A.D. 889. A monument at San Lorenzo near La Muñeca, Campeche, just north of the Guatemala border, bears the date of A.D. 928, possibly the latest one. Both dates have been calculated according to the Thompson correlation.

Dr. J. Alden Mason has maintained that Piedras Negras in Guatemala, one of the three sites in the Usumacinta Valley where, in the eighth century, the Classic civilization of the Maya Golden Age attained its culminating brilliance, must have met with a violent end. The view that the great Maya centers were abandoned under tragic circumstances was shared by Dr. Thomas A. Joyce, formerly of the British Museum, who has declared that a foreign war probably caused the extinction of the non-Yucatecan Classic Maya sites. Such an attack, he believes, was launched from the extreme northwest.

Dr. Jiménez Moreno has pointed out that the route followed by Pipil invaders can be traced from the Gulf Coast to the Atlantic, yet in the entire Yucatán Peninsula not a single vestige of the Pipil invasion exists. He could discover no trace of Pipil occupation in archaeological remains, in the Maya language as spoken in Yucatán or in regional place names. The *Books of Chilam Balam* mention the arrival on the Peninsula of Nahuatl-speaking mercenaries proceeding from Xicalango, near Laguna de Términos, and other areas in Tabasco, but it is known that these warriors were brought in to help quell domestic conflicts during a relatively recent epoch at the request of Hunac Ceel, ruler of Mayapán at the close of the twelfth century. Pipil place-names are not found beyond the Lacantun River, a southern tributary of the Usumacinta, which drains eastern Chiapas and northern Guatemala. This indicates that even though the non-Yucatecan Classic Maya centers may have been overthrown in an invasion, such an event did not affect the Yucatán Peninsula.

What, then, could have brought about the decline and eventual fall of the great Yucatecan cities of the Late Classic period during which were developed the Puuc, Chenes and Río Bec architectural styles, the period of the formation of the League of Mayapán? Apparently for two centuries the League functioned: between A.D. 987 and A.D. 1185, according to Thompson, and from A.D. 987 to A.D. 1194, according to Dr. Morley. What could have so weakened the cities during the Mexican-Toltec period, marked by the ascendancy of Mayapán, from A.D. 1194 to A.D. 1441?

A native version of many calamitous events was recorded by Bishop de Landa, in his *Relación de las Cosas de Yucatán,* written in Spain about 1566. These catastrophes decimated the majestic cities and left them easy prey to enemy invaders:

The tribes enjoyed more than 20 years of abundance and health, and they multiplied so that the whole country seemed like a town. At this time they erected temples in great numbers, as is today seen. Everywhere, in going through the forest, there can be seen in the groves the sites of houses and buildings marvelously worked.

Succeeding this prosperity, there came on, one winter night at about six in the evening a storm that grew into a hurricane of the four winds. The storm blew down all the high trees, causing great slaughter of all kinds of game; it overthrew the high houses which, being thatched and having fires within for the cold, took fire and burned great numbers of the people, while those who escaped were crushed by the timbers.

The hurricane lasted until the next day at noon, and they found that those who lived in small houses had escaped as well as the newly married couples, whose custom it was to live for a few years in cabins in front of those of their fathers or fathers-in-law. The land thus then lost the name it had borne, that of "the turkey and the deer," and was left so treeless that those of today look as if planted together and thus all grown of one size. To look at the country from the heights it appears as if all were trimmed with a pair of shears.

Those who escaped aroused themselves to building and cultivating the land, and multiplied during 15 years of health and abundance, the last year being the most fertile of all. Then, as they were about to begin gathering the crops, there came an epidemic of pestilential fevers. Those attacked swelled and broke out full of sores, so that from this pestilence many people died and most of the crops remained ungathered.

After the passing of the pestilence they had 16 other good years wherein they renewed their passions and feuds to the end that 110,000 men were killed in battle. With this slaughter they ceased and made peace, and rested for 20 years. After that there came again a pestilence, with great pustules that rotted the body, so that the members fell in pieces, within four or five days.

Since that last plague more than 50 years have now passed. The mortality of the wars was 20 years prior, the pestilence of the swelling was 16 years before the wars, and 22 or 23 after the destruction of Mayapán. Thus, according to this count, it has been 125 years since the overthrow, within which the people of this country have passed through the calamities described,

> besides many other afflictions sent by God; so that it is a marvel there is any population left, small as it is.

Clearly, the days of supreme achievement by the Maya were over. Even before the Conquest the creative impetus that had made "The People of the Serpent" at one time among the greatest in history had become inert. Yet who is to say that another "Maya Renaissance" is not possible or that racial genius dormant for centuries may not be revived in a brilliant, if different, manifestation? Dr. Paul Richard, author of *Dawn Over Asia,* in summarizing the three processes of history, has observed: "Nations die. Other nations go to sleep, to awaken after centuries or millennia with fresh vigor. New nations are born."

CHAPTER XV

Bonampak

IN THE JUNGLES OF eastern Chiapas long-hidden examples of the art of the ancient Mayas were discovered only a few decades ago. For centuries the secret of the existence of the ruined temples adorned by frescoes had been closely guarded by the remnants of the rapidly diminshing Lacandones, an offshoot of the Maya. But in the spring of 1946, Kayom, a spokesman of a Lacandón *caribal,* a cluster of houses around a forest clearing that is located between the Lacanha and the Usumacinta, shared the secret of the site with Carlos Frey, a young conscientious objector who had sought refuge in the nearby village of El Cedro. A warm friendship had developed between them; the Indian had even offered Frey one of his five wives, the beautiful Nakim. Welcomed into the tribe, Frey soon acquired a working vocabulary of their tongue. This, of course, endeared him to the 250-odd remaining Lacandones, who, in their isolation, continued their polygamous customs and their worship of ancient gods. Eventually Kayom led Frey to a ruined site in the heart of the forest, a ceremonial center containing nine structures and several scattered stelae.

Deeply impressed by its beauty and antiquity, Frey felt obliged to notify federal authorities. After considerable efforts on his part and also on the part of a fellow American, John G. Bourne, taken to the site by Frey to arouse interest, some Mexican archaeologists made exploratory visits. Frey later led Giles G. Healey, an American photographer who had been commissioned by the United Fruit Company to make a film, *The Maya Through the Ages,* to the ruined site. In the winter of 1947 Healey returned to film a sequence on the area. This expedition, under the direction of the National Institute of Anthropology and History and sponsored by the United Fruit Company and the Carnegie Institution, included several artists concerned with the state of the murals within the structures. After

The ruined site in a jungle clearing revealed to Carlos Frey by the Lacandones received its name, Bonampak ("Painted Walls"), from the masterly frescoes found in its interior chambers.

cutting away the brush that blocked the entrance to an interior chamber and removing a calcium deposit from the walls, the members of the expedition were able to view what are conceded to be the finest frescoes of the early Maya period. A bath of kerosene made the colors visible temporarily but contributed to their subsequent deterioration by lessening their adhesion. Most of the original colors have now disappeared. Only a faded tint remains to indicate their former radiance. Antonio Tejeda, a Guatemalan artist and anthropologist, copied and Augustín Villagra Caleti traced the murals they found in the so-called "Painted Temple," designated as "Building #1." On a subsequent visit Villagra Caleti copied the murals in two other rooms. Their outlines and original colors were reproduced in *Las Pinturas de Bonampak,* published by the National Institute of Anthropology and History.

The fame of the site, **Bonampak,** or Bonnanpak, named by Dr. Morley from two Maya words meaning "Painted Walls," spread and aroused scholarly interest and speculation everywhere. In April 1949, an expedition sponsored by the National Institute of Fine Arts was organized by Frey, who personally enlisted the aid of Mexico's outstanding artists. This group, guided by Frey, included an archaeologist, an architect, a photographer, a chemist, artists and others. Raúl Anguiano, who executed the murals of the Maya Hall of the new National Museum of Anthropology, was commissioned to draw and paint the tropical forest and its inhabitants. During the expedition he made some seventy sketches, many of which were later developed into canvases and lithographs. The works were reproduced in his diary-record, *Expedition to Bonampak,* published by the Institute of Esthetic Investigations of the National University of Mexico. While this expedition laid a foundation for future scientific research, Carlos Frey lost his life in a futile attempt to save the engraver Franco Lázaro Gómez when their canoe overturned in the turbulent waters of the Lacanha.

The features of an ancient warrior found on a stele at Bonampak have been likened to those of Kayom, tribal head of the remaining Lacandones.

In the opinion of Anguiano, who regards the architectural complex, reliefs and sculpture of Bonampak as among the highest achievements of Maya art, these elements are no less important than the frescoes. He found in the faces of the Lacandones, notably that of Kayom, a striking resemblance to the features of the ancient warrior depicted on Stele #3. In *Bonampak: La Ciudad de los Muros Pintados* Román Piña Chan, who believes both the site and the Lacandones, "constitute a Mexican heritage of incalculable value," declared, "More and more each day the monuments suffer from the impact of the vegetation, threatening complete collapse." Other scholars who have concerned themselves with this region are Teobert Maler, whose *Researches in the Central Portion of the Usumacinta Valley* were published in two volumes in 1901 and 1903 and Karl Ruppert, coauthor, with J. Eric S. Thompson and Tatiana Proskouriakoff, of *Bonampak, Chiapas, Mexico,* published in 1955 by the Carnegie Institution. Many scholars have pleaded for the preservation of the natural and man-made wonders of the area.

According to the Mexican archaeologist Carlos R. Margain, Bonampak was built between the seventh and eighth centuries A.D. At least fourteen similar ceremonial centers were founded and flourished during the Middle Classic period. Other sites at which were recorded a date corresponding to A.D. 692 included, according to Dr. Morley, Quiriguá, Tzendales, Lacanha and Quexil. As in all the great cultural centers of Mexico, a high degree of aesthetic and ideological integration was achieved at Bonampak. There is perfect harmony among the architectural, sculptural and decorative elements; all symbolize the ritual purpose of the structure. Of course one must rebuild, in one's imagination, the whole complex, long since covered with a labyrinth of trees and bushes that now conceal the stairways and upper levels. Each of the temples, according to A. T. Arai's calculations, reached a height of more than 150 feet.

When discovered, three of Bonampak's finest lintels were still in place over the entrances to the structure known as the Temple of the Frescoes. The bas-reliefs have a warlike motif, representing scenes of the capture and death of prisoners. The rhythmical movement of the warlike figures, juxtaposed with the classical serenity of the composition, makes a singularly harmonious unit with the paintings on the interior walls and the stucco frieze in high relief above the exterior façade. The lintels still preserve vestiges of the original polychrome, and in the depressions may be seen an almost imperceptible residue of red.

Within this temple are three chambers decorated with frescoes that start almost at floor level and extend to a small projection that encircles the room, continuing without interruption at each corner. The high arched roofs are also decorated. Painted fragments indicate that the entire exterior surface must once have been covered with frescoes, as Anguiano observed, "a veritable orgy of forms and colors, from its exterior walls right up to the most hidden corners of the vaulted roof." He has deplored the popular appellation, "The Sistine Chapel of the Americas," which has frequently been given to this temple. Painted six centuries before Giotto, the frescoes of Bonampak are strictly two-dimensional, with depth and perspective cleverly suggested by line and color. They might be better compared, he believes, with the art of Persia and Japan and with the paintings that have been found at Pompeii. The graceful attitudes of some of the figures, the smooth and rhythmical movement of the hands, bear a similarity to the forms in exquisite Persian miniatures. The positions in which other figures are seated recall Chinese drawings and Japanese prints. The scene depicting a foreshortened, recumbent figure among several captives being judged evokes particularly, it has been claimed, the "Sleeping Maenad" of Pompeii. The art of the Bonampak Maya, he has observed, while it may bear some resemblance to the art of other cultures, is not only original but of the highest order. The artists of Bonampak had gained a maturity in portraying the human form and had apparently mastered the true fresco technique. It seems to have been little known elsewhere in the New World. The paintings found at Teotihuacán, Monte Albán and Chichén Itzá do not equal those of Bonampak in conceptual beauty or in technical development. A marked contrast may be noted between the observation of reality and a synthetic realism evident in the

representation of the human figure. A fanciful stylization dominates in delineation of body and costume.

Perhaps the most impressive panel is the one which depicts a ceremony or feast. The ruler may be identified easily by his enormous headdress of emerald quetzal feathers, elaborate breastplate, earrings, bracelets and sumptuous garments. This figure—with its slanting eyes, open mouth and sharp teeth, the features meticulously drawn, the hands shapely and expressive—suggests a masterly Japanese print. Servants may be seen at the right placing a bracelet on the ruler's wrist. A container of perfume or paint to complete the regal accouterments is ready, carried by other servants, shown against a "Venetian" red background. Sienna and a dull Indian red are used for flesh tones, creating an effective contrast to the vivid green headdresses of the priests and nobles. On the lower frieze may be seen dancers wearing masks of lizards, crabs and iguanas, accompanied by a troupe of musicians who are blowing on large trumpet-like instruments. On another section of this superbly decorative panel may be seen drummers using both an upright *huehuetl* and a tortoise-shell drum which was played with deer antlers. Other musicians play single and double rattles and ocarinas. All wear high headdresses adorned with white feathers outlined in black. Added brilliance has been given to the ornaments by leaving the white surface of the lime unpainted. On another wall of the same chamber, nobles garbed in rich vestments are shown conversing.

One of the Bonampak frescoes depicts a troupe of musicians. Some wear fanciful headdresses, others grotesque animal masks.

A servant stands upon a platform bearing in his arms a child, perhaps the son of the ruler.

The dynamic mural of the second, or central, room of the temple represents a battle scene. Paul Westheim has observed of it, "In no epoch or continent has a battle scene been painted in a more grandiose or fascinating manner. . . . Here we see the combatants in their sumptuous garments, their shoulders covered with tiger-skins and their heads adorned with green and yellow feathers, attacking their enemies with lances, clutching them by a lock of hair to take them prisoners . . . a seething mass of enraged figures in impassioned movement—a chaos of bodies, crowds and colors. Each figure, each gesture, is stupendously observed and transcribed on the wall with consummate artistry."

In the third chamber the frescoes show a festival with dancers wearing quetzal-feather headdresses surrounding men apparently performing a human sacrifice. As in the first chamber, masks of the rain god Chac decorate the ceiling frieze.

CHAPTER XVI

Palenque

WITHIN THE WHOLE ORBIT of Maya culture, the dependence of the present on the past is nowhere more apparent than at **Palenque** in northern Chiapas where, with few exceptions, the villagers have existed with only the barest essentials. As a result of increased interest in the ruins of Palenque following the discovery, in 1952, of a sumptuous mortuary chamber below its Temple of the Inscriptions, there has been a modest improvement in their lot. The streets, however, are still unpaved, and one must cross open fields and farmyards to reach various sections of the village. The little *chozas*, or huts, of the town below offer a dramatic contrast to the temples and palaces, with their stucco bas-reliefs, carvings and inscriptions, which border the immense sunken plaza of a once-great ritual city. Palenque's name comes from a Spanish word meaning "palisade" or "paling."

Hailed as the Teotihuacán of the South, Palenque was abandoned long before the arrival of the Conquistadores, who were evidently unaware of its existence, although Cortés must have passed within 20 or 30 miles of it on his march across Guatemala to Honduras. The ruined city was visited by a Spanish artillery captain, Antonio del Río in March 1785. He recorded his impressions, drew plans and maps and, according to Thompson, "bulldozed" the ruins. A translation of his report was published in English and illustrated by Frédéric de Waldeck, who, in the course of his work in Central America, inserted into some of his drawings of Maya glyphs such exaggerations and inaccuracies as elephant heads. This spurious elephant motif led to many repercussions, including its utilization as support for proponents of the "lost Atlantis" theory. The del Río account of Palenque was analyzed by Dr. Paul Felix Cabrera in *A Description of the Ruins of an Ancient City Discovered near Palenque,* published in

London, in which he sought to show that the monuments had Old World origins.

Dr. Leonard André Bonnet, who first visited Palenque in 1911, maintained that it was occupied over a longer period than is generally conceded. Most scholars believe the city flourished at least from the fifth through the tenth centuries, dating its finest art and architecture from the seventh and eighth centuries. He believed that the stream known as the "Queen's Bath," winding through the ruined site, was once a tributary of the Usumacinta, the sacred river of the Maya, and that a series of ceremonial centers was built along the banks. Apparently he found Palenque in 1911 just as John Lloyd Stephens and the engraver Frederick Catherwood had seen it about a half-century earlier. Stephens' *Incidents of Travel in Central America, Chiapas and Yucatán* appeared in 1841, Catherwood's drawings shortly thereafter. Stephens described Palenque, observed Thompson, "free of all the twaddle about Atlantis and Egypt."

In the pioneer explorer's own words, what met their eyes was grand, curious and remarkable, "all that remained of a cultivated, polished and peculiar people who passed through all the stages incident to the rise and fall of nations, who had reached their golden age, and perished entirely unknown. The temples and pyramids of Palenque are the only memorials of their footsteps upon the earth. . . . We lived in the ruined palaces of their

Palenque is believed to have flourished from the fifth through the tenth centuries. John Lloyd Stephens, who visited the ruined structures bordering its sunken plaza in the mid-nineteenth century, described Palenque as "grand, curious and remarkable."

kings. We went up to their temples and fallen altars and wherever we moved, we saw the evidences of their taste, their skill in the arts, their wealth and their power." The visitor to Palenque today can well understand why Stephens declared that nothing ever impressed him more forcefully than "the spectacle of this once lovely city, overturned, desolate and lost, overgrown for miles around with trees, with not even a name to distinguish it." Perhaps he can picture the people who once lived there as they "ascended the terraces of the palaces and the steps leading to the temples in a scene of unique and gorgeous beauty that realized the creations of the Oriental poets."

The Palace is the largest and the most impressive architectural unit facing the sunken plaza. It stands on a spacious terrace 40 feet high and, with its complex of courts and inner chambers, encompasses an area approximately 225 by 175 feet. Various sections of the building are connected by profusely adorned passageways. The delicately executed figures, heads and paneling are often considered the apex of Maya sculpture in stucco.

Over the course of time the ruins have deteriorated considerably, and the primary task has been that of reconstruction. The financial assistance of the Institute of Andean Research has made possible the restoration of the four-story square tower of the Palace, a unique feature in Maya architecture. Archaeologists of the National Institute of Anthropology and History, under the supervision of Dr. Alberto Ruz Lhuillier, director of Maya Studies at the National University, maintain that their authority for the restoration was a seventeenth-century engraving. Some critics have declared that the cap of the tower suggests "a cross between a Chinese pagoda and a French mansard roof." There are, however, other examples of exotic architectural styles at Palenque as well as vertical, centrally located roof combs with intricate, lacy stonework that recall the structures of India. There is, obviously, a glaring contrast between the raw look of the new material used in the restoration and in the age-mellowed original stone, but time and weather should eventually blend the two into greater harmony.

With recent grants, exploration was undertaken on the north side of Palenque's sunken plaza. Examples of pottery of the Pre-Classic period were unearthed in 1959. Structures corresponding to the Puuc culture of northern Yucatán were also found beneath the Palace. According to the director of research operations, "Important clues to the antiquity of the Palenque site were found and the period of its occupancy by people of an advanced culture has been pushed farther back into antiquity." A second tomb came to light as the result of a clue similar to that which led to the sensational discovery of the superb sarcophagus beneath the Temple of the Inscriptions. A hole was noticed in a floor slab of a small temple designated as 18-A, located near the Temple of the Foliated Cross. Investigation revealed that the hole led to a tube, about 5 inches in diameter, which connected with a tomb below the floor of the temple. The tube, known as a psychoduct, is thought to have been intended as a conduit for the spirit of the deceased. The tomb contained jade, jewels and a skeleton in an outstretched position. In one corner was another skeleton in an upright, sitting position, probably a servant entombed with his master. Outside the crypt were the remains of four other persons, who may have been sacrificed at the time of the interment. There were, however, no exquisite bas-reliefs such as those which had adorned the massive lid of the sarcophagus of the earlier and more celebrated discovery, with the following background.

Dr. Ruz Lhuillier and his crew began work in 1949 on the Temple of the Inscriptions. The floor of the sanctuary surmounting the important structure was made of large flagstones instead of the usual stucco. Carefully plugged holes were found to be handholds whereby some stones could be removed. A stone wall that continued down behind the flagstones was a clue that there was something below. First excavators found only rubble, but they kept digging and reached at last a flat stone more than 6 feet long, with the ends imbedded in sloping, converging walls. They realized that they were in a Maya corbelled vault. Digging below, they struck a step made of stone slabs with a stucco finish. They had found a vaulted stairway 5 feet wide which had been deliberately filled with pieces of coarse masonry.

For the fewer than three dry months of each year, over a period of four years, in choking dust and almost unbearable humidity, the work went on. By 1952, 71 steps had been uncovered and the excavators were at the bottom, about 73 feet below the floor of the sanctuary. But now the way was barred by a wall of tightly packed rubble. Beyond it was a second very thick and firmly constructed wall of mortared stones. At this point, after the fourth year of labor, Dr. César A. Saenz asked his superior, "What do you think we'll find behind all this?" "I can't imagine," replied Dr. Ruz Lhuillier, "but I hope with all my soul that it will be a magnificent tomb."

And so it was. The first find was a stone container holding beautiful ornaments of jade and a teardrop pearl a half-inch long. After forcing an entrance through the thick wall, a casket was found. This held a mass of bones, which later proved to be those of six young persons who were probably sacrificed in order to serve as companions to the deceased on his journey to the next world. Probings in the side wall disclosed a grotto that suggested a vision, Dr. Ruz Lhuillier recalls, "from a fairy tale. The interior sparkled and glistened with the effect of snow crystals. Delicate festoons of stalactites hung like the tassels of a curtain, and the stalagmites on the floor looked like the drippings from a great candle. Raised above the floor was an enormous stone slab, in perfect condition."

Two days later, on June 15, 1952, Dr. Ruz Lhuillier was able to crawl into the mysterious chamber, "the first person to tread those floors in more than ten centuries." The room was about 10 by 30 feet. "Across the walls marched nine great low-relief stucco figures of sumptuously garbed priests in larger-than-natural size." The figures are thought to represent the nine lords, or gods, of the underworld. Even more impressive was a carved stone slab, 12 by 6 feet, edged by 54 Maya hieroglyphs, including dates corresponding to A.D. 603 and A.D. 633, according to the Thompson correlation. "The main central figure was that of a young man leaning back-

The central figure carved on the sarcophagus lid found in the tomb below the Temple of the Inscriptions is that of a youth seated on a mask of an earth monster, beneath a cross representing a *maíz* plant, a two-headed serpent, a quetzal-bird and the face of the rain god.

ward and seated on a large mask of an earth monster." Above him rose a cross, a conventionalized representation of the *maíz* plant. "The two arms of the cross ended in the wide-open mouths of a two-headed serpent, and a quetzal-bird with the face of the rain god perched on the top." Beneath this slab was an immense carved block.

At this exciting phase, work had to be suspended because of the rainy season, but it was begun again in mid-November. Early in the morning of November 28, after the men had worked through the night, the approximately 5-ton slab was lifted to reveal a smaller mummy-shaped slab below. With the removal of the lid of the inner sarcophagus—the first ever found in a Maya pyramid—were revealed the decayed bones of a man who had evidently been a royal personage or high priest. A jade mosaic mask covered the face. The teeth had been painted red but not mutilated as was the usual practice among the Maya nobility. The man was estimated to have been about 5 feet 8 inches tall, some 6 inches above the average height for the Maya type. There were quantities of jade objects and jewelry. Two magnificent sculptured heads were found under the sarcophagus. The profiles showed the nosepiece commonly added to emphasize the distinctive Maya profile.

The discovery of the impressive tomb beneath the Temple of the Inscriptions, according to Dr. Ruz Lhuillier, has led to "considerable modification of certain established concepts concerning the function of the American pyramid. Formerly it was regarded solely as a solid base for supporting a temple, unlike those of Egypt, which are vast mausolea." In his opinion, "Palenque's royal tomb brings us closer to the Egyptian concept, once we grant that the pyramid which hid it, although supporting a temple, was also constructed to serve as a grandiose funeral monument." As in the case of the Egyptian pyramids, "Thousands of hands were required to build and adorn the colossal sarcophagus . . . entirely covered with bas-reliefs of extraordinary aesthetic quality." The heavy stone lid, now raised a few feet above the sarcophagus, is a priceless example of the stone engraver's art. Perhaps the most perfect example of Maya bas-relief that has yet come to light, it may now also be seen in a reproduction of the entire crypt at the new National Museum of Anthropology.

Dr. Ruz Lhuillier has suggested that the mask, rich jade ornaments, jewelry and other finery found with the skeleton signified, in terms of expense and toil, the existence of a theocratic system similar to that of Egypt in which the all-powerful priest-king was considered during his lifetime or after death to be a real god. Fragments of the jade mosaic mask found inside the sarcophagus have been fitted together, providing still another similarity with Egypt and even with ancient Greece, where the faces of dead Achaean royalty of the Mycenaean period were covered with masks of thin beaten gold.

The sumptuousness of the tomb might also suggest a comparison between the Maya attitude toward the death of the *halach uinic,* or "true man," who, in the manner of the Egyptians, was the hereditary head of each Maya city-state. Dr. Ruz Lhuillier does not, however, support the claim advanced by some archaeologists that the use of pyramids as tombs by both the Egyptians and the ancient Maya requires "a complete revision of American continental history" or a change in previously held concepts of Middle-American cultural origins. He believes that the resemblance is purely coincidental and attributable to various similarities in physical environment and climate that often produce parallels in folkways, social customs and religious rites. A similarity in the funeral rites of ancient Egypt and Palenque does tend, however, to underline the parallels. In a royal pyramid-tomb of Egypt, retainers of the pharoah might be sealed in the tomb along with his corpse. Similarly, in the Palenque crypt were found six skeletons of what were believed to be the children of high-ranking nobles, evidently sacrificed to accompany and serve the dead personage in the other world. Their nobility was indicated by cranial deformations and dental mutilation.

A jade mosaic mask covered the face of the royal personage or priest buried in the colossal sarcophagus beneath the Temple of the Inscriptions.

A decorative symbol that provides a striking link between Egypt and Palenque is the cruciform motif, sometimes represented as a tree or as a stylized *maíz* plant. This is found in the Temple of the Foliated Cross. Such a cross was a symbol of the Egyptian deity Osiris, worshipped as the active power of nature, the good spirit, the bestower of all virtue, prosperity and joy. The cross of Palenque is believed to be a symbol of life triumphant over death. Other hillside temples at this site include the Temple of the Sun, the Temple of the Beautiful Bas-Relief and the Temple of the Count, all similar in plan to the Temple of the Inscriptions, with an open portico leading to three inner chambers and a central altar. Tablets of the most exquisite type of Maya decoration, one bearing a date corresponding to A.D. 692, were taken in the late nineteenth century from the Temple of the Sun or possibly from the Temple of the Foliated Cross. They are now in Palenque's Church of Santo Domingo. Carved limestone slabs showing a clearly defined cross in the form of a large tree were removed from a temple and installed in the Gallery of Monoliths in the National Museum in a setting that approximates the original. Other inscriptions were left in place in the Temple of the Beautiful Bas-Relief and the Temple of the Foliated Cross. No sculpture has been found to date in the Temple of the Count.

The typical Maya corbelled arch is seen in the ruined Temple of the Foliated Cross which contains an example of the cruciform motif, represented as a *maíz* plant or "tree of life."

Palenque provides many striking analogies with Asian art such as the sacred tree, or cross. On a relief in the Temple of the Foliated Cross a carving, which bears a kind of monster mask at its center and a bird in the upper branches, has a counterpart in a sculptured panel at Angkor Wat in Cambodia. Although the Khmer relief dates from the twelfth century and could not have been a precursor of the Palenque cross, the motif, in the opinion of Dr. Gordon Ekholm, could have had a long history in southeast Asia. Palenque also provides a counterpart to a shadow-play puppet from Java representing a celestial tree on top of Mount Meru, the "Cosmic Mountain." The Javanese design, like the Palenque relief, has a monster mask at its center. In both cases the cross, or tree, is raised on a platform.

The sacred "tree of life" is shown flanked by two figures in this replica of the sanctuary within the Temple of the Foliated Cross. An Asian counterpart of the monster mask of the horizontal panel has been cited by Dr. Gordon F. Ekholm in his study of Asian-American analogies.

A monster mask forms the central motif in this Cambodian relief from Angkor Wat.

Since 1950, increasing indications of possible Asiatic influence on Middle American cultures have been cited as a result of various explorations in Mexico. Dr. Ekholm has brought together analogous elements from the art and architecture of India and southeast Asia and the Maya region of southeastern Mexico in support of his theory that historical contacts existed between these widely separated ancient cultures. Research at Maya sites has served to deepen rather than to solve the mystery that surrounds the antiquity of man in the New World. No adequate explanation has as yet been found for those architectural elements that predate their parallels in Asia. Dr. Ekholm has pointed out that while coincidences in cultures are common in all archaeological fields, they become significant when a number of them occur in one place.

Perhaps the most striking similarity of decorative motifs is evident in a group of three drawings of architectural border designs from widely separated regions—one from the Temple of the Jaguars in Chichén Itzá, another from Cambodia and a third from Ceylon. All represent a lotus plant in stylized form and were used to frame panels. At the center of each is a jawless monster and at the lower end, all are finished with a leaping fish design. The intervening spaces show sinuous lotus plants undulating around masks, buds, flowers and other decorative motifs. The similarity is so dramatic that it can hardly be attributed, Dr. Ekholm suggests, to mere coincidence. The lotus design, occurring in Asiatic art in infinite

At the right of the figure in this Palenque relief may be seen a lotus plant, a decorative motif frequently encountered in Asian art.

variety, was carried, he believes, from Egypt to Greece, then to India and finally to the New World. In his opinion Palenque provides the best Middle-American example of a figure of a divinity holding a lotus stem or flower, a common design in Hindu-Buddhist art. The Palenque examples bear a remarkable resemblance to those which adorned an image from Khasaparna in India. A stylized lotus blossom used as a throne has been found at Palenque. The lotus design, frequently used in Asia during the third century, received its fullest delineation at the celebrated shrine of Amarāvatī in Madras and in Sanchi, Bhopal State. Continuing in use for many centuries in India, it was carried to Cambodia, Indonesia, China and other areas. In Palenque's Temple of the Foliated Cross is the only known ancient American example of a design in which a lotus is shown growing from a conch shell. This motif may be seen on a Javanese relief dating from the middle of the ninth century at Borobodur near Nagelang. It is one of the numerous decorations from the ruins of a complex of great Buddhist temples built of volcanic rock in which the life of Buddha was portrayed in more than 2,000 relief representations and 430 life-sized images in eight galleries. One of the panels has been compared, in both composition and placement of the figures in bas-relief, to Wall Panel #3 from Structure 0-13 at Piedras Negras. This site in Guatemala is stylistically closely related to the Palenque complex. The panel is regarded as one of the finest pieces of Maya sculpture found to date.

A lotus plant is used to link various elements in a relief from Stupa, India (*left*). The stone carving (*center right*), reminiscent of serpent heads of Middle America, is from Sumatra. The lintel from Piedras Negras, Guatemala (*bottom*), framed by panels adorned with hieroglyphs, is considered one of the finest of Maya carvings. It has been compared to a panel at Borobodur, in Java.

Animal figures also provide points of comparison. In the exhibition prepared by Dr. Ekholm for the American Museum of Natural History in 1949, "Across the Pacific," he showed comparative pictures of a stone animal from Sumatra, a seated lion from Borobodur, and a stone jaguar from Tula. Atlantean figures used as decorative supports for the large table-like altars at Chichén Itzá were in use in southeast Asia as early as 100 B.C.

Maya codices have been compared in format to Sumatran "Books of Divination." The paper, made from the bark of Yucatecan trees, was treated by beating it to a fiber and was rendered almost indestructible by a lustrous white varnish. The books, many measuring a yard or more in length, were folded like a fan or an accordion.

Dr. Ekholm cited several features common to both ancient American and Asiatic structures. At Palenque a trefoil arch was used over doorways and as a frame for niches on upper walls. It was used similarly in India following the Mohammedan invasion of the twelfth century. The jaguar throne is another feature common to both areas in antiquity. A figure from Hahoba in India has been compared to a sculptured slab in Palenque in which a deity is seated on an animal-throne. At Palenque is a sanctuary within a temple similar to those found in the seventh-century rock-cut cave temples of Ajanta in India. The sculpture and bas-relief of La Venta have also been compared to Ajanta. At Labná a columned entrance typical of the Puuc period bears a striking resemblance to one in a Cambodian palace. Similar columns may be found in Sayil's Palace.

Pre-Columbian codices such as the *Codex Vaticanus* shown in facsimile (*opposite page, left*), which are books of history, medicine, religion, astronomy, ethics, philosophy and mathematics, painted on varnished bark and folded like fans or screens, greatly resemble Sumatran books of divination (*opposite page, right*). This sculptured slab on a wall in the western corridor of House E of the Palace at Palenque, showing a dignitary seated on a jaguar throne, is comparable to a similar figure in Hahoba, India.

CHAPTER XVII

Comalcalco

LARGE-SCALE ARCHAEOLOGICAL explorations under the direction of Dr. Ekholm were launched in 1957 at Comalcalco in Tabasco in order to study possible trade links and other interrelationships between the ancient Maya of southeastern Mexico and the Nahuas of the Central Plateau. To date only trade pieces have been found. The site was selected for long-range study because of its unique position. Situated directly east along the coast from Coatzalcoalcos, known today as Puerto Mexico, and only a short distance east of La Venta, famed for its huge Olmec monolithic heads, **Comalcalco,** hub of the Chontalpa region, is the westernmost of the major Maya cities and therefore represents the farthest penetration of Maya culture in the direction of Tenochtitlán.

Until 1925, when the late Frans Blom, in company with the late Oliver La Farge, investigated Comalcalco for Tulane University, there is no record that the ancient city had been visited by scientists since November 1880 when the French explorer Désiré Charnay mapped the site and described the ruins in *Les Anciennes Villes du Nouveau Monde* (*The Ancient Cities of the New World*), published in 1885. In this work, which appeared in an English translation in 1887, Charnay spoke of Comalcalco's "three-storied towers" and described the structures as "immense." He cleared the main mound and left a ground plan showing three ruined temples to the north of what is known as the "Palace" mound, a vast architectural complex.

The map made by Charnay was used by Blom and La Farge in their investigation of Comalcalco. In *Tribes and Temples*, published in 1926–1927 by Tulane University, they told how the building known as Temple I was uncovered the first morning of their research. The mayor of the town, himself an ardent amateur archaeologist, had provided them with twenty unpaid assistants who, possibly fired with the hope of unearthing treasure, worked as eagerly as though they were to receive a high rate of hourly pay.

Seated figures with arms outstretched form a double frieze on one of the sculptures excavated at Comalcalco. The ruins have been dated by Dr. Gordon F. Ekholm between A.D. 500 and 900.

They were performing their share of public work in lieu of paying taxes, a system adopted by the municipalities of the region for the collection of revenues from the greater part of the Indian population and based on a pre-Columbian custom.

Instead of the usual cut limestone, which was not available, all the structures of Comalcalco had been built of brick, laid in a thick mortar. Blom and La Farge reported that the remains of rooms containing Maya corbelled vaults were still standing. From the highest buildings they were able to look out over an absolutely flat country, dotted with innumerable mounds. Clusters of what appeared to be tall trees were later found to be low trees growing on elevations.

Most of the uncovered Comalcalco temples are built on high artificial mounds, one of them about 114 feet high and extending 596 feet along its eastern base Segments of brick facing in various parts of the mound indicate that the structure was built of earth and held up by brick retaining walls. The elevation faces west. From either end extends a masonry arm, the two enclosing a plaza. Around the "Palace" mound, or "Acropolis," were found incised bricks and some elaborate examples of stucco ornament.

All the walls, as well as the steps leading up to the temple, showed indications of having been covered with a thick layer of mortar with a highly polished surface. The palace, the largest of the structures, stretches from south to north for a distance of 260 feet; it contains two parallel galleries apparently divided into rooms.

Dr. Ekholm's party, using eighteen laborers during a four-month season, worked in several buildings and made numerous test-pits primarily in order to obtain ceramics which would establish the sequence and relationships of culture at the site. Dr. Ekholm has dated the buildings, which are of Late Classic style, somewhere between A.D. 500 and 900 and has described them as representative of a culture aesthetically related to Palenque although more primitive than that of the magnificent ritual city. The general plan of the Comalcalco buildings is similar to that of Palenque, and in both places there is a wide use of stucco sculpture.

Among the important discoveries was a complete small pyramid adorned with a number of separate figures and surmounted by a roof. On one side emerged a fine mask of unusual size and effective design. The site also yielded a collection of smaller masks, stucco ornaments and incised

An unusually large architectural mask carved in deep relief is a feature of Comalcalco.

bricks. A number of the thin bricks show amusing examples of pre-Columbian "doodling." The brickmakers had drawn birds, crude animal forms and pictures of their own thatched huts on many of the damp surfaces.

Operations at the Comalcalco site have coincided with an increase in the commercial importance of the region, which is now profusely planted in cacao and other tropical products. Another factor in Tabasco's economic revival is the new all-weather highway from Coatzalcoalcos. During the era of the Conquest, Tabasco was a great trade center; it lay at the crossroads of a route that led from the Valley of Mexico to the Gulf Coast. Many storehouses for cacao and other products had been built there. "If the region was commercially important in Colonial times," Dr. Ekholm has pointed out, "it must have been so in pre-Conquest days. It is our hope to trace, in our research at Comalcalco, the extent and the scope of this ancient commerce, with its inevitable cultural impact."

No evidence of royal interment has been found during recent excavations, although several opened tombs in the vicinity of the great mound were explored. The existence of sumptuous tombs at Comalcalco was indicated by a burial chamber excavated by Blom and La Farge in 1925. On

Excavations at this site, once a crossroads of trade, yielded this finely modeled head, small masks and incised bricks.

its walls was uncovered a large bas-relief showing a dead chieftain surrounded by nobles and servants, each figure finely delineated.

The people of this land have dispersed, but the record of their lives and their achievements remains, carved upon walls and columns in designs and descriptions not yet deciphered. Bishop de Landa wrote of their fate in his *Relación de las Cosas de Yucatán:*

> Before the Spaniards conquered these lands, the natives lived in towns well arranged, and their lands were clean and free from weeds and planted with good trees, and the houses were arranged in this way: In the middle of the towns were the temples around handsome squares and around the temples were the homes of the rulers and the priests and after them were those of the principal people, and in this way the richest and most highly esteemed lived nearest them. And toward the edges of the towns there were the homes of the lower classes and where there were wells, these were near the houses of the nobles; and they had their inherited lands planted with fine trees and some with cotton, pepper and *maíz,* and in these congregations, for fear of being captured by their enemies and as a result of the Spanish Conquest, they scattered into the forest.

CHAPTER XVIII

The Campeche Area

The population of the present state of Campeche, in the southeastern part of the Yucatán Peninsula, numbering about 150,000, is the result of racial mixture—Spanish with Maya, Chontal and other Indian tribes. Anthropologists maintain that no pure Maya Indians have survived the long process of *mestizaje* in this Gulf Coast territory, which covers 19,672 square miles. It is bounded by what are now Yucatán and Tabasco and by Quintana Roo and Guatemala, in all of which the Maya culture flourished and inexplicably declined.

Many of Campeche's ancient cities were founded more than a millennium before the Spanish Conquest; 217 pre-Columbian sites of the region are listed in the most recently compiled *Arqueologico de la Republica Mexicana-Campeche,* published by the National Institute of Anthropology and History. Three cultural horizons, Pre-Classic, Classic and Post-Classic, embrace several distinct architectural styles. The oldest sites—in the Upper Pre-Classic, or Formative stage into the Early Classic—are usually dated 600-100 B.C. to the end of the third century A.D.

In her chronological survey of early Maya cultures Professor Florencia Muller pointed out that during the latter period waves of people or influences from Petén in northern Guatemala penetrated southeastern Campeche. The remote era in which these movements occurred is indicated by the date on the oldest stele of Balakbal, 35 miles north of Uaxactún. This stone bears a carved date corresponding to A.D. 408, only eighty years later than the stele dated 8:14:10:13:15 (A.D. 328) which was found at Uaxactún in the Petén area.

The route of the migrant peoples evidently passed through the center of the present-day state of Campeche, near the ruins of Etzná, and from there to the island of Jaina, 25 miles north of Campeche's capital. Later they moved down the coast, touching at Campeche, Río Sabancuy, Aguacatl and finally Atasta on the Laguna de Términos. According to the Maya chronicles the Itzá tribe, having discovered Lake Bacalar in the present territory of Quintana Roo, arrived at Chichén Itzá but left the site between A.D. 692 and 711 in order to settle in Champotón, where they remained for 260 years before returning to their abandoned capital.

A strategic point along the route of the roving Maya was Acallán on Lake Civiltuc. At the time of the Conquest this was the center of thriving trade relations with distant points. There are references in the *Annals of the Cakchiquels* to the presence of an Aztec garrison at Xicalango, maintained by Moctezuma II not only to guard his coastal colony and traders but also, as R. L. Roys suggested in his *Political Geography of the Yucatán Maya,* to exact tribute. Continued excavations at Aguacatl in Campeche by Brigham Young University investigators have indicated that the site may eventually be identified as the historical Xicalango. The merchants of Acallán knew various land and sea routes in their far-flung trading operations. On one such route they would set out from Xicalango, at the entrance to Laguna de Términos, sail around Cape Catoche and the northeastern side of the Yucatán Peninsula, touch at Pole on the mainland coast, then proceed across the channel to the port of Cozumel.

The epoch of Spanish rule in Campeche opened with the expedition of Francisco de Montejo, who, after coming to Mexico with Cortés, returned to Spain before the Conquest and in 1526 received from the Spanish king the right to conquer and settle a land believed to be the island of Yucatán, together with the island of Cozumel. Failing in his first attempt to take possession, Montejo ordered Alfonso D'Avila, his second-in-command, to join forces with him for such a conquest. According to Fray Diego López de Cogolludo in his *Historia de Yucatán,* written in 1656, Champotón was converted into a base and a second expedition was organized there.

The native leaders and their followers put up strong resistance, but Montejo succeeded in making alliances with the rulers of the provinces of Campeche and Maní. The city of Campeche was founded in 1540 on the site of an old Maya town known as Kim-Pech. The modern city, it is claimed, is built over a series of enormous artificial caverns which appear to have been used in ancient religious rituals. The Maya of the region were not fully pacified, and an opportunity for reprisal came while the conquistadores were celebrating their victory. Montejo was, in fact, dragged from his horse by the Indians, who wanted to sacrifice him, but he managed to escape, and subsequently, with tightened military control, the Mayas' hope of staging another rebellion faded. The conquest of Yucatán was completed in 1547.

Perhaps no spot in all the Campeche area evoked for the conquered and enslaved Maya more poignant visions of their ancient splendor than **Etzná,** 5 miles from Tixmucuy and 42 miles southeast of the present capital of Campeche. Etzná has now become the focal point of a comprehensive research project under the direction of Román Piña Chan. In the ceremonial center the principal structures rise around a spacious court. The builders' calculated aim—to produce an effect of magnificence—is dramatically clear.

Etzná's Pyramid of the Five Floors is a reminder of the ancient splendor of the Maya during the Middle Classic period.

These sensitively wrought figures from a 400-grave cemetery on the island of Jaina are "portrait statuettes." Women subjects in particular were treated with genuine feeling. Miguel Covarrubias has remarked on their makers' skill and realistic knowledge of form and movement.

Dominating the central ensemble on the east is the Great Acropolis, with a series of structures that provide a rhythmic balance at either side. Toward the south is a group known as the Little Acropolis, and on the northeast a ball court forms another complex of horizontal benches and vertical laterals. Nearby are the mound known as La Vieja and other minor structures.

The principal temple in the central plaza, the Pyramid of the Five Floors, rests upon a quadrangular base measuring 196 feet to a side. The height of the structure, including the tall *crestería,* or roof crest, is 102 feet. On three sides are annexes reaching to the fourth terrace. The fifth is crowned by a sanctuary reached by a broad stairway, with arched underpasses serving as the base for the terrace of the story above.

Characteristic of the Puuc-Chenes style of architecture prevailing in eastern Campeche and southern Yucatán, the several-storied structures incorporate typical features: stairways in ramps, entrances divided by columns, varied stone-mosaic ornamentation on façades and friezes, with such decorative motifs as thatched huts, Greek-type frets, latticework panels, small attached columns, and masks of Chac. The architecture, on the whole, displays restraint. The moldings are simple and the ornamentation provided by masks and stuccoed figures is concentrated chiefly on the *crestería.* A few hieroglyphs carved in stairways and stelae that bear dates corresponding to the Early Classic period have been found at the site, together with altars and ceramics of the same epoch.

Of the fourteen centers founded by the Maya during the Middle Classic period, which ended in A.D. 731, Etzná, together with Quiriguá in Guatemala, was destined to become a site of outstanding importance, Quiriguá, according to Dr. Morley, "because of its superlatively fine sculptured monuments," and Etzná "because of its striking and extensive architectural remains." In both of these cities, he stated, the Maya "stood at the threshold of their Great Period; they were ripe for an extraordinary cultural florescence. The curtain was about to rise on the most brilliant act of the Maya drama." It was during this same period that Palenque attained its culminating splendor.

At the beginning of the 18th *katun* of the 9th *baktun*—coinciding with A.D. 790—the Classic Maya area reached its widest extension. Nineteen cities erected period-markers to commemorate the ending of this *katun.* Etzná is one of a chain of five sites, also including Santa Rosa Xtampák, Holactun, Oxkintok and the Island of **Jaina,** in the western region of the Yucatán Peninsula in which monuments and buildings show definite dates.

CHAPTER XIX

The Cities of the Low Hills: Uxmal, Kabáh, Sayil and Labná

UXMAL, KABÁH, SAYIL AND LABNÁ have become objectives for an ever-increasing army of tourists. These four Yucatecan cities, linked by the same aesthetic tradition, form what is popularly known as the "Puuc Safari." Uxmal has been described by Dr. Morley as "uniquely situated in a great valley in the form of a cup immediately behind the 'Low Hills,' or Puuc range, which runs from northwest to southeast." Recent discoveries seem to indicate that it was abandoned by its inhabitants before A.D. 1441, the date of the destruction of Mayapán.

In once-magnificent **Uxmal,** 47 miles from Mérida, the proximity of past and future is dramatically evident. Here, despite the destructive fury of natural forces that have made a shambles of some of the walls, is an orderly complex of temples and palaces. These frozen harmonies in stone afford an ample basis for the claim made for Maya art by Dr. Spinden as being "one of the four really coherent expressions of beauty that have come into manifestation in the entire history of the human race."

The impression of solemnity, grandeur and mystery produced by the greatest works of autochthonous architecture has been attributed to these qualities: accentuated rhythm, with repetition of a motif, often prefabricated; stylization; ornamental or decorative character; symbolism; and religious or magic sense. The essence of the rhythm, Teodoro Lipps observed in his *Fundamentals of Esthetics,* is a "succession of elements, alternately accentuated and non-accentuated, in a series of moments of tension and moments of rest and principally in the assembly of the series in smaller units."

In its conception and in its structural unity Uxmal is also related to the latest trends advanced by urban planners. Architects of our own era have responded to the subtle balances and to the satisfying linear and spatial relationships demonstrated in its mass and profile. This acknowledgment of the heritage of the past may be found in many of Mexico's finest new public buildings and in the effort of "organic" architects to apply "sculptural theory to architectural reality." Professional, industrial and scientific groups who meet in various parts of Mexico often include in their itineraries a visit to Uxmal. Such delegations, especially those of learned societies, are reminiscent of Uxmal's Golden Age, an era when the city was the main objective of philosophers, astronomers and legislators from distant places.

The name "Uxmal," or "Oxmal," means "thrice rebuilt" and refers to the site's remote history on which only a few scattered legends shed any light. Modern scholars are indebted for knowledge of pre-Cortesian legend and for details of the culture of the region to Bishop de Landa, who recorded many ancient Maya traditions. Perhaps much more would be known of the Maya had it not been for the wholesale destruction perpetrated by the same bishop when, in July 1562, he demolished some 5,000 images and burned 27 hieroglyphic scrolls which he was unable to read but condemned as "works of the devil." He did, however, copy the hieroglyphics, indicating the symbols for the days and the months. This work has served as a key for the translation of the volumes known as the *Books of Chilam Balam,* which were written after the Conquest. These have preserved a chronology of the principal events during the last five centuries before the arrival of the Spaniards. They state that Uxmal was built in *katun* 2 Ahau or during the twenty years following A.D. 987 and that, for ten epochs, the people of King Ah Zuitok Tutul Xiu occupied the city. One of the chronicles states that a date corresponding to A.D. 1544 was 870 years after the destruction and abandonment of Uxmal.

Bishop de Landa recorded that Uxmal was founded by the Xiu, a Mexican-Maya tribe who entered Yucatán at least before the end of the tenth century. In *Yucatan Adventure,* Leonard Clark noted that Uxmal was once the greatest metropolitan city-state of the Late Classic period in Yucatán, with a population of possibly more than a million people living within its extensive environs. It was one of the three components of the League of Mayapán. General prosperity reigned during the period of its peaceful functioning, and in both Uxmal and Chichén Itzá temples and palaces attained new grandeur, with the Puuc culture achieving its most brilliant expression in Uxmal's celebrated Palace of the Governor.

The era of peace was short-lived and war developed from the rupture of the League. Bishop de Landa believed that the Xiu of Uxmal were not involved and that their ruler did not consent to the reduction of the Maya to slavery by the powerful Cocom of Mayapán after the fall of the Itzás in 1185. Unrest continued until the arrival of the Spaniards, with whom the Xiu sided, refusing to trade salt and fish with their inland rivals, the Cocom. Soon after, locusts and famine plagued the country, depopulating the areas, and with but slight resistance Spanish rule was imposed.

In the region surrounding Uxmal there are no *cenotes,* or wells formed by openings in the limestone rock above subterranean rivers. The one source of water is rainfall; from April to the end of October rains are heavy and the rainwater is stored in huge pits for use during the dry season. One theory advanced for the decline of Uxmal's glory is that wells and cisterns may have once existed but later dried up. Drought seems a logical enough cause for desertion of the "Low Hills" cities, although pestilence and famine, the result of devastating locust plagues as well as hurricanes, were probably contributory factors.

To date archaeologists have found no objects at the site dating from the Pre-Classic period. Most of the monumental ruins belong to the Classic Maya period extending from about the seventh to the tenth century. At about the time of the Toltec penetration of Chichén Itzá, the Xiu, it is believed, arrived from the Mexican Plateau, bringing with them religious and cultural ideas such as that of the plumed serpent. "It seems safe to conclude," wrote Dr. Morley, "that during the last half of the tenth century

A steep stairway leads to the various levels of El Adivino, which is actually the substructure of five superimposed temples.

The ruins of El Adivino, known both as "The House of the Magician" and "The House of the Dwarf," and Las Monjas, or "The Quadrangle of the Nuns," were sketched by Frederick Catherwood. John Lloyd Stephens called the ruins of Uxmal, "in picturesque effect, almost equal to the ruins of Thebes."

several groups of closely related peoples, probably of Mexican origin so far as their leadership was concerned, although all spoke the Maya language, entered the Peninsula from the southwest and proceeded to assume the political direction of northern Yucatán, establishing Maya-Mexican dynasties at the capitals of the three leading city-states: the followers of Kukulcán at Chichén Itzá, the Cocom at Mayapán and the Xiu, or Tutul Xiu, at Uxmal."

According to Dr. E. Wyllys Andrews of the Middle-American Research Institute of Tulane University, who explored Uxmal and Dzibilchaltún, the evidence might be interpreted to suggest that the Puuc and Mexican-Toltec influences, both of which he regards as expressions of the "Florescent" tradition, were the result of "intrusion and subsequent withdrawal of distinct ethnic groups. When these left, the native populations apparently reverted to their original cultural techniques over which they had lost mastery during the long period of control by intrusive Florescent elements."

Following the era characterized by violence, the powerful cities gradually became hidden under tropical brush and almost forgotten for many centuries until adventurers and explorers rediscovered the ruins and described their disintegrating splendor. In 1831 a leading London gazette published the observation that if the remarkable Maya ruins were more accessible they would have created a sensation rivaled only by Pompeii or Herculaneum. Waldeck visited the Uxmal site in the late 1830's but was unable to make detailed observations because the ruins were so overgrown.

He spent an entire year in Yucatán, including eight days in Uxmal, and brought out in a large handsomely illustrated folio edition his *Un Voyage Pittoresque et Archaeologique dans la Province de Yucatán Pendant les Années 1834–1836* (*A Picturesque and Archaeological Voyage in the Province of Yucatan during the Years 1834–1836*). Apparently the natives cleared the site in order to plant *maíz* there shortly before the visit of John Lloyd Stephens in 1841. In his *Incidents of Travel in Central America, Chiapas and Yucatán,* published in 1841 with engravings by Frederick Catherwood, Stephens recalled his initial impressions of Uxmal: "Emerging suddenly from the woods, to my astonishment we came at once upon a large open field strewed with mounds of ruins and vast buildings on terraces and pyramidal structures grand and in good preservation, richly ornamented, without a bush to obstruct the view and, in picturesque effect, almost equal to the ruins of Thebes." Désiré Charnay, a few decades later, made a study of Uxmal and other ruined cities. After years of painstaking study, the California journalist and publisher J. T. Goodman deciphered some of the hieroglyphics on Maya monuments and began publishing the work of Sir Alfred P. Maudslay in 1897. Goodman was particularly interested in calendrical correlations. Maudslay's exploration in the Maya region (1881–1894) were described in the section on archaeology in *Biologia Centrali-Americana,* which appeared in 1889–1902 as the first major scientific publication on the subject of the Maya civilization. Detailed drawings were made of many ancient sites for this work. Beginning in 1881, the Peabody Museum of Archaeology and Ethnology of Harvard University sent a series of expeditions to this area. Up to 1946 the Carnegie Institution sponsored twenty-five expeditions, many of them directed by Dr. Morley.

To the contributions to knowledge of the ancient past of this area should be added independent research, especially that conducted by the Mexican government. An extensive archaeological program had been planned by Felipe Carrillo Puerto when he became governor of Yucatán in 1921, but its fulfillment was cut short by his assassination in 1924. Dr. Alvar Carrillo Gil, who in his *Arte Maya* deplored the fact that wholesale vandalism and unchecked exportation of ancient objects had, through the centuries, depleted the Maya treasure-trove, stated that since the time of the founding in Mérida of the Archaeological and Historical Museum of Yucatán by Governor Carrillo Puerto this phase of Yucatecan culture had been neglected. Other subsequent governors did carry forward, however, the plans of their predecessor, sponsoring the Maya Foundation, which was organized to restore such ruined cities as Uxmal, to build new roads and improve old ones and to expand the Museum in Mérida.

The principal section of Uxmal's ceremonial center extends approximately six-tenths of a mile from north to south and 2,000 feet from east to west. The massive pyramidal edifice El Adivino is known both as "The House of the Magician" and "The House of the Dwarf." A legend about the origin of one of its popular names concerns an old woman whose son, miraculously hatched from an egg and of diminutive stature, possessed such phenomenal strength that he even succeeded in defeating the ruler in a contest.

El Adivino is in the form of a steep pyramid with a tremendous *perron*, or stairway, to the various levels of the façade. There are, in all, five distinct superimposed pyramid-temples. The ground plan is more or less elliptical, although usually such pyramids are square or rectangular.

The Lower West Temple has a double file of rooms with five doors in front and a room at each end. The frieze is beautifully carved. Above the entrances are masks of the rain god Kam Chac, representing a deity corresponding to the Mexican rain god, Tláloc. The ornamental molding above and on both sides of the opening contains Greek-style frets, interlacings, astronomical symbols and human figures with merlons in the form of a

A reconstruction of Uxmal's ceremonial center made by Professor Ponciano Salazar Ortegón shows a ball court in the foreground, Las Monjas at left and El Adivino at right. *Drawing by Hipólito Sanchez Vera.*

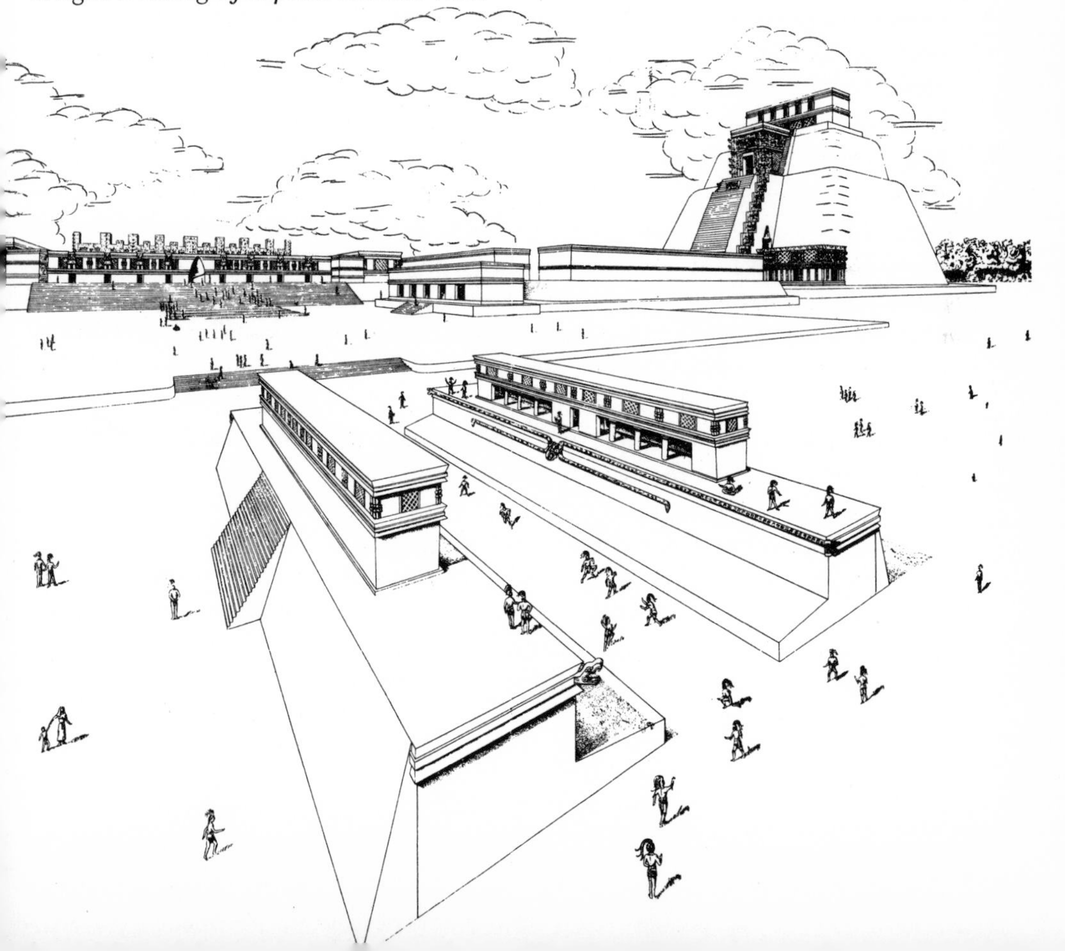

"tau," or Greek "T," and a row of attached columns as well as what appears to be the vertebral column of a serpent. This was the earliest known temple to be constructed at this location. Later some of the interior rooms and part of the exterior rooms were filled in to serve as part of the next base, which terminated at the height of the first stairway.

Resting on the platform of the latter is the Interior East Temple, excavation of which has not been completed. A serpent's form is painted on the stucco of the floor of the central room. The Interior West Temple is not visible from the outside as it was buried by later construction. Its façade reveals a more remote antiquity and the probable influence of other Maya centers. Later, using the façade as a wall, another temple was added. This has a single chamber which can be reached from the west by a unique beam-supported stairway, one of the most imposing in Maya architecture. Ornamentation of this temple is confined to the Puuc-style frieze. In the Chenes style, found largely to the south, there is, as a rule, an extraordinary profusion of decoration. On this temple the façade represents the rain god's head, with its open mouth the entrance. Elsewhere in Chenes-style buildings the mask may be repeated many times.

In the fifth period a larger base was added to the pyramid, hiding the interior temples and covering part of the lateral façade and the rear of the Chenes-style structure. Upon this base was built another temple, approached by stairways flanked by masks. The decoration of the façade is a latticed arrangement of bands, footprints and intertwined serpents. At the back is a niche in the form of a hut which may have contained a stone image.

Stephens wrote that he had stood at the main entrance of El Adivino as the sun went down, throwing from the buildings "a prodigious breadth of shadow, darkening the terraces on which they stood and presenting a scene strange enough for a work of enchantment." He was impressed by these pyramid-temples, the varying styles of which he described as "strange and incomprehensible, very elaborate, sometimes grotesque but often simple, tasteful, beautiful." Elsewhere he referred to it as "an extraordinary mass of richness and complexity" and termed its effect "both grand and curious." In his day the Maya Indians regarded Uxmal's ruined temples with superstitious reverence and would not go near them at night. They believed that an immense treasure was hidden in the ruins.

The structure known as Las Monjas, or the Quadrangle of the Nuns, is a veritable gem of Puuc-style architecture. It is composed of four buildings which surround a large court. Because of its numerous rooms and profuse latticework the Spaniards called this complex a convent. Fray López de Cogolludo referred to it, almost certainly in error, as the dwelling of the Maya "Vestal Virgins," who kept the "Sacred Fire." The patio, which may

Because of its numerous rooms and extensive latticework the Spaniards termed the quadrangular architectural complex (*top*) surrounding a court, a convent, or nunnery. The relief (*bottom*), suggesting death, was found on one of the altars in the court of Las Monjas.

be entered through an arch on the south, measures approximately 250 by 200 feet. The structures around it are built on low platforms of different heights.

Two-headed serpents adorn the façade of the East Building of Las Monjas (*top*). In the distance rises the Palace of the Governor. The frieze of the West Building (*bottom*) has a profusion of symbolic decoration, including serpents and thatched huts.

At the lowest level is the South Building, which measures 261.6 feet in length. The stairway which originally extended the entire width of the structure is partially destroyed. Each of the eight outside rooms has a separate entrance. Two small chambers were later added at each end, all facing on the court. Above each door is a niche containing a *naa,* or miniature Maya hut, a type of humble dwelling that has remained unaltered in Yucatán to this day.

On the inner walls of the arch of the central portico are painted red hands. The colors red and black indicated wisdom, but red signified the greater wisdom. The true meaning of the symbol is unknown, but Abbé Brasseur de Bourbourg maintained that the Maya believed that by impressing the red hand upon their temples they were invoking the spirit of Itzamna, also known as Kabul or Kab Ul, the "Celestial," or miraculous "Creative Hand." Others have interpreted it as the mystical sign of some ancient political society, as evidence of murder in high places or as the mark of Kukulcán. The historian Ethel D. Turner has called attention to the fact that the "red hand" symbol has been found on cliffs in Lower California, in India and elsewhere.

The largest and highest of the four units is the North Building; it is more than 260 feet long and contains eleven outside rooms, each connecting with an interior chamber. Access is by a stairway more than 90½ feet wide, flanked by two structures. The one to the west is known as the Temple of Venus because a motif adorning the frieze is believed to represent the planet Venus; it may, however, be a stylized rain god. According to one theory, Uxmal was built with reference to the relative position of the known planets. The principal frieze of the North Building is a composition of decorative elements, mainly life symbols. Masks of the rain god are placed over the doors. Stylized two-headed serpents alternate with thatched huts. Under the architrave are small figures representing prisoners with bound hands. Rising from the center of one of the steps of the broad staircase is a stele bearing a hieroglyphic inscription now almost illegible.

The East Building, 156 feet long, is the smallest and simplest of the group. Its two corridors are divided into compartments; those on the outside connect with a similar number of interior rooms. In addition to the rich latticework above its five entrances are decorations of carved serpent heads, an owl, the rain god and medallions.

A wide stairway leads to the terrace of the West Building, which is 176 feet long and contains seven chambers within its 34-foot width. The vertical frieze adorning the façade is decorated with a profusion of striking symbolic detail. Enormous plumed serpents, carrying in their fauces human heads, span the façade on either side of a central motif. They are inter-

Detail of the façade of the West Building of Las Monjas. The frets and bands are believed to comprise the original decoration, with the plumed serpents and figures in niches added later.

twined at intervals with *maíz* foliage against a latticework. On either side of a sumptuous throne, surmounted by a canopy of plumes, is the head of an old man with the body of a turtle. It is believed that the intricate background, formed of frets and indented bands in a harmonious arrangement and likened to the rich wall-embellishments of the Colonial era, was the original decoration and that the huge plumed serpents were added at a later date, at the time of the Mexican-Toltec and Xiu penetrations. The warriors and the nude tattooed figures imbedded in the niches of the frieze are said to belong to the latest epoch.

Of the seven rooms of the West Building, Leonard Clark has observed: "The only clue I had found to a seven-chambered temple was contained in the *Popul Vuh*, the sacred book of the Guatemalan Quiché Maya, which states in translation that their Sacred Mysteries were revealed to the priests in seven rites performed in seven rooms in the temple at Xibalba which, whether by coincidence or common origin, corresponds to the Egyptian Seven Halls of Death."

Adjacent to Uxmal's ruined Ball Court are the ruins of a structure known as the House of the Turtles, so named because of the carved turtles on its upper façade. The balance of proportion and austere elegance of decoration recall the classic architecture of ancient Greece.

An important group of four buildings built around a court 200 by 70 feet and known as the Quadrangle of the Doves has not yet been excavated. Stephens was of the opinion that the name might have stemmed from the high ornamented roof-comb along the top which, from a distance, looked like a row of dovecotes.

Considered by Dr. Morley as the finest example of ancient art in the Americas, the Palace of the Governor crowns a natural elevation, with a broad stairway rising on the east. This rests on another terrace that serves as the platform of the Palace. The building contains some 325,000 cubic feet of space. The long central structure, with its two smaller extensions, has a double corridor, with two great halls and four compartments on either side. The annexes are each divided into four rooms. Their doors face north and south respectively, but everything else is centered on the east side.

The broad frieze has been photographed countless times, but to each observer it offers a new experience in integrated architecture. Still in a good state of preservation, the principal motif is the symbol of the rain god, repeated and combined in original and harmonious forms. About 20,000 mosaic elements were used in the Greek-style frets and latticework panels that alternate in the frieze. The excellent quality of workmanship

A high roof-comb gives this structure, known as "The Quadrangle of the Doves," the look of a row of dovecotes.

This sculpture, found at Uxmal—a center of eroticism and phallical cults carried to Yucatán during the Mexican period—has been called "The Maya Queen."

in the carvings as well as what have been called the "inevitable" proportions of the building, which contains more than 200,000 cubic feet of solid masonry, have aroused the never-ending admiration of artist and layman alike.

Stephens expressed astonishment that all the lintels were made of wood and that most of them were still in place over the entrances throughout the immense ruin. The wood, which was very hard and rang under the blow of a *machete,* had come from distant forests, possibly 300 miles away. Dr. Morley noted that Stephens found at Uxmal a single wooden beam of *Sapodilla zapote* (chewing-gum tree) which he took with him when he left Yucatán. It was, however, destroyed in 1842 in a fire. Dr. Morley called this an "irreparable loss." "The inscription," he said, "could very well have borne the date of this structure." Another loss, that of the Maya library, has also been mourned by scholars. In 1878, after thirty years of research among the ruins of Uxmal and Chichén Itzá, Dr. Augustus Le Plongeon asserted in *Archaeological Communication on Yucatán* that the

The principal motif on the paneled frieze of the Palace of the Governor, the building considered by Dr. Sylvanus G. Morley to be the finest example of architectural art in ancient America, is the symbol of the rain god (*top*). A detail of the façade is shown (*bottom*).

great bulk of Maya literature was concealed in the temples of the two cities. Uxmal was regarded by many scholars as a center of the occult arts. Although several excavations have been made at different levels in the terraces on which the Palace of the Governor stands, no trace of the lost Maya volumes has been found.

Still awaiting excavation and restoration within Uxmal's ceremonial center are an enormous mound, almost completely covered with brush, designated as the Great Pyramid; a two-storied, partially destroyed Templo de Chimez; the building known as The House of the Old Woman (Who Mothered the Mighty Dwarf); The Temple of the Phallus and the so-called Cemetery Group, with its sculptured emblems relating to death.

Just outside Uxmal, about 1½ miles south of the Palace of the Governor, stands an isolated arch on a spacious platform. Its similarity to an arch in Kabáh, 12 miles east of Uxmal, has led to the belief that both were terminal points of a *sacbe,* or sacred road, which once connected the two cities.

Kabáh's majestic arch rests on a broad platform, its detachment from other construction endowing it with isolated grandeur and ideological significance. It impresses the visitor as one of the most dramatic notes in the entire architectural symphony of Yucatán's Puuc region. The platform and arch have been restored by the National Institute of Anthropology and History, so that in its sparkling whiteness the structure presents a strikingly modern aspect.

A few hundred feet beyond the arch is a still-unexplored section, a thickly wooded area containing scores of brush-covered mounds. The partially concealed monuments are of varying shapes and dimensions, some equaling or surpassing in size both Kabáh's Teocalli and Codz-Pop, or Palace of the Masks. Between the arch and the wooded section, on a slight elevation, is a stone image of a female deity said to be a benign fertility goddess but popularly known as "The Witch." One is sure to find at the base of this "shrine" offerings of copal and freshly cut forest flowers.

Dominating the horizon at the entrance to the archaeological zone of Kabáh is the great Teocalli, which rises to a height of 80 feet. At its base the austere pyramid-temple measures 180 feet on each of its four sides. A broad stairway, partially restored, extends to the top. On a causeway leading from the Teocalli to a smaller temple was found a monumental nude male figure, probably Kab-ul or Kab Ul, which gave the city its name; "Kabáh" signifies "He of the Powerful Hand." The figure holds a serpent in his left hand; the right hand hangs at his side.

The restored arch at Kabáh (*top*) presents a startlingly modern aspect in its solitary grandeur. The Codz-Pop, or "Palace of the Masks" (*bottom*), features rows of bizarre masks extending across its entire length.

In the rooms of some of the smaller structures were found other figures in pairs; one warrior was shown standing while his twin, in a kneeling position, held a flint-encrusted wooden weapon. Both wore grotesque masks and *penachos*, or richly plumed headdresses. For many years an elaborate pair of warrior figures provided the chief attraction of Yucatán's original Archaeological Museum in Mérida.

The profusely carved façade of the Codz-Pop, its rows of masks bordered by ornate moldings, gives an impression of massiveness.

The Codz-Pop was described by Dr. Morley as Kabáh's most interesting building. It is 151 feet long and contains ten chambers arranged in two lines of five rooms each, with one outer door for each pair of rooms. The building rests on a low platform and, unlike most Maya structures, has a rich molding above a single line of masks. Running through the lower half of the façade are three rows of masks which extend uninterruptedly across the length of the edifice. The medial molding is quite ornate. On the upper half of the façade are three additional rows of masks, the upper one crowned by another ornate molding. The profusely carved façade gives an impression of massiveness. Professor Salvador Toscano, who has called its architecture "capricious, impressive and of a very bizarre conception," has termed Kabáh "a city in transition."

To visit the cities of Sayil and Labná, a driver must proceed with caution along the narrow route in order to avoid thrusts from projecting branches. The only apparent signs of life during the trip are occasional mule-drawn carts with their burdens of recently felled logs or primitive beehives set by the Indians among the trees. Emerging from the jungle, one comes suddenly upon the vast central quadrangle of **Sayil.** While it is not known which Maya group built it, archaeologists of the National Institute of Anthropology and History have been able to ascertain a few facts about the city's later "transitional" period, which may date from A.D. 850 to 1000 and perhaps continuing beyond.

The ruins of Sayil are under the joint jurisdiction of Campeche and Yucatán, since its archaeological zone lies on the boundary line of the two states. The Palace, estimated by Thompson to have been built about A.D. 850, is Sayil's dominating monument. The impressive structure, crowning a triple-terraced mound, is a distinctive example of the Puuc style. Its hundred rooms are distributed among three floors. In the opinion of Federico Mariscal, the Palace is one of the most structurally unified of all Maya buildings. The columns are plain; built up of stone drums, they are cylindrical or of an exaggerated bulbous form with squared capitals. The roof of each of the first two floors serves as the base of a terrace for the story above. Keyed to a note of elegant restraint, the effect of great dignity created seems to stem chiefly from the repeated panels of the attached columns as well as the friezes framed by moldings and decorated with *tamborcillos*, tiny attached columns, interspersed with masks of Chac, the rain god. The slender spool-like columns here and at Labná have been compared by Dr. Gordon F. Ekholm to similar architectural features of a Cambodian structure.

The Palace at Sayil (*top*), with its 300 rooms distributed among three floors, is the largest Maya structure of this type found to date. El Mirador, near Sayil (*bottom*), is known for its high roof-comb. This technique was used by Maya architects to exaggerate the height of their buildings.

An earthquake or natural disintegration as a result of the pressure of vegetation between the building blocks apparently caused the collapse of the southern end of the upper tier of chambers. The large oval-shaped stone cistern at the base of the Palace is completely dry most of the time. Despite its symmetrical proportions and superior workmanship, it strikes a melancholy note, for it mutely testifies to one possible reason for the wholesale abandonment of the once-flourishing Maya cities of Yucatán.

Reconstruction of the Palace was undertaken in 1954 by Dr. César A. Saenz and Dr. Alberto Ruz Lhuillier. At that time the *zocle,* or flat square underbase, of the second-floor pedestals was repaired and the section to the west of the great stairway was partially restored. All the cracks in the stucco coating were closed and missing stones in the southwest corner of the building were replaced. Repairs were also made in sections of the façade where the panels are adorned with small triple columns. Numerous cracks in the cistern were also filled with mortar to conserve water during the rainless seasons.

A notable example of a typical roof-comb of the Late Classic period may be seen at El Mirador, or "The Lookout." This was placed at the front of the roof and was known as a "flying façade." In the Early Classic period it was customarily heavy, placed at the rear of a building and faced with stucco adorned with deities and masks, as seen, for example, at Tikal in Guatemala. During the Middle Classic period the *crestería* was usually reduced, as at Palenque, to a lacework extension in the central part of the roof. El Mirador is raised upon a high pyramidal base and has but a single entrance. From its vaulted roof along the front wall rises a tall *crestería* adorned with a series of rectangular perforations. The façade is simple and without decoration except for the stucco and its painted coating. Some sculpture survives in the ornamentation of the buildings of Sayil and the adjacent Maya cities of this period, but most in evidence are the frets, rhomboids and framed squares which are typical of the Puuc and Chenes styles.

Some 10 miles beyond Sayil in a southeasterly direction, **Labná** lies at "journey's end," deep within the heart of the jungle. The name means, in Maya, "Old Ruined Buildings" and was given to the abandoned city by the Indians of the region. No one may trace with certainty matters concerning the development of its unique ceramic art or designate the ancient dynasty under whose rule its distinctive arch and palace were constructed somewhere in the middle of the ninth century. Thompson and other archaeologists admit that no clue has yet been found to the origin or the history of this once-proud city. In the literature dealing with the ancient

The Palace at Labná is divided into three sections, which were apparently built at different periods.

monuments of Yucatán there are only a few scattered references to Labná, most of which are concerned with its aesthetic rather than historic aspects.

It is possible that of the three known codices of Maya origin (the authenticity of a fourth, in Mexico, is still controversial) one, the *Codex Tro-Cortesianus,* now in the National Library of Madrid, may have been painted at Labná or, at least, in Yucatán. The *Codex Peresianus* is in the Bibliothèque Nationale of Paris. The *Codex Dresdensis,* taken from Dresden by the Russians after World War II, led to Russian scholars' efforts to decipher ancient Maya glyphs.

The Palace of Labná is located on a terrace 315 feet long and 162½ feet wide. The façade, about 276 feet in length, is divided into three sections distinct in style and apparently built at different periods. Another important building, El Templo Mayor, now in a state of ruin, rests upon a truncated mound. The vestiges of its high roof-comb show that it was once elaborately adorned with stucco figures and laboriously detailed designs. Two chambers open upon the central portico. All along the upper part of

The high roof-comb of El Templo Mayor, or "The Lookout," was once adorned with stucco figures.

the wall extended a row of protruding skulls below which ran a high-relief frieze of human figures.

Labná's chief feature is a magnificent arch, the largest in Maya territory, which, along with that of Kabáh, Professor Toscano has hailed as an outstanding example of this type of construction in Yucatán. Spacious and harmonious in line, the monument has an entrance about 10 feet wide and 20 feet high; the whole design is realized with sober elegance. The lower part of the exterior façade is plain, all the ornamentation being reserved for the entablature. The decoration consists of three bands of geometrical motifs, with a fret pattern predominating. The interior lacks the austere simplicity of the exterior façade, being more complicated and less lyrical. Its upper frieze is richly decorated with large squares formed by rhomboid figures, united at their vertices to create a lacy openwork pattern. These sections are divided by stone models of typical Maya huts with niches in which small pieces of sculpture were probably placed.

Dr. Bernal has commented that, "The structures of Sayil and Labná and others in this area demonstrate not only a perfectly dominated esthetic and technique but a material wealth and possibilities of work until then unknown in the Yucatán Peninsula." Under Toltec influence, the architecture of Labná was evidently enriched with a finer, less massive type of building. Structures were adorned with small polished pieces of stone in geometric designs.

The decoration of the arch at Labná consists of bands of frets and small stone replicas of Maya thatched huts.

CHAPTER XX

Chichén Itzá

ANCIENT TRADITION HOLDS that the Itzás of **Chichén Itzá** emerged out of the west from a place known as Tulapan, possibly at the mouth of the Usumacinta in Chiapas. In the opinion of J. Eric S. Thompson they were Toltecs or a Tabascan-Maya group such as the Chontal who had adopted Toltec culture and the Quetzalcóatl cult. The *Books of Chilam Balam* of Chumayel give the date of the arrival of the migrants in Chichén Itzá as approximately A.D. 455, according to the Thompson correlation. It tells how the Itzás occupied this site, 75 miles east of Mérida, for 12 *katuns,* or about 250 years. About A.D. 692 they were said to have abandoned the city for Chakanputun—today known as Champotón—but between A.D. 948 and A.D. 987 they evidently returned to Chichén Itzá, this time as allies of the Toltecs from the Valley of Mexico.

It is not altogether certain, according to Dr. Morley, whether the reoccupation of the site by the original Itzás, who had come from the southeast via Cobá and Yaxuna four and a half centuries earlier, was accomplished peacefully or by conquest. Uncertainty also exists as to the time of arrival of the deity Kukulcán in Chichén Itzá. Bishop de Landa stated that the Itzás themselves differed on this point, some claiming that Kukulcán, regarded as a god, was already in Chichén Itzá, and others that he arrived with the homecoming wanderers.

At any rate, for the next two and a half centuries, the eleventh and twelfth, an era known as the "Maya Renaissance," Chichén Itzá was to become the greatest Maya-Mexican center. Art and architecture flourished during this period of peaceful coexistence with the two northernmost Yucatán cities, Uxmal and Mayapán, under the aegis of the flourishing League of Mayapán. But the tranquil prosperity was doomed by the civil war that broke out in 1194 between Chichén Itzá and Mayapán. The *Books of Chilam Balam* of Maní and Tizimin attribute the rupture to the lawlessness of Chac-Xib, a ruler of Chichén Itzá who kidnapped the bride of Al Ulil of Izamal, whose ally, Hunac Ceel of Mayapán, espoused Al Ulil's cause. Hunac Ceel summoned mercenary troops from the Mexican garrison of Xicalango, consolidating his victory by an act of personal bravery—diving into the sacred well—from which he emerged to proclaim that the gods below had appointed him as sole ruler. He selected as his capital Mayapán and established a dynasty, the House of Cocom.

Political intrigue robbed Chichén Itzá of her influence, while Hunac Ceel's legions wrought the destruction of what was described as once "the most brilliant jewel in the Maya-Itzá crown." The city was abandoned; some of its lords became vassals of the Cocoms, and its population dispersed. Yet it was the descendants of the Itzás, lingering in their ancestral region, who represented the last organized resistance to the invading Spaniards. During the period of the conquest of Yucatán, when Francisco de Montejo the younger had established his headquarters at Chichén Itzá, a revolt of the Cupules, allied with chieftains of Sotuta, Cochuah and Ekab, forced him to withdraw and reestablish himself in the Chel province on the north coast. Nine years later, in 1537, he returned to try to complete the conquest.

The lofty Pyramid of Kukulcán, its nine bodies crowned by a sanctuary, was named "El Castillo" by Francisco Montejo the Elder because he believed it to be a fortress. In the opinion of R. L. Roys the use of slave labor in such enormous public construction was a negligible factor in Middle America.

The Itzás maintained their independence at Tayasal, in north-central Petén, Guatemala, resisting several armed expeditions until March 13, 1697, when their island stronghold was conquered by Martín de Ursúa.

Of the hundreds of ruined structures in Chichén Itzá, which occupy an area stretching 2 miles from north to south and ½ mile from east to west, only about thirty may be visited today. Everywhere in the enormous zone, except in the limited area of the ceremonial center surrounding the lofty Castillo (Pyramid of Kukulcán) so named by Francisco Montejo the elder because he believed it was some sort of fortress, scores of mounds are still covered by tropical brush. But even with a large percentage of its architectural gems hidden from view, Chichén Itzá offers a structural aggregate of remarkable precision and beauty, obvious proof of an amazing civilization.

In the area known as "Old Chichén," about 1½ miles long, most of the buildings are overgrown with trees or entirely covered with earth. Among the excavated structures is the important "Date Group," so called because here were found the only complete dated hieroglyphic inscriptions. The dates cluster around A.D. 889 in the Christian calendar according to the Thompson correlation. A date-bearing lintel from the Classic Maya period was evidently re-used, as it is now supported by two Atlantean figures of the later Mexican-Toltec period which were clearly not part of the original construction.

A date-bearing lintel from the Classic Maya period was apparently later reused in conjunction with two Atlantean figures of the Mexican-Toltec period.

An important building in this area is the Temple of the Three Lintels. The base of this handsome structure is adorned with a Puuc-style latticework motif. Masks of Chac appear on the upper corners of the façade and at intervals on the wide frieze. One of the few remaining examples of the Classic Maya period, built between the seventh and the tenth centuries, is the Chichán-Chob, or "Red House." A red band painted on the wall of the portico has given the building its popular name. The walls are smooth-surfaced and all of the decoration is concentrated on the upper front section, known as the flying façade, which carries three masks of the rain god and a central roof-comb, where stepped frets form a latticework.

Like Uxmal, Chichén Itzá has its so-called Las Monjas, or "Nunnery," a many-roomed building which reminded the Spaniards of convents in their own country. On the northwest side is a superstructure with various galleries and chambers which is known as the "Nunnery Annex." The façade of this building, solidly covered with masks of the rain god, is a striking example of the Chenes style. Another typical Chenes feature is a doorway composed of the mouth of a mask surrounded by fanglike hooks.

East of the "Nunnery" are two other buildings of the Classic Maya period: the so-called Iglesia, or church, with its ornate exterior wall, and

On the northwest side of the multiroomed building called Las Monjas, or "The Nunnery," is a structure known as "The Nunnery Annex" (*opposite page*), covered with masks of the rain god. La Iglesia, or "The Church," has an ornately carved façade (*top*), with serpent heads protruding at the corners (*bottom*).

a long structure known as the Akab-Dzib, "The House of the Obscure Writing" or "The House of the Writing in the Dark." The central part of this building—one of the oldest in Chichén Itzá—is a fine example of the more restrained Puuc style. Undeciphered hieroglyphs inscribed around an incense burner on the underside of a stone lintel gave the building its name. Red hands painted on the wall of the east wing of the vault in the second chamber have been interpreted as a symbol of Kabul or Kab Ul, an attribute of the god Itzamna, or the "Heavenly Hand of the Worker."

Chichén Itzá's impressive astronomical observatory, known as El Caracol, or the snail, is an outstanding example of circular construction. So named because of the interior stairway that winds toward the top in the form of a spiral, the structure is the result of a series of superimpositions upon a double rectangular platform over which was erected a 41-foot tower. Reinforcements in the form of lower circular and rectangular plat-

El Caracol received its name of "The Snail" from the small spiral stairway leading to a chamber near the top of the observatory. A 41-foot tower was erected upon a double rectangular platform.

forms were added later to create the effect of a foundation supporting a triple terrace. The stairway begins at the second floor and leads to a small chamber where astronomers presumably studied the movements of heavenly bodies. Small openings in the walls may have pointed to cardinal directions or certain fixed astronomical lines of sight.

The association of El Caracol with the cult of the wind god has not, as in the case of many other ancient circular buildings, been clearly established. Numerous stone censers in the form of human heads and masks of the rain god are among its exterior adornments. A dubious date from this structure, if correct, would give a reading of A.D. 653, as correlated by Dr. Spinden, or a reading of A.D. 909, as calculated by Thompson, which would assign to this impressive monument an antiquity prior, by at least thirty-nine years, to the close of the Old Maya period. Thompson believes that the structure may date from before the beginning of the Mexican-Toltec period, its non-Maya ornamentation apparently having been added later. The vaulting is of a type that characterized a purely Maya period at Chichén Itzá, as are the lintels over the doorway. But confusion as to its dating has arisen because of the general design of the tower, which has been identified with the Mexican-Toltec period.

The Ossuary, or Grave of the High Priest, with its serpent balustrade, may be reached by a square stone-lined shaft extending downward from the floor of a temple above it. The shaft leads to a small opening with stone steps that lead in turn to a cavern 36 feet deep. Here, surrounded by offerings of jade, rock crystal and copper bells, were found the remains of priests and exalted personages.

Directly north of the Grave of the High Priest is the Great Ball Court. One of the seven courts at Chichén Itzá, it is the largest and most elaborate construction of its type in ancient Mexico. Its two high stone walls, running parallel for 150 yards, are perpendicular instead of sloping, as in earlier ball courts, and enclose a field of play 40 yards wide. The Aztecs called the game *tlachtli* and the ball court, *tlacho*. Spanish chroniclers described *tlachtli* as played in Tenochtitlán as a religious activity but also as a sport. Members of rival teams tried to toss a hard rubber ball through the hole in a stone ring set in the wall at a height of 18 feet, bringing into play only the hips, knees and elbows. Sculptured representations show that the contestants wore various protective coverings. The difficulty of the feat was acknowledged by the great honors and rich rewards customarily showered upon the victor. As his prize he was permitted to go among the spectators and collect from them as many costly cloaks of fine feather-work as he could carry away with him.

The walls of the *tlacho,* or Great Ball Court, are perpendicular and enclose a field 40 yards wide (*top*). Temples or reviewing stands were erected at either end of the court. The *tlachtli* players had to buffet a hard rubber ball into a stone ring set into the wall (*right*) without using their hands.

At ground level the walls of the court are decorated with bas-relief panels. A small temple, or reviewing stand, for the priests and nobles, rises at either end of the court and may be reached by a wide stairway from the outside. The friezes on the lower walls and the sculptures in the north reviewing stand, known as The Temple of the Bearded Man, symbolize death and renewal in fertility rites and, according to some interpreters, indicate that sacrifice was practiced by the players.

On the east wall of the Great Ball Court stands the Upper Temple of the Jaguars, so named because of a frieze of jaguars across the façade. This is separated from a lower frieze by spool ornamentation resembling that of the Mercado, or market, to the south of the Temple of the Warriors. The limestone reliefs on the doorjambs depict Toltec warriors. Mural decorations on the southwest wall of the inner chamber present a remarkably detailed portrayal of a siege, with women watching embattled warriors with great concern from their little houses. This painting is believed by some to depict the Toltec conquest of Chichén Itzá.

A construction at the base of the foundation of the Upper Temple of the Jaguars which A. P. Maudslay, who first explored it in the 1880's, designated as "Chamber E," contains on its interior walls remarkable processional reliefs dating from the twelfth century. Recalling his discovery in the monumental *Biologia Centrali-Americana,* he related that he found the outer half of the roof collapsed and the chamber filled with debris to the top of the columns. The removal of the fallen stones and rubbish, he commented, was "heavy work, but the full view of the sculptured wall repaid the labor." He also noted that the whole of the surface of the stone in the interior of the chamber, as well as the exposed ends of the walls and the square pillars which supported the roof, were covered with carving in low relief and that this surface was probably coated at one time with a thin layer of plaster.

The famed El Castillo of Chichén Itzá is crowned with a sanctuary of severe ornamentation dedicated to the Toltec deity Quetzalcóatl, or Kulkulcán. The pyramid of nine bodies reaches an over-all height of 90 feet. Each of the four sides, 180 feet long, has its own stairway leading to the upper temple. The four flights, each of 91 steps, make up a total of 364 steps. The additional step to the highest platform brings the figure to 365, or the number of days in the solar year. Excavations have indicated the existence of a substructure beneath the superimposed building. The earlier temple is a transitional building, largely in the Maya style, with some Mexican-Toltec motifs. In its sanctuary is a stone jaguar about 2¾ feet high, described by Dr. Morley as the most important object found in the Maya area. The jaguar has menacing white stone teeth, glaring jade eyes and a jade-encrusted tail. Seventy-four inlays of jade form the animal's spots. On its back was found a turquoise plaque depicting, in the opinion of Leonard Clark, the sacred serpent, the clouds, the rain and the earth. Copal offerings had been burned on the plaque.

At a short distance from El Castillo is the grandiose architectural complex known as "The Group of a Thousand Columns." In 1924, at the start of the Carnegie Institution's research in Yucatán, only an occasional bit of masonry of this extensive structure was visible above the dense growth. An army of machete-wielding Maya Indians worked for a season to clear the area occupied by this group, measuring 170 yards from north to south and 155 yards from east to west, before the archaeologists could begin their long-range task of exploration and restoration.

Dr. Jorge Acosta, who supervised the restoration of the Quetzalcóatl pyramid at Tula, has noted the theme carried out both in the columned vestibule of the pyramid at Tula and the Temple of the Warriors at Chichén Itzá. In each case two columns are located on the ninth step.

A panel in "Chamber E" showing a procession of warriors (*top*) was reproduced by A. P. Maudslay in the section on archaeology in *Biologia Centrali-Americana*, the first major scientific publication on the Maya civilization. In both the Pyramid of Quetzalcóatl at Tula and the Temple of the Warriors at Chichén Itzá (*bottom*) two columns are located on the ninth step. The complex known as "The Group of a Thousand Columns" covers an area 170 by 155 yards.

Found at Chichén Itzá were a stone relief of a jaguar (*top*) and a jaguar throne with eyes and spots of inlaid jade (*bottom left*). Copal had been burned on a turquoise plaque on its back. Several Chac-Mools (*opposite page*), varying in size from small to life size, were discovered, one at the entrance to the Temple of the Warriors, another in the colonnade facing the plaza.

Dr. Ruz Lhuillier has cited many Toltec elements carried from the Mexican Plateau to Chichén Itzá, such as the Chac-Mool immediately above the staircase. Possibly representing the idea of reincarnation, one Chac-Mool was found at the entrance to the Temple of the Warriors, another in the colonnade facing the plaza. Fourteen figures in all, varying in form from simple to ornate and from small to more than life-size, were discovered. Buried within the terraced platform of the Temple of the Warriors is what is known as the "fossil" Chac-Mool Temple. Only a short period of time separated the construction of this temple and that of the Temple of the Warriors.

Figures in the friezes of buildings of Tula and Chichén Itzá appear to represent the same rulers and warriors, wearing the same type of tunics, headdresses and ornaments. Such a phenomenon, of course, is only natural in the custom of colonists who, having settled in a new land, attempt to duplicate familiar details in the surroundings they have left behind. Other

The head (*top*) and caryatid altar (*bottom*) are elements of the Temple of the Warriors.

The pair of massive columns at the head of the stairway of the Temple of the Warriors represent serpents with fanged mouths and upright bodies ending in flattened tails. The columns are decorated in low-relief designs of undulating *maíz* leaves and serpent scales.

Technicians were able to copy a fresco found in the Chac-Mool Temple showing scenes of figures in canoes, temples and thatched huts before its obliteration.

Toltec elements include porches and galleries of colonnades; pillars in the form of inverted plumed serpents; intertwined serpents on the balustrades; a mythological being with elements of serpent, bird and man; the *talud*, or sloping wall base, of temples; the use of merlons on the front of roofs; Atlantean caryatids; columns adorned with warriors; bas-reliefs of jaguars and eagles devouring hearts; a *tzompantli*, or skull rack; and representations of such Mexican deities as Quetzalcóatl, Tezcatlipoca, Tlalchitonatiuh, Chicomecóatl and Tláloc.

The square patio enclosed by tall slender columns is believed to be the remains of a market. Nearby is a structure known as the Temascal, which may possibly have been a steam bath, another Central Mexican feature. This was equipped with low benches and there were two small apertures in the wall. A *cenote*, known as Xtoloc or Toloc, south of the market, supplied drinking water.

Typical aspects of daily life could once be seen in a fresco of the Chac-Mool Temple. The scenes included fishing boats, dwellings with thatched roofs, various domestic activities and religious ceremonies. Although weathering all but obliterated it, technicians were able to copy it before it faded.

Popular interest has mounted in the legends surrounding the treasure which was believed to have been cast during certain ceremonies into Chichén Itzá's brackish "Well of Sacrifice" in the period of the city's cultural and political preeminence (between the tenth and thirteenth centuries). The pool measures 180 feet or more in diameter, its tranquil surface, from 65 to 80 feet lower than the surrounding wooded area, suggesting a slab of pale jade. In 1961 the National Geographic Society sponsored an effort to recover ancient objects from its depths. Among the items of equipment used for this project, initiated by Pablo Bush Romero, a leading underwater explorer, was a large floating platform on which salvaged material could be sorted and cleaned before being sent to an improvised laboratory. A motor and winch to move and control the suction and hoisting apparatus, a swinging boom, a compressor and derricks were installed on the banks. Trucks, station wagons and a few tents formed a camp for the technicians. During the three-month working season a unique airlift operation, under the direction of the National Institute of Anthropology and History and Professor Ponciano Salazar Ortegón, the supervisor of the Southeast Archaeological Zone, yielded a considerable quantity of pre-Columbian artifacts, jewels, ceramics and objects of gold and other metals.

The sacred *cenote* of Chichén Itzá, the largest among scores of others

Salvaged from the Cenote Sagrado, or "Well of Sacrifice," in a recent airlift operation were many pre-Columbian artifacts, including objects of gold and other metals.

in the area, is a natural phenomenon peculiar to limestone regions such as the north-central region of the Yucatán Peninsula. The stark, white walls of the great circular well plunge down to a subterranean river that flows to the sea. The ritual pool of the "holy Itzás" is reached by an age-old limestone, plaster-covered causeway 25 feet wide and cracked by tree roots, known as the Via Sacra or "Sacred Way" that leads north for 300 yards from El Castillo. At its terminus, the legendary Cenote Sagrado ("Well of Sacrifice") opens like a wide cavernous mouth in the tropical jungle. Professor Antonio Bustillos Carrillo, in his *El Sacbe de los Mayas,* described it as the "short, mystic *sacbe* [road] par excellence, the one that best guards the Maya traditions of the past."

In the late afternoon, when divers and mechanics had completed their day's labor, silence would envelop the scene. Without interruption one could then study the almost-perfect symmetry of its circular rim and the dazzling whiteness of its perpendicular walls, their horizontal markings evenly eroded as though carved by some master sculptor. Only an enigmatic-eyed iguana might emerge in the silence to blink at the intruder.

Although the process of restoration is gradually endowing some of the buildings of Chichén Itzá with a semblance of their former grandeur, the *cenote* alone seems changeless. Except for the presence of more modern hoisting machinery and vehicles, the well seemed remarkably the same in 1961 as in the early 1920's, when the fantastic story of the treasure long hidden within its forbidding waters was first told to the author by the discoverer himself, Mr. Edward Herbert Thompson. That narrative revealed how, around the turn of the century, he had brought to the surface, with dredging and primitive diving methods, ancient objects of intrinsic and historic value. Thereafter, for many years, the well's remaining secrets remained inviolate.

Mr. Thompson's account of his explorations of the *cenote,* of which he had been the sole guardian, was first made public by the author who, on her first assignment as a correspondent for *The New York Times Magazine,* had accompanied scientists from the Carnegie Institution on their preliminary study of Chichén Itzá in February 1923. On that occasion the veteran explorer related, in the nature of a confession, how he had purchased the vast archaeological site, with all its monuments, for the equivalent of seventy-five dollars. He had come to Yucatán as a United States consul and occupied the rambling Colonial *hacienda* nearby, which later served as temporary headquarters for the Carnegie Institution investigators. An active antiquarian, he hoped to pursue his studies while serving in the consular post. He spoke the Maya language fluently and knew the native customs and traditions. Throughout Yucatán he was affectionately addressed as Don Eduardo.

Edward Herbert Thompson, who came to Yucatán as a U.S. consul (*left*), related the story of his own diving operations in the "Well of Sacrifice" to the author (*bottom right*), shown with Mrs. Earl Morris, a member of the Carnegie Institution expedition of 1923, as they prepared to descend into Chichén Itzá's Grave of the High Priest.

Sitting on a dislodged stone of the little temple on the rim of the huge pool, the aging explorer described to his fascinated listener, in vivid detail, the tragic ceremony often enacted, according to the old legends, at the brink of the *cenote.* His dramatic account seemed to summon for the author, then in her impressionable youth, a lovely sad-eyed phantom from its depths, for his narrative pictured a maiden of flawless beauty, wearing a bridal wreath of white roses, emerging from the sanctuary that crowns El Castillo. He told how black-masked priests led her from the frescoed chamber down the imposing stairway to the beating of a death drum, the shrill screech of a reed whistle and the mocking notes of a high-pitched flute. Below, in solemn procession, according to his story, the nobles and other priests awaited her descent. Trembling and helpless, the maiden joined them in their march along the sacred way. They paused at the edge of the pool and while the ominous music increased in volume, the maiden was led to the portico of the little shrine. Here the nobles and priests, their voices raised in loud supplication, formed a line around the rim of the *cenote* into which they threw precious jewels, treasured ornaments and vessels of smoking incense.

Then came the moment for the appeasement of the offended deity: the moment of supreme sacrifice. One priest chanted while another tore the rattle from a tiny copper bell worn by the maiden around her neck. To the Maya the act signified death. Her entire life had been a preparation for this hour. She had been taught that her symbolic marriage with Chac, the rain god, in the depths of the sacred *cenote* would save her people from impending doom and that her submission would open the door to immortal happiness. She had been drugged with *balche,* the sacred nectar, yet the natural urge to live and love was sometimes stronger than drug or faith, and a shriek of despair might pierce the forest as she was hurled into the murky waters.

Over the centuries, as Don Eduardo explained, this cruel ritual was performed whenever pestilence, famine or military defeat threatened the Itzás. Invariably, the spectators waited a while for the possible return of the lovely victim, believing that such a miracle would mean an immediate answer to their prayers. Occasionally, it was said, a maiden did return.

His tale finished, Don Eduardo then related the equally dramatic story of how he had substantiated the tradition of the sacrificial well and how, after years of constant solitary labor, he proved to his own satisfaction that the Cenote Sagrado of Chichén Itzá was the place of human sacrifice reported by Bishop de Landa. Don Eduardo's conclusions were strengthened by his reading of accounts of such ceremonies by the seventeenth-century historian Fray Diego López de Cogolludo and other chroniclers.

One of the legends that served to spur his determination to investigate was contained in a report rendered to Charles V of Spain by the *alcalde* (mayor) of Valladolid, Don Diego Sarmiento de Figueroa, who wrote in 1579:

> The lords and principal personages of the land had the custom, after sixty days of abstinence and fasting, of arriving by daybreak at the mouth of the *Cenote* and throwing into it Indian women belonging to each of these lords and personages, at the same time telling these women to ask for their masters a year favorable to his particular needs and desires. The women, being thrown in unbound, fell into the water with great force and noise. At high noon those that could, cried out loudly and ropes were let down to them. After the women came up, half dead, fires were built around them and copal was burned before them. When they recovered their senses, they said that below, there were many people of their nation, men and women, and that they had received them. When they tried to raise their heads to look at them, heavy blows were given them on the head, and when their heads were inclined downward beneath the water they seemed to see many deeps and hollows, and they, the people, responded to their queries concerning the good or the bad year that was in store for their masters.

"It was the mysterious, foreboding aspect of the *cenote* itself," said Don Eduardo, "that impressed me as much as its tradition of human sacrifice and offerings to the gods. For years I experienced a growing belief in the accuracy of the Spanish historians, although they made it clear that they were reporting merely from hearsay the terrible religious rites practiced here until the Conquest. My own intuitions on the close association of the Maya religious concepts with physical nature were also a strong factor in my decision to search for proof of human sacrifice in the turbid waters of the *cenote*. If human beings were actually consigned to a watery grave to avert the anger or win the favor of a deity, I reasoned that this would be the logical place of their doom. I had seen the *cenote* under all conditions—at flaming sunrise, brilliant noonday and in the silver moonlight—and always there was the suggestion of solemnity, mystery and tragedy."

When Don Eduardo decided to verify the strange tradition he was confronted, he said, by obstacles on all sides. His conviction met with ridicule from the layman and discouragement from the scientist. The scholar W. H. Holmes, who visited Chichén Itzá in 1895, deprecated his project: "There has been some talk of exploring the bottom of this *cenote* with the expectation of securing works of art or other treasure, but the task is a most formidable one and will require the erection of strong windlasses and efficient dredging apparatus. It is doubtful if promised results warrant the expenditure necessary for the carrying out of the work in a thorough manner."

Don Eduardo admitted that he agreed with Holmes about the formidable nature of the task, especially since funds for "strong windlasses" and "efficient dredging apparatus" were not available. Beneath 40 feet of water was a mud bed about 35 feet deep. Unable to obtain financial support for the expensive undertaking, Don Eduardo decided to pursue less costly research methods. He learned the diver's art from a Captain Ephraim Nickerson of Long Wharf in Boston, and day after day descended into the *cenote,* in many instances narrowly escaping death. (According to the *Books of Chilam Balam* of Chumayel, Hunac Ceel of Chichén Itzá and Mayapán was supposed to have set a precedent for his exploit and, as a survivor of the plunge, was signally honored; Richard Halliburton claimed to have descended twice.) By 1903 Don Eduardo had installed a simple dredging apparatus, with windlasses operated by the Indians. After "worried days and sleepless nights" the dredging at last yielded results. The first object to be brought up was a ball of *pom,* the sacred resin burned by the Maya as incense. Later human bones were brought to the surface, lending support to the theory that ceremonial sacrifices had been made at this spot. When, after months of dredging, the well ceased to yield results, he and his assistants began to dive. Gradually beautiful objects began to make their appearance in the scooped-up silt. The assortment included jade, gold, copper, ebony, balls of copal, obsidian knives, weapons ornamented with turquoise mosaics and even fragments of ancient textiles.

As the salvaged treasure began to reach the Peabody Museum of Harvard University via the consular mail pouch, Thompson succeeded in winning the interest and aid of Stephen Salisbury of Worcester, Mass., and Charles P. Bowditch of Boston. A signed article by the author describing this venture, in *The New York Times Magazine* in March 1923, brought many repercussions, including a lawsuit initiated by the Mexican government to repossess the ancient material. The sum demanded for the loss to Mexico of the Maya treasure was fixed at $2,000,000, the estimated value of the following objects, sent by Thompson to the Peabody Museum: a gold jar, 12 inches in diameter and weighing approximately a pound; 42 gold discs ranging from 4 to 10 inches in diameter, repoussé or engraved; an elegant tiara, 8 inches long and 4 inches wide, with serpents entwined in an openwork pattern; 20 gold rings and 100 gold bells of various sizes; 40 gold discs, 1¼ inches in diameter, used for scales; seven slabs or plates of jade, 3 by 4 inches in diameter; 14 jade spheres, 1½ inches in diameter; thousands of knives, flint points and beads of archaeological value; and, most precious of all, a small clear jade figure 4 inches high and 2 inches wide, wearing an elaborate headdress and seated on a small stand. This piece, perfectly worked, polished and well preserved, is regarded by some authorities as the finest small figure of Maya art found to date.

The bitterly fought suit, which marked a point of minimal cooperation in the relations between the neighboring republics, was heard in the lower courts and finally reached the Supreme Court. There, in Mexico's highest tribunal, it was ruled that since at the time Thompson dredged the well there were no adequate local or federal laws in force to prevent the exportation of archaeological treasure and since Chichén Itzá, where the objects had been found, was Thompson's property, Mexico had no redress. The decision was received in Mexico with considerable resentment; the treasure of the *cenote,* it was argued, represented an important cultural heritage. In the early 1930's the Peabody Museum offered to return half of the collection, but the Mexican government rejected a compromise settlement. In December 1959, however, during the 58th Congress of American Anthropologists, 94 precious pre-Columbian objects—gold discs bearing hieroglyphic inscriptions—were returned to Mexico in the name of the Peabody Museum by the curator, Dr. J. O. Brew, reflecting a new era of closer cultural cooperation between the United States and Mexico.

CHAPTER XXI

Mayapán: The Mayan Collapse

In 1950 the Department of Archaeology of the Carnegie Institution initiated a research project, supervised by H. E. D. Pollock, among the ruins of **Mayapán,** about 35 miles southeast of Mérida. It was once the most flourishing and potentially important city of northern Yucatán. The excavations have uncovered a number of mounds which have revealed both public and private buildings. The ancient homes cover a large portion of the central section of the city, which is enclosed by what may have been a defensive wall. A continuous construction, its rough stone base extends for about two miles. Originally faced and presenting a smooth surface, the wall is pierced by eight main portals. There are standing vestiges of a platform.

At first glance the ruins resemble those of Chichén Itzá in their late Maya, Toltec-influenced style. This is notably true of the colonnaded structures, built along the lines of Chichén Itzá's Temple of the Warriors. All are in a poor state of preservation and suffer by comparison with the striking monuments built by the "Holy and Learned Men at the Mouth of the Great Well." As at Chichén Itzá, the main edifices of Mayapán lie close to the circular rim of a large *cenote*. A round temple is situated in the central ceremonial group about 325 feet south of the Castillo, or great pyramid. The building faces east and looks across a plaza to a temple with a serpent column. On the plaza's southeast corner stands what archaeologists believe may have been a ritual center. Sections of a causeway connect the two main groups of buildings, each cluster forming a quadrangle around a court. From the size and quality of workmanship, these may have been reserved for official use. The colonnaded northern group, of palatial proportions, appears to be domiciliary in character. The dwellings follow a basic three-unit pattern. *Metates* for grinding *máiz*, crude utensils, red jars and bowls

Four round structures were found in the walled city of Mayapán (*top*). Also discovered here were a serpent head (*bottom*) and the remains of a long colonnaded hall similar to the portico of Chichén Itzá's Temple of the Warriors.

and heaps of bird and animal bones have been found in what may have been the kitchen area of each group.

Scientists have found ample traces of remains that almost certainly date from an era earlier than the great epoch of Mayapán. These remains, in the form of loose or reused building stones, are believed to belong to the Puuc period. No complete structure of the Puuc or the Toltec period has yet been identified at the site.

Dr. Ekholm, who has conducted extensive research in the Tampico and Pánuco regions in quest of vestiges of Huastec and Totonac cultures, has stated that the almost complete disintegration of Mayapán "seems to prove that the city had not been occupied up to the time of the Conquest but had been deserted years before the arrival of the Spaniards." In the opinion of Oswald Spengler, the story of the Maya collapse could remain forever in the realm of mystery. "The cluster of great cities in the virgin forests of Yucatán," he wrote, "succumbed swiftly to the attack of vegetation, and we do not really know the old name of any one of them. Of their literature three books survived, but no one can read them." He pointed out that the Maya empire is the one example of a civilization that ended in "violent death," not "starved, suppressed or thwarted but murdered in the full glory of its unfolding, destroyed like a sunflower whose head is struck off by one passing by."

Archaeologists have succeeded in tracing the general outlines of the Maya decline. The brilliant period of the Old Empire, which lasted up to about A.D. 629, occurred during the time it embraced a territory that extended from Central Honduras and the high plateau of Guatemala as far as northern Yucatán and included what are now Chiapas and Tabasco. From that date, however, a steady deterioration may be noted during three centuries, marked by various kinds of natural and man-made disturbances.

During this time many of the noblest Maya structures were swallowed up by the jungle, its lush vegetation even concealing some of the highest pyramids. Shortly after the middle of the tenth century there appears to have been an awakening. The stones of the old cities served in some cases to build new ones, less glorious, perhaps, but still preserving much of the architectural grandeur of the ancient palaces, temples and public monuments.

The tripartite League of Mayapán was weakened and finally destroyed by a long period of wars and revolutions, but during the time it flourished, according to Spengler, it exercised an influence and controlled resources far superior to those of the states of Hannibal's day. It could claim a comprehensive policy, a carefully ordered financial system and highly developed legislation. Its "administrative ideas and economic tradition," he observed, "were such as no minister of Charles V could ever have imagined."

Harmonious relations with Uxmal and Chichén Itzá were disrupted and soon afterward came the fall of Chichén Itzá. The conquerors, the haughty Cocoms, obliged the dethroned Maya rulers to live within the walled city of Mayapán. But in 1441, uniting under the leadership of Ah Xupan Xiu, the Maya chiefs attacked Mayapán, killed the ruler and all but one of his sons, who happened to be absent on a trading expedition. When Mayapán fell, as Dr. Morley pointed out, all centralized authority in the northern half of the Yucatán peninsula collapsed and complete political disorganization ensued. The disintegration of Maya culture was all but complete.

Excavations at Mayapán seem to confirm the claims of the ancient chronicles, that when the intruders from the Mexican plateau arrived in Yucatán, they were influenced to some degree by the native population, even to adopting their language and customs while retaining many of their own traditions and imposing some of their own aesthetic principles. But, as Spengler suggested, the once-powerful Maya cities of Yucatán, like Athens and Alexandria under imperial Rome, sank into apathy under their Nahua masters.

The incense burner of badly fired clay shown is one of many such objects produced in Mayapán under a military regime during which the arts declined.

CHAPTER XXII

Quintana Roo:
Chunyaxché, Tulum, Cozumel, Isla de Mujeres and Cancún

THE VAST TERRITORY OF Quintana Roo, occupying the eastern and central sections of the Yucatán Peninsula, is perhaps the least known and, in terms of ancient treasure, perhaps the richest of the world's still unexplored regions. While the ruins of a chain of former coastal cities provide evidence that a Maya maritime empire once flourished here, the population is sparse and there are few settlements save for scattered *chicle* stations. But its isolation is soon destined to end. In 1962 Dr. Eusebio Dávalos Hurtado announced that the seacoast citadel of Tulum would be linked by road with the ruins of Chunyaxché, 31 miles to the south.

One of the string of cities, including Xelha and Acumal, which once marked the coastal road at regular intervals for a distance of 300 miles, is Tancah, which lies north of Tulum. Investigators counted at this site more than a hundred mounds and ruins of buildings, some in fairly good condition. Club de Exploraciones y Deportes Acuaticos de Mexico (C.E.D.A.M.) explorers have made an intensive study of the region, finding, during recent expeditions, a network of roads and a watercourse of man-made canals connecting the sites of Boca Paila, Muyil and Chunyaxché. Emmett Gowen, a hunting and fishing expert, has on occasion penetrated as far as 6 miles into the jungle, where he found traces of ruined buildings, as well a couple of exceptionally beautiful *cenotes* with caverns. In one of these was a stalagmite carved into the likeness of a human face. It is Gowen's prediction that within a few years the stretch between Bahía Ascensión and Bahía Espíritu Santo on the central Quintana Roo coast will become an important objective for scientists and tourists. "There are many buildings," he remarked, "extending along the shore and back into the marshes. In one

C.E.D.A.M. explorers have discovered in Quintana Roo a network of roads and a watercourse of canals connecting Boca Paila, Muyil, the site of this ruin, known as the "High Castle," and Chunyaxché, a site spotted from the air by Charles Lindbergh in 1929.

structure was a Chac-Mool, the head of which had been broken off but later set back in place."

In 1963 Aarón Merino Fernández, then the governor of the Quintana Roo Territory, officially inaugurated a major research project at Chunyaxché, with Dr. Román Piña Chan in charge. Initial efforts have concentrated on ascertaining the extent of the ceremonial center, with its numerous palaces, temples, stelae and ball courts. According to Piña Chan, the ruins are, like those of Tulum, which they closely resemble, of a relatively late period, indicating Mexican-Toltec influence. Many of them are so low that they appear to have been built for children or for an undersized population or, what is more likely, designed as ritualistic structures for token worship. The traces of mural decoration do not approach, however, the aesthetic importance of the superb wall paintings of Tulum's Temple of the Frescoes.

Michel Peissel, author of *The Lost World of Quintana Roo,* focused attention on the site in 1958 when he made a 250-mile trek along the coast and claimed to have "discovered" the ruined inland city of **Chunyaxché.** He had started from Cozumel in a small boat, which he had hoped would take him as far as Belize and permit him to go ashore whenever he sighted a likely ruin. Left stranded on a lonely beach, with no equipment other than a chart, hammock, camera, flannel sports outfit and sandals, hardly designed for hiking over coral rocks, he was dependent upon isolated groups of Indians whom he encountered on his journey to Belize by foot. They befriended him and shared with him their knowledge of the territory and their scant supplies.

After crossing Lake Chunyaxché and Lake Muyil, C.E.D.A.M. explorers were guided to Chunyaxché, where they found ruins covering a broad expanse and, in one of the larger monuments, the remains of a tunnel.

Despite the hardships he endured, Peissel felt amply rewarded by the results of his adventure. He found a number of sites which had not been noted on his chart. Chunyaxché, however, had been spotted from the air by Charles Lindbergh in 1929 and reported, along with other ancient sites in southeastern Mexico, Guatemala and Honduras, to the Carnegie Institution. The site of Chunyaxché had evidently been explored even earlier.

An expedition by water to Chunyaxché was organized early in 1959 by Pablo Bush Romero, founder and president of C.E.D.A.M. This trip was a preliminary survey of the Boca Paila region of the coast, which was scheduled for investigation by members of the group during the following season. The immediate aim of the survey was to locate, by diving, the remains of submerged ancient sites and historic wrecks in the Boca Paila waters.

A party of ten left Cozumel at midnight March 3, 1959, on the *Marlin*. This included an underwater photographer, a diver, an archaeologist, a Maya representative of the National Institute of Anthropology and History and the Ministry of the National Patrimony, a teen-age native guide, C. W. Ennis, Jr., of San Antonio, Texas, and James Webster of Chattanooga, Tennessee. They crossed two lakes on the far side of the Boca Paila lagoon. The three bodies of water are connected by two canals, the first 9 miles in length.

Shortly after entering Lake Chunyaxché a propeller of a launch scraped against an unknown object, but the guide was sure that at this point the water was many fathoms deep. A hammerhead shark attacked, almost overturning the launch. The journey was resumed, however, and in a few minutes the group saw a small Maya temple on the left bank. Going ashore to examine it, the men observed that the site had been partially cleared of tropical brush and that the stone walls had been newly broken. Ancient artifacts and fragments of sculpture and ceramics were strewn around, giving mute evidence of recent plundering.

After crossing the immense expanse of Lake Chunyaxché, which lies more than 6 miles from the coast, they entered another canal, approximately .6 mile in length. Both canals, they believed, represented the work of ancient engineers. On the banks of Lake Muyil, where the party landed on a small wharf, they found a breach in the wall closed by giant ferns and a dense tangle of vines. Forging into the jungle, they reached a clearing and a few huts inhabited by Indian families and were able to induce a Maya boy to lead the way to Chunyaxché, buried for a millennium under a living emerald blanket.

"The ruins," Bush Romero later reported, "are numerous and cover a large expanse. There are monuments and important palaces of more than 39 feet in height. Most of them are totally covered with brush, but one can see that some have been partly cleaned and plundered as well. We found a tunnel in one of the larger monuments and explored its interior. The tunnel led for several feet before we reached a double chamber of the Tulum type. Apparently, this structure had an interior temple, reached by crossing the tunnel, and here a small pyramid had been constructed. In various wall niches were venomous Nayuacas, known as the *Cuatro Narices,* or four-nosed snakes."

Without further incident the party recrossed Lake Muyil, but on their way back to the Boca Paila landing, as they reentered Lake Chunyaxché, the launch pulling the canoe sank in shallow water. Investigation of the ruins on the Boca Paila banks revealed stone walls, resembling corrals, extending into the water. In some remote epoch the water level at this site may have been lower, lending support to the legend of a submerged Maya city, a provocative point that may be illuminated by future subaqueous explorations. The possibility that a subterranean passage may be found leading from the sea to Tulum's temple citadel also awaits further investigation by C.E.D.A.M. divers and archaeologists.

The sacred walled city of **Tulum,** connected with Cobá and with Chichén Itzá by a *sacbe,* rises at a central point on the east coast of Quintana Roo, almost opposite the Island of Cozumel. Tulum looks out over majestic rocks against which the waves of the Caribbean eternally dash,

Walled Tulum, situated on a 40-foot cliff overlooking the Caribbean, gives the impression of a citadel. The 25-foot-high Castillo in the center is flanked by smaller structures.

to produce what Miguel Angel Fernández, in his report on the Mexican government restoration project of 1938, called "a rumbling symphony."

Rising upon terraces that take advantage of the different elevations of the site, the extensive complex gives the impression of a citadel. The Castillo, or great temple, the tallest of the structures, is situated in the center. To the north and south, at points equally distant from the central complex, small temples rise on promontories overlooking inlets with small sandy beaches. Two types of construction are to be found. The more ancient is characterized by very large chambers with columned interiors covered with a flat roof of true concrete sustained by wooden beams. The second type is a superimposition with the typical primitive Maya arch, such as may be seen at Chichén Itzá and Uxmal.

The principal structure, Temple #5, is known as The Temple of the Descending or Diving God because of a large figure in a headlong position over the main entrance. This motif is repeated in other buildings at Tulum. In Temple #16, known as The Temple of the Frescoes, are notable murals. Although varnished with a preservative by Carnegie Institution experts in 1922, they were found by Miguel Angel Fernández to be seriously deteriorated before he made his own restoration in 1938. The frescoes decorate part of the north gallery and the entire extension of the south and west galleries. The symbolism attributed by S. K. Lothrop, who explored the site under the auspices of the Carnegie Institution in the early 1920's, to the free-hand paintings corresponds to the Prometheus myth. From the mouth of a deity seated upon a jaguar and representing the sun issues the sacred breath, which is transformed into a hand. The god is about to produce fire. The small flaming rods that have produced the contact with the divine breath may be clearly seen.

The list of scholars who have explored Tulum in the past century and a half includes Stephens, Holmes, Morley, H. H. Bancroft and others. Some archaeologists have identified Tulum with Zama, the largest of the several sites apparently seen by Grijalva in 1518 as he sailed along the east coast of the Yucatán Peninsula. The "highest tower," mentioned by him in his account, is believed to be the Castillo. The Grijalva flotilla, consisting of four ships supplied by Governor Velásquez of Cuba and manned by some two hundred sailors and soldiers, left Cuba on April 8, 1518, or, according to some historians, on May 1, 1518. One of the ships was commanded by Francisco de Montejo. The flotilla anchored in a large bay which they named Bahía de Ascensión because of its discovery on Ascension Thursday.

Tulum, on the mainland, looks across to the enchanted, timeless isle of **Cozumel**. Its glistening white beaches, bands of sapphire, emerald and

At the southwest end of Tulum is the Temple of the Diving, or Descending, God (*top*). This deity, represented in a headlong position over the doorway, has been identified as Ah Muzen Cab, the bee god. Galleries in Temple #16 are decorated with frescoes (*bottom*) which, according to S. K. Lothrop, represent the creation of fire by a sun god seated upon a jaguar.

turquoise waters like some vast cloisonné tiara, and an atmosphere of unrivaled peace and tranquillity are all now within an hour, by air, of Mérida. Besides its idyllic natural beauty and mild climate, the potent lure of buried treasure adds to Cozumel's appeal that currently draws numbers of vacationers, skin-divers, fishermen and marine scientists.

The route of Spanish vessels sailing northeast, laden with plunder taken from Maya, Aztec and Inca palaces of Central Mexico and South America, was usually through the Yucatán Channel. Cozumel has been over the centuries a logical stopover point for vessels in need of fresh water and supplies. In the sudden gales that can change the usually calm aquamarine waters into tumultuous seas, especially during the fall hurricane season, many of the treasure-laden galleons were sunk here. Today the coral-encrusted cannon, anchors and hulls of at least two ancient wrecks may be traced in eerie white outline by divers hoping to locate within the holds chests which may still be filled with gold bullion and Spanish doubloons.

Long-submerged ships have yielded some of their secrets to persistent investigators. Already, frogmen diving off Matanceros, hand-drilling through thick coral caps, have salvaged thousands of objects from the wreck of the *Matanceros,* an eighteenth-century Spanish merchantman. In the opinion of Dr. Mendel Peterson, curator of the Armed Forces History Department of the Smithsonian Institution, the cargo retrieved by C.E.D.A.M. explorers is "the largest and most varied yet found in American waters." Included among the recovered objects are wine bottles still containing topaz-colored dregs, crystal goblets, silver and pewter tableware, crucifixes, coins, religious medallions, elaborate metal shoe buckles, a handsome gold watch, thimbles and packaged needles. Anchors and cannon of various sizes are all that remain of the vessel's heavier equipment.

In the realms of the sea anemone, shark and barracuda, there may still lie imbedded beneath the coral other objects of great historic and intrinsic value. The *Matanceros* merchantman is only one of scores of vessels that met their doom among the reefs of Quintana Roo, Cozumel, Isla de Mujeres and the Chinchorro atoll. Ever since the Age of Discovery at the turn of the sixteenth century, treasure has literally rained down upon the floor of the Caribbean. It has flowed from ships lost in naval warfare between European rivals for control of the American continents and seas and has drained in golden streams from hulls crushed by mountainous waves hurled by hurricanes or from vessels boarded by marauders under the black flag of piracy.

Such a heritage cannot but impart a fabulous aura to the tropical paradise of Cozumel. Beneath the slumberous façade of sun-drenched tranquillity vibrates the undercurrent of suspense that accompanies strange and marvelous adventures. Legends, myths, traditions, tales of corsair gold and precious archaeological relics are rampant. The visitor to Cozumel is bound to hear, almost immediately, at least one exciting account of a quest or even the actual recovery of buried treasure. Foreign "prowlers" may be seen among the coves which indent the island's shoreline, furtively tapping likely stretches of sandy beach with metal detectors or, with chart in hand, pacing off the distance between a storm-bent palmetto and "yon rocky cliffs." Yet, more often than not, such a search yields, as the old Spanish proverb has it, "many husks but few nuts."

One intriguing account of a "find that vanished" concerns a local inhabitant who was caught in a violent "norther" as he coasted along the southern tip of the island. He sought shelter in a cave and, while waiting for the storm to subside, crept around an inner ledge from which he could see, as he later related, a spectacular array of ancient Maya art. Pieces of

Many coves, purported to hold buried pirate gold and archaeological relics, indent the shoreline of the island of Cozumel.

sculpture, masks, gold and jade ornaments were, he said, stored in an upper chamber that seemed to have been hollowed out of a perpendicular wall. Without a ladder, however, he was unable to reach the treasure. When he returned on the following day he could find no opening among the rocks. It was almost as if the sea had sealed overnight the entrance to the cavern, with its long-held secret.

Whether the tale was fact or fantasy is hard to say. As Cozumel's *cronista,* Professor Gonzalo de Jésus Rosada Iturralde, author of *Breve Historia de Cozumel,* has said, "All has vanished, all has passed. The Indian weeps for the departed glory of his race and land. But his cry echoes vainly from the *cenote*'s depths." The island's name, Professor Rosada Iturralde has explained, was originally Cuzamil, meaning "Where the Swallows Fly Over the Blue Sea." The ancient deities were said to visit men in the form of swallows, or *golondrinas,* and they were often represented in this guise on temple walls.

Almost as inaccessible as the coral-encrusted pirate treasure and lost loot of the Conquistadores are Cozumel's ancient ruins on the side of the island facing the mainland. Some of the major sites can be reached directly by an air safari, or tourists may make a day's journey through the jungle on horseback from San Miguel, Cozumel's largest town, with about 3,000 inhabitants. A highway encircling the island has recently been completed.

Historically, Cozumel reached the peak of its prestige in the complex Maya cultural scheme during the epoch of the Holy Itzás. In the transitional period near the close of the tenth century, and probably for centuries before, the island was a sanctuary, the sacred goal of pilgrims from the splendid cities on the mainland across the 12-mile Yucatán Channel and from still more distant points in Central America. The continuous flow of travel between Cozumel and the mainland kept it in close touch with the events and cultural progress of the entire Maya world.

At the time of the arrival of the Spanish conquerors, Cozumel was still a renowned "Mecca" at the eastern end of a line of sacred cities. Izamal was the seat of worship of Itzamna. Other "holy" cities were Chichén Itzá and Mayapán. Journeying over the "four roads," pilgrims came not only to worship but to be healed at Chichén Itzá's "Well of Sacrifice." Another shrine was Cobá, celebrated both as a religious and trade center. Located near the eastern coast, it was connected by a broad causeway with a town known as Yaxuna, a few miles from Chichén Itzá. The road, or *sacbe,* the longest in the ancient Maya area, stretched for 62½ miles, with an average width of 32 feet. It averages 2 feet in height, crossing swamps at an elevation of as much as 8 feet. The base was constructed of large boulders methodically integrated with small stones and bound together with a kind of cement. The surface, now almost completely destroyed, was of cement or stucco. Near Cobá's suburbs, a type of platform about 40 feet long and 16½ feet high was erected along the road at which, according to Thompson in *The Rise and Fall of the Maya Civilizations,* religious processions halted in order to offer sacrifices before entering the city. Cobá itself is the axis of a series of roads, one of which extends to ruins now known as Kucikan, about 5 miles south-southwest.

Juan de Grijalva landed off the east coast of the Island of Cozumel on May 3, 1518, the day of the Holy Cross, and, in consequence, named it Santa Cruz de Cozumel. His men, as the chronicles relate, walked along its glittering beach, where beautiful native women offered them white *jícaras,* or gourds filled with *pozole,* a corn mush sweetened with wild honey; *jícamas* and *yucas,* root vegetables; *camotes,* a kind of sweet potato; *atole de maíz,* a corn gruel; and other products.

For centuries, according to Professor Rosada Iturralde, these ancient island people had lived on land consecrated by the ashes of their fathers, ever mindful of the early times when their ancestors had first cultivated the soil. Their chieftain's title was Ah-Naum Poot. There were settlements at Cozumel's three main ports. One was at the northern end of the island, another at the northeast end and a third was X-La-Pak, or "Old Wall."

The people of these towns, known to Grijalva and Bernal Díaz, were models of amiability; a smile, it was recorded, was their "talisman." Professor Rosada Iturralde described this idyllic period: "Their tranquil happiness constituted the secret of their lives; through it they attained longevity and expressed their thoughts without fear, and in this same spirit of gentleness they received the benediction of their deities, who poured out the good crops of the field in those lands wherein grew the *maíz,* the divine grain that provided their daily sustenance."

Cortés arrived at Cozumel in February 1519, at the port known today as San Miguel. It was at San Juan, to the west, that he assured his 508 soldiers and 109 mariners that if they reached Tabasco they would find their fortunes. With him were Pedro de Alvarado and adventurous men of the sea, all apparently willing to follow their captain "wearing on their brows the crown of victory" or "finding with him their tombs in the hills of Mayab." Cortés declared the beautiful shrine to Ixchel idolatrous and ordered his men to tear down the images and erect in their place a statue of the Virgin and wooden crucifixes. In one corner he placed a large wooden cross, which may now be seen in the National Museum of Mexico. In the opinion of Professor Rosada Iturralde, the ruined structure at San Gervasio is the one in which was said the first mass in the Americas. Nearby is an imposing temple with thick walls 52 feet high. It has two entrances and traces of a small altar, at the center of which are half-erased bas-reliefs representing the goddess of agriculture and Chac, the god of rain. It is not clear whether the dominant influence of the second altar is Mexican-Toltec or late Maya. On the walls are three superimposed murals which include a red hand; possibly each was painted at a different period.

Beyond the southern *faro,* or lighthouse, rises a curious pyramid some 20 feet high, topped by a platform formed by conch shells. There are indications that incense was burned in the small ground-level chamber over a long period. The fact that even today a loud roaring sound is created as the southeast wind blows through the shells gives support to the theory that this small pyramid may once have served as a signal station to warn of approaching cyclones or storms. The sundial, known as the "Cozumel Compass," is said to have been part of the structure.

On the mystery-enveloped **Isla de Mujeres,** just off the northern coast of the Quintana Roo mainland, are some scattered remains of pre-Hispanic life—a small temple, an isolated stone image emerging from the tropical jungle, an occasional covered mound that may conceal traces of ancient habitation. But these meager vestiges shed faint light on the early history of Isla de Mujeres or the nearby Cancún. Life on Isla de Mujeres appears to have been lived almost in a vacuum since the completion of the observatory temple high on its southern promontory. It is almost impossible to reconstruct authoritatively the true history of these two enigmatic Caribbean isles. One can only hope that real clues to the historic truth may still lie on the ocean floor.

More than four centuries have passed since the discovery of these islands by the Spaniards, but the riddle of the richly adorned and flower-bedecked female deities they found on Isla de Mujeres still intrigues the imagination. One wonders what kinship, if any, they may have had with Isis, Astarte, Venus and other goddesses of fertility worshipped in the ancient world. Perhaps when the secrets of sculptured stones are finally deciphered, the Maya will be found to share in a deep reverence for the continuity of life. John Lloyd Stephens, whose courage, erudition and aesthetic awareness opened up to the English-speaking world the splendors of southeastern Mexico, once observed that the architectural ornamentation of America's ancient buildings had a significance, a symbolic meaning. "Each stone," he said, "is part of an allegory or fable, hidden from us, inscrutable under the light of the feeble torch we may burn before it, but which, if ever revealed, will show that the history of the world yet remains to be written."

In pre-Columbian times Isla de Mujeres, some 6 miles long and ½ mile wide, may have been used as a resting-place by Maya pilgrims who were traveling to the island shrine of Ixchel on Cozumel. The pilgrims came to pay homage to the goddess, the "Isis" of the Maya pantheon, over whose sanctuary presided the high priest, a member of the reigning Pat family. These pilgrimages were of the most profound significance in Maya ritual. Bishop de Landa noted a parallel between them and Christian pilgrimages to Jerusalem and Rome. Both Ixchel and Itzamna, the "Supreme Initiator," who might be considered the Maya equivalent of "Osiris," were wholly Maya deities, and it is likely that their cults reached a peak of influence long before the Mexican-Toltecs appeared on the scene.

According to the chroniclers, the mainland of the old province of Ekab (taken from Ek-kab, meaning "Black Bee"), now Quintana Roo, once had a great population, strong enough, in any event, to prevent the advance of the Spaniards until they returned with reinforcements of Xiu warriors from the west. But, in a statement rendered by the grandee of Ekab in 1579, La Isla de Mujeres, a part of the province, was reported "uninhabited." Ekab, one of the seventeen districts listed by Bishop de Landa, extended, in the late sixteenth century, to an unidentified southern boundary bordering on Lake Bacalar near Chetumal in southern Quintana Roo.

The island was evidently inhabited, however, between 1517 and 1519, according to accounts left by men who accompanied the de Córdoba expedition in 1517. After living in Cuba, Francisco Hernández de Córdoba, a wealthy landowner, applied to the governor in January 1517 for a permit to discover and settle new lands. Governor Velásquez agreed to risk a ship and provisions if de Córdoba supplied two more vessels. With 110 young Spanish soldiers of fortune, de Córdoba sailed from Cuba in February 1517. One of the members of the group was the celebrated soldier-chronicler Bernal Díaz, then only twenty-five, who later recalled that, "We steered toward the setting sun, trusting to luck, knowing nothing of the depth of the water, nor of the currents, nor of the winds that usually prevail in that latitude."

After covering a distance of 150 miles and surviving a heavy storm, the Spaniards mistook for an island what was probably Cape Catoche, the northeastern cape of the Yucatán Peninsula. As they neared the shore they were astonished to see "a large town standing back about two leagues from the coast." This, they thought, must be a rich place, even a source of gold. But since they did not disembark there or travel inland, de Córdoba and his men saw nothing of the glorious Maya cities of Yucatán in which art, architecture, agriculture and the science of astronomy had flourished for centuries. According to Bernal Díaz, when the de Córdoba vessels were at anchor close to shore, ten canoes filled with men dressed in cotton jackets and loincloths came out to meet them and, when invited to come aboard by the Spaniards, more than thirty of them did so. They appeared to be friendly and by means of signs indicated that they would return on the following day and conduct the Spaniards ashore, where they would be given water and supplies. Each native received a gift, a string of green beads.

When the natives returned, the Spaniards, who had taken the precaution of arming themselves, boarded their boats and headed for the beach. There they were given a cordial reception by a chieftain and a multitude of people. But, marching two abreast, the Spaniards were ambushed and attacked by warriors wearing quilted cotton armor and carrying arrows, javelins and slingshots. Fifteen Spaniards were wounded in the fray. The Maya warriors, who had never before seen firearms, steel weapons or crossbows, fled in dismay, leaving fifteen of their party dead. Fifteen days later, according to Bernal Díaz, during the first week of March, de Córdoba apparently reached the coast of Campeche.

The first among the Spanish chroniclers to mention Isla de Mujeres was Bernaldino Yñiguez, the *veedor,* or overseer of the portion of booty known as the "king's fifth," who had accompanied de Córdoba on his expedition. Considerable confusion exists, however, concerning the sequence and locale of some of the incidents of this voyage. The same lack of precision is true of the expedition of Francisco de Montejo the elder, particularly during his two-month stay in the region in the spring of 1519. Most authorities believe that Montejo's extended visit took place not on the Isla de Mujeres but on the long crescent-shaped island of Cancún. On March 5, 1519, Juan Velásquez de León visited the shrine of the female deities on Isla de Mujeres and examined various inland salt deposits, which are still the basis for one of the local industries, and in the same month Hernán Cortés also anchored in the little harbor.

The remains of what may have been a temple or an observatory crown a small promontory of Isla de Mujeres.

CHAPTER XXIII

Balancanche

SOME 2½ MILES west of Chichén Itzá is a cave known as **Balancanche,** or Bala'en K'amcho, "The Throne of the Balam," or "Jaguar Priest." One afternoon in September 1959, José Umberto Gómez, a tourist guide, decided to return to this cave at Kalakoop for a closer inspection of what he had seen earlier in the day with his tourist group. He had noted at that time what appeared to be several hand-inserted rocks in the natural stone wall at the rear of the cave. After discovering one to be loose he decided to pry them out. The opening he made led to a lower vestibule and a series of six or more chambers stretching for some 81½ feet. The most remote contained a reservoir fed by springs.

Gómez, as he gained entrance, must have experienced an emotion akin to that of Ali Baba in the cave of the thieves, for the prospect he surveyed was no less incredible. Scattered through the passages were carved incense-burners or lamps. On all sides he saw hundreds of offerings; large, ornate censers and urns with effigies of Tláloc, the Toltec god of rain, represented as Chac; other urns bearing the symbol of Xipe Tótec, his face covered by a flayed skin, personifying the spring which, after each winter, reappears in new splendor; and scores of ceremonial *metates,* or corn-grinding stones, each with its *mano,* or hand stone, similar to a rolling pin. Many of the urns were 3 feet high, painted blue, green, red and yellow. There were bowls, jars, vases, miniature clay spindle whorls and tiny plates on which, according to the Maya Foundation's later report, "The paint looks as though it were applied only yesterday, having been protected from the elements for nearly a thousand years in sealed chambers." All the various objects were found just as they had been placed when, somewhere between A.D. 1194 and 1441, Toltec priests sealed the grotto and cunningly disguised its entrance to prevent desecration. During the entire time cycle—possibly a span of almost 800 years—evidently no one, not even archaeologists working elsewhere in the zone, guessed what a store of treasure lay behind the grotto's wall. The collection, as a whole, represents the largest and most sensational array of Mexican-Toltec ceramics unearthed to date.

Among the archaeologists who studied Balancanche is Dr. E. Wyllys Andrews, whose work was sponsored by the National Geographic Society, the Middle American Research Department of Tulane University and the National Institute of Anthropology and History, and carried out with the cooperation of the Barbachano Travel Service. Recent improvements include the lighting of the vast underground center, the widening of difficult passages and the chiseling of stairs and apertures from the rock. Before the grotto could be opened to the public, the various objects found had to be classified and arranged in suitable spots, a burdensome task because of the intense heat within the cave. From the center of a circular pool known as the "Sacred Lake" a stone image of Chac dramatically surmounts a pyramidal-shaped rock. The water, while crystal clear, contains quantities of blind shrimp and fish and looks quite black. Geologists believe the cave is an outlet of a subterranean river and that in four or five thousand years the limestone roof will collapse, thus forming a *cenote* like the many others to be found in Yucatán. Near the entrance is a passageway leading to a cavern which has not yet been fully explored.

Effigies of Tláloc, the Toltec rain god, decorate vividly colored urns and censers in the Balancanche cave. The relics were sketched by Gene Stuart.

For a short time after the opening of the cave to the public all seemed tranquil, but before long a feeling of resentment grew among the people of Kalakoop, and a rumor was spread that a curse would befall anyone entering the sacred abode of Chac and Balam. Even laborers would fall under the malediction, since to violate Balancanche, it was said, was a great sacrilege. The intense heat of the interior was undoubtedly only a warning of other calamities to follow. To avert impending disaster the local H'men, or priests, suggested a ceremony of appeasement in the hope that the outraged deities would be placated and their wrath deflected. Items requested in order to conduct a propitiation ceremony included a turkey, hens, incense, black wax candles, a quantity of *maíz* in order to make a paste known as *saka,* ritual breads, tobacco leaves, squash seeds, rock salt, honey, black pepper, garlic, spices, *achiote,* a vegetable known as bixe or anotta.

The officiating priest and his helpers were to be duly compensated for their part in the ceremony. An accomplished linguist was asked to transcribe the prayers and chants, and arrangements were made to record the ritual. On the eve of the ceremony the chief priest entered the first chamber of the grotto, called the Altar. In the center of this is a small eminence from which descends a dark brown stalactite resembling the trunk of a lofty *ceiba* tree, with numerous smaller formations representing its branches and foliage. Here, from the *zu-huy-ha,* or virgin water, of the spring he prepared *balche,* the ritual mead, leaving it overnight to ferment.

A chamber of the stalactite-ceilinged grotto, with its various offerings left just as they were placed centuries ago by Toltec priests before sealing the entrance, was painted by Luis Covarrubias.

According to Sr. Fernando Barbachano, who, along with several archaeologists, linguists, historians and sociologists, was permitted to attend the ceremony, the people of the region realized that "from then on the cave would be under the vigilance of the National Institute of Anthropology and History and they might not have a similar chance again. They were reconciled to the opening of the cave, for they knew that, with the exception of three or four pieces which would be removed to museums, the vast collection of sacred objects would be kept intact where it had been found." Sr. Barbachano gave the following account of the ceremony:

> We entered the cave at dawn on the date coinciding with the autumnal equinox, October 17th, and remained there until dawn of the following day. During that time no man was permitted to leave or enter and no women were allowed. From the adjacent villages 13 priests had assembled; also present were seven children, each child seven years of age. Thirteen ceremonies were performed before the four Chacs representing the world directions. The ceremony honoring Yuum Chac—corresponding to Tláloc—was performed at the main altar of the sacred lake. For this ceremony wild turkeys were prepared and offered with young *maíz* and the ritual *balche*. The H'men recited from memory from the astro-magico books but gave the impression that they were reading from them. A circle was formed by 12 of the H'men, the 13th standing outside the circle, and each priest had his turn at conducting one of the rites. After their presentation before the altar, the sacrificial animals were killed and baked underground near the entrance. There was singing by the children, all imitating the sounds made by some jungle bird or beast. The strange notes from the soft, infantile voices, like the croaking of toads and frogs—Tláloc's favorite musicians—echoing through the cavern, created a weird, mystical atmosphere. About halfway through the ritual honoring the rain god, torrential rains, completely out of season, began to fall and the cave dripped in many places. Basically this "revival" ritual had a twofold object: one was to seek forgiveness that something profoundly sacred had been disturbed, the other was to purify the site after it had been profaned.

The H'men, Sr. Barbachano concluded, were so convinced that their traditional prayers and offerings had brought the unseasonable rain to the parched Yucatecan earth that they sought permission to hold a brief thanksgiving ceremony two days later, affirming their faith in their ancient deities.

CHAPTER XXIV

Mul-Chic

Was the plumed serpent a Maya symbol before the arrival of the Toltecs in Yucatán? This provocative question, enmeshed with the very essence of pre-Columbian religion, social customs and concepts of cosmic order, was raised by the discovery of mural paintings at **Mul-Chic** north of Mérida. Their existence may uproot cherished theories regarding the respective roles played by intrusive and indigenous elements in the development of the Maya culture in the Yucatán Peninsula as well as affect appraisals of its origins and antiquity.

In the opinion of their discoverer, Díaz Bolio, author of several books on Maya culture, the wall decorations of a small temple 12 miles from Uxmal may reverse the belief that the cult of *La Serpiente Emplumada* entered Yucatán as a result of the first or second Toltec invasion, both events occurring late in the Maya story. Mul-Chic's walls, he believes, provide evidence that the worship of Quetzalcóatl antedated the penetration of any influence from the Mexican plateau. He maintains that rather than constituting a late arrival in the land of Mayab the Quetzalcóatl-Kukulcán cult can now be identified with the so-called "Old Empire" that flourished centuries earlier in Uaxactún in Guatemala.

Here he found the venerated symbol, with its serpent's body, rattles and bird's plumage. Apparently a quetzal or a stylized bird, its rich dark green plumage bears touches of orange, red, white, blue and yellow; its tail, which has a graceful sweep, opens in two parts. The serpent-bird resembles other representations of the deity in southern Classic-period Maya sites. One motif, in fact, recalls the mask of E-VII-Sub of Uaxactún, shown as Plate 58 in *The Ancient Maya* by Dr. Morley. Both interpretations are adorned with a rhomboidal design inspired by the markings of the serpent's skin. In the Mul-Chic version the motif resembles that shown in the polychromed vase of Uaxactún, reproduced by Dr. Morley in Plate 87 of

The four-storied structure known as Mul-Chic, adorned within by serpent-bird motifs, has been restored (*top*). A stucco panel depicting a man with a deer (*bottom*) decorated a wall of the sub-temple.

his book. The emblem of the diagonal bar appears both in the mural and in the celebrated vase. Díaz Bolio does not regard Mul-Chic as a copy or imitation of Uaxactún but, rather, finds the serpent heads unique. The rattles are stylized. From one of the serpents emerges a human body, suggesting to him the concept of a "Creator Being" and "Racial Totem." The same idea, symbolized by a rattlesnake with an emerging human figure, is seen at other Maya sites, including Labná, Chichén Itzá and Palenque. "The rattlesnake regally dominates Mul-Chic's walls," he has explained, "and it is this same rattlesnake that is the axis of the Maya and Middle American cultures generally." He has also cited the ideographic elements in the composition of the name "Cuculcán" or "Kukulcán" and has characterized Maya art as a great *crotaloplastica,* or "plastic serpent."

This small temple owes its chance discovery to a group of students and amateur archaeologists, the "Grupo Ximbal," who had made regular visits to archaeological zones and monuments within easy access of Mérida. Díaz Bolio proposed that they visit a certain mound where he had learned there were traces of colored paint on walls projecting from the enveloping brush. The mound is topped by the remains of a roof-comb. Three of the more enterprising explorers decided to follow a narrow passage which had been opened up. Díaz Bolio, Silvio Díaz Rubio and the Yucatecan sculptor Octavio Briseño, stumbling over loose rubble and keeping a sharp lookout for the rattlesnakes common among such abandoned sites, literally slid into a decorated chamber. It was typically Maya in character, even to a corbelled arch. Further study, under the supervision of Román Piña Chan, showed that the subtemple with the decorated chamber was covered by a pyramid of four vertical-walled bodies. The superstructure may have collapsed or it may have remained unfinished, leaving the *crestería* of the building an intact projection. The exterior of the subtemple, like that of the Temple of the Seven Dolls at nearby Dzibilchaltún, was originally covered with stucco. The best of what remains, notably a panel depicting a man on foot in front of a deer, has been compared with the finest examples at Palenque, including the heads from the sepulcher found under the Temple of Inscriptions.

Briseño made sketches and Díaz Bolio took photographs of the murals. Those on the east wall had almost disappeared, but those on the west wall were in better condition, along with a frieze containing hieroglyphs in black and white. In order to study and repair the frescoes under laboratory conditions they were carefully removed by experts, transferred to gesso sheets and sent to Mexico City.

CHAPTER XXV

Izamal and Dzibilchaltún

ONE OF THE HIGHLY venerated centers of native worship is **Izamal,** a sacred city of the Itzás, which lies midway between Chichén Itzá and Dzibilchaltún in northern Yucatán. Its once stately temples and palaces built on hilltops overlooking broad lowlands were leveled by the Spaniards and the sculptured stones used to rear ecclesiastical edifices upon the ancient foundations. The city was once the shrine of Itzamna, "The Dew of Heaven." Legend recalls the splendor of its Papalchach, Temple of the Kabul or Kab Ul and Hunpiktok. Désiré Charnay, who explored the ruins of Izamal, observed that from the remains of the pyramidal temple of Hunpiktok he noted the existence of a "network of roads, one of which led to Aké." Only meager traces now remain of what was once a wide, white-tiled highway connecting Izamal with Aké, one of the largest and most populous cities of the New Empire. Upon the substructure of the pyramid known as the Castle of the Kings, rising to 40 feet and measuring 200 yards at each side of the base, the Spaniards superimposed a multiarched convent, converting the ceremonial plaza into a vast elevated courtyard.

Explorations have recently been undertaken at another once-populous center, **Dzibilchaltún,** or "Where There Is Writing on Flat Rocks." Work on the project, headed by Dr. E. Wyllys Andrews and financed by the National Geographic Society and Tulane University, was continued by grants-in-aid from the National Science Foundation and the American Philosophical Society. Dr. Andrews explained, at the outset of his preliminary survey in 1956, that the unique significance of Dzibilchaltún lay in its extended period of occupation. The great cities of the southern lowlands, he pointed out, were all abandoned in the seventh century, according to the Spinden correlation, or by the end of the ninth century, according to the Thompson correlation, with possible sporadic reoccupation. The more famous cities of Yucatán, such as Uxmal, Chichén Itzá and Mayapán, were inhabited only for a few centuries and their periods of occupation by no means always overlapped. He also pointed out that, up to that time, no remains of the early period of grandeur were known in Yucatán. "Our record therefore," he said, "was an incomplete one. We had no yardstick covering the many phases of the rise and fall of Maya civilization."

As work at the site progressed Dr. Andrews soon realized that Dzibilchaltún was what had so long been sought. It appeared to have been the seat of a large population since early Pre-Classic times, possibly 2000 B.C. or earlier, and occupied into the Colonial era, an entire span of at least 2,500 to 3,500 years. In his 1961 report he announced that it had, in fact, proved to be one of the largest, very possibly the largest ancient city in the New World, covering an area of 31 square miles of hidden but densely distributed remains.

Of equal importance, this record of habitation was available in the form of layer upon layer of earth, providing a clear vertical stratigraphy, so that no doubt was left as to the precise sequence of the many temporal components. Furthermore, the early phase could be correlated by comparison of abundant examples of trade pottery which have been fitted into

the time sequence established for the southern cities and therefore also correlated with the Maya "Long Count." The later stages could be correlated with dates of the Christian calendar.

Before 1956 the site of Dzibilchaltún was unknown even to professional tourist guides. This was not surprising, since access to the site was difficult, necessitating a long walk over a narrow dirt road that turned off the highway and an even longer distance over a trail that led through tangled brush. But the hardy adventurer was amply rewarded when he finally arrived at the sun-baked brambly plain where the "gaunt, gray ruins" of Dzibilchaltún rose in full view. Although they are scattered over an area a third the size of Mexico City the site, part of a vast *henequen hacienda,* had not been studied. Today, as the result of systematic excavations, the remains of the old city, beginning with the second phase of the Pre-Classic period and extending to the Post-Conquest era, provide at least a partial view of the radically changing settlement patterns that characterized the various periods.

Its central area displays pyramidal temples, palaces and buildings of vaulted stone, with thatched houses on masonry foundations crowded between the more massive structures. The restored Templo de las Siete Muñecas, or The Temple of the Seven Dolls, derives its name from the

The Temple of the Seven Dolls, notable for its use of windows, rarely known in Middle America, is shown as it has been restored.

seven misshapen dolls found within. Its unique feature is the presence of windows, hitherto unknown in ancient Middle America. Wood from a lintel of this long-buried pyramid temple has been dated by means of the Carbon-14 process by one laboratory at A.D. 458 plus or minus 200 years and by a second laboratory at A.D. 508 plus or minus 200 years. Supporting these dates is an abundance of ceramic trade wares from the second phase of the Classic period corresponding to a date between the fourth and seventh centuries or seventh and tenth centuries, depending on the correlation used. Thus the temple was in intermittent use for over a thousand years.

The existence of trade relations between Dzibilchaltún and the famed Classic-period cities of the Guatemala lowlands was definitely established by the recovery of seventy-five small pieces of ceramic ware that had clearly been imported from Uaxactún. These shards were recently identified by Robert E. Smith of the Carnegie Institution, and the author of a study of the ceramic sequences of Uaxactún, which reached the peak of Classic culture for the Petén area. Since a wealth of archaeological inscriptions uncovered at Uaxactún were datable, when artifacts from Uaxactún were found at Dzibilchaltún they served to fix a date for this site. Dr. Morley believed Uaxactún, 40 miles north of the eastern end of Lake Petén Itzá, to be the site of the earliest Maya stone architecture and sculptured stone monuments in Guatemala, dating from the first quarter of the fourth century. Tikal has, however, since then yielded earlier dates.

Dr. Andrews' findings at Dzibilchaltún have affected the broader view of the fundamental pattern of the prehistory of this area. It is his belief that a cultural continuum can now be established from the totality of this study. All available evidence, he states, points to three basic cultural traditions in the Post-Primitive Maya civilization which could be considered as horizons in time. These may be summarized as follows:

Reconstruction of Temple of the Seven Dolls.

The Early Period is characterized by true masonry construction. Walls were built of large stone blocks which actually bore the weight of structures. Vaults were made of flat, unworked slabs of native rock, with each projecting somewhat beyond those below, until they could be capped by a final massive stone. During the first phase of this period the wall blocks were only crudely squared; as they were not of equal size, the horizontal level was consequently uneven. In the second phase the blocks revealed a smoother finish. Although they were never ground, they were more carefully sorted. Vaults which had been given only the roughest kind of facing in the carelessly laid slabs of the first phase were more accurately constructed during the second, at which time there appeared courses of specially shaped stone for vault spring, the point at which the arch actually begins. During this entire period the finished wall surface was formed by considerable chipping and by a thick coat of stucco. Façade profiles were simple and rectangular. Architectural carved stones were rare, but examples of elaborately carved stucco for architectural decoration have been found, notably at Palenque and Acancéh. The inscriptions marked the Initial Series of the "Long Count," when dates were always given in full.

In the next stage, or Florescent Period, pure concrete construction replaced the slab-vault masonry. On the concrete walls now appeared a thin veneer of perfectly faced, rectangular blocks, ground to a fine finish, instead of being roughly pecked as in the style of the Early Period. The stone facing of the concrete vaults was now made of equally smooth blocks, deeply tenoned or imbedded at the rear to hold them into the matrix they covered. Façade profiles became complex, with multimember moldings. The naturalistic stucco carvings on the upper façades of the Early Period gave way to more elaborate, highly conventionalized mosaics in carved stone on both the upper and lower sections. Monumental art was much less emphasized and in the early stage of this period the practice of recording hieroglyphic inscriptions on stone seems to have been discontinued.

The arrival of a new influence from Central Mexico, which was reflected in art, architecture and pottery, brought to a close the first phase of this period. The Puuc cities—Uxmal, Sayil, Labná and Kabáh—were largely abandoned, while Chichén Itzá apparently became the foremost political and ceremonial center of the peninsula. Dzibilchaltún, although strongly influenced by these changes, continued as a major center of population. Dr. Andrews believes that the Mexican-Toltec influences were only temporarily superimposed on the continuum of Maya cultures, the techniques of which remained unchanged throughout both phases. New elements in design, new shapes in pottery and new plans for building appeared, but these were expressed by the same basic techniques and presumably by the same artisans.

More profound changes were to follow in the next Decadent Period. Paradoxically known as the Evolved Decadent and perhaps best exemplified at Mayapán, this period shows an almost total abandonment of the techniques that characterized the Florescent architecture and a return to those of the Early Period. Concrete and veneer were replaced by block-wall and slab-vault construction, carved stone by stucco ornamentation. But where the Mayapán architect strove to duplicate external forms of the modified Florescent, he frequently failed because the essential techniques had been lost. In terms of a return to practices of the Early Period it may be noted that several painted inscriptions of the Decadent Period at Dzibilchaltún mark a revival in the public ceremonial use of the old Maya calendar, discontinued early in the first phase of the Florescent Period.

Covering an area of 31 square miles, Dzibilchaltún may prove to be one of the largest ancient cities of the New World. This reconstruction of its ceremonial center shows the Cenote Xlacah.

Dr. Andrews envisions as his goal a stratigraphic column which will record the entire occupation of Dzibilchaltún. In the seasons ahead he hopes to move back in time through the first phase of what he calls the Early Primitive to the Formative, perhaps into three stages before the Early Period. Although the history of such a remote era is virtually unknown in Yucatán, he believes that research will be greatly aided by detailed stratigraphic studies of the period such as have been carried out in the Guatemala lowlands and adjacent regions.

Underwater explorations have provided an additional means of approach to filling in this record of occupation. During the first three working seasons a group of divers explored a deep well, Cenote Xlacah, in the central ceremonial plaza. More than 30,000 artifacts were brought up, including a surprisingly large number of pottery vessels which were intact. Most of the small artifacts, some of them exquisitely carved, recovered from the *cenote,* estimated to be from 140 to 180 feet deep, were apparently thrown in, as cult offerings, as in the Cenote Sagrado of Chichén Itzá.

On Sunday afternoons Indian boys from nearby pueblos and *haciendas* often gather at the well to stage water battles. Even on the hottest day it is delightfully cool because of the continuous flow of its waters with the current of a subterranean river. A popular legend has grown up about this *cenote,* said to be the deepest in all Yucatán. Near the *cenote,* where he played in his youth, a poor boy who managed to acquire great wealth built a splendid palace, equipped with every luxury. But his good fortune hard-

ened his heart and he forgot his aged and needy parents, who, one day, hungry and poorly clad, came to him begging for help. But he ignored their plea and ordered them from his sight, without giving them so much as a tortilla from his sumptuous table. The Maya deities, so the legend goes, decreed a fitting punishment for the ingrate. That night the palace with everything in it, including the hapless owner, was suddenly lifted into the sky and then, as suddenly, dropped into the depths of the *cenote*. The Maya of the region insist that the household utensils and water jars recovered from the bottom of the great well are the very ones that were used in the well-stocked kitchen of the unnatural son!

The vast-scale city planning, integrated architecture and evolving tech-

niques, embracing, at Dzibilchaltún, an unbroken span of four millennia, underscore Dr. Jaime Torres Bodet's address at the opening of Mexico's new National Museum of Anthropology. Reminding his audience that the young Cuauhtémoc of Anáhuac had become the venerated symbol of the entire nation's renewed and ever-renewing creative impulse, the poet-statesman declared, "The ceremony that brings us together confirms most admirably that Cuauhtémoc did not die in vain. Beside the remains of what was the grandeur of an heroic world, Mexico arises—laboring, persevering, daring and faithful. . . . In honoring the vestiges of its past, Mexico has the conviction that it honors itself, and makes loftier in a universal sense, the prestige of its present and the glory of its future."

Excavations and underwater explorations of Dzibilchaltún's Cenote Xlacah have yielded a variety of figurines and decorated pottery vessels.

Picture Credits

Dr. Jorge R. Acosta, 50–51, *bottom right.*
Manuel Alvarez Bravo photo, 155.
America, Vol. II, 136.
American Museum of Natural History, 38, *bottom;* 42, 43, 50, *center left;* 212, 265, 266, 267, 268–69, 270, 271, 314–15, *top;* 317, 318, *bottom.*
The Anáhuacalli, 25, *bottom;* 180–81, *top;* 180, *bottom left.*
Dr. E. Wyllys Andrews, 347, 357, 358–59.
Rául Anguiano, 251.
Archaeological Museum of Oaxaca, 196–97.
Archaeological Museum of the State of Colima, 185, *bottom right.*
Archaeological Museum of Yucatán, 316, *top.*
Dr Juan Armenta Camacho, 4.
Fernando Barbachano, G. R., 300, *top,* 312.
Jésus Bracamontes Aviño, 151, *left.*
Jay Chernis collection, 184, *top left.*
Club de Exploraciones y Deportes Acuaticos de México (C.E.D.A.M.), 321, 334, 345.
Club de Viajes de Pemex, endpaper maps of archaeological sites of Mexico; Otto Done photos, 18, 37, 54, 194, 244, 261, 264.
Continental Film Productions Corp., James Webster photos, 333, 338.
Department of Archaeology, State of Yucatán, Foto Alex, 298.
Dr. Jorge Enciso, 11.
C. W. Ennis, Jr., 336, 354–55.
Professor José Farías Galindo, 113, 115, 132, 204, 225, *bottom.*
Thomas S. Ferguson, 12.
Gregorio Gutierrez Balderas, 22–23, 32–33, 50–51, 74–75.
Dr. Eulalia Guzmán, 166.
Giles G. Healey, 252.
Dr. Marc Jost, 94, 95, *right;* 98, 100.
George Kubler, 189.
Mexican Government Tourism Department, 71, 107, 319.
Mexican Ministry of the Treasury, 120, *right.*
Mexican National Tourist Council, 300, *top.*
Mrs. Earl Morris, 323, *bottom.*
National Institute of Anthropology and History, 6, 20, 24, 29, 31, 34, 36, 38, *top;* 39, *bottom;* 40, 42, 52, 61, 62, 65, 76, 83, 118, 120, *left;* 124, 125, 128, 130, 134, 135, 137, 171, 172, 173, 174, 182, *top left;* 190, 193, 195, 215, 223, 225, *top;* 226, 232, 254–55, 258, 263, 273, 274, 275, 279, 280, 290, *bottom;* 297, 300, *bottom;* 303, 304, 316, *bottom;* 318, *top;* 329, 331, 351.
National Museum of Anthropology, Jose Nash photo, 25, *top;* 46, 95, 179, 213, 312, *right.*
New World Archaeological Foundation, 236.
Dr. Rául Noriega, 82, 84, 86–87.
The Orion Press, Inc., Reg Van Cuylenberg photos, 63, 117, 144, 146.
Dr. Philip Orr, Santa Barbara Natural History Museum, 3.
Osuna photo, 200.
Dr. John Paddock, 202–3.
Ralph Payne, 293, 294, *top.*
Ruben Poblano Cordero, 45.
Alma M. Reed photo, 323, *top.*
Dr. César A. Saenz, 56.
Mary Saint Albans, 230, *top;* 231, 306, 307, 308, 310, 314–15.

Professor Ponciano Salazar Ortegón, 287.
Spa Ixtapan de la Sal, 5.
Dr. Herbert J. Spinden, 151, *right*.
Dr. Kurt Stavenhagen collection, 19, 30, 174, 177, *bottom;* 178, 181, *bottom right;* 182, *top right;* 183, *top left;* 184, *top right;* 185, *top right, bottom;* 211, *left;* 219, 220, *top right, bottom left;* 221, 280. Ferdinand Anton photos, 19, left; 30, 174, 178, 181, *bottom right;* 182, *top right;* 183, *top left, top right;* 184, *bottom;* 219, *right;* 220, *bottom;* 221. Irmgard Groth Kimball photos, 19, *right;* 220, *top left*. Ricardo Salazar photo, 280, *bottom right*.
Dr. Guy Stresser-Pean, 211, *right*.
Edward Weston photo, 154.

Sources

Annals, Chronicles, Codices and Other Early Accounts

Anales de Chimalpahín (see *Codex Chimalpopoca*)
Anales de Cuauhtitlán
Unos Anales Históricos de la Nacion Mexicana, 1528.
Annals of the Cakchiquels, 1554. Edition published by the Société de Philologie of Paris, 1885; Edition published by University of Oklahoma Press, Norman, Oklahoma, Delia Goetz translation. Edition published by Fondo de Cultura Económica, Dionisio José Chonay translation, 1950.
Badianus Manuscript (see *Codex Barberini*)
Books of Chilam Balam
Cartas de Relación (Hernán Cortés's letters to Charles V). Commentary by Eulalia Guzmán in *Clarifications and Rectifications of the Invasion of Anáhuac*, Libros Anáhuac, Mexico City, 1958.
Codex Aubin
Codex Barberini, 1552. Martín de la Cruz, compiler; Juan Badiano, translator into Latin. *Codice Badiano*, Seguro Social, Mexico City, 1964. *De la Cruz-Badiano Herbal*, published by the Maya Society, Baltimore, Maryland, 1939; *The Badianus Manuscript*, Emma Walcott Emmart, editor, Johns Hopkins Press, Baltimore, Maryland, 1940.
Codex Borbónico
Codex Borgia. Eduard Seler: *Eine Altmexikanische Bilderschrift der Congregatio de Propaganda Fide* (Roma), 3 vols. *Comentarios al Codice Borgia*. M. Frenk translation, Fondo de Cultura Económica, Mexico City, 1963.
Codex Boturini
Codex Chimalpopoca
Codex Cospi
Codex Dresdensis. William Gates translation, Maya Society, Baltimore, Maryland, 1932.
Codex Florentino
Codex Magliabecchi. Codex Magliabecchi: The Book of Life of the Ancient Mexicans, Containing an Account of Their Rites and Superstitions, Zelia Nuttall, translator and editor, Berkeley, California, 1903.
Codex Matritense de la Academia
Codex Mendoza
Codex Nuttall
Codex Peresianus. Tzental Perez Codex Commentary, William F. Gates, Peabody Museum, Cambridge, Massachusetts, 1910.
Codex Ríos

Codex Telleriano-Remensis
Codex Tro-Cortesianus. Abbé Brasseur de Bourbourg "translation."
Codex Vaticanus
Codex Vienna (see *Codex Vindobonensis*)
Codex Vindobonensis
Codex Xólotl
Codex Zouche (see *Codex Nuttall*)
The Conquistadors. (First-person accounts by various conquistadors assembled, edited and and translated by Patricia de Fuentes, The Orion Press, Inc., New York, 1963.)
Crónica de Nueva España by F. Cervantes de Salazar.
Crónica Mexicayotl by F. Alvarado Tezozomoc, translated and edited by Adrián León.
De la Cruz-Badiano Aztec Herbal (see *Codex Barberini*)
General Archives of the Indies
Historia de la Conquista de Mexico by Francisco López de Gómara. Published as *Cortés: The Life of the Conqueror by his Secretary Francisco López de Gómara,* translated and edited by Lesley Byrd Simpson, University of California Press, Berkeley, California, 1964.
Historia de las Indies and *La Crónica de la Nueva España* by F. Diego Durán, issued with *The Atlas* (illustrated). Published as *The Aztecs,* translated by Doris Heyden and Fernando Horcasitas, The Orion Press, Inc., New York, 1964.
Historia de los Indios de la Nueva España by F. Toribio de Benavente (Motolinia). Edition published in Barcelona, 1914.
Historia General de las Cosas de Nueva España by F. Bernardino de Sahagún.
Historia Verdadera de la Conquista de la Nueva España by Bernal Díaz del Castillo. Translation by A. P. Maudslay, *The Discovery and Conquest of Mexico, 1517–1521,* Farrar, Straus & Cudahy, Inc., 1956, New York.
Lamentations (*Netzahualcóyotl*)
Lienzo de Cholula
Lienzo de Tlaxcala
Manuscript of Sotuta
Mapa de Tepechpan
Mapa Quinatzin
Popul Vuh. Popul Vuh: The Sacred Book of the Ancient Quiché Maya edited by Delia Goetz and Sylvanus G. Morley, University of Oklahoma Press, Norman, Oklahoma, 1950.
Relación de las Cosas de Yucatán by Diego de Landa. Edited by Abbé Brasseur de Bourbourg, 1864; English translation by William Yates, *Yucatan Before and After the Conquest,* No. 20, Maya Society, Baltimore, Maryland, 1937.
Relaciones of Gabriel Roja
Tira del Museo (see *Codex Boturini*)
Tira de la Peregrinacion (see *Codex Boturini*)
Vocabulario, 1555, Toribio de Benavente (Motolinia).

Sagas, Testaments and Other Chronicles

The Apocalypse
The Book of Daniel
The Book of Genesis
The Book of Mormon (1830)
The Book of Revelation
Critias by Plato
Giron Gagal
The Imranas
Timaeus by Plato

Books, Publications, Proceedings, Scientific Journals, etc.

Acosta, Jorge E., *El Palacio de las Mariposas de Teotihuacán,* Bulletin 9, National Institute of Anthropology and History, Mexico City, 1962.

Amaya Topete, Jésus, *Atlas of the Mexican Conquest,* Fondo de Cultura Económica, Mexico City.

Cholula, Ciudad Sagrada, Centro de Estudios Históricos de Puebla, Puebla, Mexico, 1965.

Anguiano, Raul, *Expedition to Bonampak,* Institute of Aesthetic Investigations, National University of Mexico.

Beaumont, Pablo de la Purísima Concepción, *Crónica de Michoacán,* Talleres Graficos de la Nación, Mexico City, 1932.

Bernal, Ignacio, *Archaeology of the Mixteca,* CER/BEO, 1958.

Bibliografia de Arquelogia y Ethnografia en Mesoamerica y Norte de México, National Institute of Anthropology and History, Mexico City, 1962.

Exploraciones en Cuilapan de Guerrero, 1902–1954, National Institute of Anthropology and History, Mexico City, 1958.

Mexican Wall Paintings of the Maya and Aztec Periods, William Collins Sons & Co., Ltd., New York, 1963.

Beyer, Hermann, *Studies on the Inscriptions at Chichén Itzá,* No. 483, Carnegie Institution, Washington, D.C., 1937.

Blom, Frans, *The Conquest of Yucatan,* Houghton Mifflin Company, Boston, 1936.

Blom, Frans and La Farge, Oliver, *Tribes and Temples,* Tulane University, New Orleans, 1926-1927.

Boland, Charles Michael, *They All Discovered America,* Doubleday & Company, Inc., New York, 1961.

Bolio, Antonio Mediz, *The Land of the Pheasant and the Deer,* Mexico City, 1937.

Brinton, D. G., *The Maya Chronicles,* Philadelphia, 1882.

Burgoa, Padre Francisco de, *Historia Geografica,* 1674.

Bush Romero, Pablo, *Matanceros–Cancún,* C.E.D.A.M. pub. No. 2, Mexico City, 1961.

Bustillos Carrillo, Antonio, *El Sacbe de los Mayas,* Costa Amic, 1964.

Cabrera, Paul Felix, *Description of an Ancient City Discovered Near Palenque,* translated from the report of Captain Antonio del Río, London, 1822.

Calder, Ritchie, *The World Man Created,* Simon and Schuster, Inc., New York, 1961.

Carrillo Gil, Alvar, *Arte Maya.*

Carter, George E., "Evidence for Early Contacts with America," *Southwest Journal of Anthropology,* Vol. 6, No. 2, 1950.

Plant Geography and Culture History in the American Southwest, Viking Fund Publications No. 5, New York, 1945.

Pleistocene Man at San Diego, Johns Hopkins Press, Baltimore, Md.

Caso, Alfonso, *Las Exploraciones en Monte Albán 1934–35,* Instituto Panamericano de Georgrafía y Historia, Mexico City, 1935.

Ceram, C. W., *Gods, Graves and Scholars,* Alfred A. Knopf, Inc., New York, 1951.

Charnay, Claude Joseph Désiré, *Les Anciennes Villes de Nouveau Monde,* 1885. *The Ancient Cities of the New World,* 1887. Translation by J. Gonino and Helen S. Conant.

Churchward, James, *The Lost Continent of Mu,* Xanadu Library edition, Crown Publishers, Inc., New York, 1961.

Clark, Leonard, *Yucatan Adventure,* Hutchinson & Co., Ltd., London, 1959.

Clavijero, Abbé Francisco, *Historia Antigua de México.*

Cogulludo, Diego López de, *Historia de Yucatán,* 1656, Madrid, 1688.

Colum, Padraic, *Orpheus: Myths of the World,* The Macmillan Company, New York, 1930.

Cordan, Wolfgang, *Secret of the Forest,* Doubleday & Company, Inc., New York, 1964.

Covarrubias, Miguel, *Indian Art of Mexico and Central America,* Alfred A. Knopf, Inc., New York, 1957.

Mexico South, Alfred A. Knopf, New York, 1946.
The Eagle, the Jaguar and the Serpent, Alfred A. Knopf, Inc., New York, 1954.
Cuevas, Fray Mariano, S. J., *Historia de la Iglesia en México.*
d'Alviella, Count Goblet, *The Migration of Symbols,* London, 1894.
de Camp, L. Sprague and Catherine C., *Ancient Ruins and Archaeology,* Doubleday & Company, Inc., New York, 1965.
Disselhoff, Hans-Dietrich and Linné, Sigvald, *The Art of Ancient America,* Crown Publishers, Inc., New York, 1962.
Donnelly, Ignatius, *Atlantis: The Antediluvian World,* Xanadu Library edition, Crown Publishers, Inc., 1961.
Drucker, Philip, *Ceramic Stratigraphy of La Venta,* Bulletin 153, Smithsonian Institution, Bureau of American Ethnology, Washington, D.C., 1952.
Dupaix, Guillermo, *Antiquités Mexicanes,* 1834.
Ekholm, Gordon F. and von Heine-Geldern, Robert, "Significant Parallels in the Symbolic Arts of Southern Asia and Middle America," *Selected Papers of the XXIXth International Congress of Americanists,* edited by Sol Tax, Chicago, 1951.
Encisco, Jorge, *Design Motifs of Ancient Mexico,* Dover Publications, Inc., New York, 1953.
Sellos del Antiguo México, Mexico City, 1947.
Farías Galindo, José, *Xochimilco Histórico y Arquelogico,* Sociedad Mexicana de Geografía y Estadistica, Mexico City, 1964.
Fastlich, Samuel, *The Art of Dental Mutilations,* National University of Mexico, Mexico City, 1952.
Ferguson, Thomas Stuart, *One Fold, One Shepherd,* Books of California, San Francisco, California, 1958.
Fernandez, Justino, *Coatlicue,* Instituto de Investigaciones Esteticas, Mexico City, 1959.
Francisco, José, *Arco Iris de Paz,* 1768.
Frankfort, Henri, *Stratified Cylinder Seals from the Diyala Region,* University of Chicago Press, 1955.
Gallegos Ruíz, Roberto, *Exploraciones en Zaachila,* Bulletin 8, National Institute of Anthropology and History, Mexico City, 1962.
Gamio, Manuel F., *La Población del Valle de Teotihuacán,* Vols. 1–3, Dirección de Antropología, Mexico City, 1922.
Gann, W. F., *Glories of the Maya,* London, 1928.
García Payon, José, *Archaeological Explorations in Totonocapan Meridional, Anales,* National Institute of Anthropology and History, Mexico City, 1947.
García Vega, A., "Exploraciones en el Tajín, 1934–38," *Proceedings of the XXVIIth International Congress of Americanists,* Mexico City, 1939.
Gardiner, C. Harvey, *Naval Power in the Conquest of Mexico,* University of Texas Press, Austin, Texas, 1956.
Gates, William, *An Outline Dictionary of Maya Glyphs,* No. 1, Maya Society, Baltimore, Maryland, 1931.
Goncalves de Lima, Oswald, *El Maguey y El Pulque.*
Gonzalez Ulloa, Mario, *La Medicina en Mexico,* Cyanamid de Mexico, S.A.
Goodman, J. T., "The Archaic Maya Inscriptions," *Biologia Centrali-Americana,* London, 1897.
Guzmán, Eulalia, *La Genealogia y Biografía de Cuauhtémoc.* Ediciones del Diario de Culiacan, 1954.
Manuscritos sobre Mexico en Archives de Italia, Sociedad Mexicana de Geografía y Estadistica, 1964.
Heyerdahl, Thor, *Aku-Aku: Secret of Easter Island,* Allen & Unwin, London, 1958.
American Indians in the Pacific: The Theory Behind the Kon-Tiki Expedition, Rand-McNally & Co., New York, 1953.
Irwin, Constance, *Fair Gods and Stone Faces,* St. Martin's Press, New York, 1963.
Jiménez Moreno, Wigberto, "Tula y los Toltecas," *Revista Mexicana de Estudios Antropologicos,* 1940.

Tula y Los Toltecas Segun Las Fuentes Históricas, Mexican Anthropological Studies, Mexico City, 1941.
Jost, Marc, *Medicina Precortesiana,* Grupo Roussel, S.A., Mexico City, 1955.
Joyce, Thomas Athol, *Maya and Mexican Art,* London, 1927.
Keleman, Pál, *Medieval American Art,* The Macmillan Company, New York, 1943.
Kelly, Isabel and Palerm, Angel, *The Tajín Totonac,* Smithsonian Institution, Institute of Social Anthropology, Washington, D.C., 1952.
Kingsborough, Lord, *Antiquities of Mexico,* London, 1831–1848.
Kirchhoff, Paul, *Civilizing the Chichimecs,* Latin American Studies, 1948.
"Mesoamerica," *Acta Americana,* Vol. 1, 1943.
Krickeberg, Walter, *Altmexikanische Kulturen,* Berlin, 1956. *Las Antiguas Culturas de Mexico,* Fondo de Cultura Económica, 1961.
Los Totonaca, 1933.
Kubler, George, *Chichén Itzá and Tula,* 1961.
The Art and Architecture of Ancient America, Penguin Books, Inc., 1961.
Leip, Hans, *River in the Sea: Story of the Gulf Stream,* Jarrolds, London, 1957. G. P. Putnam's Sons, 1958.
León, Nicolas, "Las Yácatas de Tzintzuntzan," *Anales del Museo Michoacano 1888–91,* Morelos. Dionisio José Chonay translation, Fondo de Cultura Económica, Mexico City, 1951.
León-Portilla, Miguel, *Imagen de México Antiguo,* Universidad de Buenos Aires, Buenos Aires, Argentina, 1963.
La Filosofía Nahuatl, Instituto Indigenista Interamericano, Mexico City, 1956.
Los Mexicanos Antiguos a Través de Sus Crónicas y Cantares, Fondo de Cultura Económica, Mexico City, 1961.
Visión de los Vencidos, National University of Mexico, Mexico City, 1959.
Le Plongeon, Alice Dixon, *Here and There in Yucatán,* J. W. Lovell Company, 1889.
Le Plongeon, Augustus, *Archaeological Communication on Yucatán.*
Queen Moo and the Egyptian Sphinx, London, 1896.
Sacred Mysteries among Maya and Quiché 11,500 Years Ago, R. Mawy, New York, 1886.
Lipps, Teodoro, *Fundamentals of Aesthetics. Aesthetik: Psychologie des Schönen und der Kunst,* Theodor Lipps, L. Voss, Hamburg, Leipzig, 1903–06, 1914–20. Second edition, Daniel Jorro, Madrid, 1924.
Lothrop, Samuel K., *Metals from the Cenote of Sacrifice: Chichén Itzá,* Peabody Museum, Cambridge, Massachusetts, 1952.
Tulum: An Archaeological Study of the East Coast of Yucatan, Pub. 335, Carnegie Institution, Washington, D.C., 1924.
Lumholtz, Carl, *El México Desconocido,* Charles Scribner's Sons, New York, 1902.
Maler, Teobert, *Researches in the Central Portion of the Usumacinta Valley,* Peabody Museum, Cambridge, Massachusetts, 1901.
Mangelsdorf, Paul, *Races of Maize in Mexico,* Cambridge, Massachusetts, 1956.
Mann, Thomas, Preface, *Joseph and His Brothers,* translated by H. F. Lowe, Alfred A. Knopf, Inc., New York, 1934, trilogy edition, 1948.
Marett, Sir R. H. K., K.C.M., O.B.E., *Archaeological Tours from Mexico City,* Ediciones Tolteca, S.A., Mexico, D.F.
Marquina, Ignacio, *Arquitectura Prehispánica,* National Institute of Anthropology and History, Mexico City, 1951.
Maudslay, Alfred P., Section on Archaeology, *Biologia Centrali-Americana,* London, 1889–1902.
Medellín Zenil, Alfonso, *Una Palma Totonaca,* Bulletin 14, National Institute of Anthropology and History, Mexico City, 1963.
Means, Philip Ainsworth, *History of the Spanish Conquest of the Yucatan and the Itzas,* Peabody Museum, Cambridge, Massachusetts, 1917.
Mendoza, Vicente de, *Panorama de la Música Tradicional de México.*

Folk Songs of Zacatecas, Secretaria de Educación Publica, Mexico City, 1952.
Morley, Sylvanus G., and Brainerd, George W., *The Ancient Maya,* third edition, Stanford University Press, Palo Alto, California, 1956.
Morris, Ann Axtell, *Digging in Yucatan,* Doubleday, Doran & Co., Garden City, 1931.
Morris, Earl H., Morris, Ann Axtell and Charlot, Jean. *Temple of the Warriors at Chichén Itzá,* Pub. 406, Carnegie Institution, Washington, D.C., 1931.
National Institute of Anthropology and History, *Arqueologico de la Republic Mexicana-Campeche,* 1958.
Las Pinturas de Bonampak.
New World Archaeological Foundation, *Papers* 1–7, Orinda, California, 1956–1960.
Noguera, Eduardo, *Ceramica de México,* Museo Nacional de México City, 1934.
Noriega, Rául, co-editor, *Esplendor de México Antiguo,* Centro de Investigaciones Antropológicas de México, Mexico City, 1959.
La Piedra del Sol y 16 Monumentos Astronómicos del México Antiguo con Símbolos y Claves, Editorial Superacion, Mexico City, 1954.
Paddock, John, "Excavations at Yagul," *Meosoamerican Notes,* IV, 1955.
Peissel, Michel, *The Lost World of Quintana Roo,* E. P. Dutton & Co., Inc., New York, 1963.
Peñafiel, Antonio; Muhlenpfordt, Eduard A. E.; Corriedo, Juan Bautista, *Monumentos del Arte Mexicano Antiguo,* 1890.
Peterson, Frederick A., *Ancient Mexico,* London, 1959, G. P. Putnam's Sons, New York, 1959, Capricorn Books, New York, 1962.
Piña Chan, Román, *Bonampak: La Ciudad de los Muros Pintados.*
Tlatilco, National Institute of Anthropology and History, Mexico City, 1958.
Las Culturas Preclásicas de la Cuenca de México, Mexico City, 1955.
Pollock, H. E. D., "The Casa Redonda at Chichén Itzá, Yucatán," *Contributions to American Archaeology,* Pub. 456, Carnegie Institution, Washington, D.C., 1937.
Prescott, William H., *History of the Conquest of Mexico,* New York, 1843.
Preuss, Konrad T., *Expedition to Nayarit,* G. B. Teubner, Leipzig, 1912.
Proskouriakoff, Tatiana, *A Study of Classic Maya Sculpture,* Carnegie Institution, Pub. 593, Washington, D.C., 1950.
Lords of the Maya Realm, 1961.
Reed, Alma M., "Aspects of Subaqueous Archaeology," *Proceedings of the Vth International Congress of the American Underwater Society,* Mexico City, 1964, C.E.D.A.M., 1965.
The National University of Mexico, Mexico City, 1958. Second edition, 1965.
Uxmal and the Low Hill Cities of Yucatán, Casas, Mexico City, 1960.
Richard, Paul, *Dawn Over Asia,* Ganesh & Co., Madras, India, 1920.
Rivet, Paul, *Cités Maya,* Paris, 1954.
Romero, Javier, *Tezcatlipoca es el Oztoteotl de Chalma,* Gobierno del Estado de Mexico, Dirección de Turísmo, Toluca, Mexico, 1957.
Rosada Iturralde, Gonzálo de Jésus, *Breve Historia de Cozumel,* Club de Libros, Mérida, Mexico, 1950.
Roys, R. L., *Political Geography of the Yucatan Maya.*
The Indian Background of Colonial Yucatán, Pub. 548, Carnegie Institution, Washington, D.C., 1943.
Rubín de la Borbolla, Daniel, *La Medicina en México Antiguo,* 1956.
Monumentos Historicos y Arquelogicos, Instituto Panamericano de Geografía y Historia, Mexico City, 1958.
Ruppert, Karl, *The Caracol at Chichén Itzá, Yucatán, México,* Pub. 454, Carnegie Institution, Washington, D.C., 1935.
Ruppert, Karl, Thompson, J. Eric S. and Proskouriakoff, Tatiana, *Bonampak, Chiapas, México,* Pub. 602, Carnegie Institution, Washington, D.C., 1955.
Saenz, César A., *Nuevos Descubrimientos en Xochicalco, Morelos,* Bulletin 11, National Institute of Anthropology and History, Mexico City, 1963.
Quetzalcóatl, National Institute of Anthropology and History, 1962.
"Tres Estelas en Xochicalco," *Revista Mexicana de Estudios Antropológicos,* 1961.

Salazar Ortegón, Ponciano, *El Tzompantli,* Tlatoani, Mexico City, 1952.
Sanders, William T., *Ceramic Stratigraphy at Santa Cruz, Chiapas, México,* New World Archaeological Foundation, 1961.
Saville, Marshall H., *Cruciform Structures Near Mitla,* American Museum of Natural History, New York, 1900.
The Wood-Carver's Art in Ancient Mexico, Museum of the American Indian, Heye Foundation, Vol. 9, New York, 1925.
Turquoise Mosaic Art in Ancient Mexico, Museum of the American Indian, Heye Foundation, Vol. 6, New York, 1922.
Séjourné, Laurette, *Burning Water,* Fondo de Cultura Económica, Mexico, D.F.
Un Palacio en la Ciudad de los Dioses, National Institute of Anthropology and History, Mexico City, 1959.
Smith, Joseph Lindon, *Tombs, Temples and Ancient Art,* University of Oklahoma Press, Norman, Oklahoma, 1956.
Sociedad de Antropología y Historia, *El Occidente de Mexico,* 1962.
Spence, Lewis, *The Gods of Mexico,* London, 1923.
Spengler, Oswald, *The Decline of the West,* Vol. II, Afred A. Knopf, Inc., New York, 1928, 1945.
Spinden, Herbert J., *Ancient Civilizations of Mexico and Central America,* Handbook Series No. 3, 1922, third revised edition, American Museum of Natural History, New York, 1946.
A Study of Maya Art, Vol. 6, Peabody Museum, Cambridge, Massachusetts, 1913.
Stephens, John Lloyd, *Incidents of Travel in Central America, Chiapas and Yucatan,* 1841.
Stirling, Matthew, *Stone Monuments of Southern Mexico,* Bulletin 138, Smithsonian Institution, Bureau of American Ethnology, Washington, D.C., 1943.
Thompson, Edward H., *People of the Serpent,* New York, 1932.
Thompson, J. Eric S., *The Rise and Fall of the Maya Civilization,* University of Oklahoma Press, Norman, Oklahoma, 1954.
Toscano, Salvador, *Arte Precolombino de México y de la America Central,* National University of Mexico, 1952.
Vaillant, George, *The Aztecs of Mexico: Origin, Rise and Fall of the Aztec Nation,* Doubleday & Company, Inc., Garden City, revised by Susannah B. Vaillant, 1962.
Velikovsky, Immanuel, *Worlds in Collision,* Doubleday & Company, Inc., New York, 1950.
Villagra Caleti, Augustín, *Bonampak, La Ciudad de los Muros Pintados,* National Institute of Anthropology and History, Vol. 3, Mexico City, 1949.
von Hagen, Victor W., *The Ancient Sun Kingdoms of the Americas,* The World Publishing Company, Cleveland and New York, 1961.
Waldeck, Frédéric de, *Un Voyage Pittoresque et Archaeologique dans la Province de Yucatán pendant les Années 1834–1836.*
Westheim, Paul, *Arte Antiguo de México,* Mexico City, 1950.
Ideas Fundamentales del Arte Pre-Hispánico en México.
La Escultura de México Antiguo. Translation by Ursula Bernard, *Sculpture of Ancient Mexico,* Doubleday & Company, Inc., New York, 1962.
Willard, T. A., *City of the Sacred Well,* Century Company, New York, 1926.

Articles in Other Periodicals

Charlot, Jean, "Who Discovered America?" *Art News,* November, 1953.
Dávalos Hurtado, Eusebio, "Return to the Sacred Cenote," *National Geographic,* October, 1961.
Reed, Alma M., "Burial-Place of Cortés," *New York Times Magazine,* March 11, 1923.
"Carnegie Expedition to Yucatan Surveys Uxmal," *New York Times Magazine,* March 18, 1923.
"E. H. Thompson Makes Public Archaeological Finds among Maya Ruins at Chichen Itza," *New York Times Magazine,* March 18, 1923.

"Manuel F. Gamio Tells of Archaeological Excavations Near Oaxaca," *New York Times Magazine,* April 15, 1923.

"Maya Well of Human Sacrifice," *New York Times Magazine,* March 25, 1923.

Ruz Lhuillier, Alberto, "The Mystery of the Mayan Temple," August 29, 1953, *The Saturday Evening Post.*

"The Mystery of the Temple of the Inscriptions," *Archaeology,* Vol. 6, 1953.

Schliemann, Paul, "How I Discovered Atlantis, The Source of All Civilization," New York *American,* 1912.

Drama

Novo, Salvador, "La Guerra de las Gordas."

Exhibit

Ekholm, Dr. Gordon F., director, "Across the Pacific," American Museum of Natural History, New York, 1949.

Film

Healey, Giles G., "The Maya Through the Ages" (United Fruit Company).

Index

Because of space limitations, titles of books and codices have not been indexed. These are, however, listed in the Sources on page 363.

ARCHAEOLOGICAL CHART OF MEXICO
SHOWING LOCATION OF PRINCIPAL RUINS

CAPITAL OF STATE AND PORT ●

ARCHAEOLOGICAL REGION ▲

INTERNATIONAL BOUNDARY +++++

LIMIT OF STATE -----------------